On Poe

On Poe

The Best from *American Literature*

Edited by Louis J. Budd and Edwin H. Cady

Duke University Press   Durham and London   1993

© 1993 Duke University Press
All rights reserved
Printed in the United States of America
on acid-free paper ∞
Library of Congress Cataloging-in-Publication Data
appear on the last printed page of this book.

Contents

Series Introduction *vii*

Poe and Phrenology (1930)
Edward Hungerford *1*

Poe as Social Critic (1934)
Ernest Marchand *24*

Edgar Allan Poe, Cryptographer (1936)
William F. Friedman *40*

Edgar Allan Poe: A Crisis in the History
of American Obscurantism (1937)
Yvor Winters *55*

Poe and the Chess Automaton (1939)
W. K. Wimsatt, Jr. *78*

The Refrain in Poe's Poetry (1953)
Anthony Caputi *92*

Poe and His Nemesis—Lewis Gaylord Clark (1956)
Sidney P. Moss *102*

Poe as Literary Theorist: A Reappraisal (1961)
Emerson R. Marks *122*

The Comic in Poe's Fiction (1962)
Stephen L. Mooney *133*

Poe's "Metzengerstein": Not a Hoax (1971)
Benjamin F. Fisher *142*

Poe's Sense of an Ending (1973)
Paul John Eakin *150*

The Limits of Reason: Poe's Deluded Detectives (1975)
J. Gerald Kennedy *172*

Usher's Hypochondriasis: Mental Alienation and
Romantic Idealism in Poe's Gothic Tales (1976)
David W. Butler *185*

Poe and the Theme of Forbidden Knowledge (1978)
Jules Zanger *197*

"The *language* of the cipher": Interpretation
in "The Gold-Bug" (1982)
Michael Williams   *208*

The Psychology of "The Murders in
the Rue Morgue" (1982)
J. A. Leo Lemay   *223*

Poe's Re-Vision: The Recovery of
the Second Story (1987)
Cynthia S. Jordan   *247*

Index   *267*

Series Introduction

From Vol. 1, no. 1, in March 1929 to the latest issue, the front cover of *American Literature* has proclaimed that it is published "with the Cooperation of the American Literature Section [earlier Group] of the Modern Language Association." Though not easy to explain simply, the facts behind that statement have deeply influenced the conduct and contents of the journal for five decades and more. The journal has never been the "official" or "authorized" organ of any professional organization. Neither, however, has it been an independent expression of the tastes or ideas of Jay B. Hubbell, Clarence Gohdes, or Arlin Turner, for example. Historically, it was first in its field, designedly so. But its character has been unique, too.

Part of the tradition of the journal says that Hubbell in founding it intended a journal that should "hold the mirror up to the profession"—reflecting steadily its current interests and (ideally) at least sampling the best work being done by historians, critics, and bibliographers of American literature during any given year. Such remains the intent of the editors based at Duke University; such also through the decades has been the intent of the Board of Editors elected by the vote of members of the professional association—"Group" or "Section."

The operative point lies in the provisions of the constitutional "Agreements" between the now "Section" and the journal. One of these provides that the journal shall publish no article not approved by two readers from the elected Board. Another provides that the Chairman of the Board or, if one has been appointed and is acting in the editorial capacity at Duke, the Managing Editor need publish no article not judged worthy of the journal. Historically, again, the members of the successive Boards and the Duke editor have seen eye-to-eye. The Board has tended to approve fewer than one out of every ten submissions. The tradition of the journal dictates that it keep a slim back-log. With however much revision, therefore, the journal publishes practically everything the Board approves.

Founder Hubbell set an example from the start by achieving the almost total participation of the profession in the first five numbers of *American Literature*. Cairns, Murdock, Pattee, and Rusk were involved in Vol. 1, no. 1, along with Boynton, Killis Campbell, Foerster, George Philip Krapp, Leisy, Mabbott, Parrington, Bliss Perry, Louise Pound, Quinn, Spiller, Frederick Jackson Turner, and Stanley Williams on the editorial side. Spiller, Tremaine McDowell, Gohdes, and George B. Stewart contributed essays. Canby, George McLean Harper, Gregory Paine, and Howard Mumford Jones appeared as reviewers. Harry Hayden Clark and Allan Gilbert entered in Vol. 1, no. 2. Frederic I. Carpenter, Napier Wilt, Merle Curti, and Grant C. Knight in Vol. 1, no. 3; Clarence Faust, Granville Hicks, and Robert Morss Lovett in Vol. 1, no. 4; Walter Fuller Taylor, Orians, and Paul Shorey in Vol. 2, no. 1.

Who, among the founders of the profession, was missing? On the other hand, if the reader belongs to the profession and does not know those present, she or he probably does not know enough. With very few notable exceptions, the movers and shakers of the profession have since the beginning joined in cooperating to create and sustain the journal.

The foregoing facts lend a special distinction to the best articles in *American Literature*. They represent the many, often tumultuous winds of doctrine which have blown from the beginnings through the years of the decade next to last in this century. Those articles often became the firm footings upon which present structures of understanding rest. Looking backward, one finds that the argonauts were doughty. Though we know a great deal more than they, they are a great deal of what we know. Typically, the old best authors wrote well—better than most of us. Conceptually, even ideologically, we still wrestle with ideas they created. And every now and again one finds of course that certain of the latest work has reinvented the wheel one time more. Every now and again one finds a sunburst idea which present scholarship has forgotten. Then it appears that we have receded into mist or darkness by comparison.

Historical change, not always for the better, also shows itself in methods (and their implied theories) of how to present evidence, structure an argument, craft a scholarly article. The old masters were far from agreed—much to the contrary—about these matters.

But they are worth knowing in their own variety as well as in their instructive differences from us.

On the other hand, the majority of *American Literature*'s authors of the best remain among us, working, teaching, writing. One testimony to the quality of their masterliness is the frequency with which the journal gets requests from the makers of textbooks or collections of commentary to reprint from its pages. Now the opportunity presents itself to select without concern for permissions fees what seems the best about a number of authors and topics from the whole sweep of *American Literature*.

The fundamental reason for this series, in other words, lies in the intrinsic, enduring value of articles that have appeared in *American Literature* since 1929. The compilers, with humility, have accepted the challenge of choosing the best from well over a thousand articles and notes. By "best" is meant original yet sound, interesting, and useful for the study and teaching of an author, intellectual movement, motif, or genre.

The articles chosen for each volume of this series are given simply in the order of their first publication, thus speaking for themselves and entirely making their own points rather than serving the compilers' view of literary or philosophical or historical patterns. Happily, a chronological order has the virtues of displaying both the development of insight into a particular author, text, or motif and the shifts of scholarly and critical emphasis since 1929. But comparisons or trend-watching or a genetic approach should not blur the individual excellence of the articles reprinted. Each has opened a fresh line of inquiry, established a major perspective on a familiar problem, or settled a question that had bedeviled the experts. The compilers aim neither to demonstrate nor undermine any orthodoxy, still less to justify a preference for research over explication, for instance. In the original and still current subtitle, *American Literature* honors literary history and criticism equally—along with bibliography. To the compilers this series does demonstrate that any worthwhile author or text or problem can generate a variety of challenging perspectives. Collectively, the articles in its volumes have helped to raise contemporary standards of scholarship and criticism.

This series is planned to serve as a live resource, not as a homage to once vibrant but petrifying achievements in the past. For several sound reasons, its volumes prove to be weighted toward the more recent articles, but none of those reasons includes a presumed superiority of insight or of guiding doctrine among the most recent generations. Some of the older articles could benefit now from a minor revision, but the compilers have decided to reprint all of them exactly as they first appeared. In their time they met fully the standards of first-class research and judgment. Today's scholar and critic, their fortunate heir, should hope that rising generations will esteem his or her work so highly.

Many of the articles published in *American Literature* have actually come (and continue to come) from younger, even new members of the profession. Because many of those authors climb on to prominence in the field, the fact is worth emphasizing. Brief notes on the contributors in the volumes of their series may help readers to discover other biographical or cultural patterns.

Edwin H. Cady
Louis J. Budd

Poe and Phrenology
Edward Hungerford

I

"THE FOREHEAD is broad, with prominent organs of ideality."[1] So, in 1846, wrote Edgar Allan Poe of William Cullen Bryant.

Eight and a half decades of changing scientific theory have all but obliterated the meaning which Poe and his readers attached to this statement. Only a few modern readers will understand that Poe is using the language of what was once a science. And those who have some reminiscent knowledge of phrenology, will recognize it only jocularly. Unconsciously, in the speech of today, such phrases as "my bump of direction," or "my bump of order," survive. But the word *bumps* is, for most of us, all that remains of the science of *cranioscopy,* or *craniology,* or, as it came to be known, *phrenology.*[2]

There are, to be sure, many books—many, many books—which lie upon library shelves. And the phrenologist himself (or herself, rather more frequently) is not unknown in the twisted walks of life. But the student of the more humane letters does not, in these days, feel called upon to inform himself about the "organs of ideality." If he feels that he is shrewd in the science of mind he will perhaps engage in the psychoanalysis of his literary favorite, discovering, in the discreet jargon of a newer science, many an unutterable complex, fixation, and psychosis. Yet while he applies to some by-gone poet the terminology of a recent learning, many subtleties of interpretation wait upon his willingness to re-explore the half lost meanings of the old. So to "the organs of ideality," and phrenology, and Edgar Allan Poe.

In those American thirties and forties through which Poe brooded and dreamed a perilous artistry, the science of phrenology

---

[1] *The Complete Works of Edgar Allan Poe,* edited by James A. Harrison, XIII, 140. All future references to Poe will be to this edition.

[2] Gall had called his studies "craniology," or "cranioscopy," but the terms were abandoned in favor of "phrenology." Since in lectures only prominent objects could be observed by the spectators, the impression was given that the phrenologist was concerned with the art of reading bumps.

occupied a position not unlike that of the hazardous psychologies of today. In the wisdom of our enlightenment we know that phrenology was a half ridiculous pseudo-science, faulty in its assumptions, and disreputable in its associations with quackery. We may regard it as naïve of Poe that he should have studied Spurzheim, and Gall, and Combe. But we should not so misjudge Poe and his decades. The human spirit has often been dazzled by any so-called science which offers the master key to locked mysteries. And the American has been long prone to a get-rich-quick attitude toward learning or wealth. The same enthusiastic disposition which produced Jacksonian democracy, produced also an energetic desire to read the riddles of mental phenomena with a too hasty disregard for final facts and logic. And phrenology was once a serious science indeed, looking forward optimistically to practical and humanitarian utilities.[3] Not unlike the psychology of today, it hoped to provide accurate vocational guidance for the young, to revolutionize our systems of education, to revise the care of the insane, to bring wisdom into the treatment of criminals, and, like our modern eugenics, to provide dependable information upon the advisability of marriages. From 1791, when, in Vienna, appeared Gall's first chapters of his *Medico-philosophical Enquiries into Nature and Art in Health and Disease*, until the latter fifties in America, phrenology had a not dishonorable career. When Spurzheim, Gall's first disciple, died in America in 1832, he and his master had acquainted the civilized world with its principles. The Austrian government had frowned upon Gall, and France had prohibited the lectures of the enthusiasts, but they had been received sympathetically in Holland, Germany, England, Scotland and America. Scotland had been especially hospitable. Edinburgh, through the efforts of George Combe, continued the teachings of the first investigators in a *Phrenological Journal,* founded in 1832; and societies, journals, and books followed this flourishing interest in England and America. That caustic traveler, Frances Trollope,[4]

[3] See Andrew Boardman's introductory essays to George Combe's *Lectures on Phrenology.* . . . New York, 3rd edition, 1841; and Thomas Forster's "Sketch of the New Anatomy and Physiology of Brain and Nervous System of Drs. Gall and Spurzheim, considered as comprehending a complete system of Phrenology. With observations on its tendency to the improvement of education, of punishment, and of the treatment of insanity," in *The Pamphleteer,* V, 220-244 (1815).

[4] Frances Trollope, *Domestic Manners of the Americans,* 4th edition (New York, 1832), p. 71.

had found phrenology penetrated so far west as Cincinnati—and this in 1828, when Caldwell lectured there, and those vulgar, unmannered Americans tried to found a society.

But who cares now about all that? The Cincinnati society, and Mrs. Trollope, and phrenology itself have withered with her sarcasm. Modernity has declared the assumptions of the science to be untenable. The neat little system wouldn't work. It had sounded very reasonable. As the brain grows, the cranium takes shape around it. Every area of the cranium is shaped as it is because of some peculiar growth in the brain itself. And, since within the brain there are special areas[5] in which are confined some primary activity of mind, such as combativeness, or wonder, or cautiousness, it follows that the external surfaces represent the development within. There is likewise an external area called *Combativeness,* or *Wonder,* or *Cautiousness.* The size of the organ within the brain determines the degree of intensity with which the individual possesses the quality. And the bump is the index which can be read.

It *was* a neat system, and not a bad one, as systems go. One should be philosophical about such matters. It was not the first well-cargoed ship to go down. We moderns may recall how stupidly Plato thought about the intellectual functions. Think of his locating the imagination in one's liver! And Aristotle was not much better, relegating it to the heart. Truly did the Scriptures say of man that "every imagination of the thoughts of his heart was only evil continually." Surely the system was no worse than that of old Bartholomeus Anglicus, who found that "the brayne hath thre holow places, whiche physytiens calle Ventriculos, small wombes. In the foremeste celle and wombe imagination is conformed and made, in the midle, reason, in the hyndermeste, recordation and minde."[6] And yet a not far different scheme was good enough for Pico, and for Vallesio, and Agrippa, and Fernelius, and Wierus, and Bacon, and Ficino, and Nymannus, and Fienus, and others and others. Spurzheim and Gall and Combe merely followed the leaders down the paths of oblivion. And who follow them? James? and Freud? and Watson?

[5] A chart prefixed to the edition of Combe cited above names and locates the organs.
[6] *Bartholomeus de Proprietatibus Rerum,* translated by John of Trevisa (London, 1535), fol. XXXV.

To the American who read Edgar Allan Poe's essay on Bryant, the observation about his "prominent organs of ideality" would have meant just about as much as calling a man an "introvert" would mean to us. Not that the two are similar. If one had consulted one's phrenological guide one would have discovered that the organs of *Ideality* are just such organs as a good poet ought to have, and to have in a well developed state. Gall had discovered the organ of *Ideality*,[7] the outer index of which was the surface just at the upper corner (if I may use the word) of the forehead. Gall had been inclined to call the organ that of poetry, but Spurzheim, noting that poetry is the result of various organs, and that this organ gives to poetry or prose "a certain quality of beauty, elegance, perfection, or sublimity," called it *Ideality*. Now we know the implication of Poe's comment. We may question his judgment, but we know his meaning. We shall understand what qualities Poe admired in Bryant's "Oh, Fairest of the Rural Maids" when he called it "richly ideal."[8]

II

One may trace Poe's interest in the science of phrenology with considerable exactness. There is no definite indication[9] of any concern with the subject before 1836. In the previous year had appeared an American edition of a work by Mrs. L. Miles which had been printed in a different form in London. The new edition was printed in Philadelphia by Carey, Lea and Blanchard under the title: *Phrenology, and the Moral Influence of Phrenology: Arranged for General Study, and the Purposes of Education, from the First Published Works of Gall and Spurzheim, to The Latest Discoveries of the Present Period*. Poe reviewed the book for *The Southern Literary Messenger* in March, 1836.[10] His review is enthusiastic:

---

[7] George Combe, *op. cit.*, p. 217. There is an important discussion of *Ideality* in the same author's *A System of Phrenology*, 4th edition (Boston, 1842), pp. 239-249. In this Combe discusses the relation of *Ideality* to poetic ability. See also M. B. Sampson, "On the Primary Functions of the Organ of Ideality," in *The American Phrenological Journal*, I, 297-308 (June, 1839). There is a discussion of the organ in Robert MacNish, *An Introduction to Phrenology*, 2nd edition (Glasgow, 1837), pp. 111-112.

[8] *Works*, XIII, 134.

[9] Poe uses the term *ideality* in his review of "The Classical Family Library," in *The Southern Literary Messenger* in September, 1835 (*Works*, VIII, 46), but the word seems to have no connection with phrenology.

[10] *The Southern Literary Messenger*, II, 286-287; *Works*, VIII, 252-255.

> Phrenology is no longer to be laughed at. It is no longer laughed at by men of common understanding. It has assumed the majesty of a science, and, as a science ranks among the most important which can engage the attention of thinking beings—this too, whether we consider it merely as an object of speculative inquiry, or as involving consequences of the highest practical magnitude.

Some short comment on the history of the science follows, together with remarks upon its uses, and upon the particular merits of the book under review. As usual in his reviews, Poe's comments are specific. He appears to have read the book thoroughly. He refers to the London edition as if he were familiar with it; he speaks of "George Combe who wrote the 'Phrenology'"; and of the hostility of *The Edinburgh Review*. But this knowledge could be gleaned from Mrs. Miles's pages, and does not indicate that Poe had known phrenology before.[11] The interest given him by the review of Mrs. Miles's treatise led to immediate results. The review was written in March. In the April number of *The Southern Literary Messenger* there is an extensive criticism of Drake and Halleck in which phrenological terms are used significantly.[12] And in the following month, in the same magazine, he reviewed Walsh's *Didactics,* taking Walsh to task for an article hostile to phrenology. Poe regrets "to see the energies of a scholar and an editor (who should be, if he be not, a man of metaphysical science) so wickedly employed as in any attempt to throw ridicule upon a question (however much maligned, or however apparently ridiculous), whose merits he has never examined, and of whose very nature, history, and assumptions, he is most evidently ignorant."[13] After 1836, Poe's references to phrenology are numerous. Presumably, then, Mrs. Miles's book first attracted his interest in the subject. It is likely that once his interest was aroused he increased his knowledge, reading some of the scores of books and articles being written in America as well as in Europe.[14] By 1836 George Combe's *Elements*

---

[11] Miles, sig. A, and pp. 166-167.
[12] *Works*, VIII, 275-318.
[13] *Works*, VIII, 329. See "Phrenology," in Robert Walsh's *Didactics: Social, Literary, and Political*, 2 vols. (Philadelphia, 1836), II, 56-65.
[14] It is unlikely that Poe read Gall in the original. Poe uses the English terms given by Spurzheim who glozed Gall's *Dichter-Geist*, or *Talent poétique* with *Ideality*, and *Kunst-sinn, Bau-sinn,* or *Sens de mechanique* with *Constructiveness*. See Combe's *System*, appendix, p. 41. Mrs. Miles gives both the English and German names.

of *Phrenology* and his *System of Phrenology* had both passed through four editions, and his *Outlines* through six. By 1838 Poe seems to have become acquainted with Combe's *Lectures on Phrenology*. In 1839, when Poe was living in Philadelphia, Combe delivered a series of lectures in the Museum,[15] which Poe may have attended.

The review of Mrs. Miles's book was written in March, 1836. In April, we find Poe writing about Drake and Halleck. He has been discussing the necessity of arriving at a definite opinion about the nature of poetry.[16] Admitting the difficulty of defining poetry, the term, he believes that "we apprehend no difficulty in so describing Poesy, the Sentiment, as to imbue even the most obtuse intellect with a comprehension of it sufficiently distinct for all the purposes of practical analysis." Poe proceeds to declare that we have "certain faculties, implanted within us." We have, for example, "a disposition to look with reverence upon superiority, whether real or suppositious." This faculty is a primitive sentiment. "Phrenologists call it Veneration."

Mrs. Miles has discussed *Veneration*.[17] With the phrenology hint in our minds, the subsequent discussion is illuminating:

Very nearly akin to this feeling, and liable to the same analysis, is the Faculty of Ideality—which is the sentiment of Poesy. This sentiment is the sense of the beautiful, of the sublime, and of the mystical.

And now Poe begins to build up his theory of poetry, employing for literary criticism the terminology of his newly discovered science. Poetry, we find, is "the practical result expressed in language, of this Poetic Sentiment in certain individuals . . . " We must test poetry by its capabilities of exciting the poetic sentiments in others. Poe's philosophizing is peppered and salted with the new terms: "We do not hesitate to say that a man highly endowed with the powers of Causality [Mrs. Miles had a section on *Causality*][18]

Poe might have known Spurzheim from the 2nd (Boston, 1835) edition of *Phrenology or Doctrine of the Mental Phenomena*.

George Combe's *Essays on Phrenology*, 1819, his *Elements of Phrenology*, 1824, *A System of Phrenology*, 1825, *Constitution of Man*, 1828, were all first published in Edinburgh.

[15] See George Combe, *Notes on the United States of North America*, 2 vols. (Philadelphia, 1841), I, *passim*.
[16] *Works*, VIII, 281 ff.
[17] L. Miles, *Phrenology*, p. 77.
[18] *Ibid.*, pp. 145-147.

—that is to say, a man of metaphysical acumen—will, even with a sufficient share of Ideality [Mrs. Miles again], [19] compose a finer poem (if we test it, as we should, by its measure of exciting the Poetic Sentiment) than one who, without such metaphysical acumen, shall be gifted, in the most extraordinary degree, with the faculty of Ideality." And so on. We discover, for instance, that Coleridge's head "gave no great phrenological tokens of Ideality, while the organs of Causality and Comparison were most singularly developed."[20]

In the discussion of Drake which follows, the transference of phrenological terms into criticism is continued.[21] The critics of Drake's "The Culprit Fay" are at fault, Poe thinks, from this "indistinct conception of the results in which Ideality is rendered manifest." The root of the trouble is that Drake exercises the faculty of *Comparison,* but he lacks *Ideality.* Poe applies his principle intelligently; doubtless he was right in saying that neither "The Culprit Fay" nor Halleck's "Marco Bozzaris" had the highest requirements of *Ideality.* Drake had, these many years, carried *Benevolence, Comparison,* and *Causality* into the dust to which all *Benevolence, Comparison,* and *Causality* return. But poor Halleck, living down in Guilford, Connecticut, something of a town drunk, may well have gazed in his mirror wistfully, longing for bigger bumps of *Ideality.*

Halleck was not the only poet whom Poe's critical comments must have sent to the mirror. Though Poe was never in high serious mood when he penned his confessedly journalistic project, *The Literati,* the sketches were clever enough to be considered. N. P. Willis, that most elegant of the New Yorkers, must have puckered his brows to learn that his forehead "would puzzle phrenology."[22] Evert A. Duyckinck, editor of *The Library of Choice Reading,* was doubtless pleased to learn that his "forehead, phrenologically, is a good one."[23] We learn of George Bush, learned professor of Hebrew at New York University, that "His countenance expresses rather benevolence and profound earnestness, than high intelligence.

---

[19] *Ibid.,* pp. 85-87. According to Mrs. Miles, *Ideality* is quite definitely "The inspiration of poetry; feeling of the sublime and beautiful; originality of thought and expression."
[20] *Works, loc. cit.;* see Miles on *Causality* and *Comparison, op. cit.,* pp. 141-147.
[21] *Works,* VIII, 293 ff.
[22] *Works,* XV, 18.
[23] *Works,* XV, 60.

The eyes are piercing; the other features in general, massive. The forehead, phrenologically, indicates causality and comparison, with deficient ideality—the organization which induces strict logicality from insufficient premises."[24] Poe is disturbed by Charles Fenno Hoffman. His *A Winter in the West* "conveys the *natural* enthusim of a true *idealist,* in the proper phrenological sense, of one sensitively alive to beauty in every development."[25] But Poe observes with surprise that the forehead, "although high, gives no indication of that ideality (or love of the beautiful) which is the distinguishing trait of his moral nature." Perhaps, in the long testing of time, phrenology was right about Hoffman.

Other instances of the use of phrenological terms in Poe's criticism need hardly be enumerated. It is clear that his interest in phrenology intrudes itself with some frequency into his analysis of men of letters. In this he merely follows his teachers. Throughout the treatises of George Combe and others, a great deal of attention is paid to the phrenological developments of poets. Byron is a favorite, and Burns, and Pope, and Racine, and Tasso.[26] As with modern psychology, the science overflowed into literary criticism.[27] In December, 1838, one L. N. F. contributed to *The American Phrenological Journal and Miscellany,*[28] an article entitled "Application of Phrenology to Criticism," and in April of the following year appeared A. Wren's essay, "Application of Phrenology to the Analysis of the Character of Shakespeare's Iago."[29] If Poe erred in introducing his pet interest into the field of literary criticism, the whirligig of time has brought in a just revenge upon him. He phrenologized his contemporaries. Modern critics have not yet tired of psychoanalyzing him.

III

Although Poe's use of phrenology in the analysis of character comes to him legitimately and naturally from the interest similarly felt by other men of his time, there is in this interest something deeply indicative of Poe's personal taste. He was always eager to

[24] *Works,* XV, 7.
[25] *Works,* XV, 118 and 122.
[26] See Combe, *Lectures, passim.*
[27] Poe quotes a review of Drake's poem which uses phrenological terms, *Works,* VIII, 298 n.
[28] I, 65-71.
[29] I, 212-228.

arrive at exact analyses of qualities of mind. It is characteristic of him that he employed other pseudo-scientific devices for reading the disposition. He made much of his ability to read character through handwriting.[30] One catches occasional hints of similar pursuits. In his sketch of Freeman Hunt in *The Literati* we find a provoking description of the chin as "massive and projecting, indicative (according to Lavater and general experience) of that energy which is, in fact, the chief point of his character."[31] The name *Lavater,* which slips so glibly from Poe's tongue, gives us a revealing glimpse of our poet's intellectual processes. Johann Casper Lavater was the author of another character-reading system. Noses, eyes, chins, and ears, were Lavater's indices. His elaborate *Physiognomische Fragmente, zur Beförderung der Menschenkenntnitz und Menschenliebe* had been published at Leipzig in 1775. Poe used Lavater as he used phrenology.[32] He surely made less use of his science of physiognomy, but the parallelism is significant. Was he less impressed by Lavater? Is that "Science of Noses" of which he makes such fun in "Lionizing" a slur at the art? Robert's "Nosology"[33] made him great fame:

When I came of age my father asked me, one day, if I would step with him into his study.

"My son," said he, when we were seated, "what is the chief end of your existence?"

"My father," I answered, "it is the study of Nosology."

"And what, Robert," he inquired, "is Nosology?"

"Sir," I said, "it is the Science of Noses."

"And can you tell me," he demanded, "what is the meaning of a nose?"

"A nose, my father," I replied, greatly softened, "has been variously defined by about a thousand different authors." (Here I pulled out my watch.) "It is now noon or thereabouts—We shall have time enough to get through with them all before midnight. To commence then:—The nose, according to Bartholinus,[34] is that protuberance—that bump—that excrescence—that—"

---

[30] *Works,* XV, 175-261.   [31] *Works,* XV, 43.

[32] For Lavater on chins, see the above-named work, IV, 263. There is a discussion of Lavater in Paola Lombroso, *I Segni Rivelatori della Personalità* (Torino, 1902), p. 5.

[33] *Works,* II, 35-37.

[34] A reference to Thomas Bartolin, the anatomist, 1616-1680, or to Gaspard Bartholin, 1655-1738, author of *Specimen historiae anatomicae partium corporis humani* (Copenhagen, 1701).

—"Will do, Robert," interrupted the good old gentleman. "I am thunderstruck at the extent of your information—I am positively—upon my soul." (Here he closed his eyes and placed his hand upon his heart.) "Come here!" (Here he took me by the arm.) "Your education may now be considered as finished—it is high time you should scuffle for yourself—and you cannot do a better thing than merely follow your nose—so—so—so—" (Here he kicked me down stairs and out of the door)—"so get out of my house, and God bless you!"

As I felt within me the divine *afflatus,* I considered this accident rather fortunate than otherwise. I resolved to be guided by the paternal advice. I determined to follow my nose. I gave it a pull or two upon the spot, and wrote a pamphlet on Nosology forthwith. All Fum-Fudge was in an uproar.

"Wonderful genius!" said the Quarterly.
"Superb physiologist!" said the Westminster.
"Clever fellow!" said the Foreign.
"Fine writer!" said the Edinburgh.
"Profound thinker!" said the Dublin.
"Great man!" said Bently.
"Divine soul!" said Fraser.
"One of us!" said Blackwood.

And Robert, thus equipped, becomes the lion of society. In this sketch Poe's satire, as invariably in his satirical writing, loses force from its promiscuity. But the point is clear. Poe could turn his scorn upon the very foibles in which he himself indulged. It was not unintelligent of him to do so.

Indeed that very real intelligence of his made capital more than once of the contemporary rage for phrenology. It was one of the tenets of phrenology that size was an index of degree.[35] It was doubtless this theory that prompted Thingum Bob's father to observe to his son:[36] "You have an immense head, and it must hold a great many brains." There is a slur at phrenology in "The System of Dr. Tarr and Professor Fether." One of the unfortunately deranged fancied himself possessed of two heads: "One of these he maintained to be the head of Cicero; the other he imagined a composite one, being Demosthenes' from the top of the forehead to the mouth, and Lord Brougham from the mouth to the chin."[37]

[35] I. Slade, *Letters on Phrenology* (London, 1836), "Letter XIII."
[36] *Works,* VI, 3.   [37] *Works,* VI, 65.

Handbooks of phrenology were replete with illustrations of prominent men. Combe prints a mask of Lord Brougham.[38] In "Diddling Considered as One of the Exact Sciences," the hero, an arrant rogue, "has constructiveness large. He understands plot. He invents and circumvents."[39] *Constructiveness* is the organ which lies just below *Ideality*. Combe says of the organ: "It does not invent; but merely fashions or configurates, though when large it stimulates the understanding to invent what will employ it agreeably in constructing."[40] Here the term is used less satirically than sarcastically. The Diddler's *Constructiveness* fashions to none of the good purposes which that excellent organ should.

One of the neatest of Poe's light sketches takes an added grotesquery from its satire upon phrenology. Indeed, the whole point of the skit comes from the bizarre turn which Poe gives to a phrenological tenet. Gall had seriously discussed whether "the form of the head can be modified during the birth of the child, or by compression or malaxation."[41] His answer was emphatically, no. In "The Business Man" we have this description of an unfortunate, or rather of a fortunate accident to our hero: "A good-hearted old Irish nurse (whom I shall not forget in my will) took me up one day by the heels, when I was making more noise than was necessary, and, swinging me round two or three times, d——d my eyes for 'a skreeking little spalpeen', and then knocked my head into a cocked hat against the bedpost. This, I say, decided my fate, and made my fortune. A bump arose at once on my sinciput, and turned out to be as pretty an organ of *order* as one shall see on a summer's day. Hence that positive appetite for system and regularity which has made me the distinguished man of business that I am."[42] Here clearly Poe is deliberately turning theory inside out. The humor of the subsequent successes of the hero is quite lost for the modern reader unless he knows that the situation is phrenologically impossible. In the vagaries of business enterprise which follow, Poe keeps us clearly in mind that it is the organ of *Order* which makes the hero's success.

---

[38] *Lectures*, p. 267. The illustration is omitted, though referred to, in the edtiion cited.
[39] *Works*, V, 212.
[40] For *Constructiveness*, see Miles, p. 49; MacNish, pp. 74-76; Combe, *Lectures*, p. 172.
[41] F. J. Gall, *On the Functions of the Brain and of Each of its Parts*, translated by Winslow Lewis (Boston, 1835), III, 9-11.
[42] *Works*, IV, 122-123. On *Order*, see Miles, p. 122; Combe, *Lectures*, p. 247.

Four times[43] Poe emphasizes the point. The hero is hurt in an escapade: "I had to be sent home to my button-headed family in a high state of fever, and with a most violent and dangerous pain in the sinciput, all round about my organ of order." He was saved from his illness and came to be "grateful to the protuberance which had been the means of my salvation, as well as to the kind-hearted female who had originally put these means within my reach." He was enabled to discharge the onerous duties of his profession "only by that rigid adherence to system which formed the leading feature of my mind." In his very profitable occupation of mud-dabbling, he observed that "there is nothing to be made in this way without *method*. I did only a retail business myself, but my old habits of *system* carried me swimmingly along." Anyone who knows Poe's invariable habit of "pointing" his stories, will recognize at once that he is here painfully careful to emphasize the situation in which his humor lies.

Phrenology takes one more fall from the hand of Poe. It figures in the highly satirical "Some Words with a Mummy." Although this sketch is in his mannered, self-conscious style, nervously grotesque, it possesses a range and depth which his satire seldom reaches. Before an incredulous and sarcastic mummy, revivified through the use of a galvanic battery, the proud achievements of modern science and society are reviewed. Monotheism, accuracy in historical research, conceptions of cosmogony, astronomical knowledge, lenses, architecture, machines for construction work, railroads, Artesian wells, metaphysical progress, democracy, steam engines, and, as a finale, patent medicines, are described to the contemptuous mummy, who fails to find anything new in whatever is described. Phrenology has an important place in the discussion.[44] One of the interlocutors, after glancing at the occiput and then at the sinciput of the mummy, observes that the inferiority of the Egyptians in all particulars of science doubtless proceeded from the solidity of the Egyptian skull. The mummy expressed doubt as to the allusion, whereupon the whole party "detailed, at great length, the assumptions of phrenology." But the mummy silenced the proud moderns by relating "a few anecdotes, which rendered it evident that prototypes of Gall and Spurzheim had flourished and

---

[43] *Works*, IV, pp. 124, 125, and 130.   [44] *Works*, VI, 133.

faded in Egypt so long ago as to have been nearly forgotten." It is not phrenology, but the pretensions of phrenology which Poe ridicules here. The passage of a hundred years has lent a new satire to this passage, a satire which one will not perceive unless he knows that Poe in some of his most serious artistry calls upon phrenology to authenticate his subtlest interpretation of human character.

IV

The truth of the matter is, that Poe's mind was fascinated with the exciting possibilities of phrenology, and that, his mind thoroughly steeped in it, he drew more than one important suggestion from it. In that "Colloquy of Monos and Una," in which Poe, pioneer of the human spirit, goes down to the border lands of death, there are two important elements of the narrative which seem to have been inspired by phrenology. In the white luster of Poe's purest style, he describes the sensations of the mind dissolving after death. States of consciousness become defined for a space, only to be succeeded by others. At one time in the dissolution Monos becomes aware of "a mental pendulous pulsation. It was the moral embodiment of man's abstract idea of *Time*. . . . And this—this keen, perfect, self-existing sentiment of *duration*—this sentiment existing (as man could not possibly have conceived it to exist) independently of any succession of events—this idea—this sixth sense, upspringing from the ashes of the rest, was the first obvious and certain step of the intemporal soul upon the threshold of the temporal Eternity."[45] A year passes, and the sense of duration is succeeded by "that of mere locality."[46] The association of these two concepts in Poe's mind is startlingly suggestive when one finds that the sense of time and of locality were represented in phrenology by definite, primary organs. Was Poe's analysis of these psychical states caught from the science of mind? Of the organ of *Time* Gall had written: "We see persons who find amusement in a collection of watches and clocks, and must have them all go with the greatest exactness."[47] Did Poe remember this when Monos describes his abstract idea of time? "By its aid I measured the irregularities of the clock upon the mantel, and of the watches of the attendants. Their

[45] *Works*, IV, 209-210.
[46] *Works*, IV, 211.
[47] Gall, *op. cit.*, V, 95; see also Miles, MacNish, and Combe.

tickings came sonorously to my ears. The slightest deviations from the true proportion—and these deviations were omni-praevalent—affected me just as violations of abstract truth were wont, on earth, to affect the moral sense."[48]

That Poe speculated deeply upon the primary elements of mind cannot be denied. One of the greatest difficulties which phrenology had to overcome was the controversy over the primary faculties.[49] What mental activities were primary? What exactly were the organs of the brain? Twice we find Poe himself entering the lists with the proposal of a primary faculty. In "The Black Cat" we find a hideous story constructed upon the idea of sub-liminal *Perverseness*. Acting upon an otherwise gentle and kindly person, the spirit of perverseness causes him to kill a beloved cat and to endure a succession of horrors from the consequences of the act. Poe's analysis of the mental state is exact: "And then came, as if to my final and irrevocable overthrow, the spirit of PERVERSENESS. Of this spirit philosophy takes no account. Yet I am not more sure that my soul lives, than I am that perverseness is one of the primitive impulses of the human heart—one of the indivisible primary faculties, or sentiments, which give direction to the character of Man."[50] Although there is here no direct reference to phrenology, the terms are unmistakably reminiscent. This story was written in 1843. Two years later appeared "The Imp of the Perverse." In the interim Poe's ideas about perverseness had taken shape. "The Imp of the Perverse" is a brilliant definition which is then followed by a thrilling narrative which embodies the idea. The *liaison* with phrenology is explicit. The essay, for in reality it is a dramatic essay, begins: "In the consideration of the faculties and impulses—of the *prima mobilia* of the human soul, the phrenologists have failed to make room for a propensity which, although obviously existing as a radical, primitive, irreducible sentiment, has been equally overlooked by all the moralists who have preceded them."[51] Poe suggests that

[48] *Works*, IV, 209.
[49] See Gall on "The Difficulties and Means of Determining the Fundamental Qualities and Faculties, and of Discovering the Seat of their Organs in the Brain," in *On the Functions of the Brain*, III, 66 ff.
[50] *Works*, V, 146. I am indebted to Mr. Thomas O. Mabbott for pointing out to me that Poe suppressed an original direct reference to phrenology in this passage, presumably because he intended amplifying his discussion of the subject in "The Imp of the Perverse."
[51] *Works*, VI, 145 ff.

this propensity has been overlooked because it was obvious. He objects to the *a priori* method of phrenology and of all metaphysics. Having a preconceived notion of the purposes of God, the intellectual or logical man builds his innumerable systems of mind:

> In the matter of phrenology, for example, we first determined, naturally enough, that it was the design of the Deity that man should eat. We then assigned to man an organ of alimentiveness, and this organ is the scourge with which the Deity compels man, will-I nill-I, into eating. Secondly, having settled it to be God's will that man should continue his species, we discovered an organ of amativeness, forthwith. And so with combativeness, with ideality, with causality, with constructiveness,—so, in short, with every organ, whether representing a propensity, a moral sentiment, or a faculty of the pure intellect. And in these arrangements of the *principia* of human action, the Spurzheimites, whether right or wrong, in part, or upon the whole, have but followed in principle, the footsteps of their predecessors; deducing and establishing every thing from the preconceived destiny of man, and upon the ground of the objects of his Creator.

Pointing out that it would have been wiser to classify upon the basis of what man "usually or occasionally did, and was always occasionally doing," Poe declares that phrenology would thus have been brought to admit perverseness as "a radical, a primitive impulse —elementary." He argues that the phrenological *Combativeness*[52] is not in essence to be confused with perverseness. One should point out that Poe's objection is not to phrenology, but to its method of classification.

"The Murders in the Rue Morgue" presents another instance of Poe's objection, not to phrenology, but to its definition of the primary faculties. Once again the discussion serves as the introduction to an illustrative story. In "The Imp of the Perverse" the narrative is subordinate to the idea. In "The Murders in the Rue Morgue" the discussion of phrenology serves merely to launch the tale. Poe wishes to focus the mind of the reader upon the analytical power of Dupin. His method is to analyze analysis. The analytical power should be differentiated from mere ingenuity: "The constructive or combining power, by which ingenuity is usually manifested, and to which the phrenologists (I believe erroneously) have assigned a separate organ, supposing it a primitive faculty, has been so fre-

[52] See Combe, *Lectures,* p. 148.

quently seen in those whose intellect bordered otherwise upon idiocy, as to have attracted general observation among writers on morals."[53] (*Constructiveness* is the organ which Poe was to ridicule in "Diddling.") Phrenology itself is not attacked. Indeed, Poe's intention is clearly not to suggest that the phrenologists are not shrewd, but that his own mind, or that of his narrator, is still shrewder. If he had regarded phrenology as pseudo, he would not have referred to it, for it would have spoiled his effect in this story. He must give the impression that he is more scientific than science itself. That he regards phrenology as suitable for reference is unmistakable from the fact that preceding the discussion of the analytical power he twice uses terms suggesting it. He discourses upon "the reflective intellect" and "the concentrative" chess player. And subsequently, in describing Dupin, he deliberately uses a phrenological term: "At such times I could not help remarking and admiring (although from his rich ideality I had been prepared to expect it) a peculiar analytic ability in Dupin."[54] Not to remark these minutiæ of Poe's method is to lose the subtleties of his artistry. Modern knowledge of phrenology has faded, but thoroughly to understand Poe we must relearn the connotation of his allusions.

V

Indeed, it is the connotation of allusions which marks the most delicate refinement of Poe's writing. In the preceding discussion Poe's references to phrenology have been comparatively explicit. It is in his more exquisite writing that he makes use of phrenology in a far more subtle fashion. Allusion is veiled in indistinctness, but by its near-imperceptibility, it becomes more closely compacted in the delineation of character, and consequently in the exposition of artistic purposes. In "The Fall of the House of Usher" and in "Ligeia," phrenology plays a delicate but definite part. In both of these stories Poe employs phrenology with exact nicety to authenticate his character portrayal. The supposedly well-informed reader is given certain faint phrenological hints upon which his mind is intended to operate during the unfolding of the story, and which contribute both to his understanding and to his artistic excitement.

[53] *Works*, IV, 149.
[54] IV, 147, and 152.

We remember that as the narrator approaches the House of Usher he finds himself in "a singularly dreary tract of country"; it is pervaded with insufferable gloom. "I say insufferable; for the feeling was unrelieved by any of that half-pleasurable, because poetic, sentiment, with which the mind usually receives even the sternest natural images of the desolate or terrible."[55] Now, according to the phrenologists, the organ of *Ideality* "consists in a taste for the graceful, the beautiful and the sublime. All things which partake of these qualities gratify it. The savage desolation of Glenco, the awful gloom and sublimity of Chamouni, the graceful loveliness of Windermere, a beautiful woman, a lovely child, the Belvidere Apollo —all such objects stimulate the organ, and give rise to emotions of the grand or the beautiful."[56] Observe that Poe has been at some pains to assert that the scenery surrounding the House of Usher is *not such* as will arouse pleasurable emotions in the mind of one who might be gifted with the organ of *Ideality*. It excites merely gloom. "There was an iciness, a sinking, a sickening of the heart— an unredeemed dreariness of thought which no goading of the imagination could torture into ought of the sublime."[57] What, we ask ourselves, would be the effect of such a scene upon a man who had a highly developed organ of *Ideality*? Poe has clearly set the scene.

Now for Roderick Usher. Usher had sent to his friend "a wildly importunate" letter.[58] "The MS. gave evidence of nervous agitation." Notice that Usher was nervous. Usher has an "acute bodily illness," "a mental disorder"; he needs his friend for the "cheerfulness" of his society. Our minds immediately associate the gloom of the landscape with Usher's gloom. Poe describes Usher further: "I was aware that his very ancient family had been noted, time out of mind, for a peculiar sensibility of temperament, displaying itself, through long ages, in many works of exalted art, and manifested, of late . . . in a passionate devotion to the intricacies, perhaps even more than to the orthodox and easily recognizable beauties, of

---

[55] *Works*, III, 273.
[56] Robert MacNish, *An Introduction*, pp. 111-112; see MacNish's questions, "What is the character of a person who has a great endowment of Ideality?" and "What are the abuses of Ideality?" pp. 113-114.
[57] *Works*, III, 273.
[58] *Works*, III, 274.

musical science."[59] We are given to understand that Usher is an artist of considerable ability.[60] Turning to phrenology again, we find that the organ of *Ideality* conduces to "a sense of exquisiteness and enthusiasm requisite for the conceptions of the poet, painter, and musician."[61] By this time we are well prepared for the description of Usher himself, and we are by no means surprised to discover that he has "an inordinate expansion above the regions of the temple."[62] Of course this region is none other than *Ideality*. Poe leaves us in no doubt about this, for later in the story he explicitly says: "An excited and highly distempered ideality threw a sulphureous lustre over all."[63]

But Roderick Usher is a complex creature of Poe's construction. He is not altogether to be explained by *Ideality,* no matter how highly developed it may be. Poe has recourse to further phrenological suggestions. In one of Combe's chapters there is a discussion of various temperaments, of which there are four types. One of these is the *nervous*. Combe thus describes the external signs of this temperament as follows: "The nervous is indicated by fine thin hair, small muscles, thin skin, paleness of countenance, and brightness of eye. This temperament gives great vivacity of mental action."[64] Recalling that Usher's letter had indicated "nervous agitation,"[65] we are not unprepared for the description of Usher with which Poe provides us: "The now ghastly pallor of the skin, and the now miraculous lustre of the eye, above all things startled and even awed me. The silken hair, too, had been suffered to grow all unheeded, and as, in its wild gossamer texture, it floated rather than fell about the face, I could not, even with effort, connect its Arabesque expression with any idea of simple humanity."[66] Can this parallelism be accidental? Clearly Poe has delineated for us a phrenologically correct *nervous temperament*. If we have any doubt Poe dispels it immediately by taking pains to point the matter. Usher is described at once as suffering from "an excessive nervous agitation."[67] At once Poe exposes his intention to portray Usher correctly according to phrenology by adding: "For something of

---

[59] *Works*, III, 275.
[60] *Works*, III, 283.
[61] Miles, p. 86; see also MacNish, p. 112.
[62] *Works*, III, 279.
[65] *Works*, III, 274.
[63] *Works*, III, 282.
[66] *Works*, III, 279.
[64] Combe, *Lectures*, p. 113.
[67] *Ibid*.

this nature I had indeed been prepared, no less by his letter, than by reminiscences of certain boyish traits, and by conclusions deduced from his peculiar physical conformation and temperament."[68] The diagnosis is complete. Roderick Usher is of the highly *nervous temperament,* with an immoderately developed organ of *Ideality.* The gloomy scene in which he lives, the events which are taking place about him, accentuate his nature, and the art of Poe creates an amazingly intense story therefrom.

It is almost superfluous to point out the added details or interpretations with which phrenology supplies the author. Poe's first readers would have missed none of them. They would have recognized the exact propriety of characterization which made Roderick Usher facile in the improvisation of verses. Had not the phrenologist MacNish declared that a person endowed with a high degree of *Ideality* had conceptions which flowed from him "rapidly and eloquently"?[69] Had not Combe especially remarked the ability of such persons to compose verses extempore?[70] Small wonder that Usher produced such "rhymed verbal improvisations"[71] as that exquisite allegory of the mind, "The Haunted Palace." Poe's first readers would have well understood the extreme suffering of Usher under the strain to which his sister's illness subjected him. An unsigned article in *The American Phrenological Journal,* published just two months before "The Fall of the House of Usher" appeared, treated extensively of the temperaments. Poe's readers knew all about the nervous temperament which Usher possessed. They knew that "a preponderance of this temperament gives a susceptibility of exquisite enjoyment, or extreme suffering."[72] Yes, the nervous temperament of Usher and his "lofty and spiritual ideality"[73] were well drawn.

[68] *Ibid.* The delineation of the character of Usher is in keeping with Mrs. Miles's description of the abuses of *Ideality:* "Over-wrought sensibility; eccentricity: uncontrollable raptures, or wild flights of fancy; exaggerated notions of refinement; neglect of the duties and realities of life" (*Phrenology,* p. 85).
[69] MacNish, *op. cit.,* p. 113.
[70] Combe, *A System,* p. 245.
[71] *Works,* III, 284.
[72] "The Temperaments," unsigned article in *The American Phrenological Journal,* I, 368. See also J. G. Spurzheim, *Phrenology,* (London, 1908), p. 248.
[73] *Works,* III, 292.

VI

"Ligeia" is one of Poe's more successful tales. Poe himself once called it "undoubtedly the best story I have written."[74] In view of its fame, we may well scrutinize Poe's significant use of phrenology in the construction of the tale. He begins abruptly. He describes the raven-haired Ligeia. One of the first things about her to strike an impression is the "thrilling and enthralling eloquence of her low musical language."[75] We may prick up our ears at this, wondering whether Poe is going to say more about language. It is one of the organs of phrenology, and the eyes are the external index of it.[76] We have not long to wait. The description leaves us very soon peering "into the large eyes of Ligeia."[77] And very large eyes they were. "Far larger than the ordinary eyes of our own race"—"fuller even than the fullest of the gazelle eyes of the tribe of the valley of Nourjahad"—and so on. Clearly the organ of *Language* was fully developed in Ligeia, and we are well prepared for Poe's subsequent observation that she was deeply proficient in the classical tongues.[78] Now what is the purpose of all this? Ligeia's language has very little to do with the story. Is it possible that Poe had an ulterior purpose? Had he some reason for putting in these phrenological details? Very definitely, yes. Poe had an excellent reason for satisfying the reader's mind: Ligeia's eyes were large and full; she was facile in language. The reader would recognize at once that Poe knew what he was about. This was a person who was true to life, scientifically true according to phrenology. Now what was Poe's ulterior purpose? Let us take another glance at the Lady Ligeia. There is a great deal said about her beauty, but among the delectable details, one is very striking. There is a "gentle prominence of the regions above the temples."[79] Anyone who knew phrenology would know at once that this was significant. But in what way?

Turning to the chart prefixed to Combe's *Lectures,* let us examine the regions above the temples. We find various contiguous areas. That marked by the number *Nine* proves to be *Constructive-*

---

[74] Letter to Duyckinck, *Works,* XVII, 227.
[75] *Works,* II, 248.
[76] Combe, *A System,* p. 322.
[77] *Works,* II, 251.
[78] *Works,* II, 253.
[79] *Works,* II, 250.

ness. Number *Eight* is *Acquisitiveness*. The lower portion of *Seven* is near the temple. It proves to be *Secretiveness*. *Six* is not far away. It is *Destructiveness*. None of these seems to fit the character of Ligeia, and they may be dismissed. One area remains to be considered. It is very close to the temple, almost certainly the region to which Poe refers. It bears the number *Six*, followed by a letter which may be construed either as a small *a* or *b*. Now in the list of "affective propensities," we discover two regions, 6*a*, and 6*b*. The first is *Alimentiveness*, an area which denotes a taste for heavy feeding. This could hardly apply to the Lady Ligeia. The chart is confusing, because while the list enumerates both 6*a* and 6*b*, the chart pictures only one area, and this with the lettering ambiguous. If we are to rule out Ligeia's appetite, what then have we left? The area 6*b* is described as *Love of Life*.[80]

Phrenologists had speculated upon the existence of an organ denoting a tenacious desire to live. "That this feeling is manifested in different degrees by different individuals is certain," says Combe, "the bravest men being sometimes excessively attached to life, while the most timid are often indifferent to life."[81] Gall, Spurzheim, Dr. Arthur Combe, George Combe, Shurtleff, MacNish, the Fowlers—all had recognized the existence of the organ.[82] But—and hence the ambiguity in the chart—there had been considerable difficulty in locating the area. Possibly it lay beneath the mastoid process, not easily apparent on the surface. It was somewhere near the ear. In 1835 Combe had felt that in persons having small *Love of Life* "That part of the base of the brain which lies between the ear and the anterior lobe is generally narrow. . . ."[83] Presumably the converse would indicate some sort of protuberance. Doubtless the matter was definite enough for Poe's purpose.

Now let us proceed with the story:

Ligeia grew ill. The wild eyes glazed with a too—too glorious effulgence; the pale fingers became of the transparent waxen hue of the grave;

---

[80] I am indebted to Mr. Verner Clapp, of the Library of Congress, for aid in unraveling difficulties connected with this organ.

[81] *Lectures*, p. 162.

[82] See *ibid.*, p. 64; Spurzheim, *Doctrine* (Boston, 1832); A. Combe, "Case of Hypochrondriasis," *The Phrenological Journal and Miscellany*, III, 467-472 (1826); N. B. Shurtleff, *An Epitome of Phrenology* (Boston, 1835); MacNish, *op. cit.*, O. S. and L. N. Fowler, *Phrenology Proved* (N. Y. 1837).

[83] George Combe, *The Constitution of Man*, 5th American edition (Boston, 1835), p. 199.

and the blue veins upon the lofty forehead swelled and sank impetuously with the tides of the most gentle emotion. I saw that she must die—and I struggled desperately in spirit with the grim Azrael. And the struggles of the passionate wife were, to my astonishment, even more energetic than my own. There had been much in her stern nature to impress me with the belief that, to her, death would have come without its terrors;—but not so. Words are impotent to convey any just idea of the fierceness of resistance with which she wrestled with the Shadow. I groaned in anguish at the pitiable spectacle. I would have soothed—I would have reasoned; but, in the intensity of her wild desire for life,—for life—but for life—solace and reason were alike the uttermost of folly.[84]

Love of Life! How emphatically Poe marks the words! He could not have accentuated them more thoroughly if he had pointed with both hands at them. And what of the reader? He had already found Poe correct in the matter of eyes and language. Now comes this other point. The "gentle prominence of the regions above the temples," carefully mentioned among the other details of Ligeia's appearance, is suddenly invested with the deepest significance. The reader's excitement is heightened. He has enjoyed the *recognition*. He might have known, perhaps had already guessed that *Love of Life* would be the dominating quality in the lady's disposition. And now this corroboration!

But Poe is not yet satisfied. He will refer to *Love of Life* again to make the matter certain. And before his paragraph is done, come these last significant words: "Let me say only, that in Ligeia's more than womanly abandonment to a love, alas! all unmerited, all unworthily bestowed, I at length recognized the principle of her longing with so wildly earnest a desire for the life which was now fleeing so rapidly away. It is this wild longing—it is this eager vehemence of desire for life—*but* for life—that I have no power to portray—no utterance capable of expressing."[85]

By this time the point has been made beyond all cavil. Ligeia will cling tenaciously to life. And now the story proper can begin. Ligeia dies and is buried. The hero of the tale marries the fair-haired Lady Rowena Trevanion, of Tremaine, who also, in the course of time sickens and dies. Her husband sits by her bier dream-

[84] *Works*, II, 254-255.
[85] *Works*, II, 256.

ing of Ligeia, when spasmodically the dead body of Rowena stirs with life. Time after time signs of life appear in the body only to be followed by "a sterner and apparently more irredeemable death."[86] At last the body of the dead Rowena actually comes to life sufficiently to "let fall from her head, unloosened, the ghastly cerements which had confined it, and there streamed forth, into the rushing atmosphere of the chamber, huge masses of long and dishevelled hair: *it was blacker than the raven wings of the midnight,* And now slowly opened *the eyes* of the figure which stood before me. 'Here then, at least,' I shrieked aloud, 'can I never—can I never be mistaken—these are the full, and the black, and the wild eyes— of my lost love—of the lady—of the LADY LIGEIA.'"

Well, it is really pretty exciting. One has known all along that something would come of that "gentle prominence of the regions above the temples." But it was rather brilliantly thought up to have *Love of Life,* that organ which Spurzheim discovered, actually bring the lady back to life through the dead body of another woman.

One has known all along that something would come of it? No. One has known only if one understood the connotation of the allusions to phrenology. It is too bad that the subtleties of this fine story of Poe should be lost to the modern reader merely because he knows nothing more about phrenology than the word *bumps.* Interpretative footnotes are sometimes essential if we are to recapture those delicate meanings which only too often die with an age. But so long as poets will enter into the *Zeitgeist,* so long must we learn to read them historically if we are to discover true meanings. It is not the history which we want. That is a secondary matter when it comes to art. But we *do* want true meanings. And that is why it is illuminating to find out what Edgar Allan Poe had to do with the science of *cranioscopy,* or *craniology,* or, as it came to be known, *phrenology.*

[86] *Works,* II, 267-268.

Poe as Social Critic
Ernest Marchand

AS early as 1855 the notion was abroad that Poe moved about over the earth thickly wrapped in a luminous cloud, which effectually shut him off from mundane concerns; that his mind dwelt exclusively in "the misty mid region of Weir." In that year Evert and George Duyckinck, who had known Poe in the flesh, wrote: "His rude contact with the world, which might have set up a novelist for life with materials of adventure, seems scarcely to have impinged upon his perceptions. His mind, walking in a vain show, was taught nothing by experience or suffering."[1] How a man who engaged in the active practice of journalism for upwards of fifteen years, who reviewed scores of books on topics ranging from the history of the American navy, life and manners in the West, education, the ecclesiastical history of the United States, and South Sea exploration, to eulogies of departed worthies like John Marshall; who, in 1844, walked with an observant eye up and down Manhattan, noting for future comment the wretched shanties of the recent Irish immigrants, the banal architecture of the dwellings,[2] and the bad taste of the Bowling Green fountain, which he likened to a "small country jail in a hard thunder shower"[3]—how such a man could prevent the various and gaudy life of the '30's and '40's from impinging upon his perceptions, is a little difficult to understand.

Professor Parrington asserts that Poe's "aloofness from his own Virginia world was complete. Aside from his art he had no philosophy and no programs and no causes."[4] Mrs. Hazard declares that Poe has "no connection with the regional frontier or with any region

---

[1] *Cyclopædia of American Literature*, 2 vols. (New York, Charles Scribner, 1866), II, 537.

[2] *Doings of Gotham . . . a Series of Letters to the Editors of the Columbia [Pennsylvania] Spy*. Now first collected by Jacob E. Spannuth with a Preface, Introduction, and Comments by Thomas Ollive Mabbott (Pottsville, Pa., Jacob E. Spannuth, 1929), pp. 25, 59. See also Poe's *Works,* ed. James A. Harrison, 17 vols. (New York, Crowell, 1902), XIV, 171: ". . . much of our cottage architecture . . . *would* have been Gothic if it had not felt it its duty to be Dutch."

[3] *Ibid.*, p. 26.

[4] *Main Currents in American Thought* (New York, 1927), II, 57.

except [that] to which [his] magic has given a local habitation and a name."[5] Accepting the general judgment of the literary historians, Professor A. M. Schlesinger finds that Poe is "a tragic and solitary genius, the Ishmael of letters, who shows no reflection of place or time in his work...."[6] Professor Edwin Greenlaw, after an able and convincing statement of the view that literature has intimate relations with the social and cultural *milieu* from which it springs, feels obliged to say that a "sharp distinction [must] be drawn between ... the product of the solitary artist working, so far as we can see, independently of time or place, such an artist as Poe for example, . . . and that other and far larger body of imaginative writing which is transcript of the life out of which it springs."[7] The old formula also serves Professor Russell Blankenship, who writes: "a grave weakness of Poe is his intellectual detachment from his time and environment."[8] Thus Poe baffles the sociological and historical critics, and becomes one of the chief supports of those doctors of

[5] *The Frontier in American Literature* (New York, 1927), p. 84. It is true that the frontier shows little direct influence in Poe's more imaginative work, although it is clear that he delved into books of travel and exploration in the West, among them accounts of the Lewis and Clark Expedition, on which he founded his "Journal of Julius Rodman" (see Miss P. P. Crawford, "Lewis and Clark's *Expedition* as a Source for Poe's 'Journal of Julius Rodman,'" University of Texas *Studies in English*, No. 12, pp. 158 ff. (1932). See also his review of Irving's *Astoria, Works*, IX, 207, and "Von Kempelen and His Discovery," which, as he explains, in a letter to Duyckinck (March 8, 1849), was written to hoax the public, to act "as a sudden, although of course a very temporary, *check* to the gold-fever," and to "create a *stir* to some purpose." (*Works*, XVII, 341.)

That Poe was well aware of the influence of the frontier on American life and character is evident in his notice of the work of Caroline M. Kirkland. "With a fidelity and vigor that prove her pictures to be taken from the very life, she has represented 'scenes' that could have occurred only *as* and *where* she has described them. She has placed before us the veritable settlers of the forest, with all their peculiarities, national and individual; their free and fearless spirit; their homely utilitarian views; their shrewd out-looking for self-interest; their thrifty care and inventions multiform; their coarseness of manner, united with real delicacy and substantial kindness when their sympathies are called into action...." An accusation of pride, he notes, is "as destructive at the west as that of witchcraft in olden times, or the cry of mad dog in modern." (*Works*, XV, 84, 86.) See also his review of Longstreet's *Georgia Scenes, Works*, VIII, 257-265.

[6] *New Viewpoints in American History* (New York, Macmillan, 1922), p. 211.

[7] *The Province of Literary History* (Baltimore and London, 1931), pp. 99-100. Poe himself admitted some connection between environment and literature. He felt, however, that social, political, moral, or physical conditions could do no more than "momentarily repress" the development of art, whose principles "lie deep within the immortal nature of man, and have little necessary reference to the worldly circumstances which surround him." (*Works*, XI, 148.)

[8] *American Literature as an Expression of the National Mind* (New York, Holt, 1931), p. 217.

æsthetic who hold that art and the mind of the artist are gifts direct from heaven. Three generations of commentators have imposed upon the world the fiction that Poe was rather more isolated from the ordinary concerns of human life than Simeon Stylites on his pillar.

Of late, however, the traditional view of Poe has begun to meet with exception. As long ago as 1923 Professor Killis Campbell indicated briefly the variety of Poe's interests in his contemporary world.[9] Hervey Allen in the preface to his *Israfel* laments that although "conservative academic circles still continue to yawn through Mr. Emerson's doubtful Compensations, there is no knowledge, or comment upon what Mr. Poe had to say of democracy, science, and unimaginative literature about the same time. The croak of the raven is conveniently supposed to be purely lyric."[10] Professor James Southall Wilson has well shown that Poe began his career as a prose writer with satire of contemporary tastes and manners, but that his satiric purpose almost entirely missed fire at the time, and has been overlooked ever since.[11] And Professor Howard Mumford Jones has sensed the fact that the treatment of Poe in the conventional literary history, in which "literature is a static concept, not a dynamic social agency," is inadequate; when the historians are "confronted by such a phenomenon as Poe, their shallow classifications break down."[12] It is a mistake, Dr. H. S. Canby believes, to think that Poe owed nothing to the American tradition.[13]

Emerson once said, "It is impossible to extricate yourself from the questions in which your age is involved." Nor was Poe able to extricate himself from these questions. The great staples of thought and discussion in his day were democracy, social reform, and prog-

---

[9] "Poe in Relation to His Times," *Studies in Philology*, XX, 293-301 (July, 1923). In his recent *The Mind of Poe* (Cambridge, Mass., Harvard University Press, 1933) Professor Campbell has greatly extended the evidence.

[10] *Israfel* (New York, Doran, 1926), I, xi.

[11] "The Devil Was in It," *The American Mercury*, XXIV, 215-220 (Oct., 1931). I here make the suggestion that one of these early pieces, "Four Beasts in One," written in the midst of the Jacksonian era, is directed specifically against Jackson and his frontier democrats, and that the homo-cameleopard king is no less than King Mob, who so fluttered the Eastern dovecote when Jackson took office.

[12] *America and French Culture* (Chapel Hill, N. C., 1927), p. 6.

[13] *Classic Americans* (New York, Harcourt, Brace, 1931), p. 275. See also F. M. Darnell, "The Americanism of Edgar Allan Poe," *English Journal*, XVI, 185-192 (March, 1927).

ress. As a preliminary to a survey of his opinions on these subjects, it will be pertinent, as well as of intrinsic interest, to review his personal experience with the politics of the period.

II

It was his friend F. W. Thomas who first suggested to Poe the possibility of obtaining a government post by political appointment. In the spring of 1841, shortly after the death of the newly inaugurated Harrison and the accession of John Tyler, when the streets and inns of the capital were swarming with hungry office-seekers, Thomas wrote from Washington, where he himself had a small clerkship, to ask, "How would you like to be an office holder here at $1500 per year payable monthly by Uncle Sam?" After enlarging on the easy duties and the leisure which would be available for literary effort, he concludes with the invitation to "Come on and apply for a clerkship."[14] Poe, struggling with poverty in Philadelphia, was fired by the prospect. He replied:

Would to God I could do as you have done! Do you seriously think that an application to Tyler would have a good result? . . . My political principles have always been, as nearly as may be, with the existing administration, and I battled with right good will for Harrison when opportunity offered. . . . Have I any chance?[15]

During the next two years, while the negotiations continued, Poe knew something of the pains of the courtier. He tried to play the game according to the rules. He enlisted the friendly aid of John Pendleton Kennedy, then a congressman;[16] he said polite things about a poem by Robert Tyler, a son of the President;[17] he tried to secure an article for his projected magazine from Judge Upshur, Secretary of the Navy and a close personal friend of the President;[18] he made a trip to Washington but became intoxicated and damaged his cause.[19] All was in vain. In a final revelation of the meanness, pettiness, and trickery of politics, he abandoned his hopes of political

[14] Poe, *Works*, XVII, 85.
[15] *Ibid.*, XVII, 91-92.
[16] *Ibid.*, XVII, 92, 93-94, 95, 102.
[17] *Ibid.*, XVII, 105.
[18] *Ibid.*, XVII, 132.
[19] *Ibid.*, XVII, 134-137. In a remorseful letter to Thomas and Dow there is mention of "a cloak turned inside out" and "other peccadilloes of that nature," and of "making a fool" of himself at the public house of one Mr. Fuller. (*Ibid.*, XVII, 136.)

appointment. "You can have no idea of the low ruffians and boobies —men, too, without a shadow of political influence or caste—who have received office over my head. . . . I would write more, my dear Thomas, but my heart is too heavy."[20]

Thenceforward politicians and all their ways were anathema to Poe. In "Some words with a Mummy" (1845), a telling bit of satire on the notion of progress, he observes that one of the interlocutors of the revived mummy

> could not make the Egyptian comprehend the term "politics," until he sketched upon the wall, with a bit of charcoal, a little carbuncle-nosed gentleman, out at elbows, standing upon a stump, with his left leg drawn back, his right arm thrown forward, with the fist shut, the eyes rolled up toward Heaven, and the mouth open at an angle of ninety degrees.[21]

Writing from New York to *The Columbia* (Pennsylvania) *Spy* in 1844 he remarked with indignant scorn on the political corruption of the city, as a result of which miles of its streets were often left in total darkness for a fortnight at a time. He noted also that easy tolerance toward public rascality which is a peculiarly American trait. "When the question is asked—'cannot these scoundrels be made to suffer for their high-handed peculations?'—the reply is invariably—'oh, no—to be sure not—the thing is expected, and will only be laughed at as an excellent practical joke'."[22]

It is doubtful whether Poe had any clear sense of direction in the welter of cross purposes which constituted party politics. He declared as above that his political principles had always been "as nearly as may be with the existing administration"; that is, Whig, and that he had "battled with a right good will for Harrison." But Tyler was at heart a Virginia Democrat who had flirted with the Whigs and been put on the ticket with Harrison as an act of expediency. After the latter's death, it was at first uncertain which way Tyler would go, but he presently began to oppose Whig measures. Poe wrote to Thomas respecting one Smith, through whom he expected a clerkship in the Philadelphia custom-house: "Mr. Smith has excited the thorough disgust of every Tyler man here.

---

[20] *Ibid.*, XVII, 123-124.
[21] *Works*, VI, 125. See also "Fifty Suggestions," Nos. 12 and 16, *Works*, XIV, 173, 174.
[22] *Doings of Gotham*, pp. 31-32.

He is a Whig of the worst stamp and will appoint none but Whigs if he can possibly avoid it."[23] And of Judge Upshur he avowed that he thought him "as a reasoner, as a speaker, and as a writer, absolutely unsurpassed."[24] But Judge Upshur was an extreme states' rights, pro-slavery Democrat. It is obvious that in all this Poe's politics showed a disposition to be flexible, that he was seeking a job and a competence that would enable him to devote himself to his writing; but his stand on the larger general questions of social reform, democracy, and progress as it was understood by industrial Whiggery, is hardly open to doubt.

III

As a thorough-going intellectual aristocrat Poe was an individualist, but his individualism was less the economic, laissez-faire type found in Whig political theory than the product of his deep-rooted sense of the uniqueness, worth, and dignity of the individual personality. "It is only the philosophical lynxeye that, through the indignity-mist of Man's life, can still discern the dignity of Man."[25] Whatever seemed to threaten the integrity of individual personality he would oppose. Hence, he despised Carlyle's hero-worship: "... is it possible," he asks, "that it ever excited a feeling beyond contempt? *No* hero-worshipper can possess anything within himself. That man is no man who stands in awe of his fellow-man."[26] Hence, also, enthusiasm for the greatest good of the greatest number, or for the exaltation of humanity in the abstract and spelled with a capital "H" failed to move him. Bentham and Mill with their utilitarianism were his peculiar aversions.[27] He liked neither the method of their reasoning nor their conclusions. He accuses Mill of employing the word "force" in four different senses on the same page. By the same process of introducing slight variations in the meaning of his terms, Poe asserts that he himself could prove a turnip to be a leg of mutton. Bentham's positions could be overthrown by the same arguments used to support them. A priori argument, outside the mathematical sciences, is futile; "it is utterly

---

[23] *Works*, XVII, 122.
[24] *Ibid.*, XVII, 132.
[25] "Marginalia," *Works*, XVI, 161.
[26] *Ibid.*, XVI, 100.
[27] See "Mellonta Tauta," *Works*, VI, 204; "Marginalia," *ibid.*, XVI, 1, 70; "Eureka," *ibid.*, XVI, 193.

and radically inapplicable" to the subject of government.[28] In so far as he entertained an ethical theory, Poe may be called a hedonist; but the hedonism of Bentham and Mill, embodied in the central utilitarian doctrine of "the greatest happiness of the greatest number," was repugnant to him simply because it removed the emphasis from individual, and placed it on social, man.

In "Mellonta Tauta," a satire on democracy, progress, and other objects of his dislike, he avails himself of a device to be used by many others after him, from Bellamy to Wells. He projects us into the distant future to provide an opportunity for criticism of the present. It is the year 2848. The protagonist of the piece is hurtling through space at one hundred miles an hour in a vast balloon with two hundred other passengers. To relieve the tedium of the journey she writes a letter:

I rejoice, my dear friend, that we live in an age so enlightened that no such thing as an individual is supposed to exist.... Is it not truly remarkable that, before the magnificent light shed upon philosophy by Humanity, the world was accustomed to regard War and Pestilence as calamities?... Is it not really difficult to comprehend upon what principle of interest our forefathers acted? Were they so blind as not to perceive that the destruction of a myriad of individuals is only so much positive advantage to the mass![29]

IV

Poe had little faith in social reform, with its emphasis on the improvement of *society*. His age was preëminently one of reform. Hardly a human custom or institution that was not under fire from some enthusiast; capital punishment,[30] diet, dress, marriage, the position of women, education, property—all came under the critical or zealous scrutiny of the reformer. The country was dotted with social experiments, New Harmony, Brook Farm,[31] and a score of others. The teachings of St. Simon, Fourier, and Robert Owen were widely spread. Poe was hostile, even questioning the sincerity of the reforming spirit, as it appeared in such popular novelists as

[28] "Marginalia," ibid., XVI, 38.
[29] Ibid., VI, 199, 200. Cf. ibid., XVI, 170.
[30] As Poe says, a vexed topic; see his notice of the Reverend George B. Cheever's *Defence of Capital Punishment*, Works, XV, 33.
[31] "Crazyites" Poe called the people of Brook Farm. (Works, XIII, 27.)

Sue: "The cant ... about the amelioration of society, etc., is but a very usual trick among authors, whereby they hope to add such a tone of dignity or utilitarianism to their pages as shall gild the pill of their licentiousness."[32] The reformers were distinguished, he felt, chiefly by their simplicity and their devotion to mere freakishness.

The world is infested, just now [he writes in *Graham's*, in 1845] by a new sect of philosophers.... They are the *Believers in everything Odd*. Their High Priest in the East, is Charles Fourier[33]—in the West, Horace Greeley.... The only common bond among the sect, is Credulity:—Let us call it Insanity at once, and be done with it.[34]

The ground of his opposition is first, that "The modern reformist Philosophy ... annihilates the individual by way of aiding the mass,"[35] and, second, that it has no real support in human nature.

"He that is born to be a man," says Wieland in his "Peregrinus Proteus," "should nor can be anything nobler, greater, or better than a man." The fact is, that in efforts to soar above our nature, we invariably fall below it. Your reformist demigods are merely devils turned inside out.[36]

Feminism, as an element in the reform movement of the age, also received Poe's attention. His ideas on women were the thor-

---

[32] *Works*, XVI, 105. Note the familiar trick of damning the social radical by calling him "licentious." It is frequently inferred from Poe's anti-didacticism that he was free of the moral taboos of his age. But in all matters touching women, sex, marriage, "morals," no more conventional-minded man than Poe ever lived. As a reviewer he seldom fails to chide and to commend writers for the moral tendencies of their work. "A high tone of morality, healthy and masculine, breathes throughout" Kennedy's *Horse-Shoe Robinson* (*Works*, VIII, 11); the hero of Ingraham's *Lafitte, the Pirate of the Gulf* is an atrocious scoundrel, yet "he is never mentioned but with evident respect ... his portraiture as depicted, leaves upon the mind of the reader no proper degree of abhorrence" (*ibid.*, IX, 115); Mrs. Child's *Philothea* "might be introduced advantageously into our female academies. Its purity of thought and lofty morality are unexceptionable" (*ibid.*, IX, 154); George Sand (or, as Poe prefers to call her, Madame Dudevant) is a woman "who intersperses many an admirable sentiment amid a chaos of the most shameless and altogether objectionable fiction" (*ibid.*, XIV, 150); Byron's love for Mary Chaworth is pure and tender, "strangely in contrast with the gross earthliness pervading and disfiguring his ordinary love poems" (*loc. cit.*); Michel Masson, author of *Le Cœur d'une Jeune Fille*, is "A fetid batterer upon the garbage of thought.... A beast.... A pig.... A carrion-crow ... (*ibid.*, XVI, 36).

[33] Poe refers often to Fourier and his doctrines, always scornfully. In "Mellonta Tauta" he puns on the name, converting it into Furrier. (*Works*, VI, 199.) See also *ibid.*, XIII 155; XIV, 172; XVI, 100.

[34] "Fifty Suggestions," *Works*, XIV, 179-180.

[35] *Works*, XVI, 170.

[36] *Ibid.*, XVI, 161.

oughly naïve and unrealistic ones traditional in the South. In the course of a rebuke to Bulwer for some public remarks about Lady Blessington, he takes occasion to outline the aims of female education in America:

We do not put the names of our fine women in the newspapers. The business of female education with us, is not to qualify a woman to be the head of a literary *coterie,* nor to figure in the journal of a travelling coxcomb. We prepare her, as a wife, to make the home of a good, and wise, and great man, the happiest place to him on earth. We prepare her, as a mother, to form her son to walk in his father's steps.... When we have done this, we have accomplished, if not *all,* at least *the best* that education can do. Her praise is found in the happiness of her husband, and in the virtues and honors of her son. Her name is too sacred to be profaned by public breath.[37]

Men, he thought, could never penetrate "that gentle and beautiful mystery, the heart of woman."[38] Hence, the delineation of feminine character in fiction was best performed by women. His ideal heroine was "a being full of lofty and generous impulses, beautiful, intellectual and *spirituelle.*"[39] He found the "dictatorial manner" of Frances Kemble the chief fault of her *Journal,* for a "female, and a young one too, cannot speak with the self-confidence which marks this book, without jarring somewhat upon American notions of the retiring delicacy of the female character."[40]

In his reviews of their works, Poe was generally very gracious to lady littérateurs, yet he held bluestockings in contempt. In the farcical "The Man That Was Used Up," the narrator attends the rout of "that bewitching little angel, the graceful Mrs. Pirouette," in search of information about the Brevet Brigadier General A. B. C. Smith, empty fraud and prophet of progress. After a nonsensical dispute with Miss Bas-Bleu he makes his retreat "in a very bitter spirit of animosity against the whole race of the Bas-Bleus."[41] Later Poe observed that "Our 'blues' are increasing in number at a great

---

[37] *Ibid.,* VIII, 14. See also X, 102-103, for some rant against "a pack of literary debauchees," "heartless slanderers," and "wretches" who are "libelling our mothers and sisters unopposed."
[38] *Ibid.,* VIII, 95.
[39] *Ibid.,* VIII, 96.
[40] *Ibid.,* VIII, 30.
[41] *Ibid.,* III, 268.

rate; and should be decimated, at the very least. Have we no critic with nerve enough to hang a dozen or two of them, *in terrorem*?"[24]

It is in his notice of Margaret Fuller in "The Literati" that we get some indication of his views on feminism. Her *Woman in the Nineteenth Century*, he thought, was "a book which few women in the country could have written, and no woman in the country would have published, with the exception of Miss Fuller. In the way of independence, of unmitigated radicalism, it is one of the 'Curiosities of American Literature'." He conceded that it was "thoughtful, suggestive, brilliant," but added, "the conclusions reached are only in part my own. Not that they are too bold, by any means—too novel, too startling, or too dangerous in their consequences, but that in their attainment too many premises have been distorted and too many analogical inferences left altogether out of sight. I mean to say that the intention of the Deity as regards sexual differences . . . has not been sufficiently considered."[43] Later, in a letter to Thomas, he referred to this brilliant representative of the race of the Bas-Bleus as "that detestable old maid."[44]

Just as he received his views on women as the gift of his time and place, so Poe received his views on slavery and swallowed them whole, unseasoned by criticism. He brings to the defense of the South's peculiar institution the same rationalizations that issued from a thousand Southern pulpits every Sunday, and from a thousand Southern presses every day of the week for more than twenty years. In an elaborate review of two works, *Slavery in the United States,* by J. K. Paulding, and *The South Vindicated from the Treason and Fanaticism of the Northern Abolitionists,* by an unnamed author—a review in which he says little of the books under consideration—he sets out his argument, founding it on a whole theory of history and society. Social revolutions occur at either of two alternately recurring extremes of the human mind—fanaticism and irreligion. At either extreme men will be animated by the same motive —the desire of happiness. But however the moralist may insist that happiness has its sources within the individual, men will bend all their energies to acquire the external means for attaining it. "Foremost among these, and the equivalent which is to purchase all the

[42] *Ibid.,* XVI, 173-174. See also XIV, 170; XV, 245.
[43] *Ibid.,* XV, 74-75.   [44] *Ibid.,* XVII, 333.

rest, is property. . . ."[45] In normal times each enjoys his own property without casting an envious eye on that of his neighbor. But under the excitement engendered by fanaticism or irreligion "the many who want, band themselves together against the few that possess; and the lawless appetite of the multitude for the property of others calls itself the spirit of liberty."[46] The Great Rebellion in England is an example of the fanatical extreme, and the French Revolution of the irreligious. The latter upheaval offers an object lesson to the South, for

it should be remembered now, that in that war against property . . . that war on behalf of the alleged right of man to be discharged from all control of law, the first triumph achieved was in the emancipation of slaves. The recent events in the West Indies, and the parallel movement here, give an awful importance to these thoughts in our minds.[47]

After a burst of indignation against "the calumnies which have been put forth against us, and the wrongs meditated by those who come to us . . . seeking our destruction under the mask of Christian Charity and Brotherly Love," Poe's next care is to maintain that the negro is of an inferior race. It is false to argue, he says, that because negroes are, "like ourselves the sons of Adam, [they] must therefore, have like passions and wants and feelings." He now dilates on the idyllic relation which subsists between master and slave, "incomprehensible to him who drives a bargain with the cook who prepares his food, the servant who waits at his table, and the nurse who dozes over his sick bed." At this point he opens up with the full orchestra, and concludes in a burst of lyric pathos:

We have seen the dying infant in the lap of its [black] nurse, and have stood with the same nurse by the bed side of her own dying child. Did mighty nature assert her empire, and wring from the mother's heart more and bitterer tears than she had shed over her foster babe? None that the eye of man could distinguish. And he who sees the heart—did he see dissimulation giving energy to the choking sobs that *seemed* to be rendered more vehement by her attempts to repress them? *Philanthropy* may think so if it pleases.[48]

[45] *Ibid.*, VIII, 267.
[46] *Loc. cit.*
[47] *Ibid.*, VIII, 269.
[48] *Ibid.*, VIII, 270, 271, 273-274.

On several other occasions Poe recurred to the subject of slavery."[49] In a fit of irritation he wrote to Thomas in the last year of his life, "I sent a review of the 'Fable' to the 'S. L. Messenger' a day or two ago, and I only hope Thompson will print it. Lowell is a ranting abolitionist and *deserves* a good using up."[50]

V

Science and mechanical invention exercised a fascination over Poe's mind, fired his imagination, and supplied him with much material for his fictions and the more serious speculations of *Eureka*. But in its practical results on society he found it evil. It destroyed the beauty of nature, vulgarized all the relations of life, delivered men over to a sordid scramble for gain, and abetted democracy in its steady encroachment on the integrity of the individual. His distrust found expression as early as 1829 in the "Sonnet to Science." The root of his hostility to English utilitarianism rested in his perception that it was the philosophical instrument of a rising industrial middle class. "Utilitarianism," he wrote, "sees in mountains and waterfalls only quarries and manufacturing sites."[51] The same is the theme of the sketch, "Morning on the Wissahiccon." In "The Colloquy of Monos and Una," which, like "Mellonta Tauta," takes place in the distant future, Monos reviews the last age of the earth:

At long intervals some master-minds appeared, looking upon each advance in practical science as a retro-gradation in the true utility . . . these men—the poets—living and perishing amid the scorn of the "utilitarians" . . . pondered piningly, yet not unwisely, upon the ancient days when our wants were not more simple than our enjoyments were keen . . . holy, august, and blissful days, when blue rivers ran undammed, between hills unhewn, into far forest solitudes, primaeval, odorous, and unexplored.

---

[49] For passing mention, see *Works*, IX, 70, 136; XII, 218; XV, 245, Whittier's themes "are *never* to our liking." In a letter to Snodgrass, June 17, 1841, Poe mentions a lengthy criticism of "Mr. Carey's book on slavery," which Burton refused (*ibid.*, XVII, 74). Was this ever printed?

[50] *Works*, XVII, 333. For the "using up," see *Works*, XIII, 165 ff. It is a mistake to dismiss Poe's opinions on slavery as dictated entirely by his resentment toward the New England hegemony in letters; "a little rant upon the Abolitionists (in the attempt to score on Lowell)," says Dr. Canby (*op. cit.*, p. 290). Poe ranted against the abolitionists before Lowell was out of college; the review of Paulding, above noticed, is of 1836. His feelings on the subject were, I am convinced, genuine; nor did they alter.

[51] *Works*, X, 25.

... Meantime huge smoking cities arose, innumerable. Green leaves shrank before the hot breath of furnaces. The fair face of nature was deformed as with the ravages of some loathsome disease.[52]

Like Emerson in his more skeptical moments, Poe felt that America was absorbed in getting and spending. Wealth was the chief measure of worth; here, "more than in any other region upon the face of the globe, to be poor is to be despised."[53] Some years later he wrote in the "Marginalia": "The Romans worshipped their standards; and the Roman standard happened to be an eagle. Our standard is only one-tenth of an Eagle—a dollar—but we make all even by adoring it with ten-fold devotion."[54]

But the doctrine of progress, which stands in relation to science as effect to cause, seemed entirely fatuous to Poe.[55] Monos says to Una, "You will remember that one or two of the wise among our forefathers—wise in fact, although not in the world's esteem—had ventured to doubt the propriety of the term 'improvement,' as applied to the progress of our civilization."[56] Ellison, the genius of "The Domain of Arnheim," had little faith in "the possibility of any improvement, properly so called, being effected by man himself in the general condition of man."[57] In a letter to Lowell (summarized

[52] *Ibid.*, IV, 202-203.

[53] Letter to Anthon, June, 1844 (*Works*, XVII, 179).

[54] *Works*, XVI, 161. See also "Fifty Suggestions," Nos. 15 and 21, *Works*, XIV, 173, 175; "Mellonta Tauta," *Works*, VI, 212-213: churches are "a kind of pagoda instituted for the worship of two idols that went by the names of Wealth and Fashion"; *Works*, IX, 158, education is invaded by "a misconceived utilitarianism," to the peril of the classical languages.

[55] Poe was not untouched by the expansive nationalism of his day. The tone and implication of his reviews of two volumes on the subject of a proposed exploring expedition, under government auspices, to the South Sea whaling fisheries, are of considerable interest. He speaks of the "paramount importance both in a political and commercial point of view" of the men of the whaling fleet. "The Pacific may be termed the training ground, the gymnasium of our national navy"; "mighty results" are to be expected "when this vast field for national enterprise is better known and appreciated." (*Works*, IX, 85, 87.) The second review will be found in the same volume, pp. 306-314. See also in this connection the long notice of Irving's *Astoria* (*Works*, IX, 207-243).

[56] *Works*, IV, 201-202.

[57] *Ibid.*, VI, 180. See the early satire "Lionizing" for a jibe at the perfectibilians (*Works*, II, 38); the review of Bryant's "The Ages," a poem on progress where Poe condemns "the radical error of deducing a hope of *progression* from *cycles* of physical nature," *ibid.*, XIII, 133; the review of Horne's "Orion," an allegory on progress, which makes out its case but "feebly," *ibid.*, XI, 258, 261; "Some Words with a Mummy," *ibid.*, VI, 136. Poe's objections to Chivers's ideas on "man's advance towards perfection" are mentioned in letters from Chivers. (*Ibid.*, XVII, 184, 189).

by Harrison) "Poe said that the vanity of human life was a genuine not a fancied thing to him; that he lived in dreams of the future while he did not believe in the perfectibility of the race. He thought that striving and struggling would have no effect, and that men are not more wise or happy than they were six thousand years ago."[58]

The appalling wilderness of stars, the unfathomable depths of space, the vast reaches of time, the rise and fall of civilizations each confident, in its pride, that it would endure forever, gave a somber tinge to Poe's thought. The greatest names of men fall into contempt or oblivion; future savants will putter about the site of long-dead New York and make ridiculous guesses about the life that once flourished there.[59] Nor does contemplation of the loftiest pinnacled edifices of the intellect offer relief from the tragedy of man. "It is laughable to observe how easily any system of Philosophy can be proved false:—but then is it not mournful to perceive the impossibility of even fancying any particular system to be true?"[60]

VI

Being the intellectual aristocrat that he was, Poe despised the rabble with its "excitable, undisciplined, and childlike ... mind,"[61] and heaped scorn upon it early and late. Democracy was merely an attempt to give "the obtuse in intellect"[62] power over their betters. One passage from among many will serve to show his thought:[63]

Pundit ... [says] that the ancient Amiriccans *governed themselves!*—did ever anybody hear of such an absurdity? ... He says that they started with the queerest idea conceivable, viz: that all men are born free and equal—this in the very teeth of the laws of gradation so visibly impressed upon all things both in the moral and physical universe. Every man "voted," as they called it—that is to say, meddled with public affairs —until, at length, it was discovered that what is everybody's business is

---

[58] July 2, 1844, *Works,* XVII, 182-183.
[59] "Mellonta Tauta," *Works,* VI, 211 ff.
[60] "Marginalia," *ibid.,* XVI, 164.
[61] *Works,* XIII, 143.
[62] *Ibid.,* XI, 10.
[63] We should not be deceived by the fact that Poe once replied to the objections of a foreign critic of democracy (see *Works,* VIII, 112-114), or by the fact that he once or twice used as an argument for international copyright the dissemination among us in foreign books of monarchical or aristocratical sentiment dangerous to democracy (*ibid.,* XVI, 79). The motives here are obvious and, it seems to me, do not weigh much against the whole tendency of his mind as it appears throughout his work.

nobody's, and that the "Republic" (so the absurd thing was called) was without a government at all. . . . A little reflection . . . sufficed to render evident . . . that a republican government *could* never be anything but a rascally one. While the philosophers, however, were busied in blushing at their stupidity in not having forseen these inevitable evils, and intent upon the invention of new theories, the matter was put to an abrupt issue by a fellow of the name of *Mob,* who took everything into his own hands and set up a despotism, in comparison with which those of the fabulous Zeros and Hellofagabaluses were respectable and delectable. This Mob is said to have been the most odious of all men that ever encumbered the earth. He was a giant in stature—insolent, rapacious, filthy; had the gall of a bullock with the heart of an hyena and the brains of a peacock. . . . As for Republicanism, no analogy could be found for it upon the face of the earth—unless we except the case of the "prairie dogs," an exception which seems to demonstrate, if anything, that democracy is a very admirable form of government—for dogs.[64]

Near the beginning of his career as a reviewer, Poe had given voice to the eighteenth-century idea of Dr. Johnson that governments, after all, have little power to cause or cure the ills of men: "we must look for the source of our greatest defects in a variety of causes totally distinct from any such action—in a love of gain, for example."[65] Thus the source of society's ills is to be sought in the individual heart. But here there is little hope, for "To be *thoroughly* conversant with Man's heart, is to take our final lesson in the iron-clasped volume of Despair."[66]

In his views on society and government Poe took on inevitably the color of his environment. It must be remembered that he always regarded himself as a Virginia gentleman,[67] that he was reared

[64] "Mellonta Tauta," *Works,* VI, 207-209. See also "Some Words with a Mummy," *ibid.,* VI, 136; "Hans Pfaall," *ibid.,* II, 48: "we soon began to feel the effects of liberty, and long speeches, and radicalism, and all that sort of thing. People . . . had as much as they could do to read about the revolutions, and keep up with the march of intellect and the spirit of the age"; *ibid.,* IX, 18-20, where Poe ridicules the French Republicans and sneers at hoi polloi who as "the result of newly acquired rights" now have the privilege "of presenting themselves dirty instead of clean before the eyes of the magnates"; *ibid.,* XII, 212, where he refers contemptuously to "a vast number of people without coats," as constituting the audience at the Chatham Theatre in New York; "Fifty Suggestions," No. 25, *Works,* XIV, 178-179, for his cynical view of democratic unrest in Europe; the same No. 21, p. 181, " 'La Jeune France,' . . . a body without a head."
[65] *Works,* IX, 54.
[66] *Ibid.,* XVI, 162.
[67] See Joseph Wood Krutch, *Edgar Allan Poe* (New York, Knopf, 1926), Chap. II.

in the expectation of becoming heir to one of the wealthiest men in Richmond,[68] that as a youth at the University of Virginia he mingled on a footing of ostensible equality with the drinking and dicing young bloods whose families constituted the aristocracy of the South. He was conscious, moreover, of superior powers of imagination and intellect. Hence, it was easy and natural for him to assume an attitude of superiority toward the rabble. But Poe protests too much, for he was at the same time profoundly and uneasily conscious of his own origins and of his precarious position as a foster son. When his break with John Allan put the world of Virginia society out of his reach, he was constrained to assert with three-fold vehemence the feelings of an aristocrat.

His scorn for Democracy and his fear of it are the same as that excited in the breasts of the propertied classes—North or South—by the Jacksonian incursion. His theory of government as instituted for the protection of property with his easy identification of the interests of property with those of religion and morality is the theory naturally adopted by any economy which feels itself on the defensive, as the South felt itself in the '30's and '40's.[69] His suspicion of industrialism, in whatever degree it was shaped or intensified by his feelings as an artist, may well have its source in the antipathy of the slave economy toward its Northern rival. The various reform movements of the age, with their open or concealed threat to established institutions, must be suspect to the social order with which he had identified himself intellectually and emotionally from his earliest years.[70] It is thus difficult to avoid seeing in Poe's hostile criticism of democracy, industrialism, and reform, the influence of that Virginia world of which he is said never to have been aware.

[68] Hervey Allen, *Israfel*, I, 116; Poe, *Works*, XVII, 15.
[69] Observe the similarities between Poe's social philosophy and that of the Federalists of two generations earlier, when Jeffersonian Democracy seemed to threaten the prerogatives of those whom John Adams denominated the "industrious, virtuous, and deserving."
[70] A good account of the domestic and social environment of Poe's childhood and boyhood is given in Hervey Allen's *Israfel*, I, 27-62; 90-146.

Edgar Allan Poe, Cryptographer
William F. Friedman

IT IS a curious fact that popular interest in this country in the subject of cryptography received its first stimulus from Edgar Allan Poe. Should a psychologic association test be made, the word "cipher" would doubtless bring from most laymen the immediate response, "Poe" or "The Gold Bug." The fame of Poe rests not a little on his activities with cipher, and much of the esteem in which this American genius is held today rests in part on the legend of Poe the Cryptographer.

Several years ago, in an extremely interesting and penetrating analysis, Joseph Wood Krutch discussed Poe's activities in cryptography, saying:

Doubtless nothing contributed to a greater extent than did Poe's connection with cryptography to the growth of the legend which pictured him as a man at once below and above ordinary human nature; but the whole subject is still unfortunately wrapped in some obscurity, and it is impossible to be sure of the facts as distinguished from his own report of them.[1]

The popular conception of, and the reaction toward, the subject of cryptography in Poe's time—and to a certain extent today—are the remnants of a medieval point of view, which regarded it in somewhat the following light: A cryptogram is a piece of writing to which a meaning exists but is not immediately perceptible; its intelligibility is concealed, hence mysterious or occult, and thus

[1] *Edgar Allan Poe: A Study in Genius* (New York, 1926), p. 103. More recently, Professor Killis Campbell (in *The Mind of Poe and Other Studies,* Cambridge, Mass., 1933) says: "What, finally, of the fibre of Poe's mind, of his natural endowments, and of his intellectual integrity? No one, so far as I know, has ever denied to Poe the possession of a peculiarly acute and active mind. . . . That he had extraordinary powers of analysis comes out everywhere,—in his critical reviews, in his studies in sensation, in his ratiocinative and pseudo-scientific stories, in his solving of ciphers and cryptographs" (pp. 28-29). "Question has likewise been raised in some quarters as to Poe's honesty and his intellectual integrity. . . . But an even more serious indictment has been brought against him, to the effect that he at times made a display of learning or affected an erudition to which he had no claim" (pp. 30-31).

supernatural. Therefore anyone practicing the art is of necessity the associate of forces governing supernatural phenomena. The mental portrait the average layman has even today of the professional cryptographer is that of a long-haired, thick-bespectacled recluse; a cross between a venerable savant and a necromancer who must perforce commune daily with dark spirits in order to accomplish his feats of mental jiu-jitsu.

This impression was doubtless prevalent in Poe's time because authentic information concerning cryptography was extremely limited and is even today quite meager. One of the interesting anomalies in the whole field of cryptology is the paucity of sound literature on the subject. In the most extensive bibliography in print,[2] the number of treatises of real technical merit does not exceed a dozen. Such a pitiful showing for an art that has been practiced from time immemorial cannot be ascribed to a lack of interest in the subject on the part of the general public, or to a lack of usefulness as a branch of knowledge. On the contrary, cryptography is employed to a great degree every day in all countries, in diplomatic, military, naval, business, and social affairs; and as a pastime, it presents many of the elements that constitute the *raison d'être* of the best types of puzzles. Even those who have never delved into it agree that the subject intrigues and tantalizes them. Yet information concerning methods of preparing cryptograms of sound merit is very meager, and that concerning methods of solving them is abysmally lacking to all except a very small circle of professional cryptographers who remain in office only so long as they violate no governmental secrets connected with their work.

It is not strange, then, that in a field wherein popular interest is great but popular knowledge extremely limited many spurious ideas should be current. This state of affairs existed in Poe's day, and consciously or subconsciously Poe saw an opportunity to exploit it for his own purposes. To exhibit deep understanding and thorough knowledge where the stock of knowledge on the part of others is practically nil, would seem to be a pardonable source of gratification to a perfectly normal person; what could be more soothing and reassuring to the victim—according to Krutch's view—of a rather well-developed inferiority complex?

[2] André Lange and E.-A. Soudart, *Traité de Cryptographie* (Paris: Librairie Félix Alcan, 1925). The number of items in this list is approximately one hundred.

Poe's known cryptographical writings include the article "A Few Words on Secret Writing," which appeared in the July, 1841, issue of *Graham's Magazine;* three supplementary articles appearing in the August, October, and December issues of the same magazine; his tale "The Gold Bug"; and, if it may be included under the heading of cryptographical writings, a recently discovered letter written to a Mr. Richard Bolton, of Pontotoc, Mississippi. In none of them can the serious student of the subject find any evidence that Poe was more than a tyro either in the art of cryptography or in its handmaid, the science of cryptographic analysis. Long before his day, men who had made a study of these matters were far more proficient, and their names are all but forgotten.

One of the references that Poe made to cryptography occurs in connection with a review of a book entitled *Sketches of Conspicuous Living Characters of France,* which appeared in the April, 1841, issue of *Graham's Magazine.* It is as follows:

In the notice of Berryer it is said that, a letter being addressed by the Duchess of Berry to the legitimists of Paris, to inform them of her arrival, it was accompanied by a long note in cypher, the key of which she had forgotten to give. "The penetrating mind of Berryer," says our biographer, "soon discovered it. It was this phrase substituted for the twenty-four letters of the alphabet—*Le gouvernement provisoire!*"

All this is very well as an anecdote; but we cannot understand the extraordinary penetration required in the matter. The phrase *Le gouvernement provisoire* is French, and the note in cypher was addressed to Frenchmen. The difficulty of decyphering may well be supposed much greater had the key been in a foreign tongue; yet any one who will take the trouble may address us a note, in the same manner as here proposed, and the key-phrase may be in either French, Italian, Spanish, German, Latin, or Greek (or in any of the dialects of these languages), and we pledge ourselves for the solution of the riddle. The experiment may afford our readers some amusement—let them try it.[2a]

The way in which Poe puts the matter reminds one very much of the manner in which a conjurer, performing a mystifying trick, extremely simple in itself, surrounds its execution with a great deal of unnecessary stage business to make it appear more complicated and difficult than it really is. A casual inspection of the type of

---

[2a] J. A. Harrison (ed.), *The Complete Works of Edgar Allan Poe,* "Virginia Edition" (New York, 1902), X, 135-136. Hereafter cited as *Works.*

alphabet said to have been employed by the lady of forgetful memory will quickly convince even a novice that the arrangement of letters in the cipher alphabet has absolutely nothing to do with the case. The solution is entirely independent of the arrangement of letters and, of course, Poe knew it. He admits this, in fact, in his essay which he published three months later. We might be very much inclined to overlook this particular bit of hokum were it not for the fact that this incident led directly to his writing the essay which appeared in the July number of *Graham's*.

In the course of this essay Poe repeats, almost verbatim, the remarks made in the April number in connection with the Berryer cryptogram and adds that "This challenge has elicited but a single response, which is embraced in the following letter." He then gives the letter, which encloses two cryptograms composed by means of cipher alphabets of the nature indicated above. Poe solves them, gives the solutions, and says:

In the solution of the first of these ciphers we had little more than ordinary trouble. The second proved to be exceedingly difficult, and it was only by calling every faculty into play that we could read it at all.[3]

Anyone who will take the trouble to go into the matter carefully will, I am sure, be entirely at a loss to account for the difficulty Poe experienced with regard to the second example. The reader will have to take my word for it, of course, but I say that any person who, having devoted but two weeks' study to elementary cryptograms, cannot solve that particular cryptogram in two hours at the most, had better turn his attention to other pursuits wherein success will crown his efforts with less expenditure of energy. As a matter of fact the experiment was recently tried upon four persons who had just completed exactly ten days' study of cryptography. They worked independently, and each accomplished the solution in approximately thirty-five minutes.

Over half of "A Few Words on Secret Writing" is devoted to the Berryer form of cryptogram, a type which, despite its utter simplicity, is so impractical that it is employed only by novices, and then only seldom. The actual Berryer cryptogram must, indeed, be considered the concoction of amateurs or of persons whose knowl-

[3] *Ibid.*, XIV, 126.

edge of cryptography was extremely limited, for, so far as history records, no such impractical system was ever regularly employed for serious purposes. It is true that Poe comments upon its impracticability, but as to the complexity of the type, it is apparent that he thought highly of it.

In this same essay Poe refers to other writings on the subject of cryptography, which, he says, appeared "in one of the weekly papers of this city [Philadelphia]." This paper has been identified as *Alexander's Weekly Messenger*.[4]

In the discussion of an analogous subject, in one of the weekly papers of this city, about eighteen months ago, the writer of this article had occasion to speak of the application of a rigorous *method* in all forms of thought—of its advantages—of the extension of its use even to what is considered the operation of pure fancy—and thus, subsequently, of the solution of cipher. He even ventured to assert that no cipher, of the character above specified, could be sent to the address of the paper, which he would not be able to resolve. This challenge excited, most unexpectedly, a very lively interest among the numerous readers of the journal. Letters were poured in upon the editor from all parts of the country; and many of the writers of these epistles were so convinced of the impenetrability of their mysteries, as to be at great pains to draw him into wagers on the subject. At the same time, they were not always scrupulous about sticking to the point. The cryptographs were, in numerous instances, altogether beyond the limits defined in the beginning. Foreign languages were employed. Words and sentences were run together without interval. Several alphabets were used in the same cipher. One gentleman, but moderately endowed with conscientiousness, inditing us a puzzle composed of pot-hooks and hangers to which the wildest typography of the office could afford nothing similar, went even so far as to jumble together no less than *seven distinct alphabets,* without intervals between the letters, *or between the lines.* Many of the cryptographs were dated in Philadelphia, and several of those which urged the subject of a bet were written by gentlemen of this city. Out of, perhaps, one hundred ciphers altogether received, there was only one which we did not immediately succeed in resolving. This one we *demonstrated* to be an imposition—that is to say, we fully proved it a jargon of random characters, having no meaning whatever. In respect to the epistle of the seven alphabets, we had the pleasure of completely *nonplus-ing* its inditer by a prompt and satisfactory translation.

[4] Krutch, *op. cit.*, p. 104.

Unfortunately the records that remain of *Alexander's Weekly Messenger* are exceedingly fragmentary. Despite painstaking research by numerous Poe experts, not a single issue containing any cipher solutions that Poe may have published as a result of his asserted challenge has ever been found, and there seems to be no way at the present moment of corroborating Poe's statements.[5] However, we may consider, from Poe's own words, that the cryptogram employing "no less than seven distinct alphabets" represented the most difficult of all those submitted to Poe, and therefore warrants special scrutiny.

Ciphers involving a plurality of different alphabets have been known in the art for a long time. The principle is very clearly described in the oldest tract on cryptography that the world now possesses, that written by Alberti.[6] Multiple alphabet ciphers vary in complexity to a much greater extent than do single alphabet cryptograms, and it is possible to employ in one dispatch a practically unlimited number of distinctly different alphabets. In general it may be said that the greater the number involved, the more difficult becomes the analysis, but the particular manner in which the separate alphabets are employed is an equally important factor in

[5] The following is quoted from Krutch, *op. cit.*: "Now the first of these articles [in *Alexander's Weekly Messenger*] was never found by any of the editors of Poe's works and has never been reprinted; but though no complete file of the periodical in question is known to exist some numbers are extant and in one of them is an article on enigmas which does challenge the reader to submit an example of secret writing in which an arbitrary symbol is substituted for each letter of the alphabet. It is not, however, possible to check up on Poe's later statement that in response to this challenge 'Letters were poured in upon the editor from all parts of the country' and were in every case successfully read in spite of the fact that many violated the conditions imposed and one employed seven distinct alphabets in the course of a single communication. Indeed, the fact that *Alexander's Weekly Messenger*, the paper in question, was exceedingly obscure and very short-lived, coupled with the fact that the second and similar challenge in the very prominent *Graham's Magazine* certainly brought much less response, makes legitimate a suspicion that Poe's statement embodies a considerable exaggeration" (pp. 103-104). "Just how much of this mysterious power was real and how much pretense it is impossible, as we have said, to determine, and it is extremely unfortunate that the results, if any, of the article in *Alexander's Weekly Messenger* cannot be traced. It is unfortunate also that the only explanation of his method which he gives, that contained in *The Gold Bug,* applies only to the simplest sort of cryptogram, and that he nowhere discusses the method employed in solving the more complicated ones" (p. 106).

[6] Leo Baptista Alberti, *Trattati in cifra.* Vat Arch., Series *Varia Politica,* Vol. LXXX, folios 173-181. (In the bibliography referred to in footnote 2, this treatise is dated 1480, but I can find no warrant for this. The acknowledged historical authority, Dr. Aloys Meister, in *Die Geheimschrift im Dienste der Päpstlichen Kurie* (Paderborn, 1906), who prints the Latin treatise in question, assigns no date to the manuscript, stating merely that Alberti died in 1472.)

solution. It is very unfortunate that Poe's statements with respect to the seven-alphabet example he solved tell us nothing about the latter factor. Internal evidence contained in his article, especially in his supplementary remarks with reference to a system known as the *chiffre quarré,* indicates that the seven alphabets were employed in one of the simplest possible ways, probably in rotation according to sentence lengths. If such were indeed the case the problem merely resolved itself into the solution of seven separate examples, each of the single alphabet type. But granting that the seven alphabets were used in one of the more intricate ways—let us assume that they were employed in a cyclic manner, changing with successive letters of the text—the solution of such a problem still represents a relatively simple case. To give Poe the greatest credit possible, however, it might be considered an achievement for an individual who simply plays with cryptography as a hobby.

In the August number of *Graham's,* Poe published a cryptogram composed by a Doctor Frailey of Washington, and sent to him by his well-known friend, F. W. Thomas. Poe says that the solution was forwarded to its author by return mail, and offers *"a year's subscription to the Magazine, and also a year's subscription to the Saturday Evening Post, to any person, or rather to the first person who shall read us this riddle."*[7] He goes on to say, "We have no expectation that it will be read; and therefore, should the month pass without an answer forthcoming, we will furnish the key to the cipher, and again offer a year's subscription to the magazine, to any person who shall solve it *with the key."*

The September number of the magazine is entirely silent on the subject. In the October number, Poe says:

> The cipher submitted through Mr. F. W. Thomas, by Dr. Frailey, of Washington, and deciphered by us, also in return of mail, as stated in our August number, has not yet been read by any of our innumerable readers. We now append its solution . . .

Poe did not abide by the terms of his August agreement, in which he stated that he would furnish the key and again offer a year's subscription to any person who would solve it with the key. Perhaps his exuberance over his achievement had somewhat died down

---

[7] *Works,* XIV, 134. The italics are Poe's.

after the August issue. But an examination of the Frailey cipher should show what there is about it that so excited Poe.

It is unnecessary to illustrate the cryptogram here; one need only indicate that it followed very closely the Berryer type, with the sole modification that a few words and the terminations SION and TION were represented not by letters, but by single symbols. For example, £ stood for IN, and the figure 7 for ON; there were nineteen such symbols, all instances of this sort. That they were not the representatives of individual letters was obvious from a mere ocular examination. Compared with the use made of the ordinary letters of the alphabet, the symbols were relatively insignificant. In fact, the solution can practically be accomplished without an analysis of these symbols, the meanings of which can then be merely inserted from the context. What then made the cryptogram seem so intricate to Poe? Let us take a look at the "clear text," and the matter may become apparent:

In one of those peripapetic circumrotations I obviated a rustic whom I subjected to catachetical interrogation respecting the nosocomical characteristic of the edifice to which I was approximate. With a volubility uncongealed by the frigorific powers of villatic bashfulness, he ejaculated a voluminous replication from the universal tenor of whose contents I deduce the subsequent amalgamation of heterogeneous facts. Without dubiety incipient pretension is apt to terminate in final vulgarity, as parturient mountains have been fabulated to produce muscupular abortions. The institution the subject of my remarks, has not been without cause the theme of the ephemeral columns of quotidian journalism, and enthusiastic encomiations in conversational intercourse.[8]

Despite a long experience with the absurd texts that cryptographic "inventors" are prone to employ, this, I confess, is quite a gem. It is a curious thing that persons who offer samples of cryptographic puzzles of their own "invention" almost invariably contrive to produce a monstrosity of diction like the foregoing. Perhaps it tickles their sense of humor—the unreasonableness of their language seems never to occur to them.

If Frailey's cipher was difficult, therefore, it became so *not because of any inherent complexity in the method employed,* but solely because the diction was so outrageous. But after the pre-

[8] *Ibid.,* XIV, 138-139.

liminary stages in solution—that is, after a few of the most important values had been obtained, which certainly should not consume more than one or two hours at the utmost—the completion of the puzzle was merely a matter of patience and the use of an unabridged dictionary. Certainly very little use of the analytical faculties so lauded by Poe was requisite. The Frailey cipher (naturally, without any information) was presented as a simple test to the same four students referred to before. In three hours all had recovered or reconstructed the phrase upon which the cipher alphabet was based, which was: "But find this out and I give it up."

The terms in which Poe issued his challenge in regard to the Frailey cipher are startling enough in themselves, but the esteem in which he really held the cryptogram is shown and, in addition, an interesting sidelight on his character is revealed by some correspondence which appeared in the November 15, 1925, issue of the Memphis *Commercial Appeal*. A Mr. Richard Bolton, of Pontotoc, Mississippi, on November 14, 1841, addressed a letter to Poe, taking him to task in the following terms:

> The November number of your valuable magazine has just arrived. To my great surprise no notice is taken of my solution of the cryptograph proposed to your readers in the August number. This I can attribute only to accident or oversight. As you had thrown the gauntlet which I took up, I must call upon you as a true man and no craven to render me according to the terms of the defiance the honors of a field worthily contested and fairly won.
>
> A friend lent me for perusal your magazine for that month. On the ninth of September, within a month after the arrival of the magazine, my solution was mailed postage paid, addressed to the editor. Accompanying it were certificates of two subscribers, Messrs. Glokenau and L. C. Draper (the latter assistant postmaster) that I had effected the solution unaided by the key and that the September number in which the key was exposed had not arrived.
>
> My solution fully agrees with your published solution except in two words about which I will soon take occasion to remark. I therefore claim to have fully complied with the terms of the challenge and to be entitled to all the rights, privileges, and honours therein expressed.

Poe's prompt reply, couched in the most friendly terms, offered a very clear and unquestionable explanation of what appeared to Bolton as an unwillingness to a division of the honors of victory and a participation in the spoils. The explanation, of course, lay in the fact that the forms of any periodical of fair size must go to press long in advance of issue. Poe then continued as follows (italicized portions were underlined in the original):

Upon this hint you will easily see the possibility of your letter not having come to hand in season for acknowledgment in the November number. Otherwise I should have had high gratification in sharing with you *then* the reputation of a bottle conjurer—for thus the matter seems to stand. In our December number (which has been ready for ten days) you will find an unqualified acknowledgment of your claims—without even allusion to the slight discrepancies for which I believe the printer is chargeable. I mean to say that you have (I believe) solved the cipher as printed. *My* solution follows the MS.—both are correct.

Allow me, Dear Sir, now to say that I was never more astonished in my life than at your solution. Will you honestly tell me?—did you not owe it to the accident of the repetition of the word "itagi"? for "those"? This repetition does not appear in the MS.—at least, I am pretty sure that it was interpolated by one of our compositors—a "genius" who takes much interest in these matters—and many unauthorized liberties.

In Dr. Frailey's MS. were many errors—the chief of which I corrected for press—but mere blunders do not much affect the difficulty of cypher solution—as you, no doubt, perceive. I had also to encounter the embarrassment of a miserably cramped and confused penmanship. Here you had the advantage of me—a very important advantage.

Be all this as it may—your solution *astonished* me. You will accuse me of vanity in so saying—but truth is truth. I make no question that it even astonished yourself—and well it might—for from at least 100,000 readers—a great number of whom, to my certain knowledge, busied themselves in the investigation—you and I are the only ones who have succeeded.

It is with some regret that I must place beside this frank acknowledgment an extract from a letter written by Poe to F. W. Thomas, dated November 26, 1841 (for which I am indebted to Dr. T. O. Mabbott). Bolton's letter, Poe declared,

... was dated at a period long after the reception of our Magazine in Pontotoc.... He pretends not having seen my solution—but his own contains internal evidence of the fact. Three blunders in mine are copied in his own and two or three corrections of Dr. Frailey's original, by myself, are also faithfully repeated. I had the alternative of denying his claim and thus appearing invidious or of sharing with him an honor which in the eyes of the mob at least, is not much above that of a bottle-conjuror. So I chose the last and have put a finale to this business.

If Poe honestly entertained the suspicion which he directed against Bolton, the course which he followed and the complimentary letter he sent to Bolton, redound to his great credit. But I am sorry to say that after a minute investigation of the whole matter, in which no detail was too insignificant to be overlooked, I must declare that Poe had utterly no foundation for his suspicion. Internal evidence in Bolton's solution, which also appears in the newspaper mentioned, as well as all the attendant circumstances, serve to indicate conclusively that his work was accomplished without the key. Nowhere can one find "three blunders in mine which are copied in his own"; and so far as regards the "two or three corrections of Dr. Frailey's original, by myself," are concerned, who can doubt that Bolton did what every cryptographer does constantly—correct errors from the context? And there were errors—many of them in the cipher text as published by Poe, of which the latter was possibly not aware, though he was aware of the errors in the original. Furthermore, it will be noted that Poe did not, in his letter to Bolton, deny having received the latter's solution mailed on September 9. Now if Bolton mailed his solution on the date indicated, even allowing a whole month for its transit, Poe must have received it by October 9. The key to the cryptogram did *not* appear in the September number, as Bolton inadvertently stated (a slip of the pen which adds weight to his claim), but appeared in the October number, which could not possibly have arrived before September 9. In fact, as the matter stands, one could, in truth, impute to Poe an unwillingness to share the honors with Bolton, but we may accept in good faith the explanation he offered the latter.

Several inaccurate statements by Poe also occur in connection with his very brief description of a well-known cryptographic method often referred to as the *chiffre quarré*. In the December article in *Graham's,* speaking of the difficulty of composing impenetrable cryptograms, Poe said:

We may say, in addition, that the nearest approach to perfection in this matter, is the *chiffre quarré* of the French Academy. This consists of a table somewhat in the form of our ordinary multiplication tables, from which the secret to be conveyed is so written that no letter is ever represented twice by the same character. Out of a thousand individuals nine hundred and ninety-nine would at once pronounce this mode inscrutable. It is yet susceptible, under peculiar circumstances, of prompt and certain solution.[9]

In the first place, even in Poe's day to say that the *chiffre quarré* "is the nearest approach to perfection in this matter" was absurd, for almost any example of it could have been solved within an hour or two by anyone who was worthy of being considered an expert cryptographer. In the second place, the *chiffre quarré,* which Poe attributed to the French Academy, was first illustrated by Vigenère in 1586. Note that I say described, and not invented, for to all intents and purposes the same method, without actually employing the square table of Vigenère, was occasionally used at least as early as 1560 by certain Italian cryptographers in the employ of the papacy. In the third place, to say of the method that it is one in which "no letter is ever represented twice by the same character" is entirely incorrect. Furthermore, Poe's statement relative to the possibility of solving this type of cryptogram leaves room for doubt as to what he meant to convey by the qualifying phrase "under peculiar circumstances"—if he intended to give the impression that the circumstances are unusual, his statement is erroneous.

Another, almost glaring inaccuracy of Poe's is found in connection with a reference made by him to the Francis Bacon cipher. In the August, 1841, number of *Graham's Magazine,* Poe begins with the following words:

Our remarks on this head [secret writing] in the July number have excited much interest. The subject is unquestionably one of importance, when we regard cryptography as an exercise for the analytical faculties. In this view, men of the finest abilities have given it much of their attention; and the invention of a perfect cipher was a point to which Lord Chancellor Bacon devoted many months;—devoted them in vain, for the cryptograph which he thought worthy of a place in his *De Augmentis,* is one which can be solved.[10]

Again, in the December number, in connection with the question of the so-called "indecipherable cipher," Poe writes:

Perhaps no good cipher was *ever* invented which its originator did not conceive insoluble; yet, so far, no impenetrable cryptograph has been

[9] *Ibid.,* XIV, 148.   [10] *Ibid.,* XIV, 133.

discovered. Our correspondent will be the less startled at this, our assertion, when he bears in mind that he who has been termed the "wisest of mankind"—we mean Lord Verulam—was as confident of the absolute insolubility of his own mode as our present cryptographist is of his. What he said upon the subject in his *De Augmentis* was, at the day of its publication, considered unanswerable. Yet his cipher has been repeatedly unriddled.[11]

It is rather a late day to take up the cudgel for the Lord Chancellor, but to do him justice I will say in the first place that he certainly did not present his mode of secret writing accompanied by any assertion relative to its indecipherability; he merely said that he had invented it while a youth in Paris, and that [forty-five years afterward] he still thought it worthy of preservation. In the second place, the cryptogram he presented as an example was accompanied not only by a full explanation of the system, but also by the key. Poe's remarks lead one, indeed, to believe that he could not himself have examined Bacon's cipher in the *De Augmentis,* but was writing upon the matter merely from hearsay.

In the course of this discussion only casual reference has been made to "The Gold Bug." It is fairly certain that Poe identified himself with its principal character Legrand, whose very name is significant. Regarding the cryptogram in this tale Poe says that it "was of a simple species," that he solved it "readily," and that he had "solved others of an abstruseness ten thousand times greater."

We have seen that so far as the actual record goes it is doubtful whether Poe ever solved any cryptogram that can properly be said to fall outside the class of simple substitution. The Frailey cipher, which was the most difficult of those shown by the record, and about which Poe wrote so enthusiastically, was but a little more complicated than that in "The Gold Bug," of which he himself made light. Therefore, to say that he had "solved others of an abstruseness ten thousand times greater" is a considerable exaggeration, even in a tale of pure fancy.

It cannot be denied that Poe was greatly given to exaggeration. It was this foible which led him to make his most famous, and, for him, a most unwarranted, dictum on cryptography; namely, that relative to the impossibility of devising the so-called "indecipherable

[11] *Ibid.,* XIV, 147-148.

cipher." It will be well to give the exact form in which he made the assertion. In "A Few Words on Secret Writing," published in *Graham's Magazine* for July, 1841, he stated:

> Few persons can be made to believe that it is not quite an easy thing to invent a method of secret writing which shall baffle investigation. Yet it may be roundly asserted that human ingenuity cannot concoct a cipher which human ingenuity cannot resolve.[12]

He repeated the declaration in one of his supplementary articles, and, again, in practically the same form, in "The Gold Bug." Even to critical readers without cryptographic training[13] it is apparent that his dictum goes far beyond what he actually demonstrated in any of his cryptographic writings; and to the professional cryptographer it appears about time that Poe's assertion be challenged.

So far as the professional cryptographer is concerned, there has never been any question about the theoretical possibility of constructing at least one or two cipher systems, which are mathematically demonstrable as being absolutely indecipherable. It is far from being the case that the invention of such ciphers had to await modern advances in cryptographic science; their devising was possible from the very earliest days of secret writing. The difficulty has been to make such systems *practicable* for regular usage by persons having a need for the highest degree of cryptographic security.

A system which is now considered to be one of the very best for practical usage was discovered recently to have been invented by that amazing American genius Thomas Jefferson.[14] There can be no question that had Poe been cognizant of the method proposed by Jefferson he would have pronounced it absolutely inscrutable, for, as compared with the *chiffre quarré* (of which it will be remembered he said that it was the nearest approach to perfection), Jefferson's system is of a very much greater security. In fact, some of the American patriots of Revolutionary days were far better informed on secure methods of secret writing than was Poe.

[12] *Ibid.*, XIV, 116.
[13] For example, Krutch, *op. cit.*, p. 107, says: "In the course of the articles on cryptography his speculations went far beyond the concrete demonstrations which he affords. 'Human ingenuity,' he declared triumphantly, 'could not devise a cypher which human ingenuity could not solve' . . . "
[14] Jefferson's Papers, Vol. CCXXXII, Item 41575. Library of Congress, Washington.

It may perhaps be charged that it is unfair to expect of Poe a knowledge of the modern intricacies of a science which, like other sciences, must have undergone rapid development in the past half-century. On the contrary, although it is true that the state of the science is greatly in advance of what it was in Poe's day, long before his time it was much beyond what his remarks lead one to assume. As has already been intimated, four hundred years before Poe lived, professional cryptographers were daily employing and solving ciphers of much greater complexity than any which Poe illustrates and terms intricate. The basic principles for solving the type of ciphers Poe discusses were described in detail in papers written by Italian cryptographers before the dawn of the sixteenth century.[15]

The serious student of cryptography can, if he takes the trouble, see in Poe's essay and in his other writings on this subject many things which are not apparent to the layman. Against his will he is driven to the conclusion that Poe was only a dabbler in cryptography. At the same time it is only fair to say that as compared with the vast majority of other persons of his time in this or in foreign countries, his knowledge of the subject, as an amateur, was sufficient to warrant notice. Had he had opportunity to make cryptography a vocation, there is no doubt that he would have gone far in the profession.

[15] Aloys Meister, *Die Anfänge der modernen diplomatischen Geheimschriften* (Paderborn, 1902).

Edgar Allan Poe: A Crisis in the History of American Obscurantism

Yvor Winters

I AM ABOUT to promulgate a heresy; namely, that E. A. Poe, although he achieved, as his admirers have claimed, a remarkable agreement between his theory and his practice, is exceptionally bad in both. I am somewhat startled, moreover, to awaken to the fact that this is a heresy, that those who object to Poe would do well to establish their position now if ever. Poe has long passed casually with me and with most of my friends as a bad writer accidentally and temporarily popular; the fact of the matter is, of course, that he has been pretty effectually established as a great writer while we have been sleeping. The menace lies not, primarily, in his impressionistic admirers among literary people, of whom he still has some, even in England and America, where a familiarity with his language ought to render his crudity obvious, for these individuals in the main do not make themselves permanently very effective; it lies rather in the impressive body of scholarship, beginning, perhaps, with Harrison, Woodberry, and Stedman, and continuing down to such writers as Campbell, Stovall, and Una Pope-Hennessy. Much of this scholarship is primarily biographical, historical, and textual; but when a writer is supported by a sufficient body of such scholarship, a very little philosophical elucidation will suffice to establish him in the scholarly world as a writer whose greatness is self-evident. This fact is made especially evident in the work of the two critics who come closest to taking the position which I shall take: W. C. Brownell[1] and especially Norman Foerster.[2] Both approach the essential issue; neither is able, or it may be that because of its absurdity neither is willing, to define it; and both maintain the tradi-

[1] W. C. Brownell, *American Prose Masters* (New York, 1909).
[2] Norman Foerster, *American Criticism* (Boston and New York, 1928). I should like, if I had time, to examine Professor Foerster's essay on Poe at length, partly because of the similarities and the differences between his position and my own, and partly because of a matter largely irrelevant but none the less astonishing—that is, Professor Foerster's view of the nature and history of music, subjects of which he displays an ignorance nothing less than sweeping.

tional reverence for Poe as a stylist, a reverence which I believe to be at once unjustified and a source of error in dealing with his theory.

My consternation became acute upon the examination of a recent edition of selections from Poe,[3] prepared, it is true, merely as a classroom text, but prepared with great competence, by a respectable Poe scholar, the late Margaret Alterton, and by an exceptionally distinguished scholar in the field of the English Renaissance, Professor Hardin Craig. The Introduction to this text, the first and second parts of which were written by Miss Alterton and revised by Professor Craig, the third part of which was written wholly by Professor Craig, offers the best general defense of Poe with which I am acquainted; it is careful and thorough, and it makes as good a case for Poe, I imagine, as can be made. And when one has finished it, one has a perfectly clear idea of why it is wrong.

The problem is a simple one. Most of Poe's essential theory is summarized in three essays: "The Poetic Principle," "The Philosophy of Composition," and "The Rationale of Verse." Important statements can be found elsewhere, and I shall draw upon other essays, but these essays contain most of the essential ideas. Furthermore, the essential statements recur repeatedly in other essays, frequently almost verbatim. By confining oneself largely to these essays, by selecting the crucial statements, by showing as briefly as possible their obvious relations one to another, one can reduce Poe's aesthetic to a very brief and a perfectly accurate statement. In doing this I shall endeavor in every case to interpret what he says directly, not with the aid of other writers whose theories may have influenced him and by aid of whose theories one may conceivably be able to gloss over some of his confusion; and I shall endeavor to show that this direct approach is fully justified by his own artistic practice.

The passages which I shall quote have all been quoted many times before; I shall have to beg indulgence on that score and ask the reader to examine once and for all their obvious significance.

Any study of Poe should begin with a statement made in connection with Elizabeth Barrett's *A Drama of Exile*. He says: "This is emphatically the thinking age; indeed it may very well be questioned whether man ever substantially thought before."[4] This sentence dis-

---
[3] *Edgar Allan Poe*, ed. Craig and Alterton (New York, 1935).
[4] All quotations in this essay are from the edition of Stedman and Woodberry. Quotations from the criticism only are given footnotes. This quotation is from Vol. I, page 294, of the three volumes of criticism.

plays an ignorance at once of thought and of the history of thought so comprehensive as to preclude the possibility of our surprise at any further disclosures. It helps to explain, furthermore, Poe's extraordinary inability to understand even the poetry of ages previous to his own, as well as his subservience in matters of taste to the vulgar sentimentalism which dominated the more popular poets of his period, such poets as Moore, Hood, and Willis, to mention no others. One seldom encounters a writer so thoroughly at the mercy of contemporaneity. Professor Foerster writes of him: "Of this sustaining power of the past, it must be admitted, Poe himself had but a dim understanding." And he quotes Professor Woodberry (*Life,* I, 132) as follows: "He had, in the narrowest sense, a contemporaneous mind, the instincts of the journalist, the magazine writer."[5]

II

One cannot better introduce the question of Poe's aesthetics than by his well-known remarks about Tennyson, in "The Poetic Principle":

In perfect sincerity, I regard him as the noblest poet that ever lived. . . . I call him and *think* him, the noblest of poets, not because the impressions he produces are at *all* times the most profound, not because the poetical excitement which he induces is at *all* times the most intense, but because it *is,* at all times, the most ethereal,—in other words the most elevating and the most pure. No poet is so little of the earth, earthy.[6]

The italics, of course, here and elsewhere, are Poe's; it is seldom necessary to improve upon Poe in this respect. Our task will be primarily to find out what this passage means. I believe that I shall be able to show that it means this: that the poet should not deal with human, that is, moral, experience; that the subject-matter of poetry is of an order essentially supra-human; that the poet has no way of understanding his subject-matter. There will appear certain qualifications to this summary, but they are of very little importance.

In the same essay Poe states: "I hold that a long poem does not exist. I maintain that the phrase, 'a long poem,' is a flat contradiction of terms."[7] And again, thus connecting the last statement with the statement regarding Tennyson: "A poem deserves its title only

[5] Foerster, *op. cit.,* pp. 1 and 2.
[6] Stedman and Woodberry, *op. cit.,* I, 27.   [7] *Ibid.,* I, 3.

inasmuch as it elevates by exciting the soul. . . . But all excitements are, through a psychal necessity, transient." "After the lapse of half an hour at the utmost, it [the excitement] flags—fails—a revulsion ensues—and then the poem is in effect, and in fact, no longer such."[8]

This great work [*Paradise Lost*], in fact, is to be regarded as poetical, only when, losing sight of that vital requisite of all works of Art, Unity, we view it merely as a series of minor poems. If, to preserve its Unity,— its totality of effect or impression—we read it (as would be necessary) at a single sitting, the result is but a constant alternation of excitement and depression. . . . It follows from all this that the ultimate, aggregate, or absolute effect of even the best epic under the sun is a nullity:—and this is precisely the fact.[9]

From these passages it follows: first, that Poe's very conception of poetic unity is one of mood, or emotion; and second, that he regards the existence of mood to be governed by narrow mechanical rules—in other words, exaltation of spirit is merely a form of nervous excitement. The word *effect* is used here as elsewhere as a synonym for *impression;* artistic Unity is described specifically as totality of effect. There appears to be no awareness whatever of that comprehensive act of the spirit, in part intellectual, whereby we understand and remember *Paradise Lost* as a whole, seize the whole intention with intellect and with memory, and, plunging into any passage, experience that passage in relationship to the whole, an act in which the emotional element, since it is involved in and supported by the rational understanding, rises superior to mechanical necessity.

We should observe further that in these passages Poe begins that process of systematic exclusion, in the course of which he eliminates from the field of English poetry nearly all of the greatest acknowledged masters, reserving the field very largely to Coleridge, Tennyson, Thomas Moore, himself, and R. H. Horne. As we shall see, this process of elimination is not a mere accident of temperament, is not merely a series of accidents of judgment, but is the necessary corollary, in the field of particular judgments, of the general theory which we are now considering.

Poe continues: "On the other hand, it is clear that a poem may be improperly brief. Undue brevity degenerates into mere epigrammatism. A *very* short poem, while now and then producing a bril-

[8] *Ibid.*, I, 4.   [9] *Ibid.*

liant or vivid, never produces a profound or enduring effect."[10] He cites "The Indian Serenade," by Shelley, a poem of twenty-four lines, as unduly brief. He regarded one hundred lines as approximately the most effective number for a poem; the length of the lines themselves, he appears never to have considered, though if we compare two of his own poems of nearly the same number of lines, "Ulalume" and "The Raven," the former, in fact and in effect, is much the shorter.

We may observe in the preceding quotation once more the obliviousness to the function of intellectual content in poetry, and an act of exclusion which deals very shortly, not only with the epigrammatists, but also with every sonneteer in the language, including Shakespeare and Milton, and with all the masters of the short lyric, including so wide a diversity of poets as Herbert, Herrick, Donne, and Landor.

By a further act of exclusion, he eliminates the great satirical and didactic masters. In his essay on Bryant, he says: "A satire is, of course, no poem."[11] And in "The Poetic Principle":

We find it [the "epic mania"] succeeded by a heresy too palpably false to be long tolerated.... I allude to the heresy of *The Didactic*. It has been assumed that the end of all poetry is Truth. Every poem, it is said, should inculcate a moral; and by this moral is the poetical merit of the work to be adjudged. We Americans, especially, have patronized this happy idea; and we Bostonians, very especially, have developed it in full. We have taken it into our heads to write a poem simply for the poem's sake, and to acknowledge such to have been our design would be to confess ourselves radically wanting in true poetic dignity and force; but the simple fact is, that, would we but permit ourselves to look into our own souls, we should immediately there discover that under the sun there neither exists nor *can* exist any work more thoroughly dignified, more supremely noble, than this very poem—this poem *per se*—this poem which is a poem and nothing more—this poem written solely for the poem's sake.[12]

Now if Poe had merely intended to exclude some of the unsatisfactory didactic poetry, let us say, of Longfellow or of Lowell, we should have very little complaint to make; however, these poets are bad not because they are didactic, but because they write badly, and

[10] *Ibid.*, I, 6.
[11] *Ibid.*, I, 111.
[12] *Ibid.*, I, 8.

because their didacticism is frequently unsound in conception, and because the lesson which they endeavor to teach is frequently connected only arbitrarily with their subjects. The didactic close of Bryant's great lyric "To a Waterfowl," on the other hand, is merely an explicit statement, and a fine statement, of the idea governing the poem, an idea inherent, but insufficiently obvious, in what has gone before, and it is foolish to object to it; and in the poetry of Samuel Johnson, of Dryden, and of Pope, as in Milton's sonnets, we have yet another form of didacticism, the loss of which would leave us vastly impoverished.[13]

Poe appears never to have grasped the simple and traditional distinction between matter (truth) and manner (beauty); he does not see that beauty is a quality of style, instead of its subject-matter, that it is merely the most complete communication possible, through connotation as well as denotation, of the poet's personal realization of a moral (or human) truth, whether that truth be of very great importance or very little, a truth that must be understood primarily in conceptual terms, regardless of whether the poem ultimately embodies it in the form of description, of narration, or of exposition. A sound attitude toward a major problem, communicated with adequacy of detail, is what we ordinarily mean by sublimity. It is through the neglect of these fundamental ideas that Poe runs into difficulty.

With as deep a reverence for the True as ever inspired the bosom of man [he continues] I would, nevertheless, limit its modes of inculcation. I would limit to enforce them. I would not enfeeble them by dissipation. The demands of Truth are severe; she has no sympathy with the myrtles. All *that* which is so indispensable in Song, is precisely all *that* with which *she* has nothing whatever to do.... In enforcing a truth ... we must be in that mood which, as nearly as possible, is the exact converse of the poetical.[14]

Poe appears oblivious to the possibility that we may come to a truth with an attitude other than that of the advocate; that we may, in brief, contemplate, with Dante, rather than enforce, with Aquinas.

---

[13] It is instructive to compare "To a Waterfowl" with "The Chambered Nautilus." Both follow the same rhetorical formula, but in Bryant's poem the "moral" is implicit throughout; in Holmes's, it is a rhetorical imposition. Holmes's poem is impressively written notwithstanding, but it illustrates the more vulgar procedure.

[14] Stedman and Woodberry, *op. cit.*, I, 9.

It follows that he would not recognize the more complex procedure of contemplating the enforcement of truth, the procedure which results, for example, in the didacticism of Pope and of Dryden; nor yet the contemplation of the need of the enforcement of truth, the procedure which results in the satirical poetry of the same writers; nor the contemplation of a discrepancy between personal experience and a standard truth, a procedure which results in much of the poetry of Donne. Yet these are all major human experiences; they all require individual perception and moral adjustment; according to the traditional view they are thus legitimate material for poetry.

Poe sees truly enough that the enforcement of truth, in itself, does not constitute poetry, and on the basis of that elementary observation he falls into the common romantic error, which may be stated briefly as follows: truth is not poetry; truth should therefore be eliminated from poetry, in the interests of a purer poetry. He would, in short, advise us to retain the attitude, but to discard the object of the attitude. The correct formula, on the other hand, would be this: truth is not poetry; poetry is truth and something more. It is the completeness of the poetic experience which makes it valuable. How thoroughly Poe would rob us of all subject-matter, how thoroughly he would reduce poetry, from its traditional position, at least when ideally considered, as the act of complete comprehension, to a position of triviality and of charlatanism, we shall presently see.

Poe's passion for exclusion, and the certitude that he has no concept of moral sublimity in poetry, appear very clearly in the essay on Horne's *Orion:*

> We shall now be fully understood. If, with Coleridge, who, however erring at times, was precisely the mind fitted to decide such a question as this—if, with him, we reject passion from the true, from the pure poetry—if we reject even passion—if we discard as feeble, as unworthy of the high spirituality of the theme (which has its origin in the Godhead) —if we dismiss even the nearly divine emotion of human *love,* that emotion which merely to name causes the pen to tremble,—with how much greater reason shall we dismiss all else?[15]

The dismissal appears to be inclusive enough, by this time, in all conscience. There would appear to be some confusion in Poe's

[15] *Ibid.,* I, 268.

mind between a passionate or violent style, which (in spite of the magnificence of *King Lear*) he might reasonably regard as inferior to a style more serene, regardless of subject, as if the poet were to rise superior to his passions in his contemplation of them, and passion as subject-matter. It is his fundamental confusion of matter and manner, to which I have already alluded.

In the same essay, and on the same subject, he writes:

Although we argue, for example, with Coleridge, that poetry and passion are discordant, yet we are willing to permit Tennyson to bring, to the intense passion which prompted his *Locksley Hall*, the aid of that terseness and pungency which are derivable from rhythm and from rhyme. The effect he produces, however, is purely passionate, and not, unless in detached passages of this magnificent philippic, a properly poetic effect. His *Oenone*, on the other hand, exalts the soul not into passion, but into a conception of pure *beauty*, which in its elevation, its calm and intense rapture, has in it a foreshadowing of the future and spiritual life, and as far transcends earthly passion as the holy radiance of the sun does the glimmering and feeble phosphorescence of the glow-worm. His *Morte-d'Arthur* is in the same majestic vein. *The Sensitive Plant* of Shelley is in the same sublime spirit.... Readers do exist ... and always will exist, who, to hearts of maddening fervor, unite in perfection, the sentiment of the beautiful—that divine sixth sense which is yet so faintly understood, that sense which phrenology has attempted to embody in its organ of *ideality*,[16] that sense which speaks of God through His purest, if not His *sole* attribute, which proves, and which alone proves his existence ... the origin of poetry lies in a thirst for a wilder beauty than earth supplies.... Poetry itself is the imperfect effort to quench this immortal thirst by novel combinations of beautiful forms....[17]

In the remarks on "Oenone," we may seem at first glance to have the hint that Poe has approached the concept of moral sublimity, but the last sentence quoted brings us back abruptly to the trivial; the exaltation is not a moral exaltation, not the result of the exercise of the intelligence and of character, but is the result of manipulation and of trickery. And were we to allow ourselves the luxury of worrying about Poe's minor obscurities, his use of the word *beautiful* in the last sentence would complicate our problem inextricably: that is, it appears that we achieve the beautiful by new

---

[16] See Edward Hungerford, "Poe and Phrenology," *American Literature*, II, 209-231 (Nov., 1930).

[17] Stedman and Woodberry, *op. cit.*, I, 267-268.

combinations of items which are already beautiful; we have again his helpless inability to separate matter from manner, the poem from its subject.

It is obvious, then, that poetry is not, for Poe, a refined and enriched technique of moral comprehension. It can be of no aid to us in understanding ourselves or in ordering our lives, for most of our experience is irrelevant to it. If, indeed, certain human experiences are admitted as legitimate subjects, they are admitted, as we shall see, because the poet cannot write without writing about something; and those are admitted which seem to involve the minimum of complexity. They are admitted, moreover, not as something to be understood, but as ingredients in a formula by means of which something outside our experience may be suggested. If Poe moves us most to indignation when defining his exclusions, he perplexes us most profoundly when he endeavors to approximate a definition of what he would include.

He writes in "The Poetic Principle":

An immortal instinct, deep within the spirit of man, is thus, plainly, a sense of the Beautiful.... This thirst belongs to the immortality of man. It is at once a consequence and an indication of his perennial existence. It is the desire of the moth for the star. It is no mere appreciation of the Beauty before us, but a wild effort to reach the Beauty above. Inspired by an ecstatic Prescience of the glories beyond the grave, we struggle by multiform combinations among the things and thoughts of Time to attain a portion of that Loveliness whose very elements, perhaps, appertain to eternity alone. And thus when by Poetry—or when by Music, the most entrancing of the Poetic moods—we find ourselves melted into tears, we weep then, not as the Abbate Gravia supposes through excess of pleasure, but through a certain petulant, impatient sorrow at our inability to grasp now, wholly, here on earth, at once and forever, those divine and rapturous joys, of which *through* the poem, or *through* the music, we attain to but brief and indeterminate glimpses.[18]

Briefly, Poe implies something like this: the proper subject-matter of poetry is Beauty, but since true Beauty exists only in eternity, the poet cannot experience it and is deprived of his subject-matter; by manipulating the materials of our present life, we may *suggest the existence of Beauty,* and this is the best that we can do. As we may

[18] *Ibid.,* I, 10-11.

discover from other passages, especially in "The Philosophy of Composition," Poe had certain definite ideas in regard to which forms of human experience lent themselves best to this procedure, and also in regard to the rules of the procedure. Having decided, in an astonishing passage to which I shall presently return, that a melancholy tone most greatly facilitated his purpose, he wrote: " 'Of all melancholy topics, what, according to the universal understanding of mankind, is the *most* melancholy?' Death—was the obvious reply. 'And when,' I said, 'is this most melancholy of topics most poetical?' From what I have already explained at some length, the answer here also is obvious—'When it most closely allies itself to Beauty; the death, then, of a beautiful woman is, unquestionably, the most poetical topic in the world. . . .' "[19] In other words, we are not concerned with understanding human experience; we are seeking, rather, the isolated elements, or fragments, of experience which may best serve as the ingredients of a formula for the production of a kind of emotional delusion, and our final decision in the matter is determined again by our inability to distinguish between the subject and the style of poetry, by the conviction that beauty is the subject of poetry.

The reader should note carefully what this means; perhaps he will pardon me for restating it: the subject-matter of poetry, properly considered, is by definition incomprehensible and unattainable; the poet, in dealing with something else, toward which he has no intellectual or moral responsibilities whatever ("Unless incidentally," says Poe, poetry "has no concern whatever either with Duty or with Truth"),[20] should merely endeavor to *suggest that a higher meaning exists*—in other words, should endeavor to suggest the presence of a meaning when he is aware of none. The poet has only to write a good description of something physically impressive, with an air of mystery, an air of meaning concealed.

An air of mystery, of strangeness, will then be of necessity, not an adjunct of poetic style, but the very essence of poetic style. In "Ligeia" there occurs the well-known passage which it is now necessary to quote: " 'There is no exquisite beauty,' says Bacon, Lord Verulam, speaking truly of all the forms and genera of beauty, 'without some *strangeness* in the proportion'." But in Poe's terms,

[19] *Ibid.*, I, 39. [20] *Ibid.*, I, 12.

strangeness and beauty are, from the standpoint of the practical poet, identical. Related to this concept is his concept of originality, which I shall take up later and separately.

Poe is, in brief, an explicit obscurantist. Hawthorne, in his four last, and unfinished, romances, gives us the physical embodiment of allegory without the meaning to be embodied, but he appears to hope for a meaning, to be, somehow, pathetically and unsuccessfully in search of one. Henry James, in many stories, as in *The Spoils of Poynton,* to choose an obvious example, gives us a sequence of facts without being able to pass judgment upon them, so that the stories remain almost as inconclusive as Stockton's trivial *tour de force* "The Lady, or the Tiger?" Both men frequently write in advance of their understanding, the one as an allegorist, the other as a novelist. But in Poe, obscurantism has ceased to be merely an accident of inadequate understanding; it has become the explicit aim of writing and has begun the generation of a method. Poe's aesthetic is an aesthetic of obscurantism. We have that willful dislocation of feeling from understanding, which, growing out of the uncertainty regarding the nature of moral truth in general and its identity in particular situations which produced such writers as Hawthorne and James, was later to result through the exploitation of special techniques in the violent aberrations of the Experimental School of the twentieth century, culminating in the catastrophe of Hart Crane.[21]

Poe speaks a great deal of the need of originality. This quality, as he understands it, appears to be a fairly simple mechanical device, first, for fixing the attention, and second, for heightening the effect of strangeness. We may obtain a fair idea of his concept of originality of theme from his comment on a poem by Amelia Welby, quoted in the series of brief notes entitled "Minor Contemporaries":

The subject has *nothing* of originality:—A widower muses by the grave of his wife. Here then is a great demerit; for originality of theme, if not absolutely first sought, should be among the first. Nothing is more clear than this proposition, although denied by the chlorine critics (the grass-green). The desire of the new is an element of the soul. The most exquisite pleasures grow dull in repetition. A strain of music enchants. Heard a second time, it pleases. Heard a tenth, it does not displease.

[21] See a volume by the present writer entitled *Primitivism and Decadence,* listed for publication in 1937 by The Arrow Editions, New York City. The techniques mentioned are therein studied in detail.

We hear it a twentieth, and ask ourselves why we admired. At the fiftieth it produces ennui, at the hundredth disgust.[22]

Now I do not know what music most delighted Poe, unless perchance it may have been the melodies of Thomas Moore, but if I may be permitted to use exact numbers in the same figurative sense in which I conceive that Poe here used them, I am bound to say that my own experience with music differs profoundly. The trouble again is traceable to Poe's failure to understand the moral basis of art, to his view of art as a kind of stimulant, ingeniously concocted, which may, if one is lucky, raise one to a moment of divine delusion. A Bach fugue or a Byrd mass moves us not primarily because of any originality it may display, but because of its sublimity as I have already defined the term. Rehearing can do no more than give us a fuller and firmer awareness of this quality. The same is true of *Paradise Lost*. Poe fails to see that the originality of a poem lies not in the newness of the general theme—for if it did, the possibilities of poetry would have been exhausted long before the time of Poe—but in the quality of the personal intelligence, as that intelligence appears in the minutiae of style, in the defining limits of thought and of feeling, brought to the subject by the poet who writes of it. The originality, from Poe's point of view, of the subjects of such poems as "The Raven," "The Sleeper," and "Ulalume" would reside in the fantastic dramatic and scenic effects by means of which the subject of simple regret is concealed, diffused, and rendered ludicrous. From the same point of view, "Rose Aylmer" would necessarily be lacking in originality.

In "The Philosophy of Composition" Poe gives us a hint as to his conception of originality of style. After a brief discourse on originality of versification, and the unaccountable way in which it has been neglected, he states that he lays no claim to originality as regards the meter or the rhythm of "The Raven," but only as regards the stanza: "nothing even remotely approaching this combination has ever been attempted."[23] Again we see Poe's tendency to rely upon the mechanically startling, in preference to the inimitable. This fact, coupled with his extraordinary theories of meter, which I shall examine separately, bears a close relationship to what appears

[22] Stedman and Woodberry, *op. cit.*, III, 284.
[23] *Ibid.*, I, 42.

to me to be the clumsiness and insensitivity of his verse. Read three times, his rhythms disgust, because they are untrained and insensitive and have no individual life within their surprising mechanical frames.

Before turning to the principal poems for a brief examination of them, we should observe at least one remark on the subject of melancholy. In "The Philosophy of Composition" after stating that, in planning "The Raven," he had decided upon Beauty as the province of the poem, Poe writes as follows:

> Regarding, then, Beauty as my province, my next question referred to the *tone* of its highest manifestation—and all experience has shown that this tone is one of *sadness*. Beauty of whatever kind, in its supreme development, invariably excites the sensitive soul to tears. Melancholy is thus the most legitimate of all the poetical tones.[24]

Now if the reader will keep in mind the principles that we have already deduced; namely, that Beauty is unattainable, that the poet can merely suggest its existence, that this suggestion depends upon the ingenious manipulation of the least obstructive elements of normal experience—it will at once be obvious that Poe is here suggesting a reversal of motivation. That is, since Beauty excites to tears (let us assume with Poe, for the moment, that it does), if we begin with tears, we may believe ourselves moved for a moment by Beauty. This interpretation is supported solidly by the last two sentences quoted, particularly when we regard their order.

"The Philosophy of Composition" thus appears after all to be a singularly shocking document. Were it an examination of the means by which a poet might communicate a comprehensible judgment, were it a plea that such communication be carefully planned in advance, we could do no less than approve. But it is not that; it is rather an effort to establish the rules for a species of incantation, of witchcraft; rules whereby, through the manipulation of certain substances in certain arbitrary ways, it may be possible to invoke, more or less accidentally, something that appears more or less to be a divine emanation. It is not surprising that Poe expressed more than once a very qualified appreciation of Milton.

We may fairly conclude this phase of the discussion by a passage from "The Poetic Principle," a passage quoted also by Miss Alter-

[24] *Ibid.*, I, 36.

ton: "It may be, indeed, that here this sublime end is, now and then, attained in fact. We are often made to feel, with a shivering delight, that from an earthly harp are stricken notes which *cannot* have been unfamiliar to the angels."[25] It should now be clear what Poe had in mind when he referred to Tennyson as the most elevating and the most pure of poets; what Tennyson might have thought of the attribution is beside the point.

III

Before turning to the poems themselves, we should examine very briefly Poe's general theory of metre, as it appears primarily in "The Rationale of Verse." And before doing this we should recall to mind in very general terms the common methods of scansion. They are: first, the classical, in which the measure is based upon quantity, or length of syllable, and in which accent is a source merely of variation and of complication; second, the French, or syllabic, in which the measure is a matter wholly of the number of syllables in the line, and in which the primary source of variation is quantity, if the language be one, like French, which lacks mechanical stress; third, the Anglo-Saxon, or accentual, in which the measure is based purely upon the number of accents, variation being derived from every other source possible; and fourth, the English, or accentual-syllabic, which resembles the classical system in its types of feet, but in which the foot and measure are determined by accent instead of by quantity.

Since it is with English verse, primarily, that we are dealing, we should note one or two other points in connection with it. First, the language is not divided into accented and unaccented syllables; within certain limits, there is an almost infinite variation of accent, and no two syllables are ever accented in exactly the same way. Consequently, for metrical purposes, a syllable is considered accented or unaccented only in relationship to the other syllables in the same foot. For example, let us take Ben Jonson's line:

Drink to/ me on/ly with/ thine eyes.

The accent of the first foot is inverted; in each of the other feet the accent falls on the second syllable. Yet the word *with*, which even in normal prose receives more accent than the last syllable of *only*, is

[25] *Ibid.*, I, 12.

less heavily accented than the word *thine;* so that in the last two feet we have a mounting series of four degrees of accent. This variety of accent is one source of variation in English meter; another is quantity; another is the normal procedure of substitution.

We may observe the obvious playing off of quantity against accent in the first foot, a normal iambic one, of this line from Robert Bridges:

Nay, barren are the mountains, and spent the streams.

The first syllable of the foot, *Nay,* is long and unaccented; the second and final syllable, *bar-,* is short and accented. On the other hand, length and accent may be brought to coincide; or there may be immeasurably subtle variations between the two extremes. These sources of variation, when understood and mastered, provide the fluid sensitivity to be found in the best English verse, within even the most rigid of patterns.

But to all of this Poe appears oblivious. He says: "Accented syllables are of course always long."[26] This initial confusion is obviously related to Poe's preference for metres dependent upon a heavy, unvaried, and mechanical beat. He makes little use of quantity except as a reinforcement of accent; where it does not reinforce the accent, the failure is an accident and usually results in a clumsy variant rather than a pleasing one.

In "The Rationale of Verse" Poe offers a new system for marking scansion, based in part upon the heresy which I have just mentioned, in part upon the equally gross concept that all syllables can be grouped into general classes, each class having a fixed and recognizable degree of accent. He is even so rash as to attempt the scansion of Horace on this basis, and to state that French verse is without music because the language is without accent. Poe had a mind for only the crudest of distinctions.

IV

The poems on which Poe's reputation as an important poet must rest are the following: "The City in the Sea," "The Haunted Palace," "The Conqueror Worm," "Ulalume," "The Raven," and "The Sleeper." "The City in the Sea" is sometimes, and I believe rightly, regarded as Poe's best performance. After the first five lines, which

[26] *Ibid.,* I, 60.

are bad enough to have been written by Kipling, the poem displays few gross lapses and some excellent passages. There is admirable description, and there is throughout an intense feeling of meaning withheld. We have, in brief, all of the paraphernalia of allegory except the significance. The poem falls short of being one of the romantic masterpieces of obscure emotionalism chiefly by virtue of the loose and undistinguished metre, and by virtue of a number of weak phrases: it remains one of Poe's most startling and talented failures.

In "The Haunted Palace," the physical material has allegorical significance which is perfectly definite. The palace of the monarch Thought is the head; the windows are the eyes; the door is the mouth; the spirits are his thoughts, which issue as words. This, however, is not the real explanation of the poem, for the subject is the change from sanity to insanity. The change occurs in the fifth stanza, suddenly and without motivation: we have feeling divorced completely from understanding; the change itself is mad, for it is inexplicable.

"Ulalume" contains very much the same problems as the other poems not yet considered. In examining this poem, we must confine ourselves strictly to what Poe offered us, namely, the poem, and refrain from biographical entanglements, which are both gratuitous and uncertain. If the poem is not self-sufficient, it is obscure; and, as critics of art, we are bound to rest with the assumption that the obscurity was satisfactory to Poe.

The poem opens with allusions to unidentified places, places with dark but unexplained histories: Weir, Auber, ghoul-haunted woodlands; we have, in other words, a good deal of ready-made Gothic mystery. These items are introduced to evoke emotion at small cost: they are familiar romantic devices, but they are none the less deliberately obscure. In the passage opening with the alley Titanic, and ending with Mount Yaanek and the Boreal Pole, we have an explicit reference to a period of violent feeling in the history of the protagonist: the cause and nature of the feeling are alike unexplained at the time, and even the loss of Ulalume, which is a very general sort of datum, is an inadequate account of feelings so grotesquely violent. In lines twenty to twenty-nine, there are dark references to a past event, references which are ultimately cleared up when we learn of the burial of Ulalume, but which, as we come to them, have the effect of gratuitous emotionalizing. Lines thirty to forty are the best in the poem: they hint of the strangeness of the nocturnal turning toward dawn, and then describe the appearance of Astarte, as the rising moon; if this strangeness has any spiritual significance, however, we are given no clue to it. The protagonist wishes to accept Astarte as a guide; Psyche distrusts her; they argue at length but darkly—darkly, in that the purpose of the protagonist and the fears of Psyche alike are not given us, so that the argument is like one in a dream. Psyche yields, but as she does so, they are led by Astarte to the door of the tomb, which brings the protagonist up shortly, with a cold realization of his loss. Lines ninety-five to one hundred and four, omitted by Griswold and by most of the cheap popular editions, but important, it would seem, to the poem, state the possibility that Astarte may have been conjured up to prevent their further irresponsible wandering in the haunted woodlands (which I take to represent the loose feelings through which they have been moving) by recalling them to a sense of definite tragedy.

In other words, the subject of grief is employed as a very general excuse for a good deal of obscure and only vaguely related emotion. This subject is used exactly as we should expect to find it used after examining Poe's aesthetic theory. The poem is as surely an excursion into the incoherencies of dream-consciousness as is the "Larme" of Rimbaud; yet it lacks wholly the fine surface of that poem.

In "The Raven," that attenuated exercise for elocutionists, and in "The Sleeper," the general procedure is identical, but the meter in the former and the writing in both are so thoroughly bad that other considerations appear unnecessary. "The Sleeper" is a kind of Gothic parody of Henry King's imperfect but none the less great "Exequy": a comparison of the two poems will show the difference between moral grandeur and the sensationalism of a poet devoid of moral intelligence. It is noteworthy that King is commonly and justly regarded as one of the smaller poets of his period.

In "The Conqueror Worm," the desire for inexpensive feeling has led to a piece of writing that is, phrase by phrase, solidly bromidic.

V

In his criticism of Hawthorne's *Tales,* Poe outlines his theory of the short story. He defends the tale, as preferable to the novel, on the same grounds as those on which he defends the short poem in preference to the long. He states the necessity of careful planning and of economy of means.

He says: "... having conceived, with deliberate care, a certain unique or single *effect* to be wrought out, he [the skillful literary artist] then invents such incidents—he then combines such events as may best aid him in establishing this preconceived effect."[27] Now the word *effect,* here as elsewhere in Poe, means impression, or mood; it is a word that connotes emotion purely and simply. So that we see the story-teller, like the poet, interested primarily in the creation of an emotion for its own sake, not in the understanding of an experience. It is significant in this connection that most of his heroes are mad or on the verge of madness; a datum which settles his action firmly in the realm of inexplicable feeling from the outset.

"Morella" begins thus: "With a feeling of deep yet most singular affection I regarded my friend Morella. Thrown by accident into her society many years ago, my soul, from our first meeting, burned with fires it had never before known; but the fires were not of Eros, and bitter and tormenting to my spirit was the gradual conviction that I could in no manner define their unusual meaning or regulate their vague intensity." And "Ligeia": "I can not, for my soul, remember how, when, or even precisely where, I first became acquainted with the Lady Ligeia. Long years have since elapsed, and my memory is feeble through much suffering." "The Assignation": "Ill-fated and mysterious man!—bewildered in the brilliancy of thine own imagination, and fallen in the flames of thine own youth." "The Tell-Tale Heart": "True!—nervous—very, very dreadfully nervous I had been and am! but why *will* you say that I am mad?" "Berenice": "... it *is* wonderful what a stagnation there fell upon the springs of my life—wonderful how total an inversion took place in the character of my commonest thought." "Eleonora": "I am come of a race noted for vigor of fancy and ardor of passion. Men have called me mad; but the question is not yet settled, whether madness is or is not the loftiest intelligence—whether much that is

[27] *Ibid.,* II, 31.

glorious—whether all that is profound—does not spring from disease of thought—from *moods* of mind exalted at the expense of the general intellect." Roderick Usher, in addition, is mad; "The Black Cat" is a study in madness; "The Masque of the Red Death" is a study in hallucinatory terror. They are all studies in hysteria; they are written for the sake of the hysteria.

In discussing Hawthorne, however, Poe suggests other possibilities:

We have said that the tale has a point of superiority even over the poem. In fact, while the *rhythm* of this latter is an essential aid in the development of the poem's highest idea—the idea of the Beautiful—the artificialities of this rhythm are an inseparable bar to the development of all points of thought or expression which have their basis in *Truth*. But Truth is often, and in very great degree, the aim of the tale. Some of the finest tales are tales of ratiocination. Thus the field of this species of composition, if not in so elevated a region on the mountain of the Mind, is a table-land of far vaster extent than the domain of the mere poem. Its products are never so rich, but infinitely more numerous, and more appreciable by the mass of mankind. The writer of the prose tale, in short, may bring to his theme a vast variety of modes of inflections of thought and expressions (the ratiocinative, for example, the sarcastic, or the humorous) which are not only antagonistic to the nature of the poem, but absolutely forbidden by one of its most peculiar and indispensable adjuncts; we allude, of course, to rhythm. It may be added here, *par parenthèse,* that the author who aims at the purely beautiful in a prose tale is laboring at a great disadvantage. For Beauty can be better treated in the poem. Not so with terror, or passion, or horror, or a multitude of other such points.[28]

Poe speaks in this passage, not only of the tale of effect, already alluded to, but of the tale of ratiocination, that is, of the detective story, such as "The Gold Bug" or "The Murders in the Rue Morgue." It is noteworthy that this is the only example he gives of the invasion of the field of fiction by Truth; in other words, his primary conception of intellectual activity in fiction appears to be in the contrivance of a puzzle. Between this childish view of intellectuality, on the one hand, and the unoriented emotionalism of the tale of effect on the other, we have that vast and solid region inhabited by the major literary figures of the world, the region in which human ex-

[28] *Ibid.,* II, 32.

perience is understood in moral terms and emotion is the result of that understanding or is seen in relationship to that understanding and so judged. This region appears to have been closed to Poe; if we except the highly schematized and crudely melodramatic allegory of "William Wilson," we have no basis for believing that he ever discovered it.

VI

If Poe's chief work is confined to the communication of feeling, what can we say of the quality of that communication? Poe rests his case for art on taste, and though we may disagree with him, yet we are bound to examine his own taste, for if he has no taste, he has nothing. It is my belief that he has little or none.

Every literary critic has a right to a good many errors of judgment; or at least every critic makes a good many. But if we survey Poe's critical opinions we can scarcely fail to be astonished by them. He understood little or nothing that was written before his own age, and though he was not unaware of the virtues, apparently, of some of the better stylists of his period, as for example Coleridge, he at one time or another praised such writers as R. H. Horne, N. P. Willis, Thomas Hood, and Thomas Moore as highly or more highly; in fact, he placed Horne and Moore among the greatest geniuses of all time. He praised Bryant above his American contemporaries, but he based his praise upon poems which did not deserve it. He was able to discover numerous grammatical errors in one of the lesser novels of Cooper, but the faultless, limpid, and unforgettable prose of the seventh chapter of *The Deerslayer,* the profundity of conception of *The Bravo,* the characterization of *Satanstoe* and *The Chainbearer,* were as far beyond his powers of comprehension as beyond his powers of creation.

To illustrate the weakness of detail in his poems and stories is an easy matter; to illustrate the extent of that weakness is impossible, for his work is composed of it. In his poems one may enumerate the following passages as fairly well executed: "Ulalume," lines thirty to thirty-eight, provided one can endure the meter; "The City in the Sea," lines six to eleven, lines twenty-four to the end; "To One in Paradise," the first stanza and perhaps the last; the early poem "To Helen," especially the first three or four lines; "The Spirits of the Dead," lines five to ten. Perhaps the only passage of his prose which displays comparable ability is the opening of "The Assignation": the conception is merely that of the typically Byronic man of mystery, and the detail, in its rough identity, is comparably typical, but there is a certain life in the language, especially in the rhythm of the language, that renders the passage memorable.

For the rest we are met on every page of his poetry with such resounding puerilities as "the pallid bust of Pallas," and "the viol, the violet, and the vine." We encounter prose such as the following: "As if in the superhuman energy of his utterance there had been found the potency of a spell, the huge antique panels to which the speaker pointed threw slowly back, upon the instant, their ponderous and ebony jaws." "It was a voluptuous scene, that masquerade. But first let me tell of the rooms in which it was held. They were seven—an imperial suite." "Where were the souls of the haughty family of the bride, when, through thirst of gold, they permitted to pass the threshold of an apartment *so* bedecked, a maiden and a daughter so beloved?" "Morella's erudition was profound. As I hope to live, her talents were of no common order—her powers of mind were gigantic."

The poetry is composed almost wholly of such items as these:

Ah, broken is the golden bowl!—the spirit flown forever!
Let the bell toll! a saintly soul floats on the Stygian river:—
And, Guy de Vere, hast *thou* no tear?—weep now or never more!
See! on yon drear and rigid bier low lies thy love, Lenore!

    At midnight, in the month of June,
    I stand beneath the mystic moon.

    For, alas! alas! with me
      The light of Life is o'er!
    No more—no more—no more—
      (Such language holds the solemn sea
    To the sands upon the shore)
      Shall bloom the thunder-blasted tree,
    Or the stricken eagle soar!

    That motley drama—oh, be sure
      It shall not be forgot!
    With its Phantom chased forevermore
      By a crowd that seize it not,

> Through a circle that ever returneth in
> To the self-same spot,
> And much of Madness, and more of Sin,
> And Horror the soul of the plot.
>
> And the silken, sad, uncertain rustling of each purple curtain
> Thrilled me—filled me with fantastic terrors never felt before.

This is an art to delight the soul of a servant girl; it is a matter for astonishment that mature men can take this kind of thing seriously. It is small wonder that the claims of Chivers have been seriously advanced of late years in the face of such an achievement; they have been fairly advanced, for Chivers is nearly as admirable a poet. If one is in need of a standard, one should have recourse to Bridges's "Eros," to Hardy's "During Wind and Rain," or to Arnold's "Dover Beach." And in making one's final estimate of the quality of Poe's taste, one should not fail to consider the style of his critical prose, of which the excerpts quoted in the present essay are fair, and, as specimens of taste, are random examples.

VII

On what grounds, if any, can we then defend Poe? We can obviously defend his taste as long as we honestly like it. The present writer is willing to leave it, after these few remarks, to its admirers. As to his critical theory, however, and the structural defects of his work, it appears to me certain that the difficulty which I have raised is the central problem in Poe criticism; yet not only has it never been met, but, so far as one can judge, it has scarcely been recognized.

There are, I believe, two general lines of argument or procedure that may be used more or less in support of Poe's position; one is that of the Alterton-Craig Introduction, the other is that (if I may cite another eminent example) of Professor Floyd Stovall.

The argument of the Introduction appears to be roughly that Poe is an intellectual poet, because: first, he worked out in *Eureka* a theory of cosmic harmony and unity; second, related to this, he held a theory of the harmony and unity of the parts of the poem; and third, he devoted a certain amount of rational effort to working out the rules by which this unity could be attained.

But this intellectuality, if that is the name for it, is all anterior to the poem, not in the poem; it resides merely in the rules for the practice of the obscurantism which I have defined. The Introduction cites as evidence of Poe's recognition of the intellectual element in poetry, his essay on Drake and Halleck, yet the intellectuality in question here is plainly of the sort which I have just described. As a result, Professor Craig's comparison of Poe to Donne, Dryden, and Aquinas, is, to the present writer, at least, profoundly shocking.

The only alternative is that of Professor Stovall, as well as of a good many others: to accept Poe's theory of Beauty as if it were clearly understood and then to examine minor points of Poe criticism with lucidity and with learning. But Poe's theory of Beauty is not understood, and no casual allusion to Plato will ever clarify it.

Poe and the Chess Automaton
W. K. Wimsatt, Jr.

IT WAS GRISWOLD who wrote in his *Memoir* of Poe that the stories of ratiocination had been thought "more ingenious" than they were, that there was about them, besides a method, an "air of method." The fate of the unfriendly Griswold at the hands of subsequent scholars has been so forlorn, the praise of Poe has been for over fifty years so sustained on almost every score, that the present writer only with a certain diffidence in nonconformity ventures this nibble at Poe's ratiocinative reputation, in the way of a study of his essay "Maelzel's Chess-Player."

"The essay on the Automaton *cannot be answered,* and we have heard the Editor challenges a reply from Maelzel himself, or from any source whatever. The piece has excited great attention." Such was the comment of the *Norfolk Herald,* quoted by Poe in the "Supplement" to the July issue of the *Messenger.* Applause is quoted from six other papers too—the *Baltimore Gazette,* the *Baltimore Patriot,* the *United States Gazette,* the *Charleston Courier,* the *Winchester Virginian.* Only one, the *New Yorker,* finds a fault—that too much space is sacrificed to the essay.[1]

Forty-four years later the biographer Ingram gave the literary world the following opinion: "The poet demonstrated by clear, concise, and irrefutable arguments, that the machine then being exhibited before the citizens of Richmond must be regulated in its operation by *mind*—that, in fact, it was no automaton at all, but simply a piece of mechanism guided by human agency."[2] Next, Woodberry, after a somewhat more critical examination, wrote in a state of indecision. Poe "demonstrated that Maelzel's Chess Player must be operated by human agency, and solved the methods used." But on the same page, the essay "has been vastly overrated, as anyone may convince himself by comparing it minutely with Sir David Brewster's 'Letters on Natural Magic,' to which it stands confessedly

---
[1] *Southern Literary Messenger,* II, 518-523 (July, 1836). The essay on the "Chess-Player" had appeared in the April issue (II, 318-326).
[2] John H. Ingram, *Edgar Allan Poe, His Life, Letters and Opinions* (London, 1880), I, 135.

obliged, and from which it is partly paraphrased."[3] Poe's most romantic biographer writes as follows: "Chief of these essays was *Maelzel's Chess-Player* in which he exposed the method by which a dummy chessman, that had gone the rounds of American cities winning games from living opponents, was operated. Many persons had been more mystified than amused by the manoeuvres of the automatic man, and the *exposé,* although only partly correct, created quite a little furor. It was the first of Poe's work in which he emerged as the unerring abstract reasoner, and foreshadowed the method he followed later in his detective stories such as the *Murders in the Rue Morgue.*"[4]

The purpose of this article is to insist, more specifically than seems yet to have been done, that the essay on the automaton "has been vastly overrated," that it was "only partly correct," to add that it was based on no original thinking, and hence to suggest that so far as Poe emerges from it as anything at all, it is not as an "unerring abstract reasoner," but as an artist with a certain method.

There were two chief mysteries presented by the automaton. First, if one assumed, as most writers did, that there was a human player within, how was he concealed during the opening of the doors and drawer? Secondly, how was this player aware of the moves of his adversary made by Maelzel on the top of the chest, and how did he direct the automaton's arm in making his own moves? With the second of these Poe's only connection is that he was ignorant of the solution. The fact that the correct solution had been both guessed and betrayed before April, 1836, is not the pith of this argument, for Poe had no periodical indexes foreign or domestic, and if, unaware of the most recent publications, he had reasoned honestly to an independent solution, there would be no

[3] George E. Woodberry, *The Life of Edgar Allan Poe* (Boston, 1909), I, 178. Woodberry wrote more specifically but not so happily (*The Works of Edgar Allan Poe,* ed. Edmund Clarence Stedman and George Edward Woodberry, Chicago, 1895, IX, 315): "The portions other than those pertaining to the analysis of the Chess-Player are from Sir David Brewster's 'Lectures [sic] on Natural Magic,' partly in acknowledged quotation, partly in close paraphrase. . . . The analysis itself follows closely Brewster's method, but is more exact and detailed, and adds much to the explanation. The pamphlet, of which the solution is given by Brewster, and which Poe identifies with an article in a 'Baltimore weekly paper,' possibly the 'Saturday Visiter,' to which Poe contributed, has not been found; but, doubtless, Brewster's account is accurate, and it would appear probable from Poe's language that he did not himself write it, although perhaps it directed his attention to the theme."

[4] Hervey Allen, *Israfel: The Life and Times of Edgar Allan Poe* (New York, 1934), I, 323-324.

obstacle to his credit. Still some notice of the real working of the automaton is necessary—to make clear Poe's debt to a source that was only partly correct.

The method of conducting the game, by a kind of pantograph and by magnetized chessmen, had been approximated as early as 1789 in a pamphlet written by Joseph Friedrich, Freiherr zu Racknitz.[5] And both the method of conducting the game and that of concealing the player within the chest had been completely exposed, almost two years before Poe's essay, in an article appearing in *Le Magasin pittoresque*,[6] based on a betrayal of the secret by Mouret, a Parisian chessplayer, who was at one time the operator of the machine.[7] In 1838 Maelzel died in passage from Havana to Philadelphia; the automaton was bought at auction in Philadelphia and resold to Dr. John Kearsley Mitchell, Professor in the Jefferson College of Medicine, who together with a group of friends rehabilitated it, operated it till the novelty was gone, then deposited it in the Chinese Museum in Philadelphia, where it was destroyed by fire on July 5, 1854.[8] By 1857 Dr. Mitchell had dictated an account[9] of the construction and operation of the automaton, which was published in the *Chess Monthly*. This remains not only the most authoritative but the clearest statement and together with the article in the *Magasin pittoresque*, which it completely corroborates, constitutes the extant evidence of how the automaton actually worked.

The chest was divided into two apartments above, and a drawer beneath. In the smaller apartment, occupying about a third of the longitudinal dimensions of the box, was placed a number of pieces of brass, made very

[5] *Über den Schachspieler des Herrn von Kempelen und dessen Nachbildung* (Leipsic and Dresden, 1789), esp. pp. 33-44 and plates.

[6] *Le Magasin pittoresque, publié sous la direction de MM. Euryale Cazeaux et Edouard Charton* (20 Livraison, 1834), II, 155.

[7] G[eorge] W[alker], "Anatomy of the Chess Automaton," *Fraser's Magazine for Town and Country*, XIX, 728 (June, 1839); and G[eorge] A[llen], "The History of the Automaton Chess-Player in America," *The Book of the First American Chess Congress*, ed. Daniel Willard Fiske (New York, 1859), p. 423 n.

[8] George Allen, *op. cit.*, pp. 474-484.

[9] George Allen (*op. cit.*, p. 480 n) says that Dr. John Kearsley Mitchell dictated an explanation which was communicated to the *Chess Monthly*. The two parts of the article in the *Chess Monthly* are unsigned, but in the index are credited to "S. W. Mitchell," doubtless S. Weir Mitchell, son of John Kearsley. See *Dictionary of American Biography*. George Allen's fine collection of chess books was purchased after his death by the Library Company of Philadelphia and is now at the Ridgway Branch. Here also S. Weir Mitchell deposited a box containing newspaper clippings and manuscripts about the automaton and a small chessboard and pattern of the knight's tour which would seem to be relics of the famous machine.

thin, and designed only for the purpose of deception. . . . Behind this movable back of the drawer, there was therefore left an unoccupied space of the whole length of the chest, and rather more than a foot in breadth. In this trough was fixed an iron railroad . . . upon which was placed a low seat. . . . The left arm of the Turk, part of a pentograph, communicated, through his body, with the interior of the chest, where, by means of a lever, the operator, concealed within it, was enabled to give every desired motion to the arm, hand, and fingers of the figure. . . . On the under side of the chest appeared a chess-board directly beneath that upon the upper surface. . . . The squares were numbered from one to sixty-four, under each of which hung a little lever, well balanced, to which was attached a small disk of iron. These disks, when attracted by magnets [one in each chess-man], placed on top of the box, swung up into the excavations and remained there quietly until liberated by the removal of the magnets, when they vibrated for some seconds like a well-hung bell. In front of the operator was placed . . . another chess-board. . . . This was also numbered to correspond exactly to that above his head, and was perforated by holes . . . in order to prevent the possibility of his chess-men being disarranged.[10]

Poe makes much of his reasoning that the automaton cannot be a pure automaton, that only a human mind can act with the endless variety necessary to make the choices of a chess game.[11] Again, he suspects that the operator of the machine was a certain assistant of Maelzel's, Schlumberger, during whose illness, on a former visit to Richmond, the automaton did not play.[12] The truth is that Schlumberger *was* the "director" of the automaton in most of its American exhibitions.[13] But how Poe guessed, or knew, it, is an-

---

[10] "The Last of a Veteran Chess Player," *Chess Monthly: An American Chess Serial*, ed. Daniel Willard Fiske, I, 41-44 (Feb., 1857). Two significant passages I quote later in a more specific connection.

The most scholarly treatment of the subject is the extensive bibliography in Antonius van der Linde, *Geschichte und Litteratur des Schachspiels* (Berlin, 1874), II, 339-352. But van der Linde, although he describes the *Magasin pittoresque* and *Chess Monthly* articles, has not seen either and is consequently inaccurate in his notion of the true solution. The history of writings on the automaton both before and after Poe is one of complicated plagiarism, misinterpretation, and irresponsibility which I have been able only to hint at within the limit of this article.

[11] *Works of Poe*, ed. James A. Harrison (New York, 1902), XIV, 9-11. All references to the "Essay" are to this edition.   [12] *Op. cit.*, p. 35.

[13] George Allen, *op. cit.*, pp. 436 ff. Schlumberger, an Alsatian imported from the chess cafes of Paris, was actually ill during a visit of the automaton to Richmond in August and September, 1834. The second visit, during which apparently Poe gathered the data for his excellent description of a performance, took place in December, 1835, and January, 1836 (*ibid.*, p. 463 n).

other matter. This seems the place to glance at a possibility that long before Poe wrote of the automaton he had ample testimony not only that a man was concealed in the machine but that it was Schlumberger.

About the end of May, 1827, while Maelzel was exhibiting in Baltimore, two boys actually saw Schlumberger emerge from the automaton after a performance and recognized him.[14] On Friday, June 1, the Baltimore *Federal Gazette* carried the following:

The Chess Player Discovered. This ingenious contrivance of M. Kempelen . . . has at length been discovered. . . . an accidental circumstance exposed . . . the concealed agent as he emerged from the case, just after the conclusion of an exhibition of the Automaton.[15]

Four days later the *Gazette* was more circumstantial:

The Automaton Chess Player. The Editor of the United States Gazette expresses some doubt as to the discovery of the Agent in the Box or Table . . . because we did not vouch for it in our paper of Friday last. . . . It was not necessary *here* to vouch for a fact which was very generally known, and as generally believed. Two persons, one in his fifteenth, the other in his nineteenth year, at the same time witnessed the transaction. . . . We take this opportunity of noticing an observation made by the Editor of the Baltimore Republican on Saturday last, "that the boy who states he made the discovery demanded money for disclosing it. . . ." When the report had partially circulated of the discovery of the concealed Chess Player, a number of curious enquirers successively pressed for a relation of the circumstances, until it became "very annoying" to the elder youth, who was tired of telling "the oft repeated tale," and to his employer, whose business was interrupted by so many curious intruders.[16]

And on the following day the *Gazette* reverted to the topic again, this time in answer to a gibe in the *New York Commercial Adver-*

[14] George Allen (*op. cit.*, pp. 451-452) says they were standing on the roof of a shed in the rear of the building where Maelzel exhibited, that after the performance the automaton was wheeled into a back room and the top lifted, upon which Schlumberger climbed out. As it was a hot day, Maelzel had thrown the shutters of the room open; the boys saw everything clearly. I have been unable to find any contemporary notices which are so specific. Yet from the newspaper items which I quote it is evident that something of the sort happened. Allen gives a circumstantial history (pp. 436 ff.) of Schlumberger's connection with the automaton. There is no reason to doubt that it was he who was seen, though how much his name was connected with the story that went around is doubtful.
[15] *Federal Gazette,* June 1, 1827, p. 2, col. 5.
[16] *Ibid.,* June 5, 1827, p. 2, col. 3.

tiser.[17] There can be little doubt that the affair received some notice outside Baltimore and within the city was commonly discussed. The diary of Robert Gilmor, Baltimore merchant and art patron (1774-1848), offers a fortunate illustration. On May 12 and 16 of this year Gilmor discusses the mystery of the automaton. On May 23 he attends an exhibition and thinks there is an *"assistant"* within the chest. Then on June 1 comes the revelation.

Called in for a moment at Meredith's to talk of the recent discovery by a boy, of the secret of Maelzel's Automaton Chess Player; which was as we all suspected moved by a man concealed in the Machine.[18]

Poe, of course, was not in Baltimore at this time; he was in Boston, publishing *Tamerlane and Other Poems*.[19] But his brother Henry Poe *was* in Baltimore—at least about this time.[20] Henry Poe's first contribution to the *North American* appeared in No. 11, July 28.[21] In No. 18, September 15, he published "The Happiest Day," taken from Edgar's *Tamerlane*,[22] so that it is certain that by that time the brothers had been in communication. There is no proof that this had taken place as early as the exposure of the automaton, but it is not unlikely. The two had been together in Richmond, on good terms, in 1825. In March, 1827, Edgar fled from Richmond. Probably in May or June he published *Tamerlane*.[23] "It is known that he sent out several copies of *Tamerlane* from Boston."[24] It would have been curious had he waited until September to send one to his brother.

The question overlaps oddly with the fact that in the first number of the *North American*, May 19, appeared an article on the "Automaton Chess Player." One cannot be sure that this is what Poe refers to when he writes: "His Essay was first published in a

[17] *Ibid.*, June 6, 1827, p. 2, col. 3. George Allen (*op. cit.*, p. 452) says the *National Intelligencer*, of Washington, D. C., believed the *Gazette* article was a publicity trick of Maelzel's, and that other papers then kept silent.

[18] "Diary of Robert Gilmor," *Maryland Historical Magazine*, XVII, 332, 333, 337, 341 (Dec., 1922). I owe this reference to the kindness of Mr. Louis H. Dielman, Librarian of the Peabody Institute of Baltimore.

[19] Hervey Allen and Thomas Ollive Mabbott, *Poe's Brother* (New York, 1926), pp. 78-79.

[20] *Ibid.*, p. 31.   [21] *Ibid.*, p. 91.

[22] *Ibid.*, p. 92. It is barely conceivable that a copy of *Tamerlane* might have come into Henry's hands without Edgar's knowledge. But a week later Edgar's co-operation is clear, for "Dreams," in No. 23, has corrections that must be due to Edgar himself (*ibid.*, pp. 49-51, 92).

[23] *Ibid.*, pp. 78-81.   [24] *Ibid.*, p. 82.

Baltimore weekly paper, was illustrated by cuts, and was entitled 'An attempt to analyze the Automaton Chess-Player of M. Maelzel.' "[25] The article in the *North American* has only one cut; however, Poe may well have remembered it but vaguely. The title in the *North American* is simpler, but what more natural than that Poe should have given it approximately the title he had before him, that of the pamphlet to which Sir David Brewster refers?[26] Unless someone points out another such article in another Baltimore weekly, there must be a strong presumption that it was to this Poe made a confused reference—in his effort to appear acquainted with the bibliography of the automaton.[27] Mr. Allen and Professor Mabbott have suggested the connection by reproducing a page of Poe's essay, with his illustration, and following that the first two pages of the first number of the *North American*, containing the automaton essay in full.[28]

The essay in the *North American*, as it derives from the same stock as Poe's ideas, leads us conveniently to the last part of our discourse. The "original," the source, the fountainhead, of the already widespread ideas which Poe adopted—the anonymous pamphlet referred to by Brewster—was: *An Attempt to Analyse the Automaton Chess Player of Mr. De Kempelen. With an Easy Method of Imitating the Movements of that Celebrated Figure. Illustrated by Original Drawings. To Which is Added a Copious Collection of the Knight's Moves over the Chess Board. London. Printed for J. Booth. . . . 1821.* 40 pp. The author of the pamphlet was a young man twenty-one years old, Robert Willis, later Jacksonian Professor of applied mathematics at the University of Cambridge.[29] In the same year this anonymous

---

[25] *Op. cit.*, p. 20.

[26] Sir David Brewster, *Letters on Natural Magic, Addressed to Sir Walter Scott, Bart.* (New York, c. 1832), *Harper's Stereotyped Edition* (on binding, *The Family Library*, No. 50), p. 248. Cf. note 48. Brewster speaks of "a pamphlet, entitled 'An Attempt to analyse the automaton chess-player of M. Kempelen' "—which of course was nearly the correct title of the pamphlet to which *he* was referring.

[27] It is extremely improbable that any article on the automaton appeared in a Baltimore paper before its visit there in 1827. Woodberry's suggestion that the article had appeared in the *Saturday Visiter* (cf. note 3) could perhaps be tested thoroughly by the file of the *Visiter* owned by the Cloud family. (See Hervey Allen, *Israfel*, New York, 1926, I, 350, n. 448.) But the discovery of such an article could not add to or detract from Poe's credit for originality. I think it is plain from what is said above and from what follows that whatever he had seen he did not remember it or rely on it, but drew entirely from Brewster. [28] *Op. cit.*, pp. 85 ff.

[29] *Dictionary of National Biography*, Robert Willis (1800-1875).

pamphlet was reviewed in the *Edinburgh Philosophical Journal,* one of the editors of which was Sir David Brewster. The review, with extracts and eleven figures of the automaton, was in effect a second publication of Willis's well-reasoned, but only partially correct, solution.[30]

Six years later, during the first tour of the automaton in America, there were at least three more republications of the same solution. The automaton came to America in April, 1826, and after a short stay in New York, moved to Boston, where it remained until the end of October[31] and provoked *The History and Analysis of the Supposed Automaton Chess Player,*[32] a pamphlet with diagrams taken, perhaps through an intermediate account, from Willis, and drawing on the solution of Willis and on some intermediate account of a misinterpretation of Racknitz which had appeared in Hutton's *Philosophical and Mathematical Dictionary.*[33] Not many months later, in March, 1827, Poe himself, let us recall, was in Boston.

The automaton moved on to Philadelphia, and the *Franklin Journal and American Mechanics' Magazine* for February, 1827, published "Some Observations upon the Automaton Chess Player,"[34] an article which included the elements of Willis's solution and mentioned both the review in the *Edinburgh Philosophical Journal* and the Boston pamphlet. It employed one simplified diagram, with but three letters. By May the automaton had moved on to Baltimore, and the *North American* published its article, borrowing both diagram and text from the *Franklin Journal.*

In 1832 Sir David Brewster published his *Letters on Natural Magic, Addressed to Sir Walter Scott, Bart.,* in which, perhaps reminded of Willis's pamphlet from his editing of the *Edinburgh Philosophical Journal,* he drew again on the same source, giving the title, though not the name of the author, which he may not have known. And this brings us to Poe.

There is no reason to suppose that Poe drew on any writing but that of Sir David Brewster. He does not pretend to have seen Brewster's source, the pamphlet, but only its "original" in a Balti-

[30] *Edinburgh Philosophical Journal,* IV, 393-398 (April, 1821).
[31] For the itinerary of the automaton, see George Allen, *op. cit.,* pp. 435, 442, 447.
[32] George Allen's copy, the only one I have located, is at the Ridgway Branch of the Library Company of Philadelphia.   [33] See note 35.
[34] *Franklin Journal and American Mechanics' Magazine,* III, 125-132 (Feb., 1827).

more paper, and this if it was the *North American* article, we have already seen he could hardly have remembered very well. Concerning the pamphlet of 1789 by the Freiherr zu Racknitz, Poe has plainly learned everything from Brewster.[35] The same is true of the "large pamphlet printed at Paris in 1785 . . . the first attempt of which we ourselves have any knowledge";[36] and the same, of Poe's history of the automaton, its invention in 1769 by Baron von Kempelen of Presburg in Hungary, its exhibition in Presburg, Paris and Vienna, its visit to London in 1783 and 1784, von Kempelen's calling it a *bagatelle*.[37] Poe's knowledge that "the plume

[35] Cf. Poe, *op. cit.*, p. 19, and Brewster, *op. cit.*, p. 247. Cf. note 5. Brewster's description, including the quotation, is taken from the *Edinburgh Encyclopedia* (Edinburgh, 1830), II, 65, of which he himself was the editor. The article in the *Encyclopedia* professes to have drawn (through an intermediate work, I think. Cf. above, p. 145) on an account by Thomas Collinson in a "Supplement to Hutton's Mathematical Dictionary, Art. Automaton." I have not seen the edition of Hutton's *Encyclopedia* with the "Supplement," but in the article "Automaton" in the edition of 1815, the account of the chess-player is quoted from Collinson, who, it appears, had a slight acquaintance with Kempelen and Racknitz but was ignorant of German. His "boy . . . thin and small . . . concealed in a drawer almost immediately under the chess-board" is a misinterpretation too complicated to be treated here (Charles Hutton, *A Philosophical and Mathematical Dictionary*, London, 1815, I, 194). Brewster makes the "thin and small" boy "thin and tall." Poe acquires from him this mistake, the original misinterpretation, and the amusing "Mr. Freyhere."

[36] Cf. Poe, *op. cit.*, p. 19, and Brewster, *op. cit.*, p. 247. This "pamphlet" is Decremps, *La Magie blanche devoilée* (Paris, 1784), a volume of 287 pages. George Allen's copy, the only one I have located, is at the Ridgway Branch of the Philadelphia Library Company. Decremps's solution is plainly what Brewster and Poe are describing.

[37] Cf. Poe, *op. cit.*, pp. 11-12, and Brewster, *op. cit.*, pp. 243-248. It is worth noting that Poe omits a second visit to England in 1819-1820 (the occasion of Willis's *Attempt*) and attaches Maelzel's name to the 1783-1784 visit, where it does not belong. It was Maelzel who brought the automaton to England in 1819-1820 (H. J. R. Murray, *History of Chess*, Oxford, 1913, p. 877). Poe's account of the other automata, the coach of Camus, the magician of Maillardet, the duck of Vaucanson, the calculating machine of Babbage (pp. 6-9), he seems to have taken also from Brewster. He admits the debt for the first three, and the fourth is there too; they are all in the same Letter as the chess automaton (Letter XI, pp. 241-243, 256-257, 263-267). "We copy the following account of it [Maillardet's magician] from the *Letters* before mentioned of Dr. B., who derived his information principally from the Edinburgh encyclopedia" (Poe, *op. cit.*, p. 7). We must not assume from this that Poe had seen the *Edinburgh Encyclopedia*—not even when he adds, "Under the head *Androides* in the Edinburgh Encyclopedia may be found a full account of the principal automata of ancient and modern times" (p. 9 n). Brewster had put a footnote to his account of Maillardet's magician: "See the Edinburgh Encyclopedia, Art. Androides, vol. II, p. 66" (p. 257 n). Brewster's Letter XI begins with an account of ancient automata; and in the same letter (p. 260) there is a second mention of the *Edinburgh Encyclopedia*—besides a few more in other parts of the book—ample premises for Poe to guess that most of the Letter on automata was from the *Encyclopedia*. (It is to be remembered, however, that Willis's solution was not in the *Encyclopedia*. See *Edinburgh Encyclopedia*, Edinburgh, 1830, II, 64-65, "Androides.") Finally, had Poe turned to the *Encyclopedia* and found that the editor was none

... on the automaton's turban was not originally worn"[38] he could easily have got from the diagrams in Brewster. His note that "The making the Turk pronounce the word *echec,* is an improvement by M. Maelzel" could have been gathered from Brewster,[39] though what he adds, "the figure originally indicated a *check* by rapping on the box with his right hand," came from some other source, for Brewster says it shook its head thrice. Poe's idea might have been picked up as easily at the exhibition room as anywhere else. I have found it in no other writing.[40]

We come then to consider how much of his solution Poe owed to Brewster; and the answer is: almost everything, all that was correct, as well as much that was incorrect. As far as Brewster is right, Poe is right. Where Brewster is wrong, Poe is wrong. He who likes may compare point for point the opening of the three front doors, of the drawer, of the two back doors, the successive postures assumed by the operator within the box.[41] The mere X-ray like diagrams in Brewster, the shadowy figure of the man, first bent forward, then sitting upright, then up in the body of the Turk, shout the story. The fact that according to Brewster the operator extended his own left arm into that of the Turk, while according to Poe he brought his right arm across his chest to actuate some machinery, makes no difference—both were wrong. Poe has the operator's legs behind the drawer only when it is pulled out, and in a footnote calls attention to Brewster's "untenable" supposition that the drawer is a false drawer and does not extend to the back of the box. Brewster was nearer to the truth than he. "The drawer, which when drawn out, seemed to be of the entire hori-

---

other than David Brewster, LL.D., it would have seemed pointless to accuse Brewster of deriving his information "principally from the Edinburgh Encyclopedia." ·

[38] *Op. cit.,* p. 12.

[39] Cf. Poe, *op. cit.,* p. 17 n, and Brewster, *op. cit.,* p. 245.

[40] Or perhaps Poe has remembered confusedly something from the *North American* article: "The right hand rests upon the table, and if a false move be made, the figure notices it by striking this hand repeatedly upon the table, and shaking his head" (p. 2). There is good evidence that Brewster gives the correct account of how the figure originally gave check. Racknitz, who says he has observed the automaton carefully (p. 3), writes: "Both die Figur dem Könige Schach: so neigte sie dreimal, bei Schach der Königin nur zweimal, den Kopf" (p. 9). (See note 5.) Windisch, an early and circumstantial first-hand reporter, writes: "Beym Schache der Königinn nickt er zweymal, so, wie beym Schache dem Könige dreymal mit dem Kopfe; bey einem falschen Gange aber schüttelt er denselben" (Karl Gottlieb von Windisch, *Briefe über den Schachspieler,* Basel, 1783, pp. 31-32).

[41] Cf. Poe, *op. cit.,* pp. 22-24, and Brewster, *op. cit.,* pp. 248-255.

zontal dimensions of the chest, was also deceptive, as its back end was so constructed as to move upon wheels, by means of which it did not press backwards with the sides more than a foot and a half."[42]

Having adopted the explanation of Sir David Brewster, Poe alleges as the foundation of his "result" seventeen "observations taken during frequent visits to the exhibition."[43] Some of them are acute

[42] *Chess Monthly,* I, 42 (Feb., 1857). Cf. note 10.

[43] 1. The moves of the Turk are made at irregular intervals. Since it would have been easy to limit the time allowed to the opponent for each move, and, if the automaton were a pure automaton, to set its replies at a fixed interval, and since this would favor the operation of a pure automaton, the irregularity argues a human agency. (This argument is not in Brewster.) 2. When the automaton is about to make a move, the drapery over the left shoulder may be seen in agitation. If the opponent retract his move, even before Maelzel retracts the move on the automaton's board, the movement of the arm will be withheld. (Since the operator was not looking through the chest of the Turk, as Poe supposed, but depended for his information on Maelzel's moves on the board on the chest, it would appear that Poe's imagination beguiled him.) 3. A pure machine would win all games; but the automaton does not. (Not in Brewster.) 4. The Turk shakes his head and rolls his eyes only when the game is easy, i.e., when the operator has time to think about it. (Not in Brewster.) 5. When the doors in the trunk of the Turk were opened and the automaton was swung around, it seemed to Poe that pieces of machinery within shifted their position—an effect which he attributed to mirrors. (Again imagination—induced by his notion that the operator sat up in the trunk of the Turk.) 6. The appearance and movements of the automaton are artificial and awkward, not natural, like those of the rope-dancers and other automata of Maelzel; this is to support the illusion of pure mechanical operation. (Not in Brewster.) 7. When the automaton is wound up, the sound is not like that of an axis connected with "either a weight, a spring, or any system of machinery whatever." (Brewster quotes from his source [Willis]: ". . . the axis turned by the key is quite free and unconnected either with a spring or weight, or any system of machinery" [*op. cit.,* p. 253]. Poe argued from the sound of the turning axis. Willis had argued from the fact that widely varying numbers of moves were the result of windings of the same length [*op. cit.,* pp. 20-21]—perhaps a better argument.) Maelzel will never directly affirm that the automaton is a pure machine. (Not in Brewster.) 9. When Maelzel holds the candle at the rear of cupboard No. 1 and the automaton is wheeled about, the machinery to the rear of the cupboard seems to move—evidence that it is swung out of position when the man straightens up into that space. (Not in Brewster. Perhaps the machinery did move; it was movable, but not for the reason Poe supposed. The player prepared to *play the game* by "swinging the whole interior furniture—wheels, partitions, and all—against the outer doors and walls of the box, so as to throw all the subdivisions into one large apartment" [S. W. Mitchell, *loc. cit.,* p. 4. Cf. note 10.].) 10. He corrects Brewster's statement that the Turk is only life-size. 11. The chest is designed so as to seem to have less capacity than it has. (Not in Brewster.) 12. The cloth which lines the interior of the main compartment is in places a false partition, easily removed. (Poe indulges in the same weakness for which he berates Brewster so severely—speculating on the interior arrangements. The Brewster solution makes much the same use of the cloth. It is not clear from Mitchell's explanation just how near either Poe or Brewster is to the truth; each is at least partly wrong.) 13. The antagonist is seated away from the automaton, lest he detect the breathings of the man within. (Not in Brewster.) 14. Maelzel occasionally deviates from his routine of showing the interior of the box, but never in any essential. (An attempt to refine on Brewster's argument: "This ingenious explanation of the chess automaton is, our author states,

and well applied, but these all tend to establish, not the way the machine worked, but, as Poe confesses in a footnote, the fact, already amply established, that the machine must be regulated by *mind*. Willis had given sufficient attention to this preliminary matter. Sir David Brewster had assumed it was obvious and dwelt on it but momentarily.[44]

It remains to be said that Poe's consciousness of his debt to Brewster is best proved by his studied attempts at disparagement. The long complaint beginning with "The solution consists in a series of minute explanations"[45] is but a red herring. "It was altogether unnecessary," he says, "to devote seven or eight pages for the purpose of proving what no one in his senses would deny— viz.: that the wonderful mechanical genius of Baron Kempelen could invent the necessary means for shutting a door or slipping

---

greatly confirmed by the *regular and undeviating* mode of disclosing the interior of the chest" [*op. cit.*, p. 253]. Poe's example, "he never opens the main compartment without first pulling out the drawer," etc., is probably not significant, for as we have seen, the back of the drawer moved on rollers, and the operator's legs could have been behind it even when it was closed.) 15. There are six candles on the chest before the Turk, to enable the operator to see through the material, "probably fine gauze," of the Turk's chest. The candles are of different heights to prevent by the dazzle of the crossing rays, the spectators' having a clear view of the gauze chest. (Wide of the mark.) 16. About Schlumberger. (See above, pp. 141-143.) Also, a story about an Italian in the suite of Baron von Kempelen, suspected of being the operator, ill once at a time when the automaton did not play. (I have not seen this in any other account. Poe might have heard it in the gossip of the exhibition room, or he might have invented it without much fear of contradiction.) 17. The Turk plays with his left arm—not by accident, but in order that the operator, sitting in the body of the Turk, may reach his right arm across his chest to operate machinery in the left shoulder of the Turk. (Again wide of the mark. Poe takes occasion to remark: "The early writers of treatises on the Automaton, seem not to have observed the matter at all, and have no reference to it. The author of the pamphlet alluded to by Brewster, mentions it, but acknowledges his inability to account for it." The first of these statements is simply irresponsible. The early writers *do* observe the matter. Racknitz's plates show a left-handed player, and he comments [p. 39] on the fact that Kempelen's is left-handed, rejects an explanation by Windisch and offers one of his own. Willis takes the matter fully into account [*op. cit.*, pp. 30-31]. If Poe's second statement could be taken as a literal reflection of his mind, it might be a clue to whether the "original" he saw was the Baltimore *North American* article, which says: "The figure plays with the left hand, which when not in action, rests upon a cushion placed near to the board" [p. 1]. But any article based on Willis's pamphlet could hardly avoid mentioning the fact at least cursorily, and Poe's addition that the author "acknowledges his inability to account for it" certainly need have been prompted by nothing more than that Poe remembered that the author did not try to account for it.)

[44] He says merely: "Upon considering the operations of the automaton, it must have been obvious that the game of chess was performed either by a person enclosed in the chest or by the exhibitor himself" (p. 246). Willis's longer treatment was repeated in a different form in the *Franklin Journal* and from that was copied in the Baltimore *North American*. [45] *Op. cit.*, pp. 20-21.

aside a pannel." So he imposes upon the reader's imagination the concept that Brewster's article is but a tangle of arbitrary carpenter's specifications. What is but the superstructure of Brewster's account is made to seem the foundation—while the real foundation Poe has shifted into his own essay without acknowledgment.[46] Another fault which he has found is even more factitious. "It is quite impossible to arrive at any distinct conclusion in regard to the adequacy or inadequacy of the analysis, on account of the gross misarrangement and deficiency of the letters of reference employed."[47] This is a monstrous exaggeration. To begin with, if there were hardly a letter of reference in Brewster's whole explanation, the eleven figures, in which the Turk and his box are cross-sectioned and anatomized from every direction, would convey the necessary ideas with sufficient lucidity. In the second place, there is not much wrong with the letters of reference—not enough to cause an interested student more than a moment's perplexity.[48] "The same fault is to be found," says Poe, "in the Attempt &c, as we originally saw it." If the "Attempt" as he originally saw it was the article in the *North American,* then he had no possible grievance, for there were only three letters, A, B, C.

What then is the merit of Poe's essay? George Allen wrote that "it was only in favor of the great mechanician [Maelzel], that the public resolutely persisted in refusing to know a secret, which had been exposed and published a dozen times."[49] Why did Poe's "exposure" attract so much notice, win the applause of so many contemporary journals? Why was he, of all who had written on the same subject, both more and less accurately than he, singled out in the public imagination as the champion who had slain the mechanical monster? Why was it that after a few years his was the only solution that people outside of a very esoteric chess world remembered at all? George Allen, for example, must have realized perfectly Poe's little claim to originality. He had the "Essay" in his

[46] It is worth while recalling that the original work of Willis was meant not only as an analysis of the automaton but a suggestion of "An Easy Method of Imitating the Movements of that Celebrated Figure." [47] *Op. cit.,* p. 20.

[48] There are two editions of the *Letters* which Poe could have used, the first edition, London, 1832, John Murray; and the American edition, undated, published at New York perhaps soon after 1832, by Harper as No. 50 of the *Family Library.* (There were a number of later impressions, or perhaps issues, of both of these, with varying title-pages.) Throughout this article I have referred to the latter, as the one Poe is more likely to have used. In that I have discovered six slight errors, and in the London edition, five.

[49] *Op. cit.,* pp. 477-478.

large collection of works on the automaton. But Ingram was apparently unaware that any such books as Allen's existed, or if he was aware, he never thought of them as possible rivals to the "clear, concise, irrefutable arguments" of Poe.

The answer, of course, is partly that Poe was Poe, and that the "Chess-Player" has been embedded in the rest of his reputation. But also there is the fact that the other men who wrote were mechanicians, journalists, or editors, while Poe was a prose master. His arguments, if not "irrefutable," *were* "clear, concise," graceful and strong. It has not been the purpose of any part of this article to deny that Poe's "Essay" was a good one, in some parts—where he was right—the best exposure of the automaton ever made. Other exposures of the automaton, that of the *Magasin pittoresque,* that of Dr. Mitchell, were rooted in the world of fact, which for artistic purposes is a scrap heap. Such writings had eminently less claim to general interest than Poe's, which sprang from the ideal soil of vision. Not what *has happened,* says Aristotle, but what *may happen.* So the quarrel is not with Poe, with an illusion which succeeded, but with the evaluation of that illusion by his critics, with the common opinion of "Maelzel's Chess-Player"—which comes sometimes even to the ears of school children. Poe emerges from the "Essay" not as a detective drawing from observed facts a conclusion which squares with other facts. He emerges as an imaginative writer, with a power of making bright and acceptable the drab, mechanic guesses of writers with an eye to reality.

> True wit is nature to advantage dress'd,
> What *oft was thought,* but ne'er so well express'd.

The Refrain in Poe's Poetry
Anthony Caputi

EDGAR ALLAN POE's use of the refrain constitutes a valuable index to his literary practice and to the relation between his practice and theory. An examination of the refrain in his poetry can be helpful in clarifying the disparity between his merits and the frequent puerility of even his best poems. Before turning to his work, however, it is perhaps necessary to distinguish the refrain as a literary device from such related devices as simple repetition, incremental repetition, and parallel structure by limiting it to thematic, patterned repetition.[1] Poe's poetry abounds in all these devices, and sometimes they seem to blur into one another. But refrain can usually be isolated on the basis of its thematic character, whether it consists of the repetition of a single word or of a unit as large as a stanza.

Poe's most complete discussion of the refrain occurs, unfortunately, in a work which critics have viewed with great suspicion. But whatever "The Philosophy of Composition" (1846) may or may not reveal about the composition of "The Raven," it probably sets forth accurately some of Poe's opinions on aesthetic and technical matters. Certainly there is no reason to question his remarks on the general nature of the refrain, since they clearly describe the theory of the refrain which he practiced in his later poems. To facilitate the examination of this theory, the crucial passage is quoted in full.

I betook myself to ordinary induction, with the view of obtaining some artistic piquancy which might serve me as a keynote in the construction of the poem—some pivot upon which the whole structure might turn. In carefully thinking over all the usual artistic effects—or more properly *points*, in the theatrical sense—I did not fail to perceive immediately

[1] This definition avoids the pitfalls of such polar definitions as have been proposed by Anne Hamilton, *Seven Principles of Poetry* (Boston, 1940), p. 129, and C. A. Smith, *Repetition and Parallelism in English Verse* (New York and New Orleans, 1894), pp. 9-18.

that no one had been so universally employed as that of the refrain. The universality of its employment sufficed to assure me of its intrinsic value, and spared me the necessity of submitting it to analysis. I considered it, however, with regard to its susceptibility of improvement, and soon saw it to be in a primitive condition. As commonly used, the *refrain,* or burden, not only is limited to lyric verse, but depends for its impression upon the force of monotone—both in sound and thought. The pleasure is deduced solely from the sense of identity—of repetition. I resolved to diversify, and so heighten the effect, by adhering in general to the monotone of the sound, while I continually varied that of the thought: that is to say, I determined to produce continually novel effects, by the variation *of the application* of the *refrain*—the *refrain* itself remaining, for the most part, unvaried.[2] [Italics are Poe's.]

Perhaps the most striking remark in the passage is Poe's claim that he found the refrain in a "primitive condition." In view of the tradition which asserts that he was incredibly unappreciative of the poets who had preceded him,[3] it is likely that he spoke the truth as far as he was aware of it. According to Poe, the refrain as he found it depended "for its impression upon the force of monotone—both in sound and thought"; the pleasure was "deduced solely from the sense of identity—of repetition." The emphasis on "monotone" and "identity" suggests that he was thinking here of refrain which is repeated without variation. This kind of refrain derives its force from the compounding effect of the repetition of a line containing an unvaried emotional content. Anne Hamilton describes it "as a device by which the poet may embolden the color of his thought."[4] Poe proposed to exploit its full possibilities "by adhering in general to the monotone of sound, while he continually varied the thought." By varying the context in which the same refrain appeared, he reasoned that he could qualify the refrain, throwing different facets of it into relief with each different context. Logically, this technique would produce unexpected combinations of ideas and emotions. It is highly probable that Poe was thinking of such combinations when he spoke of pro-

[2] *The Poems of Edgar Allan Poe,* ed. Killis Campbell (New York, 1917), p. 322. All references to Poe's work will be to this edition.
[3] The most recent statement of this opinion can be found in Yvor Winters, "A Crisis in the History of American Obscurantism," *American Literature,* VIII, 380, 381 (Jan., 1937).
[4] *Seven Principles,* p. 129.

ducing "continuously novel effects, by the variation *of the application* of the *refrain*." Certainly he was speaking of effects of this kind when he expressed his intention "to vary and graduate, as regards seriousness and importance, the queries of the lover" in "The Raven."[5]

Such, in outline, is Poe's theory of the refrain as it emerges from his most extensive discussion of it. An examination of his poetry reveals that although the theory does only partial justice to the wide diversity of uses to which he actually put the refrain, it does sketch the principles operating behind the most important of those uses.

Taken as a whole, Poe's poetry reveals that he used the refrain much more extensively in his later work than in his early work. Only two of the poems published in *Tamerlane and Other Poems* (1827) have refrains. Fourteen poems with refrains were included in Griswold's edition in 1850; and though that number included the two of the 1827 volume and at least one other early poem, "To One in Paradise," the evidence favors the conclusion that the remaining eleven were completed within the last five or six years of the poet's life. Even "Bridal Ballad," the present form of which is ascribed to 1837, reveals that Poe tinkered with its refrain considerably later. His use of the refrain in the final years of his life almost amounted to a dependence.

Traces of the theory of the refrain set forth in "The Philosophy of Composition" can be discerned in the earliest poems using the refrain. These poems might be called experimental, since each represents an attempt at quite different effects. "The happiest day . . . " (1827) repeats the initial line, "The happiest day—the happiest hour," in the fourth stanza, but hardly involves any manipulation of it for its multiple meanings. The line is deceptive in its initial occurrence; but the nostalgia which attaches to it in the first stanza, when "the happiest day" is placed in the past, is rather intensified than qualified by the repetition of the line. The "Song," "I saw thee on thy bridal day" (1827), presents the first working out of Poe's theory of the "improved" refrain. Opening with the lines

[5] "Philosophy of Composition," p. 324.

> I saw thee on thy bridal day—
>   When a burning blush came o'er thee,
> Though happiness around thee lay,
> The world all love before thee:

the poem repeats the last two lines without, and the first two with slight variation in the last stanza. The intermediate stanzas elaborate on the "burning blush," showing that it is not the conventional blush of the bride, but the result of the unlooked-for presence of an admirer. This complication renders ironic the repetition at the end of the poem of the lines

> Though happiness around thee lay,
> The world all love before thee.

It is even probable that the poet was punning on the word "before," placing emphasis on the notion of futurity in line four, but on the meaning "in front of" in line sixteen. This technique, it is apparent, could be productive of very subtle shadings in emotional complexity. Unfortunately, the repetition of lines one and two, with substitutions and additions which Poe apparently felt necessary for proper emphasis, exemplifies the rhetorical puerility which too often vitiates his most interesting effects.

In addition to the poems of the 1827 edition, at least one other early poem throws light on Poe's developing theory of the refrain. "To One in Paradise" (1835) does not use a refrain-line at all, but what might be called a refrain-word, a word, that is, which is repeated in pattern and which is the "nucleus of the poetic utterance."[6] The word which fills this function in "To One in Paradise" is "all." In the first stanza it occurs three times, constituting an intense affirmation of the fulness of the speaker's experience during his beloved's lifetime.

> Thou wast that all to me, love,
>   For which my soul did pine—
> A green isle in the sea, love,
>   A fountain and a shrine,
> All wreathed with fairy fruits and flowers,
>   And all the flowers were mine.

With an appropriate shift to the present tense the last stanza re-

---
[6] The phrase is B. Roland Lewis's (*Creative Poetry*, Stanford University, 1931, p. 191).

peats "all" twice, turning its initial implications back upon themselves by emphasizing the completeness of the reversal from fulness to emptiness, from joy to joylessness.

Poe's experimentation with the range of effects obtainable through the refrain bore fruit in the poems which hardened into final form between 1844 and 1849. Though most of these poems involve weaknesses of various kinds, behind all of them is discernible the purpose of fashioning simple materials to make them refract complexity. Like "I saw thee on thy bridal day," "Bridal Ballad" presents a vignette contrasting the surface bliss of a wedding scene with the inner struggle of the bride. The refrain, "And I am happy now," is repeated with slight variation at the end of each stanza, at first expressing the bride's joy, but gradually, as she reflects on her dead lover and her promises to him, nucleating her doubts and misgivings. It mounts in complexity with each repetition, until in the fourth stanza, where it is repeated twice, it brings the poem to a climax in the lines.

> And, though my faith be broken,
> And, though my heart be broken,
> Here is the ring as token
> That I am happy now.

However picayune the art involved in the first two of these lines, they should not obscure the fact that the passage achieves a highly effective climax: in the temporary success of the present struggling against the past the poem attains a precarious emotional plateau which is held to the end.

In "Eldorado" (1849) and "The Raven" (1845) Poe apparently turned to the technique developed in "To One in Paradise"; but instead of playing the refrain-word off against itself, he used two refrain-words, playing them off against each other. This is perhaps more applicable to "Eldorado" than to "The Raven." In "Eldorado" the refrain-words "shadow" and "Eldorado" both rhyme and contrast through four stanzas. They constitute a kind of duet in which each voice qualifies the other, while the combination of the two embodies the theme. "The Raven," on the other hand, does not represent so much a duet as conjunctive solos. Despite all that Poe has said about his selection of "Nevermore" and the method by which he qualified its meaning in successive stanzas, he failed to mention that "Nevermore" has a complement in "nothing more" in the early part of the poem. Of all the patterns of repetition worked into the poem, only these refrain-words and their interrelations constitute more than an attempt at rhetorical emphasis and phonetic lushness. Enough has been said already by Poe and others about the qualification of "Nevermore" in the last seven stanzas of the poem. It should, however, be noted that "Nevermore" functions primarily to qualify "nothing more." The first seven stanzas create the atmosphere of desolation, a desolation which is primarily spiritual, but which also vaguely includes everything beyond the door past which the speaker cannot see. This sense of desolation centers in the refrain-word in these stanzas, "nothing more." The raven introduces "Nevermore" at the end of stanza eight; and thereafter "Nevermore" serves as a reply to the bereaved questioner, finally becoming emblematic of his subjective state. As the sign of his pessimistic melancholy it is an explanation of "nothing more." Only after the raven has become symbolic, after the full extent of the questioner's loss and the degree of his perversity and self-pity are apparent, do the questioner's isolation and self-limitation to "nothing more" become meaningful.

In view of these remarks on "The Raven" Poe's claim that the poet must begin with his "*dénouement* constantly in mind"[7] clarifies another of his ideas on the subject of form. "The Raven" suggests, as "Dreamland" (1844) and "Ulalume" (1847) clearly show, that Poe was interested in the kind of circular form that can be achieved through a judicious use of refrain, a form wherein the latter part of the poem comes back upon the beginning. The first stanza of "Dreamland" sets forth in concrete terms, however vague and indefinite, the state of mind to be equated with dreaming.

> By a route obscure and lonely,
> Haunted by ill-angels only,
> Where an Eidolon, named NIGHT,
> On a black throne reigns upright,
> I have reached these lands but newly
> From an ultimate dim Thule—
> From a wide weird clime that lieth, sublime,
> Out of SPACE—out of TIME.

[7] "Philosophy of Composition," p. 318.

There is no immediate hint beyond that provided by the title that the journey described is wholly subjective. The description proceeds, detailing "bottomless vales" and "boundless floods," "seas that restlessly aspire" and "dismal tarns and pools"; but it does not establish a palpable connection with its tenor, the mind, until the penultimate stanza. By a process of suggestion the speaker gradually makes clear that he is speaking about the mind, not the mind as it becomes while dreaming, but the mind as it always is, and as it reveals itself in the dream-state. Once this connection is established, the speaker draws back at the spectacle:

> But the traveller, travelling through it;
> May not—dare not openly view it;

and the poem concludes with the repetition of the first six lines of the first stanza. The circle of the journey is completed by the substitution of "I have wandered home but newly" for "I have reached these lands but newly," leaving the reader with the impenetrable images with which the poem had begun.

"Ulalume" is ordered on much the same principle. Though "Ulalume" makes much more extensive use of incremental repetition in the interests of intensification and the kind of emphasis and intricate rhyme that can be observed in "The Raven," like "Dreamland," its theme is organized by the crucial repetition of a descriptive passage emblematic of a state of mind. The poem opens with a similar description of a place into which the speaker is journeying.

> The skies they were ashen and sober;
>   The leaves they were crisped and sere—
>   The leaves they were withering and sere;
> It was night in the lonesome October
>   Of my most immemorial year;
> It was hard by the dim lake of Auber,
>   In the misty mid region of Weir—
> It was down by the dank tarn of Auber,
>   In the ghoul-haunted woodland of Weir.

Again, there is no immediate hint that the description is wholly subjective. Only gradually, after the debate between body and soul, Psyche and Astarte, has begun and the problem of choice has arisen, does the speaker become conscious of his familiarity with the quality of mind which he is describing. First, he recognizes it as love, for he has been to this place before; and then, almost immediately, he recognizes it as love-melancholy, for the place is associated not only with love, but also with the death of the speaker's beloved. The paradox resulting from the fact that the same place, the same mind, must beget both emotions is, of course, a peculiarity of a mind of pronounced idealistic turn: the idealist can love only once; for him the *grand amour* usurps the mind completely. The poem closes on this paradox and, by a final repetition of the opening descriptive passage, turns in on itself, much as its subject, the mind, turns in on itself. Many things are to be regretted in "Ulalume," but certainly its conception is not among them.

Poe's versatility with the refrain was not exhausted, however, with "Ulalume" and "Dreamland," though it probably never took a better direction. In "For Annie" (1849) the lines "Now in my bed," "that you fancy me dead," and "the fever called living" rather anticlimactically qualify the theme of peace in death, since the theme is very baldly stated in the lines

> For a man never slept
> In a different bed;
> And, to *sleep,* you must slumber
> In just such a bed.

In "Annabel Lee" (1849?) the repetition of "Annabel Lee" and the phrase "In the kingdom by the sea" probably comes closer to purely phonetic repetition than to refrain; but the contrast between the booming-receding onomatopoeia of the latter line and the serenity of the name re-enforces the irony of lying down by the side of Annabel Lee, while she lies by the side of the sea. The poem which represents Poe's most ambitious effort with the refrain and at the same time his most colossal failure is "The Bells." "The Bells" (1849) furnishes final proof, if such proof is necessary, that ingenious technique never made poetry. Poe's purpose in the poem was apparently to synthesize the ambivalences of experience by underscoring heavily the multifaceted complexity of a single object. To accomplish this purpose, he mustered the most intricate patterns of rhyme, vowel-motives, and refrains to be found in his poetry.

Beginning with the sleigh bells, he qualifies "bells" all down the line: first wedding bells, then alarum bells, and finally funeral bells. Each repetition of the "Bells, bells, bells" refrain theoretically folds in another area of experience. Out of the welter the "Bells" refrain emerges in the last stanza in duet with the lines

> Keeping time, time, time,
> In a sort of Runic rhyme,

building to a frenzy in answer to the implicit question: "Who is responsible?" Poe's versatility was never more in evidence than here, and never more ineffectual.

But if "The Bells" marks the high tide of Poe's ineffectuality, it also bears testimony to his immense gift for poetic conception and thereby confronts us with the peculiar problem of this poet. Whatever might be said in praise of Poe's gift for poetic conception, there is a discrepancy between it and the means by which he attempted to transmute conception into poetry. Inferior technique might provide part of the answer; but it does not provide all of the answer, as many of the poems thus far reviewed attest. The rest of the answer is probably to be found in Poe's attitude toward technique, a key to which is offered by two poems which use the refrain but which were not well conceived. "Lenore" (1844) and "A Dream Within a Dream" (1849?) contain the rhetoric of certain passages of "The Raven" and "Ulalume," but no sign of a controlling intention. In "Lenore" the refrain "died so young" is introduced in the first stanza, qualified in the second, but dropped thereafter. "A Dream Within a Dream" fails to move out of the title, which is repeated at the end of each of its two stanzas. These poems almost confirm what the others too frequently suggest: that Poe was not above using the refrain for whatever return it might bring.

Poe believed that Beauty existed in eternity, that terrestrial life was graced by only the most fugitive reflections of it.[8] The best the poet could hope to do was catch as many of these reflected lights in his poetry as possible; and, as Yvor Winters has put it, "Poe had certain definite ideas in regard to which forms of human experience

[8] For a more complete statement of this view, see Winters, "A Crisis . . . ," pp. 387-389.

lent themselves best to this proceeding, and also in regard to the rules of procedure."[9]

According to Winters, "The Philosophy of Composition" is an elaborate analysis of the methods by which such reflected lights are caught, an analysis in his words, of the "ingredients of a formula for the production of a kind of emotional delusion."[10] Without going to such extremes—for it is still doubtful whether the bulk of "The Philosophy of Composition" can be regarded with sufficient eriousness to justify such a conclusion—it can be conceded that Winters's view of Poe seems just in its general outlines.

There is, therefore, every reason to believe that Poe viewed the refrain largely as a device, even a kind of trick, by which to produce emotional excitement. In the passage from "The Philosophy of Composition" quoted earlier he made reference to the "artistic piquancy" which he hoped to achieve by it and compared it to *"points,* in the theatrical sense." It was, of course, only one of the group of devices which recur in his poetry with such distressing regularity. That he was frequently successful with the refrain suggests that he probably understood it better than he understood the other devices. At his worst his use of the refrain descends to sheer rhetoric. At his best the refrain is integral in his poetic conception, though frequently submerged in rhetoric of other kinds. But even when Poe's art is most in evidence, the art which conceals art is conspicuous by its absence.

[9] *Ibid.,* p. 388.
[10] *Ibid.,* p. 388.

Poe and His Nemesis—Lewis Gaylord Clark

Sidney P. Moss

IN ONLY ONE INSTANCE has the battle between Edgar Allan Poe and Lewis Gaylord Clark been treated as a distinct episode, and then rather fragmentarily.[1] Yet the battle engaged Poe during almost his entire critical career and constitutes a case that can be isolated from the melée and studied almost clinically. Poe and Clark crossed swords time and again in defamatory and derisive articles. These, when culled and arranged chronologically, serve to document the shifting fortunes of their quarrel. More, they reveal for what reasons and under what circumstances Poe became one of the most maligned persons in literary history. For if Rufus Wilmot Griswold was Poe's posthumous nemesis, Lewis Gaylord Clark was Poe's contemporary one.

Not that a few of the charges levelled against Poe were wholly unfounded. Poe in his letters, both private and public, stands self-confessed as an unstable person and an occasional drunkard. But Clark and his friends did not proclaim Poe's faults, nor exaggerate them, nor hint at unspeakable acts of wickedness, until Poe singled them out for special attacks.

Clark, as will be seen, enjoyed a singular advantage over Poe: he had his own magazine, the *Knickerbocker*, which was widely circulated, whereas Poe had to take his stand wherever he could. And if Clark was not altogether a combatant worthy of Poe's mettle, he had more than enough allies to make up the difference.

The reasons for Clark's consistent hostility toward Poe are not obscure, as some writers believe; they are simply numerous.

First, Clark was the "specially appointed guardian of New York reputations,"[2] and Poe's assault against the literary clique that Clark

---

[1] Herman E. Spivey, "Poe and Lewis Gaylord Clark," *PMLA*, LIV, 1124-1132 (Dec., 1939).

[2] Frank Luther Mott, *A History of American Magazines, 1741-1850* (New York, 1930), I, 407. Mott elsewhere notes the conspicuous exception that Clark made of Cornelius Mathews, whom he consistently ridiculed and attacked.

represented was enough to antagonize him.³

Second, being at the head of the New York group, Clark tended to be a sectionalist and favor only New York writers.⁴ Only on this score, since the question of rivalry seems too remote, can Poe's remark be explained, that the *Knickerbocker* "refused to exchange with us [the *Southern Literary Messenger*] from the first."⁵

Third, Clark's twin brother, Willis Gaylord—a co-editor of the *Knickerbocker*—had attacked Poe on more than one occasion.⁶ Though Poe maintained a uniform respect for Willis Clark, it was only natural that Lewis Clark should bombard the same target.

A fourth reason for the mutual antagonism between Poe and Lewis Clark may have been partly "the latter's role in the 'Moon Hoax.' "⁷ While Poe in June, 1835, was hoaxing the country with his "Hans Phaall—a Tale," a similar hoax was perpetrated only a few weeks later in New York. As a contemporary narrator told it:

Mr. Moses Y. Beach had recently become sole proprietor of the *Sun*, and Richard Adams Locke was the editor. It was desirable to have some new and startling features to increase its popularity, and Locke for a consideration proposed to prepare for it a work of fiction. To this proposal Mr. Beach agreed. Locke consulted Lewis Gaylord Clark, the editor of the *Knickerbocker Magazine*, as to the subject. The Edinburgh *Scientific Journal* was then busied with Herschel's astronomical explorations at the Cape of Good Hope, and Clark proposed to make these the basis of the story. It was done. Clark was the real inventor of the incidents, the

---

³ See Sidney P. Moss, "Poe and the *Norman Leslie* Incident," *American Literature*, XXV, 294-306 (Nov., 1953). Poe alleged (*Southern Literary Messenger*, II, 460, June, 1836) that the *Knickerbocker*, among others, had engaged "in covert, and therefore unmanly, thrusts at the *'Messenger.'* "

⁴ Clark's treatment of William Gilmore Simms, for example, became so notorious that a writer signing himself "S. T." blasted the *Knickerbocker* in an article that appeared in the New York *Evening Mirror*, Nov. 7, 1845. This article was copied in part or in whole by the New York *Morning News*, Nov. 8, 1845, the New York *Weekly Mirror*, Nov. 15, 1845, and by *Godey's Lady's Book*, XXXII, 240 (May, 1846). The writer has been identified as Evert A. Duyckinck (see Mary C. Simms Oliphant *et al.*, eds., *The Letters of William Gilmore Simms*, Columbia, S. C., 1953, II, 114 n.). Simms's own letters are full of such statements as: "Clark is a creature to be kicked or spit upon not argued with or spoken to," and, "Had I been living in N. Y. I could not have refrained, long ago, to have scourged him hip & thigh for the scoundrel & puppy that he is" (*ibid.*, pp. 115 and 117).

⁵ *Messenger, loc. cit.*

⁶ Two of Willis Clark's attacks can be found in the paper he edited, the Philadelphia *Gazette and Commercial Intelligencer*, 2 (April 8, 1836) and 2 (May 10, 1836).

⁷ T. O. Mabbott's suggestion, quoted by Leslie W. Dunlap, ed., *The Letters of Willis Gaylord Clark and Lewis Gaylord Clark* (New York, 1940), p. 16 n.

imaginative part, while to Locke was intrusted the ingenious task of unfolding the discoveries.[8]

Poe was convinced that the idea was stolen from himself and periodically referred to the matter over eleven years, asserting that he left "Hans Phaall" unfinished for that reason.[9]

Whatever the background of the animosity between Poe and Clark, it was Poe's repeated bombardment of the New York coterie that caused Clark finally to cease sniping at Poe under cover of the *Knickerbocker* and to open fire at him with everything in his arsenal. Poe seemed to consider Clark contemptible and noticed him only sporadically. Nevertheless, Clark grew more and more violent, and it is not too much to say that the reverberations of his charges are still sounding today.

I

Sniping began in August, 1838. The May, 1837, issue of the *Knickerbocker* had carried Harpers' announcement of the publication of *The Narrative of Arthur Gordon Pym*,[10] and Lewis Clark's review of the book duly appeared three months later.[11] Clark began by reprinting the long title, making certain to italicize the word *incredible* in the phrase, "together with the incredible adventures and discoveries . . . to which that distressing calamity gave rise":

> There are a great many tough stories [*sic*] in this book, told in a loose and slip-shod style, seldom chequered by any of the more common graces of composition, beyond a Robinson Crusoe-ish sort of simplicity of narration. . . . We would not be so uncourteous as to insinuate a doubt of Mr. Pym's veracity, now that he *lies* under the sod; but we should very much question that gentleman's word, who should affirm . . . that he *believed* the various adventures and hair-breadth 'scapes therein recorded. . . .[12]

---

[8] Benson J. Lossing (1813-1891), *History of New York City* (New York, 1884), pp. 360-362.

[9] See, for example, Poe's letter to John P. Kennedy, Sept. 11, 1835 (John Ward Ostrom, ed., *The Letters of Edgar Allan Poe,* Cambridge, Mass., I, 74), and Poe's *Literati* article on Locke (*Godey's Lady's Book,* XXXIII, 159-162, Oct., 1846).

[10] *Knickerbocker,* IX, 529.

[11] *Ibid.,* XII, 167 (Aug., 1838).

[12] That Clark, in dealing with an imaginative story, should call attention to "Mr. Pym's veracity" is ironic. The same irony impelled Clark to question the veracity of Melville's *Typee* (*Knickerbocker,* XXVII, 450, May, 1846)—a novel that by and large was true.

Despite Clark's boast to Longfellow that Harpers "tell me, that they can lose on *no* book, now—even the *worst*,"[13] such reviews[14] as this made the book under Harpers' imprint sell "less than a thousand copies." In England, however, where no clique militated against it, "it was highly successful, running through several editions within a short time."[15]

In December, 1839, the *Knickerbocker* carried this announcement: "Notices of the following works, although in type, are unavoidably postponed till our next number: . . . Tales [of the Grotesque and Arabesque] by E. A. Poe. . . ."[16] But the promised review, "although in type," never appeared. Clark, however, in reviewing a number of *Burton's Gentleman's Magazine,* made the point that the "Journal of Julius Rodman," then appearing there, was another fabrication like *Pym*.[17]

In June, 1840, Poe began sending broadcast his "Prospectus of the Penn Magazine . . . to be Edited and Published . . . by Edgar A. Poe." In it he announced a rigorous editorial policy, since, as he said, he had "not yet been taught to read through the medium of a publisher's interest, nor convinced of the impolicy of speaking the truth."

To the mechanical execution of the work [he added] the greatest attention will be given. . . . In this respect, it is proposed to surpass, by very much, the ordinary Magazine style. The form will nearly resemble that of The Knickerbocker. The paper will be equal to that of The North American Review.[18]

---

[13] In a letter dated Nov. 2, 1834 (Dunlap, *The Letters,* p. 83). William Gowans—a man who became a distinguished bookseller—bears out Clark's statement. He wrote that *Pym* "was the most unsuccessful of all his writings, although published by the influential house of Harper & Brothers, who have the means of distributing a single edition of any book in one week" (quoted by Arthur Hobson Quinn, *Edgar Allan Poe: A Critical Biography,* New York, 1941, p. 267).

[14] See the New York *Mirror,* XVI, 55 (Aug. 11, 1838), for a curiously similar review.

[15] William F. Gill, *The Life of Edgar Allan Poe* (New York, 1877), p. 86. Quinn (*Poe,* p. 263) states that the book "ran through more than one edition" in England. Contrast these statements with Griswold's (Preface to *The Literati,* New York, 1850, p. xv): "The publishers sent one hundred copies to England, and being mistaken at first for a narrative of real experiences, it was advertised to be reprinted, but a discovery of its character . . . prevented such a result." Was it to curtail its circulation that Clark dwelt on the *incredible* nature of the tale and punned on the word *lies?* Clark must have felt that such a review was damaging, for he used the same tack in reviewing "The Journal of Julius Rodman," which began appearing serially with the Jan., 1840, issue of *Burton's Gentleman's Magazine.*

[16] *Knickerbocker,* XIV, 564 (Dec., 1839). [17] *Ibid.,* XV, 359 (April, 1840).

[18] For the entire prospectus, see Charles F. Heartman and James R. Canny, *A Bibliogra-*

Clearly, Poe intended to compete with the two magazines he most disliked, magazines which represented the two most powerful literary cliques then operating in America, the Boston and New York Groups, and which had barred their doors to him.[19] Another reason that Poe had for singling out the *Knickerbocker* and the *North American Review* may be explained by his remarks in a subsequent prospectus, in which, reiterating what he had said earlier, he added:

It shall be a leading object to assert precept, and to maintain in practice the rights, while in effect it demonstrates the advantages, of an absolutely independent criticism—a criticism self-sustained; guiding itself only by the purest rules of Art; analyzing and urging those rules as it applies them; holding itself aloof from all personal bias; acknowledging no fear save that of outraging the right; yielding no point either to the vanity of the author, or to the assumptions of antique prejudice, or of the involute and anonymous cant of the Quarterlies, or to the arrogance of those organized *cliques* which, hanging like nightmares upon American literature, manufacture at the nod of our principal booksellers, a pseudo-public opinion by wholesale.[20]

Clark soon used his chance to notice Poe's prospectus as well as the discontinuation of Burton's publication.

The 'Gentleman's Magazine,' . . . is offered for sale; 'the proprietor being about to engage in a more profitable business.' Mr. E. A. Poe, a spirited writer, and hitherto the principal editor of the miscellany in question, announces his retirement from its supervision. He has issued proposals for a new monthly magazine, 'to be executed in the neatest style, after the manner of the Knickerbocker,' to which he promises to bring great additions to the literary aid he has hitherto diverted into a different channel [*sic*].[21]

The distortions of this brief paragraph are many: first, the initial

---

phy of First Printings of the Writings of Edgar Allan Poe (Hattiesburg, Miss., 1943), pp. 54-55.

[19] In *Doings of Gotham* (ed. Jacob E. Spannuth and T. O. Mabbott, Pottsville, Pa., 1929, p. 44), Prof. Mabbott remarks that Poe's "relations with the *Knickerbocker Magazine* and Clarke its editor were uniformly unfriendly, as with the *North American Review*—he never contributed to either of them, although at one time or another he succeeded in selling something to almost every other really important magazine of the time, and many unimportant ones."

[20] Heartman and Canny, *A Bibliography*, pp. 58-59.

[21] *Knickerbocker*, XVI, 88 (July, 1840).

quotation marks are intended to be sneers of disbelief;[22] second, the assertion that Poe was "the principal editor" implies that he was responsible for the failure of the "miscellany in question";[23] and third, the misquotation of Poe's prospectus statement makes it appear that Poe intended to imitate, not to rival, the *Knickerbocker*.

The hostility that Clark felt toward Poe was not eased by the fact that Poe, editing *Graham's Magazine* (April, 1841-May, 1842), made that periodical the chief competitor of the *Kncikerbocker*.[24] Nor did it pacify Clark's feelings when Poe went on the literary warpath, hacking at the scalps of such men as Thomas Ward, popularly known as Flaccus, who was a regular contributor to the *Knickerbocker*.[25] The article was Poe's characteristic attack on the New York coterie, and to this one he signed his name, a most unusual proceeding in a period of anonymous reviewing. Poe wrote: ". . . the sum of his [Thomas Ward's] deserts has been footed up by a *clique* who are in the habit of reckoning units as tens. . . . With deference to the more matured opinions of the 'Knickerbocker,' we may be permitted to entertain a doubt whether he is either Jupiter Tonans, or Phoebus Apollo." Poe ended the review by announcing that he was throwing Ward's book to the pigs.[26]

Almost at the same time that this tomahawking occurred, Poe for the first time reached for Lewis Clark's head:[27]

The glory of the Knickerbocker is for ever departed. . . . the principal cause of its melancholy decline, may be traced to the peculiar and unappreciated talent of its editor, Lewis G. Clark. . . . The present condition

---

[22] "S. T." (probably Evert A. Duyckinck) in the New York *Weekly Mirror* (III, 96, Nov. 15, 1845) spoke of Clark's use of "inverted commas" as "one of those small typographical tricks in which the Magazine delights."

[23] "With Volume VI, beginning in January, 1840"—almost a half year before this review appeared—"Burton began to feature his own name on the front wrappers with larger display type" (Quinn, *Poe*, p. 293).

[24] Mott (*American Journalism: A History of Newspapers in the United States through 260 Years, 1690-1950*, New York, 1951, p. 319) notes that the *Knickerbocker's* "chief rival after 1841 was the Philadelphia *Graham's Magazine*."

[25] The announcement of Flaccus "as a permanent contributor of this Magazine" appears in the *Knickerbocker*, XV, 88 (Jan., 1840).

[26] *Graham's*, XXII, 195-198 (March, 1843).

[27] This article appeared anonymously, and Poe scholars have long debated whether it belongs in the Poe canon. Spivey ("Poe and Lewis Gaylord Clark") discusses the matter and cites evidence in an attempt to prove that it was written by Poe. In light of the information I have assembled, I have no doubt that the article was written by Poe. For our purposes, however, the fact that Clark attributed it to Poe is sufficient to make it figure as a shot in the continuing battle between them.

of this periodical is that of a poorly-cooked-up concern.... The sooner it dies, the better will it be for the proprietors....[28]

Three years after this article appeared, Lewis Clark claimed that Poe had first submitted it to the *Knickerbocker*.[29] This claim is very hard to believe, considering what their relations were at this time. What makes the claim even harder to believe is that Clark did not mention the rejection at once, when he could have capitalized on it, but waited three years to publish the assertion—and then only when he was frontally assailed by Poe in the *Literati* papers. The article, however, had been submitted to Epes Sargent of *Sargent's New Monthly Magazine*, who rejected it.

Clark, more concerned for himself than for his friend and contributor, Thomas "Flaccus" Ward, responded to the *New World* article in the next issue of the *Knickerbocker*:

Our friend and old correspondent, Sargent ... has thought it advisable to notice an attack in the 'New World,' by some 'rejected contributor,' upon his publication. This was unwise.... All that such a small-beer 'complainant' desires, is the notoriety of *any* notice whatsoever. If left to his native insignificance, he mourns with Meddle in the play, that he can 'get nobody to kick him.' ... Disturb not, friend Sargent, the leaden repose of a 'critic' which is even more harmless than it is malignant.[30]

It was not until July that Clark took Poe to task for his review of Flaccus, and then indirectly through a correspondent, who argued that Flaccus had at times exposed himself to Poe's charges, but that Poe could not have written Flaccus's "Epistle from my Arm-chair" or his "Address to the President of the New-England Temperance Society" (in good hexameters), except "in about a century of leap-years."[31]

Contrary to his own advice, Clark did not leave the critic to his native insignificance. Poe, an inveterate anti-Transcendentalist, had been publishing disparaging remarks about Carlyle, but only at this time did Clark attack Poe on this score. Using another person as a shield again, this time the editor of the *Louisville Daily Journal*, he wrote: "Mr. [George Dennison] Prentice ... is 'down upon'

---

[28] "Our Magazine Literature," *New World*, VI, 302-303 (March 11, 1843). Poe, in this article, curiously enough, linked Griswold's name with Clark's, claiming that Griswold was also unfit to edit *Graham's*.

[29] *Knickerbocker*, XXVIII, 368 n. (Oct., 1846).

[30] *Ibid.*, XXI, 380 (April, 1843).   [31] *Ibid.*, XXII, 89 (July, 1843).

'a gentleman of some smartness who rejoices in the euphonious name of Poe,' (a correspondent of ours spells it 'Poh!') for terming Carlyle . . . 'an ass.'" Prentice, whom he then quoted, said that what Poe lacked in Carlyleism he made up in jackassism, and that he had given repeated evidence to the public of his ability to be a judge of asses.[32]

The quarrel lapsed for a while. In the meantime, Poe's criticisms had won such favor among discerning people that Lowell observed in *Graham's Magazine* that Poe was "at once the most discriminating, philosophical, and fearless critic upon imaginative works who has written in America," and that "His analytic power would furnish forth bravely some score of ordinary critics."[33] In addition, Poe had sold "The Raven" to the *American Review,* where it appeared under the pseudonym of "Quarles."[34] It made an impression, as one writer said, "probably not surpassed by that of any single piece of American poetry."[35]

Apparently—and only apparently—veering with the critical wind, Clark published a favorable report of Poe in the *Knickerbocker,* a report conspicuous for its uniqueness:

The second number of *The American Review and Whig Journal,* . . . has made its appearance. The very best thing in its pages is an unique, singularly imaginative, and most musical effusion, entitled, *The Raven.* We have never before, to our knowledge, met the author, Mr. Edgar A. Poe, as a poet; but if the poem to which we allude be a specimen of his powers in this kind, we shall always be glad to welcome him in his new department.[36]

---

[32] *Ibid.*, XXII, 392 (Oct., 1843). Poe remembered both Prentice and Clark for their abuse. In revising his sketch, "The Literary Life of Thingum Bob, Esq." (which first appeared in the *Southern Literary Messenger,* X, 719-727, Dec., 1844) for the *Broadway Journal* (July 26, 1845), Poe wrote: "I bought auction copies (cheap) of . . . 'Prentice's Billingsgate,' (folio edition) and 'Lewis G. Clarke on Tongue.'" See James A. Harrison, ed., *The Complete Works of Edgar Allan Poe* (New York, 1902), VI, 21.

[33] *Graham's Magazine,* XXVII, 49-53 (Feb., 1845). Lowell qualified the first statement somewhat by saying that "he *might be,* rather than that always *is,* for he seems sometimes to mistake his phial of prussic-acid for his inkstand."

[34] I, 143-145 (Feb., 1845).   [35] Quinn, *Poe,* p. 439.

[36] *Knickerbocker,* XXV, 282 (March, 1845). George H. Colton, then editor of the *American Review,* was Clark's brother-in-law, and Clark may only have been doing him a good turn by favorably noting the appearance of "The Raven" in its pages. In Clark's notice of the *New World* article, he had spoken of the "ambitious 'authorling'" of a "small volume of effete and lamentable trash, full of little, ragged ideas, stolen and disguised from original inanities, which had fallen dead-born from the press, before the first fifty copies printed . . . [were] exhausted in a 'third edition!'" Clark may have had reference here to an earlier volume of Poe's poetry.

But by the time the next issue of the *Knickerbocker* appeared, Clark had revised his opinion of "The Raven" and printed a few stanzas that parodied the poem.[37]

Unable to resist the temptation of attacking Poe, Clark took issue with an unsigned review by Poe that appeared in the *Broadway Journal* for June 7, 1845, entitled, "Mr. Peter Snook":[38]

Some sage correspondent of the 'Broadway Journal' has temporarily resuscitated from oblivion an article from an old English magazine, entitled *Mr. Peter Snook*, which it lauds without stint, but the very 'plums' of which we defy any person of taste to swallow with pleasure. . . . 'Chacun à son gôut,' however; and had it not been for an indiscriminate fling at American periodicals,[39] we should not have quarrelled with the commentaries of the nil-admirari critic in question; he is simply one of a numerous class, who are 'nothing if not critical,' and even less than nothing at that.

Clark then called Poe a "literary Aristarchus," and contrasted his proclivity for foreign works with that of the *Knickerbocker* for native productions, implying that Poe was anti-American.[40]

Poe, in his ironic way, responded to the veiled attack. In the *Broadway Journal* of July 12, 1845, he called the forty-two line attack a three-line compliment, which he "sincerely" hoped it was not. He quarreled with Clark's spelling of the French proverb and with his misuse of the phrase *nil admirari*, and ended: "we have found the *Knickerbocker* sinking day by day in the public opinion in despite of the brilliant abilities and thoroughly liberal education of Mr. Lewis Gaylord Clarke."[41]

These exchanges almost led to a street fight between Poe and Clark. Thomas Holley Chivers, a rather unreliable eyewitness, who after Poe's death claimed that "The Raven" and "Ulalume" were

[37] *Ibid.*, XXV, 368 (April, 1845).

[38] A longer version of this article had originally appeared in the *Southern Literary Messenger*, II, 727-730 (Oct., 1836). Clark was aware that Poe had written the article, for Poe was announced as being "associated with the editorial department of our Journal" in the Feb. 22, 1845, and in the March 8, 1845, issues of the *Broadway Journal;* and in five weekly numbers of that periodical, from March 8 to April 5, Poe had replied to "Outis" in the so-called Longfellow war.

[39] Pretty indisputable evidence that Clark attributed the *New World* article to Poe, and that he clearly recognized the authorship of "Mr. Peter Snook."

[40] *Knickerbocker*, XXVI, 76 (July, 1845). Curiously enough, Clark in his article contrasted Griswold's pro-American literary attitudes with Poe's, whom he alluded to as an "anonymous decrier of our own periodicals."

[41] *Broadway Journal*, II, 11.

stolen from two of his poems,[42] has described the episode.[43] Chivers met Poe in New York soon after the July number of the *Knickerbocker* had appeared, in which Clark had condemned the writer of the "Mr. Peter Snook" article. Poe, it seems, was drunk, but Chivers joined him nevertheless, and as they strolled the streets, they encountered Lewis Clark. "The moment Poe saw him—maddened by the remembrance of something that he had said in a recent Number of the Magazine touching one of his own articles which had appeared in the *Broadway Journal*—he swore, while attempting to rush away from my hold, that he would attack him." Clark, however, bowed himself out of the situation as well as he could, and left Poe exclaiming "in an indignant chuckle—'A d—d coward! by God!'"

If Clark had a distaste for physical combat, he had none for editorial combat. He started the new year with an extensive review of *The Raven and Other Poems,* which had been published in November, 1845. But it was not a review of Poe's poetry so much as a sustained sneer at the man himself. Near the end of the review, Clark declared how magnanimously he had dealt with Poe:

If we were disposed to retort upon Mr. Poe for the exceedingly gross and false statements which, upon an imaginary slight [!], he made in his paper respecting this Magazine, we could ask for no greater favor than to be allowed to criticize his volume of poems. Surely no author is so much indebted to the forebearance of critics as Mr. Poe, and no person connected with the press in this country is entitled to less mercy and consideration. His criticisms, so called, are generally a tissue of coarse personal abuse or personal adulation. . . . But criticism is his weakness. . . . In ladies' magazines, he is an Aristarchus,[44] but among men of letters his sword is a broken lath.[45]

Immediately following this "review" of Poe's volume appeared Clark's notice of Longfellow's *Poems.* A eulogy of Longfellow,

[42] For the merits of Chivers's claim, see Joel Benton, *In the Poe Circle* (New York, 1899), and Samuel F. Damon, *Thomas Holley Chivers, Friend of Poe* (New York, 1930).
[43] In *Chivers' Life of Poe,* ed. Richard Beale Davis (New York, 1952), pp. 57-59.
[44] Probably a reference to the fact that Louis A. Godey of *Godey's Lady's Book* had accepted Poe's *Literati* papers on New York writers, which appeared in the summer and fall of this year. Even before publication, they provoked a storm of protest, and Godey, as he noted in his magazine (XXXII, 288, June, 1846), received "letters from New York, anonymous and from personal friends, requesting us to be careful what we allow Mr. Poe to say of the New York authors," and that "Many attempts have been made . . . to forestall public opinion."
[45] *Knickerbocker,* XXVII, 69-72 (Jan., 1846).

it was at the same time a veiled attack on Poe, who had recently accused Longfellow of plagiarism. The review concluded with this statement: "The pretentious and the self-conceited, the 'neglected' and the soured, among our self-elected poets, may be pardoned for decrying that excellence [of Longfellow's poetry] they cannot reach."[46]

Through Lowell, Poe had obtained a lecture appointment to read a poem before the Boston Lyceum on October 16, 1845. Whether he could not write a poem to order for the occasion, as seems likely, or whether he wanted to hoax the Bostonians, as he claimed, is a question that need not detain us, except to note that the episode created a furor and was discussed editorially in many newspapers and periodicals. Clark, alert to material that might be quoted to the disparagement of Poe, picked up an article from the Boston *Morning Post,* which concluded that the " 'poet' ought to have been expelled" from the hall.[47]

In the meantime, Poe's "The Literati of New York City," ominously subtitled, "Some Honest Opinions at Random Respecting Their Autorial Merits, with Occasional Words of Personality," was awaiting publication in *Godey's Lady's Book*. And in May, the first series made its appearance and caused such a sensation that Godey could not satisfy the demand. He had to put out extra editions of the magazine and finally reprint that series along with the second series in the June number.

Only two of the eight articles in the first series could have offended Clark, the introduction and the essay on Charles F. Briggs. In the first of these, Poe—true to his principles—stated: "[There] exists a very remarkable discrepancy between the apparent public opinion of any given author's merits and the opinion which is expressed of him orally by those who are best qualified to judge." The reason for this, he argued, was that public opinion was manufactured by the editors of periodicals who were friends of the contributors, but that the real opinion of these same editors bore only an inverse relation to the opinion they created and circulated. Only privately, however, did they reveal their true sentiments, and then in such a way as to make them "seem bent upon avenging the wrongs self-inflicted upon their own consciences."

[46] *Ibid.,* pp. 72-73.
[47] *Ibid.,* p. 184 (Feb., 1846).

Poe then used Longfellow and Hawthorne as examples. Hawthorne, he asserted, "is scarcely recognized by the press or by the public, and when noticed at all, is noticed merely to be damned by faint praise." The reasons for such treatment, Poe claimed, were first that "Mr. Hawthorne *is* a poor man, and, second . . . he *is not* an ubiquitous quack." Longfellow, on the other hand, "as a man of property and a professor at Harvard, [has] a whole legion of active quacks at his control—of *him* what is the apparent public opinion? Of course, that he is a poetical phenomenon. . . ."[48]

Poe's reference to Longfellow's having "a whole legion of active quacks at his control" must have stung Clark. Longfellow had contributed to the *Knickerbocker* for years; Clark appears to have acted as an intermediary between Longfellow and Harpers during the publication of *Outre-Mer;* and once Clark had connived to get Longfellow a prize. This happened in November, 1834, when the *New-Yorker* announced a story contest for a prize of one hundred dollars. Lewis Clark was appointed as one of the three judges. Clark wrote to Longfellow at once, asking that he submit a story he had seen, "The Wondrous Tale of a Little Man in Gosling Green." Longfellow complied, sending the story under the pseudonym of George F. Brown. The story was not awarded the full prize because, apparently, the other two judges disagreed with Clark's decision and preferred the story submitted by Eliza Leslie. The issue was resolved by dividing the hundred dollars—no trivial sum considering that Longfellow, with extra duties, was earning only nine hundred dollars that year at Bowdoin College—between Eliza Leslie and Longfellow.[49]

The second article that may have offended Clark was called "Charles F. Briggs." Poe began by stating: *"Mr. Briggs* is better known as Harry Franco, *a nom de plume* assumed since the publica-

---

[48] *Godey's Lady's Book,* XXXII, 194-195 (May, 1846). Poe's remark concerning Hawthorne's obscurity is at variance with the statement he made four years earlier. In reviewing Hawthorne's *Twice-Told Tales* (*Graham's Magazine,* XX, 298-300, May, 1842) he said that he had mistakenly believed that Hawthorne "had been thrust into his present position by one of the impudent *cliques* which beset our literature."

[49] For the details of this affair, see James Taft Hatfield, "An Unknown Prose Tale by Longfellow," *American Literature,* III, 136-148 (May, 1931); Clark's letters to Longfellow dated Aug. 24, Nov. 1, and Dec. 10, 1834 (in Dunlap, *The Letters,* pp. 79, 81-85); and Lawrance Thompson, *Young Longfellow, 1807-1843* (New York, 1938), pp. 198-201. It should be noted that none of these investigators interprets the event as I have. It is pure speculation on my part, but Clark's real antagonism toward Poe may have been due to Poe's knowledge of Clark's role in this story contest.

tion, in the 'Knickerbocker Magazine,' of his series of papers called 'Adventures of Harry Franco.'[50] He also wrote for 'The Knickerbocker' some articles entitled 'The Haunted Merchant,' and from time to time subsequently has been a contributor to that journal." Poe then evaluated Briggs's writings and concluded that he "has never composed in his life three consecutive sentences of grammatical English," and that "he is grossly uneducated."[51]

But what offended Clark most—or terrified him—was the news that he was to be included in the *Literati* papers. He had heard this from Louis Godey himself. As Godey reported the incident:

When during a recent visit to New York, the subscriber [Godey] informed Mr. Lewis Gaylord Clark that Mr. Poe had him 'booked' in his 'Opinions of the New York Literati,' he supposed that he was giving Mr. Lewis Gaylord Clark a very agreeable piece of information.... But it seems that, on the contrary, the information that Mr. Lewis Gaylord Clark received has put him in a perfect agony of terror.[52]

Thus apprised, Clark had his reply ready in the May issue of the *Knickerbocker*. He said that a literary snob was continually obtruding himself upon public notice, today in the gutter, tomorrow in some milliner's magazine;[53] that "Mrs. Louisa Godey" had taken this snob into "her" service; and that the snob was proving himself one of the lowest of his class infesting the literary world. Clark then quoted the *Evening Gazette and Times,* which said that Poe was "in a state of health which renders him not completely *accountable* for all his peculiarities." Clark ended by saying, "Poh! Poe! Leave the 'idiosyncratic' man 'alone in his glory.'"[54]

---

[50] This was a mistake on Poe's part; the *Adventures* never appeared in the *Knickerbocker*.

[51] *Godey's Lady's Book,* XXXII, 199-200 (May, 1846). Briggs and Poe earlier had had a falling-out when they were co-editors of the *Broadway Journal*.

[52] New York *Evening Mirror,* May 8, 1846. I am indebted to the New York Historical Society for a photostat of this article.

[53] " 'The milliner's book' was Griswold's satirical appellation for the popular monthly [*Godey's Lady's Book*]" (Joy Bayless, *Rufus Wilmot Griswold: Poe's Literary Executor,* Nashville, 1943, p. 54). Griswold had used the phrase in a letter to William Cullen Bryant dated Dec. 17, 1843 (see *ibid.,* p. 268 n.). Echoes of Griswold are often heard in Clark's writings. They are significant only in that they show a close connection between the two which, to my knowledge, has never been disclosed.

[54] *Knickerbocker,* XXVII, 461 (May, 1846). Clark's penchant for this kind of attack was noticed by "S. T." and others (*op. cit.,* p. 96): "During eight years the Knickerbocker Magazine has published various attacks upon Mr. Mathews and his writings, with a malignity and pertinacity which once induced the *Tribune* to call loudly for the private reasons which instigated such a course.... according to a cheap and favorite argument with this

The series, notwithstanding such reactions, continued. Finally, in September of that year, Poe's head-on attack on Clark appeared, even as Godey had promised. Poe spoke of the "editorial scraps" to be found at the end of each *Knickerbocker* number—an allusion to Clark's own "Editor's Table," a popular feature of the magazine— as "the joint composition of a great variety of gentlemen."

Were a little more pains taken in elevating the *tone* of this "Editors' Table," [note the deliberate transposition of the apostrophe] (which its best friends are forced to admit is at present a little Boweryish [the recent attack on Poe, for instance]) I should have no hesitation in commending it . . . as a specimen of . . . easy writing and hard reading.

When Poe turned to a discussion of the magazine itself, he wrote:

Still some incomprehensible *incubus* has seemed always to sit heavily upon it, and it has never succeeded in attaining *position* among intelligent or educated readers. On account of the manner in which it is necessarily edited, the work is deficient in that absolutely indispensable element, *individuality*. As the editor has no precise character, the magazine, as a matter of course, can have none. When I say "no precise character," I mean that Mr. C., as a literary man, has about him no determinateness, no distinctiveness, no saliency of point;—an apple, in fact, or a pumpkin, has more angles. He is as smooth as oil or a sermon from Doctor Hawks; he is noticeable for nothing in the world except for the markedness by which he is noticeable for nothing.[55]

Clark published his retort in the October number of the *Knickerbocker*.

Our thanks are due to 'J. G. H.,' of Springfield, (Mass.,)[56] for his communication touching the course and the capabilities of the wretched inebriate whose personalities disgrace a certain Milliner's Magazine in Philadelphia; but bless your heart, man! you can't expect us to publish it. The jaded hack who runs a broken pace for common hire, upon whom

---

Journal, it has been suggested that he is out of his mind. So John Neal was called in the Knickerbocker 'crazy Neal.' It is time this should cease, or that the Knickerbocker should be put into Coventry by the respectable press." He added that the *Knickerbocker* selected high game and mentioned Poe as an example.

[55] *Godey's Lady's Book*, XXXIII, 132 (Sept., 1846).
[56] It has been suggested that "J. G. H." of Springfield, Mass., may have been Josiah Gilbert Holland (1819-1881). It is interesting to note, however, that a "H. G. J." (a reversal of these initials), also of Springfield, Mass., was respectfully informed in *Godey's Lady's Book* (XXXIII, 240, Nov., 1846) "that we cannot republish any article in our 'Book,' especially the one he refers to—biographical notice of L. Gaylord Clark. He is referred to the September number of our magazine, which he can either buy or borrow."

you have wasted powder, might revel in his congenial abuse of this Magazine and its Editor from now till next October without disturbing our complacency for a single moment. He is too mean for hate, and hardly worthy scorn. In fact there are but two classes of persons who regard him in *any* light—those who despise and those who pity him; the first for his utter lack of principle, the latter for the infirmities which have overcome and ruined him.

Clark then quoted a long passage from "one of our most respectable daily journals," which stated that a poor creature in a condition of sad imbecility called at the office; that he indulged in profane ribaldry; that an aged female relative dogged his footsteps to prevent him from drinking, but that he was nevertheless inebriated; and that one could not entertain a feeling of contempt for a man who was evidently committing a suicide upon his body, as he had already done upon his character.[57] To all this, he added a controversial footnote:

He is equally unknown to those whom he abuses. The Editor hereof has no remembrance of ever having seen him save on two occasions. In the one case, we met him in the street with a gentleman, who apologized the next day, in a note now before us for having been seen in his company while he was laboring under such an *'excitement'*; in the other, we caught a view of his retiring skirts as he wended his 'winding way,' like a furtive puppy with a considerable kettle to his tail, from the publication-office, whence—having left no other record of his tempestuous visit upon the publisher's mind than the recollection of a coagulum of maudlin and abusive jargon—he had just emerged, bearing with him one of his little narrow rolls of manuscript, which had been previously submitted for insertion in our 'excellent Magazine,' but which, unhappily for his peace, had shared the fate of its equally attractive predecessors.[58]

For reasons given earlier, the first of Clark's statements—that he rejected a manuscript of Poe—is extremely doubtful. And if the second statement implies, as it certainly seems to do, that Clark repeatedly rejected a number of Poe's articles,[59] then the statement

---

[57] I have not been able to locate this article to determine whether Poe actually "sat" for such a portrait. In the extract quoted by Clark, no mention of Poe appears, only an allusion to an aged female relative, who may or may not have been Maria Clemm, Poe's mother-in-law.

[58] *Knickerbocker*, XXVIII, 368-369 (Oct., 1846).

[59] When Clark wrote about a rejected manuscript which "had shared the fate of its equally attractive predecessors," he clearly wanted to assign a disreputable motive to Poe's attacks on him in the *New World* and in the *Literati* papers.

is patently false, which casts even greater doubt on the veracity of the first statement. Moreover, Clark claimed to have met Poe on only two occasions—both, as he described them, decidedly unfavorable to Poe. He may have been forgetful or merely malicious in failing to mention a time when he and Poe, among others, proposed toasts at the famous Booksellers' Dinner held in New York City on March 30, 1837.[60]

But Poe had not discharged all his cannon. *Godey's Lady's Book* carried in its next issue Poe's paper on Charles Fenno Hoffman. In it he wrote:

Mr. Hoffman was the original editor of "The Knickerbocker Magazine," and gave it while under his control a tone and character, the weight of which may be best estimated by the consideration that the work thence received an impetus which has sufficed to bear it on alive, although tottering, month after month, through even that dense region of unmitigated and unmitigable fog—that dreary realm of outer darkness, of utter and inconceivable dunderheadism, over which has so long ruled King Log the Second, in the august person of one Lewis Gaylord Clark.[61]

Clark retaliated the following month by discharging a doublebarreled attack on Poe. One was in the form of doggerel, no doubt written by Clark himself, since he had often referred to Poe as "Aristarchus" and "Poh" in many of his diatribes:

Epitaph on a Modern 'Critic.'
'P'oh' Pudor!'
Here Aristarchus lies!' (a pregnant phrase,
And greatly hackneyed, in his early days,
By those who saw him in his maudlin scenes,
And those who read him in the magazines.)
Here Aristarchus lies, (nay, never smile,)
Cold as his muse, and stiffer than his style;
But whether Bacchus or Minerva claims
The crusty critic, all conjecture shames;
Nor shall the world know which the mortal sin,
Excessive genius or excessive gin![62]

---

[60] See the New York *Commercial Advertiser*, XL, 1 (April 3, 1837), which shows that Clark's toast preceded Poe's by only an interval of eight short toasts. The toasts Clark and Poe proposed are revealing. Clark proposed: "Protection to Home Manufactures, whether of the hands or of the intellect." Poe proposed, with what appears to be his usual taste for hoaxing, "The *Monthlies* of Gotham—Their distinguished Editors, and their vigorous *Collaborateurs*."

[61] *Godey's Lady's Book*, XXXIII, 157 (Oct., 1846).

[62] *Knickerbocker*, XXVIII, 425 (Nov., 1846).

The second attack was in the form of a quotation from the *North American Review*. Wiley and Putnam had published *Tales by Edgar A. Poe* as the second in a series entitled *Library of American Books,* and Clark, while slashing at Simms, observed: "These works [Simms's], with the 'Tales by Edgar A. Poe,' who is described as 'belonging to the forcible-feeble and shallow-profound school,' are pronounced 'poor materials for an American Library.' "[63]

The last of Poe's *Literati* papers appeared in the October number of *Godey's Lady's Book*. With Poe's counterattacks ceasing, Clark seemed satisfied to let the quarrel lapse. Only once again before Poe died did Clark mention him, and then only under the exigencies of having to defend himself against charges of personal bias against Mathews, Simms, and Poe. That occasion was in January, 1848, when Clark found an article in *Blackwood's Magazine* that would, he thought, prove him guiltless of bias and an honest editor.[64]

Poe died October 7, 1849, and Griswold began to edit his works, the reaction to which was violent. Among the protests, George R. Graham's of *Graham's Magazine* was most perceptive. In an open letter to N. P. Willis, he wrote that Poe had "in the exercise of his functions as critic, put to death, summarily, the literary reputation of some of Mr. Griswold's best friends; and their ghosts cried in vain for him to avenge them during Poe's life-time—and it almost seems, as if the present hacking at the cold remains of him who struck them down, is a sort of compensation for duty long delayed—for reprisal long desired but defered [*sic*]."[65]

Clark, a friend of Griswold,[66] felt impelled to aid him, yet it must have posed something of a dilemma to have to defend the editor and at the same time attack his subject. In the review, Clark,

[63] *Ibid.*, 452. The article from which Clark quoted may be found in the *North American Review*, LXIII, 357-381 (Oct., 1846).

[64] *Ibid.*, XXXI, 68-71 (Jan., 1848).

[65] *Graham's Magazine*, XXXVI, 224-226 (March, 1850).

[66] In a subsequent eulogy of Griswold, Clark wrote (*Knickerbocker*, XLV, 398, Oct., 1855) that "we have known him, for almost twenty years—for nearly the entire period of our connection with the *Knickerbocker*"—a claim only slightly exaggerated. Perhaps no better proof of their friendship exists than this, that in 1853 Griswold edited a magnificent gift volume in honor of Clark (*The Knickerbocker Gallery: A Testimonial to the Editor of the Knickerbocker Magazine from Its Contributors*, New York, 1855), the proceeds from the sale of which were to be used in buying Clark a cottage on the Hudson. The roster of the writers who sent manuscripts gratis for inclusion in that volume contains the familiar names of those who had in one way or another contributed to Poe's downfall—Theodore S. Fay, Charles F. Briggs, George D. Prentice, Epes Sargent, Thomas Ward, Rufus W. Griswold, and Henry Wadsworth Longfellow, to mention but a few. For details concerning the publication of this volume, see Bayless, *Griswold*, p. 237.

quite significantly, stressed "literary thefts" which Griswold himself did not point out, in print at least, until his Memoir appeared in the third volume of Poe's works—*The Literati* volume that was issued some eight months subsequent to this review. Clark asserted that the "Pit and the Pendulum" was plagiarized from "Vivenzio, or Italian Vengeance," and from a tragic scene of E.T.A. Hoffman. An investigator has shown, however, that "a careful search through the tales of Hoffman reveals no story of a pendulum used as an instrument of torture," and that if Poe borrowed in this instance, it was not from "Vivenzio," but from a tale called "The Iron Shroud" by William Mudford. His conclusion was that the *Knickerbocker's* "reviewer's wish was evidently father to the thought."[67]

Clark then maintained that Poe's "charge of plagiarism against Professor Longfellow, we happen to know, was so false that the plagiarism was on the other side [*sic*]." Longfellow, although he recognized the accusation to be absurd, did not protest this statement until September 28, and then not to Clark, who originally hinted at it, as least in print, but to Griswold.[68]

When *The Literati* volume appeared, Clark was not happy to find himself and some of his friends served up again for public amusement. He wrote: "On the score of entertainment of any sort . . . or of good taste, we trust these disjointed criticisms . . . are not considered by their editor as presenting any considerable claim to the regard of the public. Indeed, we have his implied judgment in this regard." He then said that he would content himself with a "synopsis of the extraordinary career of the author, as furnished us by Dr. Griswold, in a biography accompanying the work." Clark then repeated precisely what he himself had charged in his earlier review, and for which he now pretended to find support from Griswold: "Poe's plagiarisms are . . . pronounced by his biographer as 'scarcely paralleled in literary history.' He accused Mr. Longfellow, for example, of a plagiarism from *himself,* when it turned out that the poem of Longfellow was written two or three years before the publication of that by Poe, and was, during a portion of that time, in Poe's possession."[69] Clark was referring to Griswold's charge that

[67] D. L. Clark, "The Sources of Poe's 'The Pit and the Pendulum,'" *Modern Language Notes*, XLIV, 349-356 (June, 1929). Also see *The Literati* volume, pp. xxxii-xxxiii, in which Griswold repeated the identical charges.

[68] *Knickerbocker*, XXXV, 163-164 (Feb., 1850). Also see Quinn (*Poe*, p. 674) for a printing of the letter from the original autograph manuscript in the Boston Public Library.

[69] *Ibid.*, XXXVI, 370-372 (Oct., 1850).

Poe's "The Haunted Palace"—which had been widely circulated as a poem in "The Fall of the House of Usher"—was plagiarized from Longfellow's "The Beleaguered City." In a letter to Griswold dated September 28, 1850, Longfellow denied the charge and said that "The Beleaguered City" "was written on the nineteenth of September, 1839." But Longfellow's denial is not needed on this point, except to show that there is strong reason to believe that Clark and Griswold were collaborating in "hacking at the cold remains." "The Haunted Palace" had appeared in the *Museum* as a separate publication on April, 1839. To concur in a truth is simple; to concur in an error indicates collusion.

In November, 1856, Clark again quoted the *North American Review,* since it contained a harsh article on Poe, which ended, "we would choose to forget all that he has written." Clark concluded by recommending the *Review* "most cordially to our readers."[70]

Louis Godey, in whose magazine the *Literati* papers, as well as a number of other Poe articles and stories, had appeared, wrote to Clark to say that he was not to be counted among those to whom Poe was supposed to have been faithless. Clark replied by evading responsibility for the accusation, and implied that Godey was the exception that proved the rule.[71]

Clark's last public strike at Poe appeared in 1860 when he reviewed Sarah Helen Whitman's defense of Poe, *Edgar Poe and His Critics* (1860). Clark said that the opinions of the *Knickerbocker* had been recorded "frankly and conscientiously" several years ago and implied that those opinions remained warrantably unchanged.[72]

II

The evidence is plain. Poe began his career as a critic of high principles, and fearlessly asserted those principles, whatever the occasion, the author, the publisher, or the coterie involved. But the age as a whole was incredibly mediocre. One need simply read at random in the leading periodicals of the time to be convinced of that. To borrow a phrase of George E. Woodberry, no quotation can do sufficient justice to the writers of this period—they must be read to be properly damned. Such mediocrity prevailed, in fact,

[70] *Ibid.,* XLVIII, 514-518 (Nov., 1856). The review which Clark quoted appears in the *North American Review,* LXXXIII, 427-455 (Oct., 1856). Mott (*American Magazines,* II, p. 243) attributed this article to "a Mrs. E. V. Smith."

[71] *Ibid.,* XLIX, 106 (Jan., 1857).   [72] *Ibid.,* LV, 429 (April, 1860).

that it is really unbelievable that Poe and Hawthorne, Melville and Emerson, Thoreau and Lowell could have survived it artistically. As a practicing critic—a critic whose profession was criticism and who earned his livelihood chiefly by his critical writings—Poe continually received books from authors and publishers. It was inevitable that Poe should react to them in indignation, that he should slash at them, and that his indignation should be exacerbated by the cliques who arrogantly imposed such works on the public as monuments to American literature. Nothing—unless Poe abandoned his principles or his profession—could have stopped his clash with the authors, the publishers, and the coteries who wrote, published, and logrolled such works.

George R. Graham recognized Poe's critical integrity and the enmity he had earned by maintaining that integrity. Graham also recognized—as few of us do today—that if Poe had compromised himself and praised the authors he condemned and toadied to the coteries which he consistently antagonized, the doors of fortune would have swung open for him and that he would not have had to try to smash them open.[73]

The clash came with Poe's first slashing review of *Norman Leslie* in 1835 and continued throughout his life. The men such as Clark who contended against him were, at first, only trying to starve him out as a writer by curtailing the sale of his work, or to destroy him as a critic. Failing that, and finding that he was bringing the battle into their very camp, they then attacked him, not as a writer and critic any longer, but as a man in order to bring him into such disrepute that his critical charges would be discredited. Then, and only then, was he called a literary snob, today in the gutter and tomorrow in some milliner's magazine; a dirty critic who infested the literary world; a man whose state of health rendered him not completely accountable for all his peculiarities; a man tainted with alcoholism, plagiarism, and immorality.

The truth is that Poe as a critic was successful to the point of his own undoing. Having allowed his enemies no ground on which to stand, he drove them to discredit his criticism by discrediting him as a human being. In this they succeeded, and so well, that it may be forever impossible to deflate the Poe myth to its proper proportions.

[73] See, for example, *Graham's Magazine,* XXXVI, 226 (March, 1850).

Poe as Literary Theorist: A Reappraisal
Emerson R. Marks

THERE IS A DOUBLE MOTIVE for a fresh assessment of Edgar Poe's criticism. Every generation finds it necessary to reappraise past writers, a kind of periodic stock-taking as appropriate to dead critics as to dead poets. Often this is true because aspects of a man's work are found to answer some current need or to articulate some newly emerged aspiration of the common psyche. The poetry of Donne and Blake and the criticism of Coleridge come readily to mind in this regard. My present concern, however, is less to argue that Poe's criticism has in fact taken on such renewed utility than to investigate the question of its general value, which I take to be the necessary prior step.

Aside from this, Poe invites reconsideration because of the long-standing uncertainty about his worth as a critic and especially because of the disparity between his reputation in France, where since Baudelaire he has been idolized, and his reputation in the English-speaking world, where frequently he has been at best patronized. With us, today, Poe seems to stand highest for his stories, which still provide material for serious studies like Levin's *The Power of Blackness* as well as for amateur literary psychoanalyses. His poetry is valued almost exclusively for a few lyrics regarded as excellent examples of a very limited kind. Though his criticism perhaps fares better than his poetry, the homage paid it is mainly historical. When, rarely, his doctrines are considered on their intrinsic merits, Poe is generally credited with having propounded a poetic ontology more thoroughly defined by Coleridge a generation earlier and an analytical method destined to be elaborated by the New Critics a century later.[1] Yet even outside of France one finds occasional

---

[1] See for example Floyd Stovall, "Poe's Debt to Coleridge," *University of Texas Studies in English*, X, 70-127 (July, 1930); Marvin R. Laser, "The Growth and Structure of Poe's Concept of Beauty," *Journal of English Literary History*, XV, 69-84 (March, 1948); George Snell, "First of the New Critics," *Quarterly Review of Literature*, II, 333-340 (Summer, 1945); R. H. Fogle, "Organic Form in American Criticism, 1840-1870," in *The Development of American Literary Criticism*, ed. Floyd Stovall (Chapel Hill, N. C., 1955), pp. 75-111. Poe's affinity to the New Critics has, I think, been overstressed. The New

sharp dissent from this grudging estimate. Writers as respected and different as Saintsbury, Eliot, and Auden have rated his critical writing highly. Edmund Wilson called it "the most remarkable body of criticism ever produced in the United States."[2]

Though unanimity in such a matter is an idle hope, some reduction of disagreement now seems possible if we pose a broad initial question: In the whole context of what we believe to be the soundest criticism past and present, what features of Poe's method and theory, what specific evaluations, retain validity? The answer would require a book. I propose here only the tentative emphases of such a book, not in every case the familiar ones given in the literary histories, but those which emerge from a survey of the whole range of Poe's critical prose—the essays, the editorials, the reviews, the letters. If, except to biographers and bibliographers, the great bulk of what he wrote is almost worthless, we still have to scrutinize the trash for the clues it supplies to the value and significance of the treasure and as a check on our too ready tendency to see all Poe's ideas as facile restatements of European Romantic prototypes. When this has been done, I think we may fairly conclude that Poe is worth study today—and I mean by today's critics and literary theorists—on several counts.

In the interest of honest perspective, however, it may be well first to review his critical shortcomings. There are several. For all his insight into the importance of unity, Poe was curiously blind to the aesthetic value of a complex whole that resides in a writer's control of a great mass of material. To this failing, rather than to his misreading of Coleridge or to his romantic lyrical bias, I should ascribe his declaration that a long poem is a contradiction in terms, his preference for the tale over the novel, and his impatience with talk of "sustained power." Only a favored few, if any, he believed, were possessed of the "sculptural taste" needed to take in a novel's "totality of beauty."[3] Poe had got hold of a real critical problem here, one that Percy Lubbock was to explore decades later in *The*

Critics themselves have not claimed him as a forerunner, and their rare references to his criticism are not especially laudatory. See William K. Wimsatt, Jr. and Cleanth Brooks, *Literary Criticism: A Short History* (New York, 1957), *passim*, and Allen Tate's "Our Cousin, Mr. Poe," in *The Forlorn Demon* (Chicago, 1953), pp. 79-95.

[2] "Poe as a Literary Critic," *Nation* CLV, 452-453 (October 31, 1942).

[3] *The Complete Works of Edgar Allan Poe*, ed. James A. Harrison (New York, 1902), X, 120.

Craft of Fiction. But what Lubbock regards only as a challenge to our appreciative powers Poe declares flatly to be prohibitive. It is the same, though for additional reasons, with the long poem.

This ban on mere length is a serious theoretical restriction which produced some unfortunate results in critical practice. Poe is seldom at his best in his many reviews of novels. He resorts to long paraphrases of the plot and to fussing pedantically over minutiae of his author's grammar. His uncertainty leads him to rash and crippling generalizations: that a novel differs radically in kind from a short story; that its unity is only the "unity of the writer's individual thought"; most grotesque, that it must contain the author's observations, *in propria persona,* on the incidents of his narrative. To blame a novelist for keeping himself out of his fiction is at best questionable. To praise Defoe for doing the reverse in *Robinson Crusoe,* as Poe does, is not only hopelessly to confuse author and fictive narrator; it is to reduce the novel to a kind of didactic confessional, which by Poe's own best theory is virtually to deny it any status as an art form.[4]

Second, I should place certain ultra-romantic limitations of taste by which he condemns, among other things, English metaphysical poetry (marred by "bathos, baldness, and utter imbecility"), Greek tragedy (crude and primitive), *Pilgrim's Progress* ("ludicrously over-rated"), Molière's plays, and Fielding's novels.[5] His preferences among poems, especially his choices for the highest honors, Shelley's "The Sensitive Plant" and Keats's "Ode to a Nightingale," suggest that in Poe the nineteenth-century tendency to confine poetry to the lyrical reaches an extreme. He wonders whether a dramatic poem is not a "flat contradiction in terms"; in any case neither the dramatic nor, as he warns Lowell, the narrative has anything to do with "true" poetry.[6]

[4] *Works,* X, 201, 218; XII, 224. Ill suited to his general theory, Poe's demand for "autorial comment" in the novel also seems to clash with his insight into what Keats called negative capability, an idea Poe himself may have come on in Hazlitt. Reviewing an edition of *Robinson Crusoe* in 1836, he concluded that Defoe "must have possessed . . . what has been termed the faculty of *identification*—that dominion exercised by volition over imagination which enables the mind to lose its own, in a fictitious, individuality." Elsewhere he praises Boccaccio, Scott, Shakespeare, and, again, Defoe for displaying this faculty (*Works,* VIII, 170, 234-235).

[5] *Works,* IX, 95; XVI, 119; XII, 4; XIII, 149; XI, 89-90.

[6] *Works,* VIII, 299; XIII, 73, 112; *The Letters of Edgar Allan Poe,* ed. John Ward Ostrom (Cambridge, Mass., 1948), I, 239.

Nearly allied to this lyrical bias of taste is a relative indifference to comedy and satire that seems oddly inconsistent with his own satirical experiments and his literary hoaxes. Poe brushes aside Fielding and Smollett and is scornful of Molière. To the comic in poetic form he is downright hostile. In his view, the element of rhythm renders the ratiocinative, the sarcastic, and the humorous, though all admissible in prose fiction, foreign to the essence of poetry. Butler's *Hudibras* and Pope's *Essay on Man* he classes among "humorous pieces," not really poetry at all.[7] Yet the comic and the satiric are perhaps only the most noteworthy of many modes of human response to experience which Poe places off limits to the poet. His perverse dictum that the death of a beautiful woman is the most poetical of all subjects may be charitably excused as an apologia for a favorite theme of his own verse. But on any view his conception of the range of subject matter proper to poetic treatment is ludicrously narrow, at times even "precious"; a mountain, he observes in one place, is "more poetical than a pair of stairs."[8]

A fourth weakness, his emphasis on originality, might be forgiven if it were less obtrusive. In some sense, of course, every good writer is original, and Poe might have invoked Dr. Johnson's massive authority for his insistence on this point. Only in Poe's criticism the notion seems both obsessive and shallow, perhaps no more than a conscious elevation to theoretical dignity of his own fertile inventiveness. The morbid suspicions of derivativeness that darken many of his reviews and his strident charges of plagiarism against Longfellow are a high price to pay for whatever truth may lie in his belief that the "desire of the new is an element of the soul. . . ."[9] It is obvious, in any event, that unless the criterion of originality is restricted by far more rigorous qualifications than Poe offers, it must logically negate his deeply held conviction that poetry can be defined, that every poem belongs, in his own favorite phrase, to a species of composition.

Finally, there is a defect of an excellence. Within its limits Poe's condemnation of the didactic heresy, as he formulated it in "The Poetic Principle," is sound. Too often, though, in his practical

[7] *Works*, XI, 109, 76.
[8] *Works*, XII, 24.
[9] *Works*, XI, 277. Poe offers as evidence the enchanting strain of music which after repeated hearings gradually becomes boring and at last disgusting (*ibid.*).

criticism, he combats this heresy with the opposite heresy, thus providing ammunition for those who would picture him as a mere aesthete, a kind of early American Oscar Wilde. It is one thing—and a good thing—to insist that poetry is poetry and not metrical polemics; it is quite another to argue, as Poe does in a *Graham's* review of Charles Sprague, that "didactic subjects are utterly *beyond,* or rather beneath, the province of true poesy," or that one of Elizabeth Barrett's poems is least meritorious *because* most philosophical.[10] His proper resentment of poetry that has a design on us (as Keats so nicely put it) enables him to make some provocative remarks on the nature and limitations of allegorical verse. But his bald pronouncement that "*all* allegories are contemptible"[11] is of a kind that degrades his prosecution of the didactic heresy to the level of an inquisition.

II

Given such grave deficiencies, can we justify Edmund Wilson's opinion that Poe's criticism ought to be with us, as with the French, "a vital part of our intellectual equipment"?[12] I think we can, though my reasons for saying so may not in every instance be those Mr. Wilson would adduce. They refer primarily to four fundamental and closely related theoretical issues: the nature of artistic imitation, poetic form, the creative process, and the function of criticism itself.

Important though it is, Poe's exposure of the didactic heresy rests on shiftier theoretical grounds and is less needed today than his clear-sighted and consistent rejection of another fallacy prevalent in his times and destined despite him to be even more widely entertained after his death. It has been variously called the realist fallacy, the confusion of art and life, the fallacy of imitative form. So far as I know, Poe has yet to be given the place rightly due him among those critics and aestheticians—the very best—who have admitted the aesthetic worthlessness of fidelity of representation. "The mere imitation, however accurate," he writes in one of the *Marginalia* pieces, "of what *is,* in Nature, entitles no man to the sacred name of 'Artist'. . . ." Man can, thanks to his innate sense of beauty, de-

[10] *Works,* X, 141; XII, 15.
[11] *Works,* XII, 174.
[12] "Poe as a Literary Critic," p. 453.

light in the varied sights and sounds of real life, but repeating them orally or in writing does not constitute "poesy."[13]

In 1913 Clive Bell thought it necessary to explain that the "world of Shakespeare's plays is by no means so lifelike as the world of Mr. Galsworthy's, and therefore those who imagine that the artistic problem must always be the achieving of a correspondence between printed words or painted forms and the world as they know it are right in judging the plays of Shakespeare inferior to those of Mr. Galsworthy."[14] Bell's logic is as fine as the irony of his rhetoric, but Edgar Poe anticipated him in both by seventy years when he reasoned that if "truth is the highest aim of either Painting or Poesy, then Jan Steen was a greater artist than Angelo, and Crabbe is a more noble poet than Milton."[15]

The tendency of some to regard this concept as a mere adjunct to an "escapist" view of poetry, irrelevant to literature closely concerned with human problems, can be discredited by Poe's own reasoning. In judging specific works he applied the criterion generally and without distinction of genre. He praises N. P. Willis for achieving a truthfulness in his drama *Tortesa* which is not a mere "Flemish perception of truth." He invokes the principle again in rejecting what he calls the ill-founded charge that Dickens's characters are caricatures: "caricature seldom exists . . . where the correspondent parts are *in keeping*. . . ." Far from being an escapist crotchet, this perception shrewdly confirms Aristotle's injunction to prefer probable impossibilities to improbable possibilities. Aristotelian, too, is his observation in this same review (of *The Old Curiosity Shop*) that a detailed copying from life is precisely what makes a work of art unnatural.[16]

The truth Poe grasped here of course parallels Coleridge's distinction between a copy and a proper mimesis, but he expresses it with an air of such personal conviction and illustrates it so unerringly that it seems to have been his independent discovery. Almost every major critic has left his version of it somewhere on record, Dr.

---

[13] *Works*, XVI, 164; XI, 71. Poe extends his stricture to "imitative" music, rejecting even Giovanni Gravina's mild claim that music may imitate the language of human feeling (*Della Ragion Poetica*, 1708). Poe's retort that true music imitates nothing because it is essentially indefinite is hardly satisfactory (*Works*, X, 42-43).

[14] *Art* (New York, 1958), p. 53.

[15] *Works*, XI, 84.

[16] *Works*, X, 28, 152-153.

Johnson being a well-known exception. William Hazlitt's unfortunate habit of forgetting or ignoring the principle is usually overlooked; but not by Poe, who exposed its unhappy consequences in an otherwise laudatory review of the English critic's *Characters of Shakespeare's Plays*.[17]

Perhaps the most insidious form of the art–life confusion still prevalent is that a poem communicates to the reader some passion or passions felt by the poet. Recent critics, in understandable reaction against romantic emotionalism in poetic theory, have made much of Eliot's view that "Poetry is not a turning loose of emotion, but an escape from emotion." This aphorism has been helpful. But if we want an elucidation of the nice problem of how natural and aesthetic emotions are both connected and different, we do better to turn from the "classical" Eliot to the romantic Poe: "True passion is prosaic—homely. Any strong mental emotion excites *all* the mental faculties; thus grief the imagination:—but in proportion as the effect is strengthened, the cause surceases. The excited fancy triumphs—the grief is subdued—chastened,—is no longer grief. In this mood we are poetic, and it is clear that a poem now written will be poetic in the exact ratio of its dispassion. A passionate poem is a contradiction in terms." Poe's reviews abound in applications of this idea, by which, for an interesting example, he censures Tennyson's "Locksley Hall."[18]

When we insist today on the distinction between our experience of grief and our experience of an elegy, or between how it feels to be in love and how it feels to read a love lyric, we prefer to appeal to notions like aesthetic distance, artistic objectification, or controlling form, rather than to Poe's quasi-platonic intuition of the soul's thirst for the supernal. Yet it is no more just for this reason to deny him credit for the distinction itself than to reject Coleridge's secondary imagination along with the outmoded faculty psychology behind it. What counts—and it ought to count for a great deal—is that Poe propounded not a mere tenet of one critical school but a

---

[17] This review, one of Poe's best, appeared in 1845 in the *Broadway Journal* (*Works*, XII, 226-228). His objection to Hazlitt's book seems well supported by a distinguished contemporary critical theorist: "Because Hazlitt has an insufficient sense of the distinction between art and reality he teeters on the brink of . . . absurdities. His *Characters of Shakespeare's Plays* is partly vitiated by a view of art as a mere copy of reality" (René Wellek, *A History of Modern Criticism, 1750-1950*, New Haven, Conn., 1955, II, 205).

[18] *Works*, XVI, 56; XI, 255.

principle that can make the difference between good criticism and bad. It defines a condition of all literature, of Balzac's social novels as of Shelley's lyric poems, of *Madame Bovary* as of "Ulalume."[19] According to Joseph Joubert, a remarkable Frenchman unknown to Poe, it is the great rule, the first rule, the only rule of art.

In all this Poe was working, like any good critic, toward a definition, a sound conception of literature as a whole and of poetry as one kind. His attack on the didactic heresy is best understood as part of this broad philosophical enterprise. He does not, at his best moments, espouse a purist position, freely conceding that a poem may be didactic if its morality does not obtrude, if it remains "the undercurrent of a poetical thesis." Though his fondness for dogmatic overstatement led him into intemperate denunciations of allegory and philosophical poetry, it is clear that Poe was grappling honestly with the crucial problem of the status of moral and cognitive values in literature. Perhaps only today, when after long debate critics have begun to see this problem as an aspect of mimesis,[20] can we fully estimate the worth of Poe's pioneering efforts.

On the matter of poetic form, Poe's strong preference for the functional over the merely decorative image is especially remarkable as anticipating a principle of twentieth-century poetics. He objected to the essential splitting of form from content characteristic of poetry that presents truth wreathed "in gems and flowers." Longfellow's "Blind Bartimeus" receives his censure because its imagery (which Poe called the "upper current of meaning") depends for its *sole* interest on its explicit relation to the undercurrent of meaning. "What we read upon the surface," he complains, "would be *vox et praeterea nihil* in default of the Moral beneath."[21] His argument should not be mistaken as an earlier version of J. C. Ransom's idea that the imagery in a poem constitutes a *texture* irrelevant to its *structure* of meaning. Poe rather conceived the nexus

---

[19] In the essay on Balzac which he added to the 1919 edition of *The Symbolist Movement in Literature* Arthur Symons ably explained why Balzac felt insulted by those who praised his novels for their alleged photographic truth to reality. More recently, Henri Peyre has argued in the same vein that Flaubert, as a genuine artist, had no interest in photographic imitations of life ("Introduction" to *Madame Bovary*, Modern Library College edition, New York, 1950, p. xii).

[20] See *Literature and Belief: English Institute Essays 1957*, ed. M. H. Abrams (New York, 1958), especially Professor Abrams's own essay, "Belief and the Suspension of Disbelief," which lucidly defines the issue and reviews its history.

[21] *Works*, XI, 68, 70, 79.

of idea and image, of metaphor and meaning, to be organic and symbolic, not illustrative and arbitrary. He was clearly ahead of his time in this conception, which has for us a clarity and significance it could not have had for his own or for several generations thereafter. With him of course it remained only an insight whose ontological implications he never explored. But if in our time we "know" so much more about these things, it is also true, to paraphrase T. S. Eliot in another context, that Poe is part of what we know.

Poe's contribution to the third of the three theoretical issues named above, the nature of the creative process, can be dealt with more briefly. One measure of the stature of any critic is his capacity at once to express the best insights of his age and to resist its ephemeral excesses. By period and taste Poe was a romantic, often in the worst sense. But nothing so eloquently illustrates the superior quality of his intellect than his dissent from aspects of the romantic attitude toward art which, from our point of view at least, are dubious. Chief among these is an unfortunate brand of antirationalism in the vulgar romantic notion of how a poem gets written. The romantics' healthy restoration of the intuitive to an honored place in the creative process tended too easily to degenerate into a complete distrust of the rational. By Poe's day prevailing opinion held the two mental operations to be mutually incompatible. In sharp protest against this obscurantism, he asserted not only the possibility but the necessity of reconciling genius and artistic skill. He can thus regard the signs of deliberate technique in Bryant's poems as positive merits rather than evidences of imperfect inspiration or meretricious artificialty. Characteristically exaggerating his case, he declares the making of a poem to be a matter of purely ratiocinative calculation. Creation and appreciation depend upon entirely separate mental faculties. We respond to a poem suprarationally, by what he called, taking the term from phrenology, the "faculty of Ideality." But the poem itself, as a means of eliciting that response, is a product of the "organs of Causality and Comparison," that is, of pure intellection. The poet always knows to the smallest detail what he is about, and the wildest "effusion of the Muse" is owing to *Method* for its value.[22]

[22] *Works*, VIII, 284; XI, 133.

Though this doctrine is surely as "heretical" as any Poe deprecated, it was a useful corrective to the opposite bias of his time. More important, it motivated his concern with craftsmanship and his respect for conscious artistry. Too much has been made of the deficiencies of "The Philosophy of Composition," which are after all not so much in what is said there as in what is left out. In our current understanding that a literary work is not something ineffably mysterious before which we can only emit appreciative gasps, that it is instead an object amenable to orderly and rewarding inspection, we are as much the heirs of Poe as of Coleridge or Henry James.

Like Coleridge and James, too, Poe enforced the inevitable corollary having to do with the critical function itself. He taught us to regard criticism as an exacting and respectable discipline, not an unexamined expression of conflicting and groundless opinions on books. He is at least more nearly right than wrong in his assertion that Schelling, the Schlegels, and Goethe do not and cannot differ in their principles from Kames, Johnson, and Blair, but only in their subtler elaboration and application of them. If his faith that the "science" of phrenology would someday eliminate *all* indefiniteness from critical theory is no better than quaint, his scornful rejection of the otiose relativism of *de gustibus,* then as now a seductive escape from hard thinking about the arts, is admirable. While Poe nowhere regards criticism as an autotelic activity divorced from literature, his declaration of its autonomy is among the earliest on record and the clearest: "Criticism is *not* . . . an essay, nor a sermon, nor an oration, nor a chapter in history, nor a philosophical speculation, nor a prose-poem, nor an art novel, nor a dialogue. In fact, it *can* be nothing in the world but—a criticism. . . . Following the highest authority, we would wish . . . to limit literary criticism to comment upon *Art.* A book is written—and it is only *as the book* that we subject it to review."[23] By themselves, these words seem to place their author in the company of Whistler and Wilde. But read in the context of the total corpus of his critical writing, they associate him rather with Matthew Arnold's plea, two decades later, for critical disinterestedness. If in our time we must object that Poe has not here stated the whole truth about the critic's proper business, we ought at least to see that he has stated the first

[23] *Works,* XI, 5, 65, 6-7.

and the most important, the *point de repère* from which to take the bearing of all other claims.

W. H. Auden has expressed his astonishment that Poe, denied by his time and place issues and subjects of real importance, was nonetheless so fine a critic. Pointing to the contrast between Baudelaire's subjects—Delacroix, Constantin Guys, Wagner—and the worthless stuff assigned to Poe for review, Auden suggests that Poe's limitations were "entirely his misfortune, not his fault."[24] This argument is attractive and plausible, but as much beside the point as it is beyond proof. It is by no means certain that Poe's shortcomings would have been substantially less had his opportunities been greater. On the other hand, there is no more reason to be astounded that Poe could extract sound theory from tawdry literary material than that many a novelist has written well and truly from scanty experience of his subject. The fact is that the critic, like Henry James's novelist, need only be one of those on whom nothing is lost. That Poe was such a one some readers in the past have suspected from the grace and precision of his style, reflecting as it does the combination of his sensitivity with that rare order of intelligence which—like his own Dupin's—can infer truth from very slender evidence. But we need no longer rely on so elusive a standard for taking the measure of Poe's achievement. The revolutionary complexities of recent literature have forced upon our criticism a degree of theoretical sophistication that is producing a revaluation of the critical past. In the light of that sophistication and that revaluation, much in Poe that once seemed obscure or perverse becomes clear and compelling.

[24] "Introduction," *Edgar Allan Poe: Selected Prose and Poetry*, rev. ed. (New York 1950), p. xiii.

The Comic in Poe's Fiction
Stephen L. Mooney

THE COMIC ELEMENT in Poe's early writing was first noticed by John Pendleton Kennedy, who suggested to Poe that he write "some farces after the manner of the French vaudevilles."[1] Perhaps Kennedy did, as Professor Fagin speculates, judge "Poe's ability on the basis of previous [dramatic] work which has been lost to us."[2] But a more likely possibility is that Kennedy had read some of the "Tales of the Folio Club"[3] and had seen in them a turn for comedy that might be put to profitable use in vaudeville. The fact that Poe never followed up Kennedy's suggestion does not diminish the accuracy of the insight. Poe does have humor.

Few critics since Kennedy, however, have found in Poe an essentially comic vein. The pathological, the hysterical, the phantasmagorial, the unspeakable have all been meticulously exposed and over-exposed, but the comic has been largely ignored. Nevertheless, Poe could, "apart from any satirical purpose, . . . construct situations that are themselves intrinsically humorous,"[4] and, when he wished, was able to turn his wit on the masses of society or their rulers with trenchantly satiric effect.

The purpose of this essay is to suggest, in the light of Bergson's treatment of the comic, the subject, the means, and the object of Poe's humor, as it appears in a selected group of tales, with particular attention to comic progression: *Disguise, action, error, revelation,* and *result.* It will further be suggested that Poe's comedy is allied to vaudeville and farce, and is directed toward the exposure of a society in which heroes and rulers are shown to be deluded or irresponsible and their subjects a dehumanized, sycophantic mass.

The element of vaudeville and farce is strikingly present in

[1] Kennedy to Poe, September 19, 1835, *The Complete Works of Edgar Allan Poe,* ed. James A. Harrison (New York, 1902), XVII, 19.
[2] N. B. Fagin, *The Histrionic Mr. Poe* (Baltimore, 1949), p. 68.
[3] Poe's work was easily available to Kennedy in 1835. See Arthur H. Quinn, *Edgar Allan Poe: A Critical Biography* (New York, 1942), p. 212.
[4] Walter Fuller Taylor, "Israfel in Motley," *Sewanee Review,* XLII, 333 (July-Sept., 1934).

"Four Beasts in One," "The Man That Was Used Up," "Hop-Frog," "The Spectacles," and "The System of Doctor Tarr and Professor Fether." These five pieces will be offered as a representative group showing evidence of Poe's talent for the comic. "The Man That Was Used Up" will be examined in some detail, though not exhaustively, as a specimen of the group.

Poe's wit ran, not to sophistication and controlled urbanity, but rather to the extravagant and outrageous. It is the wit of the Grand Guignol, the Commedia dell'Arte, and the Jonsonian antimasque of the Royal Court:[5] inventive and fantastic, and charged with shocking jests and metamorphoses. Thus it partakes of the burlesque and the grotesque, qualities which in modern times shade off into Gothic horror and nightmare and, by the nineteenth century, had long since disappeared from the court, to emerge again in popular vaudeville and farce.

Poe's comic pieces reveal "the usual artifices" of Bergson's definition, "the periodic repetition of a word or a scene, symmetrical inversion of roles, and geometric development of blunders [quiproquo]," all belonging to "the art of the vaudevillist."[6] The comic pattern in the five stories under consideration follows a well-defined progression from *disguise* to *action* in disguise, the action based upon a fundamental *error* in the perception of the real, which leads to the comic *revelation* of truth as a stripping away of appearances. The following is an effort to sort out the component parts of this comic mélange.

In these, as in certain other tales,[7] Poe exploits the comic possibilities of groups of people brought together in mad pursuit of amusement at any price. The fancy soirée, the masked ball, the public entertainment—all figure as a central device for exhibiting society at its most ludicrous. The exchange of roles between animals and human beings in several stories contributes to the general grotesqueness of effect.

Poe's world of grotesque beings is a fraternity of caricatures ranged on an animal–human scale reaching from the synthetic toward the genuine. The animal when it approximates the human

---

[5] Jonson introduced the antimasque in "The Masque of Queens," 1609.
[6] Henri Bergson, *Le Rire* (Paris, 1938), p. 36 f. (First published in 1900. Translations are my own.)
[7] "Lionizing" and "King Pest" are good examples.

Comic Progression in Five Tales

Tale	Disguise >	Action >	Error >	Revelation >	Result
"Four Beasts in One"	Antiochus Epiphanes, the monarch of Syria, on all-fours disguised as cameleopard	Revolt of animals, lion, tiger, leopard, ape, against false cameleopard	Degraded monarch's delusion that he can survive a return to the primitive	Fallibility of kings. Sycophancy of masses in following a stupid ruler; their fickleness and cowardice	Escape of the monarch, who gets next year's wreath in foot-racing
"Hop-Frog"	King and seven ministers disguised as "the eight chained orang-outangs;" tarred shirts and drawers with flax coating, chain	Revenge of the dwarf Hop-Frog on his masters who, having been chained to pulley, are raised to ceiling, set on fire, and burned to death	King's naive assumption that silence and obedience signify total submission	The survival of the eiron by superior brainwork (astuteness in plotting); impotence of the aristocracy (guests at the ball)	Escape of hero Hop-Frog with beautiful dwarf friend Trippetta
"The Man That Was Used Up"	A legless, armless, chestless, shoulderless, eyeless, toothless, palateless "bundle" disguised as a handsome hero	Narrator's search for truth about hero's bravery and physical prowess	Sham hero's belief in human perfectibility and "progress"	Worship of shams, pursuit of synthetic beauty by frivolous society	Probable continued success of the synthetic man
"The Spectacles"	Myopic young hero disguising ugliness as beauty by inability to see (inversion of the disguise-device)	Amorous hero's pursuit of his own great, great grandmother, aged 82, and their sham marriage	Hero's self-delusion through egomania	Hoax played by old lady on her young great, great grandson; sham marriage revealed, egomania presumably corrected	Real marriage to beautiful young woman, inheritance of grandmother's fortune
"Tarr and Fether"	The mad masquerading as the sane; the sane disguised to suggest orang-outangs	Guest entertained at dinner by inmates of madhouse, where keepers, tarred and feathered, break out of cells and end party	Naive assumption of "rulers" that man is naturally good	Idealism insufficient to cope with dehumanized masses; impossibility of defining true sanity when the sane and the mad reverse roles	Re-incarceration of inmates; another reversal of roles

is grotesque without disguise. For the dwarf, the hunchback, the otherwise malformed, disguise is unnecessary; like Hop-Frog, he is already grotesque, formed by nature in the fixity of his affliction. The physically normal may be disguised in almost any way, except for diminution of size.

Of the five stories represented here, three make use of animal disguises: a monarch on all fours impersonating a camelopard, his tail being held up by his two principal concubines; a king and his ministers frolicking as orang-outangs; and the wardens of an insane asylum also fitted out as orang-outangs. This is a fair sampling of Poe's menagerie, with its population of horses, baboons, whales, bears, lions, tigers, apes, and even a cat and her new-born kittens.[8] The menagerie in Poe usually signifies some quality of bestiality that degrades or ruins the human characters who are associated with or compared to the beasts. Poe's wit, in this respect, carries the spirit of ancient Egyptian caricature and grotesque, with its tendency to turn men into animals, and animals into men, as part of a karmic purification mystique.[9] It is also the spirit of the antimasque, in which lions, apes, baboons, and hogs were made to sport upon the stage.[10] (There are other points of kinship, as in the gargoyles of medieval church architecture and the grotesques— e. g., a sow playing a flute—carved on the misereres of the choir stalls in certain English cathedrals.)

The action of these stories is made possible only by the presence of disguise. No true metamorphosis, spiritual or physical, takes place in any of them, but the illusion of metamorphosis is sustained long enough to trap the fool in his own folly and allow the logic of his folly to arrive at its conclusion. The action is usually focused in the character of the protagonist, whose possession of a comic flaw leaves him open to error and consequently to downfall. The revelation, to which disguise, action, and error contribute, is the final emergence of the larger meaning, the theme. The "result," a way of bringing the action to a close, may or may not be cynically treated, but in all cases the hero gets away. The camelopard-king escapes, Hop-Frog goes free, the synthetic man is equipped to charm

---

[8] Besides Morella, this cat is the only creature in Poe that reproduces her own kind.

[9] See Thomas Wright, *A History of Caricature and Grotesque in Literature and Art* (London, 1865), p. 5.

[10] Cf. Allardyce Nicoll, *Stuart Antimasques and the Renaissance Stage* (London, 1937), p. 207.

his friends again, the myopic young man marries well and gets money, and the wardens of the insane asylum break out of their cells and recapture the stronghold.

The most profitable of these five stories to notice for comedy of character and language (Bergson's major divisions) will be "The Man That Was Used Up." This tale, written early in Poe's career but not printed until 1839, has seemed to most commentators merely pointless. It has been regarded as nothing more than "a dressing up of the old joke about the person with the false teeth, the cork leg, and the glass eye."[11] Poe's own high evaluation of the story has baffled so thorough a scholar as Professor Quinn, who states that although "there may be some profound satire upon a general who is made up of cork legs, false teeth, and other artificial limbs . . . it escapes the present writer."[12] The only commentator who has found really significant meaning in the story says that it seems inconsequential and incomprehensible until we "recognize [that it is a satire] aimed at Richard M. Johnson, Vice President of the United States."[13] Although this interpretation gives historical point to the tale by showing the contemporary object of Poe's wit, we must still account for the workings of "The Man That Was Used Up" as a story.

The source of the comic in this piece is what Bergson calls

that side of a person by which he resembles a thing, that aspect of human events which, by its inflexibility, imitates mechanism and automatonism. It expresses thereby an individual or collective imperfection which calls for an immediate corrective. That corrective is laughter.[14]

The comedy of Brevet-Brigadier General John A. B. C. Smith, the used-up man, arises from his very perfection: his height (six feet, perhaps excessive in Poe, where men are sometimes four feet[15] and in one story two feet[16] tall), his brilliantly white teeth, his beautiful hazel eyes, his fine chest and shoulders and arms, but most of

[11] Taylor, loc. cit.
[12] Quinn, p. 283.
[13] William Whipple, "Poe's Political Satire," *University of Texas Studies in English*, XXV, 91 (1956). For another treatment of this tale, see Ernest Marchand, "Poe as a Social Critic," *American Literature*, VI, 28 f. (March, 1934).
[14] Bergson, p. 88.
[15] Dirk Peters in *Pym* and Hugh Tarpaulin in "King Pest" are both four feet tall.
[16] The moon-man in "Hans Pfaall" is two feet tall.

all his magnificent legs. "I wish to God," the narrator says, "that my young and talented friend Chiponchipino, the sculptor, had but seen the legs of Brevet-Brigadier General John A. B. C. Smith." The irony of these legs is of course that they are machines; as Bergson points out, "the attitudes, gestures, and movements of the human body are funny in the exact proportion that this body makes us think of a simple machine."[17] The reader's knowledge after the fact only increases the harsh humor of the story in retrospect.

The ultimate discovery that all the general's physical glories are false accounts for his more than military inflexibility and reduces his pontifications on unlimited material progress to a set of squeaking absurdities produced by a "bundle" of a man without a voice of his own. He is a "human perfectibility man," not the only one in Poe,[18] who illustrates the notion that the enlightenment of science can lead humanity to the achievement of apparent perfection, where the gods and nature fail. Half of this gentleman is in the tomb, as Poe suggests in his epigraph from Corneille, but this paradox does not deter the general from maintaining a philosophy of naïve optimism, expressed in a rich baritone in praise of such nineteenth-century mechanical wonders as parachutes, railroads, steamboats, and electromagnetic devices capable of transforming social life, art, commerce, and even literature.

This man is a nineteenth-century Waste-Lander, or Hollow Man, with whom history has not yet caught up, still capable of making the gestures of significant life and observing the rituals of the old institutions, but doing it out of mere habit and by artificial means. As Mr. Tate says, Poe was well ahead of his time.[19]

The confusion of appearance and reality in "The Man That Was Used Up" is further expressed in the dialogue of the story. Poe's comic means in this respect is a simple one, analogous to the suspended tone in music, whereby a note of one chord is held over as the tonal feature of a new chord: the two chords, two contexts of "meaning," have quite different tonal qualities (comparable to contextual meanings) but keep the one note in common. This is of course in music not a device for humor, but Poe exploits it to interesting literary effect in his story.

[17] Bergson, p. 30.
[18] Cf. the guest-list in "Lionizing."
[19] Allen Tate, *The Forlorn Demon* (Chicago, 1953), p. 93.

Similarly, Bergson notes that "a situation is always comic when it applies at once to two absolutely independent series of events, and when it can be interpreted simultaneously in two different senses."[20] This is Poe's language-situation exactly. His "suspended tone" is the word *man,* an appropriate choice for the general, who is to be revealed as half a man, and the changing context (Bergson's independent series) is first a church, then a theater, and last a "solon." The vacuity of the conversation is evident in the church scene when the narrator, during the sermon, loudly pursues the mystery of the general's identity by questioning Miss Tabitha Thus:

Miss Thus: . . . Why, you know, he's the man—
Minister: (showing anger at the whispering) Man . . . is cut down like a flower . . . .

Again, during a performance at the Rantipole Theatre, the detective-narrator is about to succeed in his noisy inquiries.

Miranda Cognoscenti: Bless my soul!—why he's the man—
Climax (the actor): . . . mandragora
Nor all the drowsy syrups of the world . . . .

And finally at the soirée of Mrs. Kathleen O'Trump, the narrator pursues Mrs. Pirouette on the same subject:

Mrs. Pirouette: I shall have to sit down and enlighten you—Smith! why, he's the man—
Miss Bas-Bleu: (interrupting) Man-*Fred,* I tell you!
Did anybody ever hear the like? It's Man-*Fred,*
I say, and not at all by any means Man-*Friday.*

Whether this device was regarded as humorous in Poe's day, something like it was highly successful a hundred years later. T. S. Eliot in *The Cocktail Party* achieves an effect of social vacuity similar to Poe's by manipulating the phrase "cry of bats:"

Julia: . . . he had a remarkable sense of hearing—
The only man I ever met who could hear the cry of bats.
Peter: Hear the cry of bats?
Julia: He could hear the cry of bats.
Celia: But how do you know he could hear the cry of bats?
Julia: Because he said so. And I believed him.[21]

[20] Bergson, p. 97.
[21] T. S. Eliot, *The Cocktail Party* (London, 1950), p. 11.

The soirée conversation of the nineteenth century thus becomes the cocktail party chatter of the twentieth.

It would be interesting to discover that many of Poe's tales have satiric objects as clearly defined as that in "The Man That Was Used Up,"[22] which Mr. Whipple has studied. It is suggested, thanks again to Mr. Whipple, that "The System of Doctor Tarr and Professor Fether" is a satire on Dickens, who in his *American Notes* describes an insane asylum reminiscent of the one Poe used in his story.[23] There is no question of the value and interest of studies dealing with Poe's use of contemporary materials, but even if all matters of sources and references were settled, we would still be faced with the pleasure of accounting for the popular survival of Poe's works.

It may be that the comic pieces are still read now and then merely because they were, most of them, the early work of the craftsman who later produced stories like "Ligeia" and "William Wilson." But the light pieces, we must admit, are indispensable to the total picture of Poe. "If we take a distant view of [his work], as a whole," Mr. Eliot suggests, "we see a mass of unique shape and impressive size to which the eye constantly returns."[24] The comic pieces are an integral part of the total work, as contributions not only to "mass and size" but to total meaning as well.

Allen Tate's judgment is that "in the history of the moral imagination in the nineteenth century Poe occupies a special place. No other writer in England or the United States, or, so far as I know, in France, went so far as Poe in his vision of dehumanized man."[25] If the comic tales share the common quality of being charades played by marionettes, the social commentary in them is nonetheless valid; the deadness of society is in fact the point that Poe intends to make. The Chaplinesque stiffness, the arbitrary

---

[22] Cornelia Varner, "Notes on Poe's Use of Contemporary Materials in Certain of His Stories," *Journal of English and Germanic Philology*, XXXII, 77-80 (Jan., 1933), comments on a probable source for "The Man That Was Used Up" and quotes an advertisement for cork legs and other artificial members that appeared frequently in the Philadelphia *Public Ledger*.

[23] William Whipple, "Poe's Two-Edged Satiric Tale," *Nineteenth Century Fiction*, IX, 121-123 (Sept., 1954).

[24] T. S. Eliot, "From Poe to Valery," *Hudson Review*, II, 327 (Aug., 1949).

[25] Tate, p. 89.

and cinematic awkwardness, the sense of a mindless puppetry moved by not-quite-invisible strings are all deliberately designed.

Always scornful of the mass, Poe in his comic tales burlesques the pretensions of society and, by implied contrast, affirms the superiority of the solitary man in pursuit of a private destiny. That the pursuit is sometimes nightmarish does not diminish its reality. If Poe "has neither Purgatory nor Heaven; and only two stations in Hell," as Mr. Tate remarks,[26] his situation makes him the kinsman of countless readers, American and foreign, and suggests one good reason for his survival.

[26] Tate, p. 90.

Poe's "Metzengerstein": Not a Hoax
Benjamin F. Fisher

SEVERAL CRITICS have treated Poe's "Metzengerstein" as a burlesque of the horror fiction widely published in American magazines of the 1820's and 1830's.[1] Others, including several who have dealt with specialized aspects of the comic in Poe's fiction, have not considered it among the more obviously humorous tales.[2] On evidence derived from the circumstances of original publication, from subsequent revisions, and from other elements within the tale, I should like to propose that it was written with no comic intention, but that it was an early venture of Poe's into Gothic fiction and followed in the sober path of numberless predecessors. Comparing the text first published with Poe's final version will, I believe, show that he refined away crudities, in an attempt to cull out extremes and to produce a more effective Gothic story, rather than to exaggerate the Gothic elements for humorous effect.

"Metzengerstein" was one of five tales entered by Poe in a competition, with a prize of a hundred dollars, sponsored by the Phila-

[1] Fred Lewis Pattee, *The Development of the American Short Story* (New York, 1923), pp. 124-125; Edward H. Davidson, ed., *Selected Writings of Edgar Allan Poe* (Boston, 1956), pp. xiv, 499; *Poe: A Critical Study* (Cambridge, Mass., 1957), pp. 137-138. Eric Carlson is more cautious in assessing the humorous potential of this tale in his *Introduction to Poe: A Thematic Reader* (Glenview, Ill., 1967), p. 572.

The possibilities for including "Metzengerstein" among a group of tales to be published in a volume, "Tales of the Folio Club," a work with humorous intent, are discussed in *The Complete Works of Edgar Allan Poe*, ed. James A. Harrison (New York, 1902), II, xxvi–xxxix; Arthur H. Quinn, *Edgar Allan Poe: A Critical Biography* (New York, 1941), p. 746. Thomas O. Mabbott points out that the criticism to be interlarded among the tales rather than the tales themselves was to be the chief vehicle for humor in the volume. See "On Poe's 'Tales of the Folio Club,'" *Sewanee Review*, XXVI (April, 1928), 171–176. There is no solid agreement about just which of Poe's early tales were to figure among the "Tales of the Folio Club," and Professor Mabbott, in a letter to me dated January 8, 1968, states that in his opinion not all the early tales are comic.

[2] James S. Wilson, "The Devil Was in It," *American Mercury*, XXIV (Oct., 1931), 215–220; Walter F. Taylor, "Israfel in Motley: A Study of Poe's Humor," *Sewanee Review*, XLII (June, 1934), 33–40; Ted N. Weissbuch, "Edgar Allan Poe: Hoaxer in the American Tradition," *New York Historical Society Quarterly*, XLV (July, 1961), 291–309; Stephen Mooney, "The Comic in Poe's Fiction," *American Literature*, XXXIII (Jan., 1962), 433–441; James M. Cox, "Edgar Poe: Style as Pose," *Virginia Quarterly Review*, XLIV (Winter, 1968), 67–89.

delphia *Saturday Courier* for the "best American tale."[3] None of Poe's tales won the prize, but they were published in the *Courier* during 1832. Edward H. Davidson notes that a chief reason for Poe's turning from poetry to prose was financial; Mabbott is more blunt: "But Poe wrote prose for bread and fame."[4]

Concerning the early tales, Poe himself wrote, "To be appreciated you must be *read,* and these things are invariably sought after with avidity. They are . . . the articles which find their way into other periodicals, and into the papers, and in this manner, taking hold upon the public mind, they augment the reputation of the source whence they originated." This attitude remained characteristic of Poe until the end of his life. In his last year he wrote about "Hop-Frog," a late tale, "It was to be published in a weekly paper of Boston, called 'Flag of Our Union,' not a *very* respectable journal perhaps, in a literary point of view, but one that pays as high prices as most of the magazines. The proprietor wrote to me, offering $5 a 'Graham page' as I was anxious to get out of my pecuniary difficulties, I accepted the offer."[5] Bread and fame indeed seem to have been important to Poe.

As published in the *Saturday Courier* for January 14, 1832, "Metzengerstein" was a more conventional Gothic tale than were the others accompanying it,[6] and it may well have been that in writing it Poe had in mind the wide audience attracted to Gothic fiction in contemporaneous magazines. Edward Wagenknecht is correct in observing that "Metzengerstein" does not go to the excessive lengths in horror to be found in many other tales of Poe's day. Such restraint would hardly be expected if burlesque had been his purpose.[7]

[3] *Saturday Courier*, May 23, 1831, p. 1. See also John Grier Varner, Jr., *Edgar Allan Poe and the Philadelphia "Saturday Courier"* (Charlottesville, Va., 1933), pp. v, 3.

[4] Davidson, *Selected Writings*, p. xiv; Mabbott, "On Poe's 'Tales of the Folio Club,'" p. 171. On Poe's financial problems see also Quinn, *Edgar Allan Poe*, pp. 207, 307ff.; and Henry S. Canby, *Classic Americans* (New York, 1939), pp. 268ff. Howard Mumford Jones remarks in *Ideas in America* (Cambridge, Mass., 1944), p. 41, that "what Poe was principally trying to do was . . . to master a market."

[5] *The Letters of Edgar Allan Poe*, ed. John Ward Ostrom, 2 vols. (Cambridge, Mass., 1948). The citations are respectively to I, 57–58, and II, 425.

[6] The other tales where "Duc de L'Omelette," "A Tale of Jerusalem," "A Decided Loss," and "The Bargain Lost."

[7] *Edgar Allan Poe: The Man behind the Legend* (New York, 1963), p. 57. For another view of "Metzengerstein" as something more than "mere parody," see Geoffrey Rans, *Edgar Allan Poe* (Edinburgh, 1965), p. 8.

In the text published by Griswold in 1850, which presumably incorporates Poe's final revisions and differs in many respects from the original appearance in the *Saturday Courier,* "Metzengerstein" appears to be no more than an initial earnest, though somewhat amateurish, endeavor in the traditional type of Gothic or "German" fiction then so popular. While I agree with Davidson that "Metzengerstein" does not present "Poe's autobiography and revelations of his inner, psychotic state of mind," I think it is important for other reasons—as an instance for one thing of Poe's following the pattern of current magazine fiction.[8]

The beginning of the first version is commonplace Gothic: "Horror and fatality have been stalking abroad in all ages. Why then give a date to the story I have to tell? I will not. Besides I have other reasons for concealment." Gothic fiction frequently tries to take the reader into strange, remote regions to emphasize the unreal horrors experienced by sensitive heroes and heroines; the reader is immediately plunged into a quandary of doubts and uneasiness in this beginning. Poe's own line, "Out of SPACE—Out of TIME," seems anticipated here. Beginnings are of prime importance in Poe's tales,[9] and the tone of this beginning is far less bantering, if it is bantering at all, than the beginnings of "Loss of Breath" and "How to Write a Blackwood Article," obvious burlesques.[10] The conventionality of the first lines may be emphasized if compared with those which open Godwin's *Caleb Williams,* a Gothic work with which Poe was familiar and which was not by any means humorous: "My life has for several years been a theatre of calamity. I have been a mark for the vigilance of tyranny, and I could not escape. My enemy has shown himself inaccessible to entreaties and untired in persecution."[11] The abrupt beginning of "Metzengerstein," rapidly drawing the reader into the midst of fright, high-

---

[8] *Selected Writings,* p. 500.

[9] See Joseph P. Ropollo, "Meaning and 'The Masque of the Red Death,'" *Tulane Studies in English,* XIII (1963), 64.

[10] The obvious burlesque element in early tales like "Loss of Breath" was quickly noted by Poe's contemporaries, e.g., in the anonymous notice on the inside front cover of the *Southern Literary Messenger,* Vol. II (Dec., 1835), after the tale reappeared there, somewhat altered from its appearance as "A Decided Loss" in the *Saturday Courier.* No contemporary of Poe's seems to have noticed comic elements in "Metzengerstein."

[11] *The Adventures of Caleb Williams: or, Things as They Are,* ed. George Sherburn (New York, 1960), p. 3. For Poe's acquaintance with *Caleb Williams* see Burton R. Pollin, "Poe and Godwin," *Nineteenth-Century Fiction,* XX (Dec., 1965), 437–454; Poe, *Works,* XI, 64.

pitched emotion, and sensationalism, is typical of Poe and surely not overdone.

The setting, "the interior of Hungary," is "German," i.e., Gothic, and the mention of supersition and the mysterious prophecy combine with geographic locale to hint to the reader of nineteenth-century periodicals that here is an instance of common terror fiction. When the tale was reprinted in the *Southern Literary Messenger* of January, 1836, it carried the subtitle, "In Imitation of the German," perhaps to attract even more certainly the reader of mystery fare. The subtitle was dropped in the *Tales of the Grotesque and Arabesque* (1840), perhaps to counteract the charges of excessive "Germanism" which Poe tried to answer in the preface, stating that terror was "not of Germany, but of the soul."[12]

The character of young Frederick, Baron Metzengerstein, suggests no humorous or exaggerated qualities which might embody burlesque or parody. "Heartless, self-willed, and impetuous from childhood, he had arrived at the age of which I speak, through a career of unfeeling, wanton, and reckless dissipation, and a barrier had long since arisen in the channel of all holy thoughts, and gentle recollections." These are the typical attributes—no more and no less—of a Gothic villain, and Frederick might easily step into the pages of Mrs. Radcliffe or those tales of terror familiar to Poe in "the earlier numbers of *Blackwood's,* those relished by every man of genius" (*Works,* XI, 109). Frederick's personality is as diabolical as the villain's in William Mudford's "Iron Shroud," a *Blackwood's* tale with which Poe was familiar, and upon which he later drew in writing "The Pit and the Pendulum."[13]

Like many another Gothic villain from the European nobility, Frederick inherits "vast possessions . . . castles without number," and an era of feudal magnificence and wealth is immediately established. His own residence contains a "vast and desolate upper apartment" with "rich, although faded tapestry hangings which swung gloomily," such as could have hung in the eerie upper chambers of

---

[12] Comments on the "Germanism" in Poe's tales may be epitomized by the following anonymous notice of "Morella": It is called "one of those wild and gloomy exhibitions of passion, heretofore belonging almost peculiarly to the genius of the German school of romance." Cover notice, *Southern Literary Messenger,* I (May, 1835). Poe's defense appears in *Tales of the Grotesque and Arabesque,* 2 vols. (Philadelphia, 1840), I, iii.

[13] Thomas O. Mabbott, ed., *Selected Poetry and Prose of Edgar Allan Poe* (New York, 1951), p. 422; David L. Clark, "The Sources for Poe's 'The Pit and the Pendulum,'" *Modern Language Notes,* XLIV (May, 1929), 349–356.

Otranto or Udolpho. On these hangings are depicted "shadowy and majestic forms of a thousand illustrious ancestors" which "startled the steadiest nerves with their vigorous expressions." Frederick's attention is held by the figure of a great fiery-colored horse, which had belonged to an ancestor of the Berlifitzings, a neighboring family long at enmity with the Metzengersteins. As if alive, the horse suddenly darts a mysteriously malign glance at Frederick, while he watches the holocaust consuming the Berlifitzing stables—fired probably at Frederick's instigation. The firelight suddenly throws his figure into relief in the place of his murderous ancestor in the tapestry, the murderer of the horse's owner. Old Count Berlifitzing dies trying to rescue horses from his burning stables, and Frederick is shortly afterward informed that a mysterious horse has been captured for him, apparently from the Berlifitzing stock. Simultaneously he learns that the portion of the tapestry picturing the horse has disappeared. The new animal is of course the reincarnated vengeful spirit of Berlifitzing, for the opening of the story deals with metempsychosis, another fad of interest in Poe's time. The supernatural creature eventually causes the death of Frederick and thus fulfills the prophecy: "A lofty name shall have a fearful fall when, as the rider over his horse, the mortality of Metzengerstein shall triumph over the immortality of Berlifitzing."

The backdrop for the villains's violent death, following a hackneyed convention in Gothic fiction, is fitting. One stormy night "the stupendous and magnificent battlements of the Chateau Metzengerstein were discovered crackling and rocking to their very foundations, under the influence of a dense and livid mass of ungovernable fire." Those watching the conflagration were suddenly startled by the great horse appearing close by, bearing a maniacally terrified Frederick, and from the onlookers' lips burst the ejaculation "Azrael!"—the name of the angel of death in Jewish and Islamic belief. "The clattering hoofs resounded sharply, and shrilly above the roaring of the flames and the shrieking of the wind, . . . and clearing, at a single plunge, the gateway, and the moat, the animal bounded, with its rider, far up the tottering staircase of the palace, and was lost in the whirlwind of hissing, and chaotic fire."

Here, as in other Gothic works, setting contributes significantly to the atmosphere of terror the writer wishes to create. Poe's careful choice of words is important in emphasizing this effect. "Crackling" and "rocking" foundations, "stupendous and magnificent" battlements, "aged oaks," "tottering" staircases, and "chaotic" fire conjure up venerable age and extreme emotion, both associated in the Gothic tradition with mystery and fear.

The mild conventionality in "Metzengerstein" is evident in the rather sparse outlay of horrors. The setting, noted above, contributes to the foreboding and mystery, but the brevity of the tale allows for none of the rhapsodic quality of some of Mrs. Radcliffe's or Maturin's descriptive passages. The conciseness and the suggestiveness of a "whirlwind of hissing and chaotic fire" anticipate the cadenced, poetic qualities of certain passages in later tales like "The Masque of the Red Death." The tone of "Metzengerstein" betrays no satiric intent, so far as I can see. Irving's "The Story of the Young Italian," with which Poe was familiar, is much more a gallery of horrors than "Metzengerstein," and it is by no means a burlesque of traditional Gothic characters and conventions. The death of Filippo is presented in much more gruesome detail than anything in Poe's tale.[14]

The citations from learned authorities in "Metzengerstein"—"as La Bruyère observes of all our unhappiness, *vient de ne pouvoir être seuls*"—and the pompous erudition—"But there were some points in the Hungarian superstition (The Roman term was religio)"—are among the objects of Poe's mirth in the later, clearly satiric "How to Write a Blackwood Article" and in its sequel, "A Predicament." Yet such bits of pseudoerudition, the foreign phrase inserted for effect, remain with Poe through his last work. "Hop-Frog," his last published tale, is sprinkled with foreign phrases.

Examples of loose construction, both minor defects and structural flaws in the tale as a whole, in the original *Saturday Courier* text, indicate an uncertain, tentative quality and possibly haste in the writing of "Metzengerstein." In the paragraph detailing the origins of the Metzengerstein-Berlifitzing feud appears the following sentence: "Indeed, at the era of this history, it was remarked by an old crone of haggard and sinister appearance, that the fire and water might sooner mingle, than a Berlifitzing clasp the hand of a Metzengerstein." Then follows the mysterious prophecy. Poe later deleted this sentence, eliminating a bit of irrelevant sensationalism

---

[14] Washington Irving, *Tales of a Traveller* (New York, 1849), p. 117; the original edition appeared in 1824. Poe pays special attention to this tale in *Works*, XII, 153-154.

and enhancing the unity of effect, which by the middle forties, the period of the final revision of the tales, had become so important to him.[15] The foreboding crone, a stock Gothic character, was probably calculated to interest magazine readers, who would be alert for such personages. Another instance of Poe's toning down the sensationalism of the early version is apparent in the following revisions: *Saturday Courier* version—"A rapid smile, of a peculiar and unintelligible meaning, shot over the beautiful countenance of the listener"; Griswold—"A rapid smile shot over the countenance of the listener."

In the *Saturday Courier* version appear two long paragraphs, one detailing Frederick's mother's death from consumption, the other, at the end of the tale, noting the disappearance of the name Metzengerstein from the Hungarian aristocracy. Deleting them in revising contributes to a tighter structure of the whole. The ending is especially improved by eliminating the original final two sentences: "Frederick, Baron Metzengerstein, was the last of a long line of princes. His family name is no longer to be found among the Hungarian Aristocracy." As the tale concludes in Griswold's version, it is much more abrupt and dramatic—and more directly related to the foundation theme of metempsychosis:

The fury of the tempest immediately died away, and a dead calm sullenly succeeded. A white flame still enveloped the building like a shroud, and, streaming far away into the quiet atmosphere, shot forth a glare of preternatural light; while a cloud of smoke settled heavily over the battlements in the distinct colossal figure of—*a horse.*

Other revisions suggest how carefully Poe proceeded in an effort to polish his work. In the *Saturday Courier* text, old Berlifitzing is Wilhelm, but he is later called William by one of the servants. He is consistently Wilhelm in Griswold. The Chateau Metzengerstein in the first version becomes a palace in Griswold, which is more in keeping with the Hungarian setting and the "Germanic" quality of the tale.[16] The early version reads, "There was a fiendish expres-

---

[15] Seymour L. Gross notes how Poe drew away from sensationalism in revising "The Oval Portrait," in "Poe's Revisions of 'The Oval Portrait,'" *Modern Language Notes,* LXXIV (Jan., 1959), 16–20.

[16] Poe's poor German, coupled with the nearby citations in French, may account for the inconsistency in the first text. Poe's faulty German is noted in Howard Mumford Jones, *The Theory of American Literature* (Ithaca, N.Y., 1948), p. 146. Mabbott also states that Poe "had a very slight knowledge of German," *Selected Poetry and Prose,* p. xii.

sion on the lips of the young Frederick" as he gazed upon the mysterious tapestry. Griswold reads, "On Frederick's lips arose a fiendish expression." In the same paragraph, "It was with difficulty that he could reconcile his dreamy and incoherent feelings, with the certainty of being awake," later reads, "It was with difficulty that he reconciled. . . ." "He could, by no means, account for the singular, intense and overwhelming anxiety which appeared falling, like a shroud, upon his senses," is tightened into "On the contrary, he could by no means account for the overwhelming anxiety which appeared falling like a pall upon his senses." Frederick's "compulsory, and desperate exertion" is compressed to "a compulsory exertion." Still other instances might be cited to show how even in the most minor ways Poe attempted to decrease the strained effect of his earlier prose.

There is, I think, little reason to place "Metzengerstein" among Poe's burlesques and hoaxes such as "Loss of Breath," "A Tale of Jerusalem," or "How to Write a Blackwood Article," which lampooned authors and fads of Poe's own day.[17] It is not necessarily, as Davidson has said, "a fantasy which out-fantasies the German tale of terror, with its baroque setting, its titanic villain, and its overwrought prose. . . ."[18] The revised prose is not nearly so overwrought as that of the first version. Indeed, "Metzengerstein" appears more a part of "that staple of popular reading consumption which so delights an unintelligent audience" than like an attack, playful or otherwise, upon such staples.[19] As a direct descendant of *The Castle of Otranto*,[20] Poe's tale seems quite close in tone and situation, characters and props to its sober ancestor.

He also remarks in a letter to me dated June 1, 1966, that Poe knew about German writings only in English and French translations.

[17] See the articles cited in n. 4 and Ruth L. Hudson "Poe and Disraeli," *American Literature*, VII (Jan., 1937), 407.
[18] Davidson, *Selected Writings*, p. xiv.
[19] Ibid., p. xiv.
[20] Lucille King, "Notes on Poe's Sources," *Texas Studies in English*, X (1930), 128–134.

Poe's Sense of an Ending
Paul John Eakin

In *The Golden Bowl* PRINCE AMERIGO recalls the wonder and the mystery of the ending of *The Narrative of Arthur Gordon Pym*, "a thing to show, by the way, what imagination Americans *could* have."[1] For all the native power of the final image of Poe's longest tale, however, Henry James himself was unsparing in his criticism of its artistic failure: "the climax fails—fails because it stops short, and stops short for want of connexions. There *are* no connexions; not only, I mean, in the sense of further statement, but of our own further relation to the elements, which hang in the void: whereby we see the effect lost, the imaginative effort wasted."[2] In this pair of observations James displays the characteristic set of responses which the conclusion of *Pym* invariably elicits: it is at once arresting and arrested, striking but unsatisfactory, somehow incomplete in the rendering.[3] Even Poe himself, in the person of the "editor" of the tale, would seem to concede the justice of such criticisms in his insistence on the incompleteness of Pym's published narrative. This insistence, however, is deliberately misleading, for the design of the tale is complete and fully executed. The charges that Poe's invention was flagging or that his intentions were shamelessly opportunistic stem, in fact, from a failure to recognize in this instance the familiar concluding strategies of his major fictions. Taking as a point of reference a passage from the "Marginalia," I want to examine these strategies, showing how they work in the angelic colloquies, the mesmerist pieces, and certain representative tales, with a view toward a deeper understanding of Poe's sense of an ending.

I

In a well-known passage from the "Marginalia" (*Graham's American Monthly Magazine*, March, 1846) Poe claimed for his

[1] Henry James, *The Golden Bowl* (New York, 1909), p. 22.
[2] *The Altar of the Dead* (New York, 1909), pp. xix–xx.
[3] See, e.g., Edward H. Davidson, *Poe: A Critical Study* (Cambridge, Mass., 1957), p. 158.

own a complex of concerns that inform the group of fictions to be studied in the later sections of this essay. Here he reports his personal experience of the farthest reach of consciousness, nothing less than "a glimpse of the spirit's outer world."[4] The passage is, in effect, his most elaborate account of his sense of an ending, an anatomy of the special "psychal impressions" that transmit such visionary experience. "They arise in the soul," he writes, "where the confines of the waking world blend with those of the world of dreams, . . . upon the very brink of sleep." This evanescent dream-state induces an ecstasy of vision remarkable for its *"absoluteness of novelty,"* for in these "psychal impressions" "there is really nothing even approximate in character to impressions ordinarily received." Poe and his heroes pursue these "fancies" because they allow a rare and privileged anticipation of the soul's destination *outre-tombe*, what Georges Poulet has so aptly termed "posthumous consciousness."[5] The revelation of "the spirit's outer world" is registered by five senses somehow "alien to mortality"; had man the power to prolong such experience he could compel "the Heaven into the Earth." So great is Poe's faith in "the *power of words*," nevertheless, that he believes he can, at least, capture his transcendent visions in language.

As Poe proceeds in the "Marginalia" passage to describe "experiments" designed to demonstrate the possibility of an accurate mortal record of "posthumous consciousness," a basic plot for the pursuit of such knowledge begins to emerge: a movement of approach and entry, in his claim that he can make this special state of consciousness supervene; and a movement of withdrawal and return, in his claim that he can startle himself from this "condition" into wakefulness in order to effect its transfer into his conscious memory. To this fundamental motion of approach to and return from a "supernal" realm of "vision" or "ecstasy" the "Marginalia" passage adds one more clarification: the moment of revelation itself, that is, the climax of this plot, can be but "an inappreciable *point of time*," and hence it is rather in terms of an image than as some

[4] *The Complete Works of Edgar Allan Poe*, ed. James A. Harrison (New York, 1902), XVI, 89. All citations from Poe refer to this edition unless otherwise noted.

[5] "Poe," in *The Recognition of Edgar Allan Poe: Selected Criticism Since 1829*, ed. Eric W. Carlson (Ann Arbor, Mich., 1966), p. 233. D. H. Lawrence speaks, similarly, of Poe as the master of "inorganic consciousness" in *Studies in Classic American Literature* (New York, 1955), p. 88.

paraphrase or other exposition that its content can be rendered (XVI, 88–89).[6]

Richard Wilbur has argued that the movement toward and entry into this state of visionary consciousness (which he terms "the hypnagogic state") provides the plot structure of a central group of Poe's narratives which he calls "dream-voyages."[7] His analysis of "the mind's progress into unconsciousness" focuses on the final descent or plunge into "the one truly paradisal state, . . . the suspended death-in-life or life-in-death of reverie."[8] Poe himself, however, in "The Power of Words," suggests important corrections to the basic thrust of Wilbur's formulation of the archetypal soul-plot of the Poe story. Here he defines the motive for the dream-journey as "the thirst *to know*" (VI, 140). Thus the drive toward insensibility or "death-wish," as Harry Levin has pointed out, is always accompanied in these stories by an insatiable and morbid curiosity which takes the form of a will to survive in order to know all.[9] The Poe protagonist either resists the end to which he is irresistibly drawn, defying it like Ligeia, surviving it like Pym; or else he discovers that the end is somehow not final, learning like Monos that to die is to be "born again."

The mortal "thirst *to know*," then, is not fulfilled in the journey out, as Wilbur's one-way formulation might seem to imply, but in the journey out and back. Further, this vital principle of the soul, which creates the dramatic tension in the dream-voyage between surrender and survival, determines Poe's paradoxical conception of the journey's end. Mortals may dream, he writes, that in the attainment of final knowledge the soul would achieve supreme felicity;

---

[6] Thus the abruptness of the ending of *Pym* accords completely with Poe's own sense of the dynamics of the transcendent order of perceptions he is attempting to capture in words. Walter E. Bezanson comments, "Poe's most important gift is in psychological projection from the mind of a troubled sleeper who wakes and then drops back into the self's midnight. . . . The question in Poe is how much flummery one will endure in exchange for his special vision." "The Troubled Sleep of Arthur Gordon Pym," in *Essays in Literary History Presented to J. Milton French*, ed. Rudolf Kirk and C. F. Main (New Brunswick, N.J., 1960), p. 173.

[7] "In 'Arnheim,' as in all of his dream-voyage tales, Poe deliberately derives his basic structure from the typical stages of the mind's approach to sleep." "Introduction" to the Laurel *Poe* (New York, 1959), p. 22.

[8] Wilbur, pp. 25, 31.

[9] Levin, *The Power of Blackness* (New York, 1960), p. 101. Roderick Usher, for example, one of Wilbur's exemplary dream-travelers, suffers characteristically from "a morbid acuteness of the senses" (III, 280).

the angels recognize such knowledge for what it is, the ultimate threat:

Oinos. But in this existence, I dreamed that I should be at once cognizant of all things, and thus at once be happy in being cognizant of all.

Agathos. Ah, not in knowledge is happiness, but in the acquisition of knowledge! In for ever knowing, we are for ever blessed; but to know all, were the curse of a fiend. (VI, 139)

In this double view of knowledge as at once desirable and deadly, this exchange poses the central dilemma for the artist who, like Poe, writes "with the *dénouement* constantly in view" (XIV, 193): man lives but for the end, in the end man lives no more. To conclude truly, then, is to preclude all pursuit, if indeed, as I have argued, narrative movement in Poe is bound up with the life of the soul. The remainder of this essay will examine the various strategies Poe adopted in his continuing attempts to deal with these problems of the soul's quest for final knowledge.

II

In his own uncanny way, in tale after tale, Poe managed to explore his sense of an ending while following to the letter his burlesque recipe for "a genuine Blackwood article of the sensation stamp." "Get yourself into such a scrape as no one ever got into before," he instructs, and report it with "the actual fact to bear you out," for "nothing so well assists the fancy, as an experimental knowledge of the matter in hand." The ending of such a story is both its point and its point of departure: "Should you ever be drowned or hung, be sure and make a note of your sensations" (II, 274). It is in Poe's angelic colloquies, however, rather than his tales in the *Blackwood* manner, that the aspirations of the "Marginalia" program receive their total, wishful fulfillment: here the novel sensations of life beyond the grave are reported *viva voce* by the angels themselves, obviating the mortal necessity of cataleptic fits, premature burials, bottled messages, and the like. The "psychal impressions" of the "Marginalia" passage become the substance for narrative in the colloquies; further, the same analogy between sleep and death obtains but reversed, death now understood as a kind of sleep. "The Colloquy of Monos and Una" provides an explicit and extended definition of the matter and the form of the root Poe story.

Una announces its theme when she tells Monos, recently arrived in the spirit world, that she burns "to know the incidents of your own passage through the dark Valley and Shadow" (IV, 201). The beginning of the soul's voyage is, she instructs, the beginning of what mortals term the end. The rise of a new "sixth" sense "from the wreck and the chaos of the usual senses" (IV, 209) marks the development of Monos's "weird narrative (IV, 201), "the first obvious and certain step of the intemporal soul upon the threshold of the temporal Eternity" (IV, 210). The unfolding of this novel mode of consciousness comes to its appointed climax with the revelation of the "secret" of Death, that the end is truly the beginning. Monos, like Una, has learned that death is not a barrier, "a check to human bliss—saying unto it 'thus far, and no farther,' " but an experience of regeneration; to know this is to be "born again" (IV, 200). There is, as Poe was to write in "The Power of Words," to be no end to the soul's *"thirst to know,"* which now stands revealed as its vital principle, the motive force of its immortal quest through an infinity of space, an eternity of time.

In "The Conversation of Eiros and Charmion," the root Poe story defined by Monos and Una is extended into an apocalyptic dimension, in which the end of the individual soul merges with the end of the world.[10] Eiros's account of his final days on earth, which recapitulates the plot of Monos's story phase by phase, is especially remarkable for his formulation of the end. Since some or all of its characteristics are to be found in many of Poe's endings, it may serve as the prototype for them all:

Let me be brief—brief as the ruin that overwhelmed. For a moment there was a wild lurid light alone, visiting and penetrating all things. Then let us bow down, Charmion, before the excessive majesty of the great God!—then, there came a shouting and pervading sound, as if from the mouth itself of HIM; while the whole incumbent mass of ether in which we existed, burst at once into a species of intense flame, for whose surpassing brilliancy and all-fervid heat even the angels in the high Heaven of pure knowledge have no name. Thus ended all.

[10] John Lynen writes, "For Poe the final catastrophe is implicit in all experience: the more an experience is understood, the more clearly it is seen in relation to universal history, the more, in consequence, emotion crystallizes into the terror of death, and the more the percipient's view approximates a vision of annihilation." *The Design of the Present: Essays on Time and Form in American Literature* (New Haven, 1969), p. 222.

The end is striking, first of all, in its brevity: the "inappreciable *point* of time" is but a point, and its rendering, consequently, must be highly concentrated. Second, the violence of the catastrophe is explicitly apocalyptic, "the entire fulfillment, in all their minute and terrible details, of the fiery and horror-inspiring denunciations of the prophecies of the Holy Book" (IV, 8). This ultimate moment is heralded by a sudden influx of light accompanied by an outpouring of sound, which Eiros has likened to the "voice of many waters" at the opening of his relation and which he now identifies as the voice of God himself. Poe invariably uses these motifs of light and sound to indicate the acceleration of history that brings the soul to the threshold of final knowledge: not merely is it to know all but specifically to know the end, which for Poe is itself the symbol of total knowledge. Finally, it is crucial that the Poe hero be in a position to witness the end *and to relate* the wonder of what he has seen. The ingenuity of Poe's solution to this problem in these narratives of Monos and Eiros is that the angelic stance permits the transcendence of the otherwise insuperable limitations of mortality (which seemed to say to Una, "thus far, and no farther"): from his privileged location beyond the veil, the hero as angel, "overburdened with the majesty of all things—of the unknown now known" (IV, 2), can utter the words which seal both the literary and the eschatological completion of the Poe story: "Thus ended all."

The angelic colloquies, however, fail by definition to offer a human solution to the pursuit of final knowledge; they do not provide for communication with the world of the living. In his pieces inspired by mesmerism, "A Tale of the Ragged Mountains," "Mesmeric Revelation," and "The Facts in the Case of M. Valdemar," Poe explores the riddle of final knowledge in terms of the human rather than the angelic condition. Mesmerism seemed to offer a means by which the barrier between the angelic and the mortal realms might be crossed by a living man. Poe values mesmeric revelation, in the piece with that title, precisely because it constitutes an anticipation of angelic experience, and the eschatological drift and the dialogue format of this narrative heighten its resemblance to the form and content of the angelic colloquies.[11] The ending of the tale makes

[11] The resemblance between "Mesmeric Revelation" and the "Marginalia" passage, between the mesmerist trance of the one and the dream-state of the other, is equally striking.

clear, however, that Poe, in his quest for final knowledge, required something more, finally, than either conversation with the living in a mesmerist trance or colloquies between the angels could offer. When "P" rouses his mesmerized subject at the last, the "sleep-waker" expires, his body assuming the condition ordinarily to be observed in the dead "only after long pressure from Azrael's hand. Had the sleep-waker, indeed, during the latter portion of his discourse, been addressing me from out the region of the shadows?" (V, 254). These final words of the story manifest the desire of the living for direct communication with those who have been truly dead; no mere similitude of death will do. Given the intransigence of this desire, nothing less would serve than a hero who could, like Lazarus, return from the dead to tell all, an old man of the Maleström, a Ligeia, and, as we shall see, an Arthur Gordon Pym.

"The Facts in the Case of M. Valdemar" show what mesmerism could and could not do to satisfy this need. In this last of his mesmerist fictions, Poe tortures the pseudo-science to extract the ultimate confession, producing what is surely the most grisly avatar of the Lazarus figure in all of Poe. As with "Berenice," however, the horror of this story, especially the loathsomeness of certain of its "facts," has worked to deny it the central place in the Poe canon which, from the nature of its concerns, it deserves. Allen Tate, though, has not allowed the matter of the tale to interfere with his keen perception of its significance. "All of Poe's characters," he writes, "represent one degree or another in a movement towards an archetypal condition: the survival of the soul in a dead body; but only in 'The Facts in the Case of M. Valdemar' is the obsessive subject explicit."[12] The narrator relates that his primary motive in his experiment with M. Valdemar, namely to mesmerize his subject *"in articulo mortis,"* was to arrest "the encroachments of Death" (VI, 155) for as long a period as possible, thus going one better than the dreamer of the "Marginalia" passage who could not prolong the point of his con-

---

The opening of the tale emphasizes man's power to induce visionary consciousness by an act of will and his power, subsequently, to effect the transfer of the preview of "the ultimate life" (V, 251) to mortal waking consciousness. In his letters Poe invites his correspondents to interpret "Mesmeric Revelation" as a statement of his own ideas. *The Letters of Edgar Allan Poe*, ed. John Ward Ostrom (Cambridge, Mass., 1948), I, 259–261, 273.

[12] "Our Cousin, Mr. Poe," in *Poe: A Collection of Critical Essays*, ed. Robert Regan (Englewood Cliffs, N.J., 1967), p. 42.

dition. The upshot of the experiment is that M. Valdemar, dying in the course of his trance, is privileged to relate, "I *have been* sleeping—and now—now—*I am dead*" (VI, 163).

The Lazarus-Valdemar figure, however, unlike the angel Monos, rarely presumes to give a more detailed account of his condition—for obvious reasons. If Poe valued the analogy between sleep and death operative in the mesmeric trance insofar as it permitted a preview of angelic experience, the premise of that angelic experience was, he argued, that death was but some sleep. But the case of M. Valdemar does not allow for the fiction—so important elsewhere—that the end is anything other than final. The extraordinary conclusion of the story reads as follows:

> As I rapidly made the mesmeric passes, amid ejaculations of "dead! dead!" absolutely *bursting* from the tongue and not from the lips of the sufferer, his whole frame at once—within the space of a single minute, or even less, shrunk—crumbled—absolutely *rotted* away beneath my hands. Upon the bed, before that whole company, there lay a nearly liquid mass of loathsome—of detestable putridity. (VI, 166)

It is death that speaks here, literally, and not some benign angelic condition in the disguise of transcendent sleep or dream. D. H. Lawrence knew that the quest of the Poe hero was doomed: "There is no end. There is only the rupture of death. That's where men, and women, are 'had.' Man is always sold, in his search for final KNOWLEDGE."[13] And it may well be that a large share of the horror with which Poe invites us to contemplate the facts in the case of M. Valdemar stems from his own reluctant if unshrinking recognition in this instance of the defeat of his ultimate aspiration. "Quoth the Raven, 'Nevermore.'"

III

Charles O'Donnell has captured the dilemma of the Poe hero's quest for final knowledge in an admirable formulation. Taking as his epigraph Hans Pfaall's determination "to depart, yet live—to leave the world, yet continue to exist," O'Donnell writes: "The question, then, is how the 'exciting knowledge,' the 'never-to-be-imparted secret, whose attainment is destruction,' can be gained with-

---

[13] Lawrence, p. 81.

out loss of identity."[14] In this regard the successful solution of the angelic colloquies is, finally, irrelevant to Poe's predicament. They fail to meet the requirements of the "Marginalia" program because they do not place supernal revelation within the grasp of mortal consciousness. Man becomes angel, man is no longer mortal man; the transfer of the "glimpse of the spirit's outer world," of the knowledge of "the gulf beyond," remains uneffected. Mesmerist trances, on the other hand, cherished for their preview of the soul's life beyond the grave, show finally as a dress rehearsal for a drama disastrous to enact: man is reduced to a "mass . . . of detestable putridity." In either case the challenge of the *Blackwood* formula remains unanswered. It was all very well to "get yourself into such a scrape as no one ever got into before," but in order to carry it off you had to get out as well, to survive to tell your tale to mortal men. The *Blackwood* formula was literally an all-or-nothing proposition, for to aspire to the knowledge of Monos was to risk the fate of M. Valdemar. There is, however, a considerable body of stories in which Poe, adopting what I have chosen to call a Lazarus plot, manages to provide for his hero's venture into the great unknown a round-trip ticket, steering a precarious middle course between death and immortality. I have selected "A Descent into the Maelström" and "Ligeia" as illustrations of the two principal varieties of Lazarus fictions in Poe, the tales of miraculous voyage in which the hero charts strange and unknown realms and the tales of the grave itself in which "the posthumous heroine"[15] descends into the mystery of the tomb and returns to the world of the living.

The opening of "A Descent into the Maelström" announces this story as a tale of the *Blackwood* stamp: "about three years past," the old man observes, "there happened to me an event such as never happened before to mortal man—or at least such as no man ever survived to tell of" (II, 225). As these words suggest, the old man's special destiny has made of him a man as rare as Lazarus, for the descent into the whirlpool is in fact a classic version of the drama of final experience in Poe. The preliminary manifestations of the old man's adventure present the familiar cluster of motifs that Poe invariably employs to signal the imminence of the end. A violent

[14] "From Earth to Ether: Poe's Flight into Space," *PMLA*, LXXVII (March, 1962), 85.
[15] Levin, p. 156.

acceleration in the speed of his fishing-boat throws him to the deck, and a sudden influx of light and outpouring of sound usher in the "singular change" (II, 237) that follows. Discovering that his watch has run down, he flings it into the ocean, for he has reached the end of time, poised, apocalyptically, between one world and the next. His account of his state of mind here on the threshold of the Maelström expresses precisely the ambition to know all and yet survive that Poe's Lazarus fictions are designed to gratify: "I positively felt a *wish* to explore its depths, even at the sacrifice I was going to make; and my principal grief was that I should never be able to tell my old companions on shore about the mysteries I should see" (II, 240). Rushing "headlong into the abyss," the old man crosses intact the barrier that seemed to stand between him and the secrets of "the gulf beyond": "I still lived" (II, 241). The ensuing imagery of revelation overwhelms him with its sublimity as he beholds with "awe, horror, and admiration" "the rays of the full moon" that "streamed in a flood of golden glory along the black walls, and far away down into the inmost recesses of the abyss" (II, 242). This vision of the ultimate dimension transforms him and it is in his new guise as one of Poe's elect, returned from the grave, that he is rescued at the last: "Those who drew me on board were my old mates and daily companions—but they knew me no more than they would have known a traveller from the spirit-land" (II, 247).

It is in the elaborate narrative frame, to which Poe devotes the first third of the tale, that the significance of the contrast between the sublime Lazarus and the ordinary mortal is made clear. The old man himself insists on the importance of the frame, leading the narrator to the top of a cliff overlooking the Maelström in order to tell him "the whole story with the spot just under your eye" (II, 226). When the narrator presently beholds the whirlpool as it takes shape and throws himself on the ground in the prone and clinging posture which the old man will assume on board the boat in his story, it becomes clear that he is reenacting in the frame situation an experience of the end that closely resembles that of the old man himself.[16] For all these carefully worked-out parallels between the nar-

[16] "The wild bewildering sense of *the novel*" which confounds the narrator as he beholds the Maelström here is invariably the hallmark of final experience in Poe: "The mountain trembled to its very base, and the rock rocked." Interestingly, he identifies the impact of "the magnificence" and "the horror" which this scene inspires as an experience

rator and the old man, however, the fundamental difference between their experiences is decisive. The narrator recoils from the brink, desirous of full knowledge yet fearful, while the old man willingly plunges over the rim to get to the bottom of it all. The narrator, as I think Poe would have us see, is what men mostly are, and the old man what men dream of being.

Even as "A Descent into the Maelström" would seem to offer the satisfaction of transcending mortal limitations, it reasserts them, for the old man's experience of the end is, in fact, strangely inconclusive. First, his initial headlong rush into the abyss proves to be only the prelude to a second and final plunge that apparently awaits all things in the whirlpool at the bottom. Then, as to the revelation itself, even though he beholds the very bottom of the gulf, his vision is incomplete: "I could make out nothing distinctly, on account of a thick mist in which everything there was enveloped" (II, 243). Endings following endings, revelations withheld in revelations granted—man's mortal limitations abide for all the ingenious doubling of final experience in the story and its frame. Poe must content himself with the fact of the old man's return in place of the final revelation finally deferred. The old man returns *as though* he were "a traveller from the spirit-land," *as though* he descended to the bottom of the abyss, whereas only his unfortunate brother, no Lazarus he, did that and was heard from no more.

The kinship of the Lady Ligeia with the old man of the Maelström will be immediately obvious, for she is what he had merely seemed, "a traveller from the spirit-land." The dying Ligeia, in "her wild desire for life,—for life—*but* for life" (II, 255), aspires to conquer "the Conqueror Worm" (II, 257), and she succeeds. She dies, only to rise once more, a monument to the vigor of the will, to man's refusal to yield himself—in the words from Joseph Glanvill ever on her lips—"unto death utterly." The narrative frame in "Ligeia" is even more elaborate than in "A Descent into the Maelström," and makes an analogous contribution to narrative design. In both tales the frame doubles thematically and structurally the story it surrounds; the result is an obsessive reenactment of the

---

of the American sublime, comparing the sudden outpouring of sound to "the moaning of a vast herd of buffaloes upon an American prairie," "an appalling voice, half shriek, half roar, such as not even the mightly cataract of Niagara ever lifts up in its agony to Heaven" (II, 228–229). In Poe's sense of an ending the novel and the sublime are frequently linked.

paradigm of final experience, of the moment in which all knowledge is to be revealed. Thus the drama of recollection in the first part of "Ligeia," the narrator's attempt to "bring before mine eyes in fancy the image of her who is no more" (II, 249), becomes no less than a literal calling back in the second part: "I would call aloud upon her name . . . as if, through the wild eagerness, the solemn passion, the consuming ardor of my longing for the departed, I could restore her to the pathway she had abandoned—ah, *could* it be for ever?— upon the earth" (II, 261).

To examine the narrator's preoccupation with the image of Ligeia, however, is to recognize that his drive to recall her is not merely the counterpart of her ambition to triumph over death but the expression as well of his own desire for ultimate knowledge. "The beauty of beings either above or apart from the earth" is, he believes, incarnate in her, and she functions, accordingly, as the medium for his aspiration to transcend his "ignorance of so much of the spiritual" (II, 251). Standing in her presence he beholds the promise of the angelic condition, "that delicious vista by slow degrees expanding before me, down whose long, gorgeous, and all untrodden path, I might at length pass onward to the goal of a wisdom too divinely precious not to be forbidden!" (II, 254). Since it is, above all, in "the *expression*" of Ligeia's eyes that the riddle of the universe resides, they become the narrator's fixation. He reports that their special aura of significance is peculiarly noticeable "in moments of intense excitement" (II, 251) (his or her own?), and, further, that this excitement betrays the intensity of her "gigantic volition," accompanied as it is by her "wild words" (II, 253) which express the urgency of her determination to master her mortality. The same passage from Glanvill on the will links the meaning of Ligeia's eyes with the meaning of her words, confirming the twinship of the narrator's quest and that of his beloved.

This likeness is instructive. If the "Marginalia" passage, in its description of the entry into and withdrawal from special states of mind, contains the latent germ of the tales of the miraculous voyage and "the posthumous heroine," conversely, such journeys into the unknown, into the grave, are always, finally, properly regarded as an objectification of a drama of consciousness. The metaphoric nature of the Lazarus plot in Poe is nowhere more clearly set forth than in the parallel relationship between the narrator and Ligeia. Further, the figure adopted by the narrator to dramatize the ebb and flow of his consciousness in its meditations on Ligeia bears this out:

There is no point, among the many incomprehensible anomalies of the science of mind, more thrillingly exciting than the fact—never, I believe, noticed in the schools—that in our endeavors to recall to memory something long forgotten, we often find ourselves *upon the very verge* of remembrance, without being able, in the end, to remember. And thus how frequently, in my intense scrutiny of Ligeia's eyes, have I felt approaching the full knowledge of their expression—felt it approaching—yet not quite be mine—and so at length entirely depart!

The loss and recovery of the image mirrors the departure and return of the beloved. "*Upon the very verge*"—this is the critical posture of the Lazarus figure in Poe. Ligeia's "large and luminous orbs" (II, 252) are to the narrator what the whirlpool is to the old man of the Maelström, a symbol of the ultimate significance.[17] As the eyes of Ligeia slowly open at the close of the story, the narrator is restored to his longed-for contemplation of the Alpha and the Omega; the departed spirit has returned, the lost image has been recaptured.

In a revealing exchange of letters with Philip Pendleton Cooke about "Ligeia," Poe offered a criticism of the ending which sets the twin Lazarus quests of the tale in a new perspective. "One point I have not fully carried out—I should have intimated that the *will* did not perfect its intention—there should have been a relapse—a final one—and Ligeia (who had only succeeded in so much as to convey an idea of the truth to the narrator) should be at length entombed as Rowena—the bodily alterations having gradually faded away" (XVII, 52). In the face of his opportunity to allow the ambitions of the "Marginalia" program to succeed, I would argue, Poe decided not to let on that "the *will* did not perfect its intention." In any case, Poe's comment, which points up the ambiguity of Ligeia's

[17] Wilbur points up the connection between the two stories, noting that the same lines from Joseph Glanvill which Poe has the narrator associate with the mystery of Ligeia's eyes serve as the epigraph for "A Descent into the Maelström." He argues, further, that the similarity of the endings of the two narratives (whirling movement and plunge) confirms his view that they are, in effect, parallel versions of the familiar dream-journey in so much of Poe's fiction. "Edgar Allan Poe," in *Major Writers of America*, ed. Perry Miller (New York, 1962), pp. 375-376, 379.

apparent triumph at the last, applies with equal justice to the narrator's success as well. Even though—*mirabile dictu*—he beholds Ligeia's eyes once more, the content of his symbolic experience of revelation remains, finally, as inscrutable as "the very bottom" of the Maelström wrapped in mist. "What was it—that something more profound than the well of Democritus—which lay far within the pupils of my beloved?" (II, 251). The answer to the question of questions is never disclosed.

The power of Poe's dream-glimpses of "the spirit's outer world" in stories like "Ligeia" and "A Descent into the Maelström" resides in his conception of a miraculous traveller who has made the journey of Lazarus. The narrator's contemplation of Poe's Lazarus hero promises a symbolic transfer of final knowledge, for as the one looks upon the other's face he shares that sense of the unutterable sublime with which the Lazarus himself beholds "the inmost recesses of the abyss." Promises, moreover, are easier to make than keep: the evocation of the wondrous appearance of this "traveller from the spirit-land" is surely more compelling than any attempted exposition of the great secret that has made him what he is. In this way Poe could make this figure larger-than-life attain the unattainable, mediating between mortal man and the annihilating splendors of the angels' final knowledge. That is to say that our willingness to assent to the possibility of the triumph over death depends precisely upon the distance between the Lazarus and the narrator in these tales. Make them one and the same individual and he must be both man and superman. Maintain a separation between them and obviate an otherwise impossible task of character integration, one which, as we shall see, was to cause Poe so much trouble in the case of Arthur Gordon Pym.

IV

So completely realized is Poe's pretense that Arthur Gordon Pym's narrative is incomplete that many unreflecting readers have been content to assume that Poe's story is unfinished as well, that Poe had more work to do and that he left that work undone. Given the logic of this misconception, it was probably inevitable that someone would eventually presume to write the rest of the story, and Jules Verne obliged with a lengthy sequel, *Le Sphinx des*

Glaces, in 1897. Given Poe's strategies for ending his tales, however, there is every indication that *The Narrative of Arthur Gordon Pym* is a completed fiction.

In the last chapter, once Poe has set his hero and his friend, Dirk Peters, together with their captive, the savage Nu-Nu, adrift "in the wide and desolate Antarctic Ocean... in a frail canoe" (III, 236), he signals the approaching end of the story in his customary fashion. In his first dated entry in many a chapter Pym himself stresses the point of transition: "Many unusual phenomena now indicated that we were entering upon a region of novelty and wonder" (III, 238). There is a "rapid change" (III, 239) in the color and temperature of the water, and the southerly current suddenly takes on a "hideous velocity," carrying the canoe inexorably toward "a limitless cataract, rolling silently into the sea from some immense and far-distant rampart in the heaven" (III, 241). "Rushing and mighty, but soundless" winds arise. The ebbing life of Pym and Peters, the death of Nu-Nu, the prophetic cries of the birds "from beyond the veil"— all confirm that Pym and his companions have reached the boundary between this world and the next. Not content to mark the advent of revelation by despatching his hero headlong into the abyss, Poe boldly supplies an image of the revelation itself: "And now we rushed into the embraces of the cataract, where a chasm threw itself open to receive us. But there arose in our pathway a shrouded human figure, very far larger in its proportions than any dweller among men. And the hue of the skin of the figure was of the perfect whiteness of the snow" (III, 242). Here final knowledge is confronted directly in the mysterious white figure rather than at one remove in the person of the Lazarus hero who has looked upon it.[18] Here Pym's narrative concludes, but Poe lets on instead that is has been merely interrupted, that the end is not the end.

The lengthy editorial note to the ending proper announces that

[18] Or does the white figure belong in the company of the ancient captain of "MS. Found in a Bottle," Ligeia, and the old man of the Maelström? Is it Poe's most literal avatar of the heroic seeker after final knowledge who must by definition be larger-than-life? Either way, I would hazard a guess that the portentous image of the colossal white figure has been remembered not so much for any intrinsic power of its own but because Poe was willing to deliver anything at all in a context that requires satisfaction of all our final expectations. Henry James was right, after all, in his conviction that the only successful strategy for the presentation of the supernatural in fiction is that of indirection: "prodigies, when they come straight, come with an effect imperilled; they keep all their character, on the other hand, by looming through some other history" (*Altar*, p. xix).

Pym survived his ordeal and returned from the end of the world with knowledge of "the Pole itself, or at least to regions in its very near proximity." Lazarus lived to tell his tale—but the man and the "two or three final chapters" of his story were destroyed in an unfortunate accident following his safe return. And then, as if "to fill the vacuum" (III, 243) left by the "missing" chapters and their account, presumably, of the world "beyond the veil," the note proceeds to decipher the mysterious *"indentures"* that Pym encountered in his wanderings on the island of Tsalal. In the light of the apocalyptic utterance of the final line of the note, which reads, "*I have graven it within the hills, and my vengeance upon the dust within the rock*" (III, 245), the decoded message about "the region of the south" purports to be nothing less than revelation divine.

Pym survived—but he died. The key to the mystery is lost—but here it is. Clearly we are in the presence of an elaborate sleight-of-hand, designed to establish Pym's extraordinary adventure as a genuine Lazarus fiction. The balance of recent critical opinion, however, emphatically rejects the editorial note and its instructions for the interpretation of Pym's narrative. Thus J. V. Ridgely and Iola S. Haverstick observe, "the 'Note' remains a curious, almost contemptuous, treatment of the credulity of the reader." Their piece on *Pym*, a massively documented and carefully researched investigation of the vicissitudes of the writing of the tale, brings to a culmination the lively interest in this subject in recent years. While their account of the facts is unlikely to be superseded, their sense of the fits and starts of Poe's composition of the story has led them, strangely, to the position that the story cannot be interpreted. "Serious meaning" for them is contingent upon structural unity, and this, they believe, they have definitively discredited.[19] Grant their contention—which seems quite likely—that Poe either lacked a plan for the whole narrative at the outset or that he shifted from one plan to another as he went along, grant that the resultant shifts and discrepancies in the unfolding of the narrative line with which they are concerned are distracting, their researches, nevertheless, can do nothing to set aside

[19] "Chartless Voyage: The Many Narratives of Arthur Gordon Pym," *Texas Studies in Literature and Language*, VIII (Spring, 1966), 63–80. For earlier treatments, see Sidney P. Moss, "*Arthur Gordon Pym*, or the Fallacy of Thematic Interpretation," *University Review*, XXXIII (June, 1967), 299–306, and L. Moffitt Cecil, "The Two Narratives of Arthur Gordon Pym," *Texas Studies in Literature and Language*, V (Summer, 1963), 232–241.

the fact that most readers of *Pym* are struck by the presence of consistently repeated pattern in each of the various parts of the story. They usually arrive at the same sense of narrative divisions as a series of voyages, beginning with the excursion of the *Ariel*, continuing with the major journeys of the *Grampus* and the *Jane Guy*, and concluding with the drift of the frail Tsalalian canoe.[20] Further, the repetitiveness of certain features in each of these situations has usually led to talk of symmetry or parallelism as a structural principle of the narrative as a whole.[21]

Now the upshot of the editorial note is an argument in favor of narrative design: although Pym's narrative seems to be incomplete, it is based on a completed manuscript unfortunately lost; the apparently meaningless "figures" of the chasms on the island of Tsalal have a meaning after all, "especially when taken in connection with statements made in the body of the narrative" (III, 244). Sidney Kaplan, for one, has interpreted these figures literally, with that "minute philological scrutiny" (III, 245) the note prescribes. Translating the message that they spell in ancient letters as a key to the concluding portions of *Pym,* he reads in Pym's adventures on Tsalal a fundamentalist allegory on race which damns the black man to the end of time.[22] This is not, however, what the figures signify when they are first encountered in the text. Only one of the series bears "some little resemblance to alphabetical characters" (III, 225); the others denote the course of Pym's wanderings in the labyrinthine chasms. That is to say that Poe establishes the figures in the text itself as symbols of the shape of Pym's experience, the configuration made by the path of the embattled self as it moves tortuously through a threatening nature. Thus the dual angle of vision permitted by text and note allows the figures to function both allegorically and symbolically, allegorically (as Kaplan persuades) in the sequence on Tsalal, symbolically in the narrative as a whole. The figures are at once the letters of ancient alphabets and the characters of a primordial language of experience, "the awful Chaldee," as it were, "of the Sperm Whale's brow." If we are to learn this second language, in the belief that the meaning of Pym's adventures is in

[20] E.g., Bezanson, p. 152.
[21] E.g., Levin, p. 114; O'Donnell, p. 89.
[22] "An Introduction to *Pym*," in Regan, pp. 145–163.

some fundamental way expressed in the very shape of his experience itself, it is to the pattern of the adventures and to the strategies of fiction devoted to the creation of such patterns, rather than to the "editor's" fancy show of Ethiopian, Arabic, and Egyptian, that we must turn.

Pym's initial adventure, his madcap, nearly fatal, escapade with his friend Augustus on board the *Ariel*, offers a paradigm for all that follows: the approach to a seemingly inevitable death followed by a miraculous return to life. Pym tastes the zenith and the nadir of sensation in brief compass when the two young men, intoxicated with drink and power, embark in a gale at night; for the intensity of heightened consciousness, that ecstasy which man's capacity to attain the ultimate reach of experience inspires, and the numbness of insensibility when this "mental energy" gives way, are always yoked in Poe, who would live the life of the dead. Poe resuscitates Pym "from a state bordering very nearly upon death" (III, 16) in the aftermath of the wreck of the *Ariel* only to restore him to it at greater length in the episode that follows. Buried alive in an iron-bound box in the labyrinthine hold of the *Grampus*, Pym is subjected to cycle after punishing cycle of the loss and recovery of consciousness as hunger, thirst, and suffocation push him over the edge of sanity into nightmare and impending annihilation. "Those only who have been suddenly redeemed from the jaws of the tomb" (III, 46) possess the knowledge that is his upon his rescue.

From this point forward in the narrative Poe pursues a systematic exploration of every imaginable form of human extremity: what counts is the isolated consciousness and its sensations in the face of the ultimate calamity. True child of *Blackwood's*, Pym identifies himself at the outset as the melancholy man whose imaginative life is consecrated to visions of death and disaster. The urgency of his sense of an ending, which functions, somewhat paradoxically, as the vital principle of his existence, is most strikingly displayed in the celebrated passage of his penultimate plunge, his *"longing to fall"* (III, 230) into the Tsalalian abyss. This central fact of Pym's character governs the design of Poe's fiction; the hero and his author collaborate to act it out at the expense of narrative itself, for no single story can suffice but rather a seemingly endless series of tales that constitute a tale without an end. Thus Poe's strategies are designed to repeat Pym's longed-for confrontation with the end, and each new situation is reduced accordingly to fit this final shape. Again and again Poe engages in a deliberate and relentless sabotage of his cast of characters and the settings they inhabit, moving Pym closer and closer to zero, to the void. The men drop like flies in the mutiny, the storm leaves the ship only a drifting hulk; hunger, thirst, and cannibalism do the rest. Once the ship and the crew have been sacrificed to satisfy Pym's—and Poe's—voracious appetite for disaster, Poe's recourse is simple: take up another ship, another crew. Predictably, the crew of the *Jane Guy* (except, of course, Pym and his friend Peters) and the ship itself are destined to be utterly destroyed in the most explicitly apocalyyptic of the many endings of *Pym*. When the ambushed crew is buried alive in the treacherous chasms of Tsalal, the shock of the concussion suggests to Pym "that the whole foundations of the solid globe were suddenly rent asunder, and that the day of universal dissolution was at hand" (III, 203). Plunged into "the blackness of darkness," Pym shares as so many times before "the allotted portion of *the dead*" (III, 205).

Pym even has occasion, disguising himself as the corpse of Rogers (in the midst of the *Grampus* sequence), to act out literally what is, symbolically, his role in each experience first and last, that of Lazarus-Valdemar. Indeed the horrible events that follow this grim and premonitory impersonation bring home to Arthur Gordon Pym the gruesome fact of the case of M. Valdemar. First he beholds the dead on board a drifting ship in "the last and most loathsome state of putrefaction" (III, 112) and presently he is himself to feed on the corpse of the luckless Parker. In these scenes of cannibalism Poe keeps coming back to a central problem of the *Blackwood*-Lazarus genre: if sensations *are* the great things after all, how is man to achieve an experimental knowledge of the secret places of the mind, to surrender to the forbidden drives that lie beneath the surface of rational consciousness, without sacrificing the power to know which reason confers? how to be drowned or hung and to make a note of one's sensations all at once? This is the fundamental difficulty of the first-person Lazarus hero which Poe so wisely avoided, for example, in "Ligeia" and "The Fall of the House of Usher." It is Pym's greater reserves of "mental energy," Poe would have us believe, that distinguish him from his friends: he must share and not share in the extremities of their common condition, going with them all of the horrible way while holding back, "retaining my powers of mind in a surprising degree, while the rest were completely prostrated in intellect" (III, 120). This dilemma is never resolved, and the form of the tale dramatizes the fundamental equivocation: the "fact" of the published narrative confirms that Pym did not yield himself unto death utterly; the fiction of its incompleteness, that he did.

Is Poe's treatment irresponsible or, worse, insulting, or does he give us a haunting double view of the possibilities of his hero's Lazarus quest? To recognize the presence of an equivocation on so central an issue as this is to confront the question of the meaning of Pym's experiences once and for all. If the diagrams of the chasms of Tsalal may be taken to represent the shape of Pym's experience, and if this shape is invariably that of an ending obsessively reenacted in each and every episode of this episodic narrative, has this shape any significance at all? Poe's presentation of the figures themselves provides a clue, for it shares in the very doubleness that I take them to symbolize. For Pym's "editor," stationed as he is at a privileged, indeed "angelic," vantage point looking down on the chasms from above, the figures have a meaning, they spell out a message. Pym's position in the earth, however, his stance within the figures, does not permit transcendence; he inhabits a significance that he fails to fathom.

The reader who would press such experience for greater certitude is certain to encounter a critical ambivalence at its very core, for the double ending of this tale states baldly what the more richly ambiguous "Ligeia" and "A Descent into the Maelström" imply, that Poe's attitude toward the experience of meaning is divided. Taking the text and the note together, the conclusion of *Pym* presents in a single extravagant and contradictory package the range of possible endings devised by Poe: either the hero is arrested in tantalizing proximity at the very threshold of revelation, as in "MS. Found in a Bottle" or "The Man of the Crowd"; or he attains the vision of "the spirit's outer world" and returns transfigured to the world of the living, like Ligeia or the old man of the Maelström: sometimes even the revelation itself is supplied, as in the angelic colloquies or the transcripts of mesmerist trances. Of these alternatives in the case of Pym, it is to the first that the imagination most readily assents for reasons which some consideration of the psychology of endings will supply. First, we want to believe that we could know all, but the urgency of our wanting is directly proportionate to our conviction of the impossibility of our knowing. Second, we believe that the knowledge we seek is by its very nature incommunicable, hence any translation of the ineffable into the language of the tribe could only prove unsatisfactory. Thus we prefer our Lazarus at one remove to the too-familiar Pym, better the sublimity of a figure rare and strange, resplendent with the aura of last things beheld but unspoken, than the inevitable banality of an editor's intrusive explication.

The equivocation, then, of the double ending of *Pym* does not cast the existence of meaning in doubt but rather man's capacity to apprehend it. Surely the recent tendency to identify the tale as an existentialist or even absurdist work is mistaken.[23] Whether Poe's endings take the hero to the brink of the abyss or plunge him into the gulf beyond, they all confirm that Poe and his heroes believe in a significant universe; they believe in its buried treasure and they dream of the man who could find it out and cry "Eureka!" to an astonished world. If the equivocation of *Pym* does not serve to make Poe our contemporary, it does assist us in placing him among his own, serving at once to align him with and to distinguish him from writers like Melville and Hawthorne. Their seekers, it is true, share the Poe hero's lust for final knowledge—Dimmesdale in his midnight fantasy of a Last Judgment when the dark problem of this life shall be made plain, Ahab in his determination to strike through the mask and read the riddle of the universe in a single blow—but the ecstasy of apocalyptic vision shows in such as these as a monstrous egotism, a monomaniac delusion. For each the moment of truth is veiled in ambiguity, displaced by the fact of death: Dimmesdale's final noon serves only to illuminate the confusion of the crowd while Ahab, neither destroyer nor destroyed, disappears forever in the tangle of his line. Poe, on the other hand, as the in-

---

[23] Helen Lee's conclusion, in "Possibilities of *Pym*," *English Journal*, LV (Dec., 1966), 1149–1154, is characteristic: "With exquisite irony [Poe] uses artistic pattern to demonstrate his theme that life has no pattern" (p. 1154). See also D. E. S. Maxwell, "Poe and the Romantic Experiment," *American Fiction: The Intellectual Background* (New York, 1965), p. 94.

genuity of his Lazarus fictions attests, was willing to go to any length to indulge his hero in his quest, which was, after all, an intimate parallel to his own "Marginalia" program.

What the equivocation of *Pym* reveals, finally, is that Poe in pushing his hero to the limits of experience was pushing himself to the limits of fiction as well. While we would surrender to the sublime bravado of the headlong plunge into the abyss, Poe compels us most when we linger upon the very verge. The epigraph from Joseph Glanvill that heads "A Descent into the Maelström" may serve as an epitaph to Poe's daring attempts to construct a fiction commensurate to final knowledge: "The ways of God in Nature, as in Providence, are not as *our* ways; nor are the models that we frame in any way commensurate to the vastness, profundity, and unsearchableness of His works, *which have a depth in them greater than the well of Democritus*" (II, 225).

The Limits of Reason: Poe's Deluded Detectives

J. Gerald Kennedy

IN A CANON OF FICTION preponderantly devoted to terror, madness, disease, death, and revivification, Poe's tales of ratiocination provide a revealing counterpoint in their idealization of reason and sanity. During the productive years 1841-44, Poe explored the theme of rational analysis in various ways: the three adventures of C. Auguste Dupin—"The Murders in the Rue Morgue" (1841), "The Mystery of Marie Rogêt" (1842-43), and "The Purloined Letter" (1844)—established the prototype of the modern detective story by focusing on the investigative methods of a master sleuth. Ratiocination led William Legrand to buried treasure in "The Gold Bug" (1843) and enabled the narrator of " 'Thou Art the Man' " (1844) to solve a backwoods murder; analytical operations figured less prominently in "A Descent into the Maelström" (1841) and "A Tale of the Ragged Mountains" (1844). But publication of "The Purloined Letter" marked the last of Poe's investigative fiction; none of the tales after 1844 returned to the subject of ratiocination. Two basic questions to be considered here, then, are why Poe initially became interested in the detective story, and why, after the technical achievement of "The Purloined Letter," he abandoned the genre, reverting to the familiar materials of horror and the grotesque.

The significance of Poe's ratiocinative phase can perhaps be best understood in the context of his broader thematic concerns. The search for the figure in Poe's fictional carpet has produced myriad interpretations: Patrick F. Quinn has termed the Doppelgänger motif the "most characteristic and persistent" of Poe's fantasies, while Edward H. Davidson states that the "central bifurcation" in Poe lies between "two sides of the self, between emotion and intellect, feeling and the mind." Harry Levin sees the essential Poe hero as an "underground man" embodying "reason in madness," while more recently, Daniel Hoffman has identified "duplicity" or "the doubleness of experience" as Poe's chief theme.[1] Behind the evident

---
[1] Quinn, *The French Face of Edgar Poe* (Carbondale, Ill., 1957), p. 197; Davidson, *Poe: A Critical Study* (Cambridge, Mass., 1957), p. 259; Levin, *The Power of Blackness* (New York, 1958), p. 164; Hoffman, *Poe Poe Poe Poe Poe Poe Poe* (Garden City, N. Y., 1972), p. 210.

diversity of opinion about Poe's fundamental fictional concerns looms a point of focus: the author's preoccupation with the relationship between the mind, or rational consciousness, and the sensational influence of the world beyond the self. Constantly in Poe's fiction irrational forces and inexplicable phenomena threaten "the monarch Thought's dominion." In an important sense, his serious tales return continually to the process of reason—the way in which the mind orders and interprets its perceptions. Poe's narrators repeatedly seek a clarification of experience, only to discover, in the tales of terror, that rational explanation is not possible.

The condition of terror and uncertainty does not obtain, however, in the tales of ratiocination. Joseph Wood Krutch once lapsed into the assertion that "Poe invented the detective story in order that he might not go mad."[2] The biographical fallacy aside, however, it is true that the ratiocinative tales posit a vision of reason and order not elsewhere evident in Poe's fiction. His detective hero, engaged in "that moral activity which *disentangles*,"[3] not only restores law and order to the world of mundane human affairs; he also explains the seemingly inexplicable, thereby demonstrating the ultimate comprehensibility of the world beyond the self. While the Gothic protagonist typically succumbs to a paroxysm of fear, uncertainty, or madness, the ratiocinator discerns the causes behind effects, proving that nature's laws are accessible to the man of reason. The emergence of this man of reason and his eventual disappearance from Poe's fiction can be observed in "The Man of the Crowd" (1840) and "The Oblong Box" (1844), tales which respectively signal the beginning and end of Poe's ratiocinative cycle.

I

Though it is impossible to determine the origin of Poe's ratiocinative interests (his 1835 essay on "Maelzel's Chess-Player" reveals an early analytical bent), the appearance of nine "Unpublished Passages from the Life of Vidocq, the French Minister of Police" in *Burton's Gentleman's Magazine* (Sept., 1838–May, 1839) likely helped to stimulate his curiosity about the investigation of crime. According to Valentine Williams, Vidocq was Poe's "fount of in-

[2] *Edgar Allan Poe: A Study in Genius* (New York, 1926), p. 118.
[3] "The Murders in the Rue Morgue," *The Complete Works of Edgar Allan Poe*, ed. James A. Harrison (New York, 1902), IV, 146. All subsequent page references to Poe's tales are to the Harrison edition.

spiration"[1]; and if Poe had not already read Vidocq's *Mémoires* in the 1828 translation of George Borrow, he surely saw the instalments in the *Gentleman's Magazine* (of which he became editor in June, 1839). Poe's onerous duties with the magazine apparently hindered his fictional efforts, for after the splendid narratives of the late thirties—"Ligeia," "The Fall of the House of Usher," and "William Wilson"—the first tales of the new decade showed little imagination.[5] However "The Man of the Crowd," the first tale published after Poe's break with Burton, gave evidence of both renewed intensity and a developing fascination with what Poe later called "the principles of investigation."[6]

Long one of Poe's most perplexing tales, "The Man of the Crowd" presents, outwardly at least, another version of the Doppelgänger motif employed in "William Wilson." Yet the theme of the double is inverted significantly: rather than flee his malevolent counterpart, the narrator of "The Man of the Crowd" actively pursues his double, seeking knowledge of the man's inner nature through a detective-like scrutiny of his outward appearance and behavior. Critical interpretation of the tale has dealt primarily with the symbolic importance of the aged peripatetic: Quinn terms the stranger a "prophetic image" of the narrator's "future self," while Davidson argues that he represents "man's abandonment of the moral prescription within which he is supposed to live." Herbert Rauter in turn links the old man to the idea of disintegration, identifying him as one of Poe's *"ruhelosen Wanderern zwischen Leben und Tod."*[7] But critical emphasis on the significance of the stranger has perhaps obscured the real conflict in the tale: the psychological tension between the narrator's detached, analytical view of human experience and his mounting subjective fascination with the "man of the crowd."

[4] "The Detective in Fiction," *Fortnightly Review*, CXXXIV (Sept. 1, 1930), 384.

[5] "Why the Little Frenchman Wears His Hand in a Sling" and "The Business Man" at best represent witty hack work. "The Journal of Julius Rodman," published serially from January to June in the *Gentleman's Magazine*, exploits the vogue for travel writing by lifting material from earlier narratives. See Stuart Levine, "Poe's *Julius Rodman*: Judaism, Plagiarism, and the Wild West," *Midwest Quarterly*, I (Spring, 1959), 245-259. John J. Teunissen and Evelyn J. Hinz argue that the work has redeeming parodic elements in "Poe's *Journal of Julius Rodman* as Parody," *Nineteenth-Century Fiction*, XXVII (December, 1972), 317-338.

[6] Letter to Joseph Evans Snodgrass, June 4, 1842, *The Letters of Edgar Allan Poe*, ed. John Ward Ostrom (Cambridge, Mass., 1948), I, 202.

[7] *The French Face of Edgar Poe*, p. 230; *Poe: A Critical Study*, pp. 190-191; "Edgar Allan Poes 'The Man of the Crowd,'" *Neueren Sprachen*, N. S. XI (Nov., 1962), 504.

As the tale immediately preceding "The Murders in the Rue Morgue," "The Man of the Crowd" stands as a transitional work between the haunting Gothic tales of the late thirties and the ratiocinative fiction of the early forties, possessing obvious qualities of both. The opening paragraphs portray a narrator suffering, like many of Poe's characters, from an indefinable mental excitation. Recovering from an unspecified illness, he derives a febrile pleasure "even from many of the legitimate sources of pain" (IV, 135), and though his mind is literally working at a fever pitch, he compares his heightened awareness to "the vivid yet candid reason of Leibnitz," the German philosopher whose vision of a rationally designed universe of cause and effect was satirized (as Poe punningly reminds us) in Voltaire's *Candide*. The narrator appropriately identifies himself with the Enlightenment tradition, for he too seeks a rational, scientific clarification of experience. Analyzing pedestrians passing before the window of a London coffeehouse, he remarks, "At first my observations took an abstract and generalizing turn. I looked at the passengers in masses, and thought of them in their aggregate relations. Soon, however, I descended to details, and regarded with minute interest the innumerable varieties of figure, dress, air, gait, visage, and expression of countenance" (IV, 135). Much like Sherlock Holmes, Poe's narrator infers from precise observation the occupations of passersby; for example, the "upper clerks of staunch firms" are known "by their coats and pantaloons of black or brown, made to sit comfortably, with white cravats and waistcoats, broad solid-looking shoes, and thick hose or gaiters.— They had all slightly bald heads, from which the right ears, long used to pen-holding, had an odd habit of standing off on end.... They always removed or settled their hats with both hands, and wore watches, with short gold chains of a substantial and ancient pattern" (IV, 136–37).

Belief in his perceptiveness tempts the narrator to a more dramatic claim: "In my then peculiar mental state, I could frequently read, even in that brief interval of a glance, the history of long years" (IV, 139)—anticipating Dupin's boast in "The Murders in the Rue Morgue" that "most men, in respect to himself, wore windows in their bosoms" (IV, 152). But the narrator of "The Man of the Crowd" is no Dupin. The narrative in fact disproves his claim that he can "read" men's lives, a circumstance foreshadowed in the opening lines: "It was well said of a certain German book that 'es lässt sich nicht lesen'—it does not permit itself to be read. There are some secrets which do not permit themselves to be told" (IV, 134). In a key essay, James W. Gargano notes that Poe "often so designs his tales as to show his narrators' limited comprehension of their own problems and states of mind."[8] The ironic structure Gargano finds in tales like "Ligeia" and "The Tell-Tale Heart" also appears to inform "The Man of the Crowd," where the narrator, a would-be detective, essentially demonstrates his failure to grasp the "principles of investigation" later used by Dupin.

This failure occurs primarily because the narrator cannot maintain a critical detachment; he confesses, "As the night deepened, so deepened to me the interest of the scene" (IV, 139). The transformation of the crowd, whose "gentler features" give way to "harsher ones," corresponds to a subtle shift in the narrator's attitude from dispassionate objectivity to subjective fascination. By his own admission, the "wild effects" of the gas lamps have "enchained" him to "an examination of individual faces." Gradually fancy subverts abstract reason. Like many of Poe's Gothic protagonists, he falls under the influence of vague sensations; the rational mode of cognition is steadily undermined by irrational impulses. In such a state he glimpses the face of the old man, significantly regarding it in imaginative rather than analytical terms: "I well remember that my first thought, upon beholding it, was that Retzsch, had he viewed it, would have greatly preferred it to his own pictural incarnations of the fiend" (IV, 140). Wishing to remain ratiocinative, the narrator struggles "to form some analysis" of the haunting visage but receives only conflicting impressions of "vast mental power, of caution, of penuriousness, of avarice, of coolness, of malice, of blood-thirstiness, of triumph, of merriment, of excessive terror, of intense—of supreme despair." Overwhelmed by a "craving desire" to keep the stranger in sight, he quits his observation post—the coffeehouse window—to plunge into the chaos of the streets, symbolically abandoning a detached, analytical perspective for a more visceral involvement in the world of human striving.

While the narrator's account of his nocturnal adventure draws attention to the stranger's peculiar and seemingly perverse actions,

[8] "The Question of Poe's Narrators," in *The Recognition of Edgar Allan Poe*, ed. Eric W. Carlson (Ann Arbor, Mich., 1966), p. 309.

it simultaneously reveals, on another level of understanding, the egotism and self-deception of the narrator. Much like the narrator of "The Tell-Tale Heart," whose "sagacity" betrays his madness, the aspiring sleuth exposes his foolishness even as he celebrates his investigative prowess. One of the many delusions plaguing the narrator is his intuition that the stranger (an incarnation of "the fiend") conceals a terrible secret: "How wild a history," the narrator assumes, "is written within that bosom!" Predictably, his perceptions begin to "confirm" his suspicions; close examination of the man leads him to remark, "My vision deceived me, or, through a rent in a closely-buttoned and evidently second-handed *roquelaire* which enveloped him, I caught a glimpse both of a diamond and of a dagger" (IV, 140–41). The tantalizing ambivalence of his statement, like the description of the ruby-colored drops in "Ligeia," reveals more about the narrator's state of mind than about the physical reality of the situation. Entering a realm of fantasy and hallucination (objectified in the nightmarish cityscape), the narrator believes he has seen, by the "fitful and garish lustre" of gas lamps, emblems of the old man's sinister nature. Unlike Dupin, who calmly withholds judgment until the evidence has been weighed, he begins his investigation already convinced, by the illogic of the subconscious, that the old man is somehow evil.[9]

The narrator's second major delusion arises from his method of surveillance. Throughout the latter portions of the tale, he refers frequently to his own stealth, as if to reassure both the reader and himself. He speaks of following the man "closely, yet cautiously, so as not to attract his attention" (IV, 140) and says again, "Never once turning his head to look back, he did not observe me" (IV, 141). He later remarks, "It required much caution on my part to keep him within reach without attracting his observation" (IV, 142). A fourth insistence on his discretion—"At no moment did he see that I watched him" (IV, 142)—produces ironic reverberations of the sort heard in "The Tell-Tale Heart." The narrator's "stealth" is moreover called into question by his constant proximity to the

---

[9] Davidson hints that the narrator may be "so terrified of admitting who or what he is that he projects himself into this desperate and wholly imagined fugitive." See *Poe: A Critical Study*, p. 191. G. R. Thompson suggests that the tale may be read as the "deluded romanticizing of the tipsy narrator, who perversely attributes a Romantic significance to an old drunk." See *Poe's Fiction: Romantic Irony in the Gothic Tales* (Madison, Wisc., 1973), p. 170. Neither critic explores the implications of the narrator's unreliability, however.

stranger: he follows closely enough to study the texture of the man's clothing; he walks "close at his elbow" for half an hour; he pursues him through "many crooked and peopleless lanes." At length he even adopts the plural pronoun: "A blaze of light burst upon our sight, and we stood before one of the huge suburban temples of Intemperance" (IV, 144). That the narrator has actually escaped detection seems unlikely, particularly in light of numerous references to the stranger's visage—to the eyes that "rolled wildly from under his knit brows," to his "wild and vacant stare," to the "intense agony of his countenance"—which indicate that the narrator has been virtually face to face with his counterpart.

Significantly, just after the half-hour at the "elbow" of the stranger, the narrator notes a change in behavior: the wanderer crosses and recrosses streets "without apparent aim," retraces his path around a square several times, and then wheels about "with a sudden movement." An obvious explanation for the man's singular conduct (and his affinity for crowds) is his awareness of the narrator's presence. Indeed, the narrator has already marked himself as a threatening figure, for in wrapping a handkerchief about his mouth (IV, 141), he has unconsciously (or perversely) assumed the mask of a felon. If the man of the crowd were aware of his pursuer, as the details of the narrative tend to suggest, then the tale hinges on the theme of mutual suspicion. Such a reading must, however, remain speculative, since Poe never permits us to share the thoughts of his enigmatic old man. And this is as it should be; the story is after all concerned with the limits of knowledge and the ambiguities which frustrate our efforts to penetrate the veil of appearances. Regardless of what we may infer from his actions, the man of the crowd retains the ultimate inscrutability of Melville's white whale, symbolizing (if anything) man's inability to ascertain, by means of reason, any absolute knowledge of the world beyond the self.

The ironic form of "The Man of the Crowd" seems finally a manifestation of Poe's own ambivalence toward his art, for the tale is poised between rationality and irrationality, between understanding and terror. Read as the account of a reliable observer who correctly recognizes aberrant behavior, the story leads plausibly to the diagnosis, "This old man . . . is the type and the genius of deep crime. He refuses to be alone" (IV, 145). Yet the headnote to the tale (*"Ce grand malheur, de ne pouvoir être seul."*) applies as well to the narrator, a meddlesome detective guilty of what Dupin, in "The Mystery of Marie Rogêt," called "romantic busy-bodyism" (V, 34). Through the ironic design of "The Man of the Crowd" Poe expresses his own unfulfilled rage for order and clarity; even as the narrator seeks enlightenment about the old man, he sinks into the darkness of subconscious fantasies. The "mad energy" of the stranger only mirrors the narrator's compulsive behavior—his monomaniacal attempt to become the man of reason, to read the book that will not permit itself to be read.

II

In "The Murders in the Rue Morgue," Dupin says of Vidocq, the French minister of police: "He erred continually by the very intensity of his investigations. He impaired his vision by holding the object too close" (IV, 166). His remark succinctly defines the shortcoming of the bedeviled detective in "The Man of the Crowd." Poe describes precisely the opposite difficulty, though, in "The Oblong Box," a parody of the ratiocinative tale.[10] Here the analytical narrator attempts to solve from a distance the mystery of an oblong box brought aboard a ship bound for New York. With comic pertinacity, he constructs an utterly wrongheaded interpretation, reached through an abstract contemplation of events. Considerably less complex than "The Man of the Crowd," "The Oblong Box" nevertheless employs the motif of self-deception, as Poe again pokes fun at "romantic busy-bodyism" and the inclination to play detective.[11]

At the outset, the narrator offers another version of the heightened-consciousness syndrome: "I was, just at that epoch, in one of those moody frames of mind which make a man abnormally inquisitive about trifles" (V, 275). A puzzling circumstance arouses his curi-

[10] "The Oblong Box" was published in the September, 1844, number of *Godey's Lady's Book*, at about the same time "The Purloined Letter" appeared in *The Gift* for 1845 (issued in the fall of 1844). See John Cook Wyllie, "A List of the Texts of Poe's Tales," in *Humanistic Studies in Honor of John Calvin Metcalf* (Charlottesville, Va., 1941), I, 333-334.

[11] A detective story of sorts lies behind the only articles heretofore published on "The Oblong Box." C. V. Carley's "A Source for Poe's 'Oblong Box,'" *American Literature*, XXIX (Nov., 1957), 310-312, closely parallels Clifford Carley Vierra's "Poe's 'Oblong Box': Factual Origins," *Modern Language Notes*, LXXIV (Dec., 1959), 693-695. The extraordinary resemblance between the articles (the same source and details appear in both) indicates plagiarism, but the similarity of the authors' names suggests a Poesque hoax perpetrated on the scholarly community.

osity: Cornelius Wyatt, an artist-friend, has reserved three staterooms for a party which apparently includes only Wyatt, his new bride, and his two sisters. The intrigued narrator confides: "I busied myself in a variety of ill-bred and preposterous conjectures about this matter of the supernumerary state-room. It was no business of mine, to be sure; but with none the less pertinacity did I occupy myself in attempts to resolve the enigma" (V, 275). In busying himself with the affairs of Wyatt, the narrator identifies himself as a Poesque Paul Pry, a detached spectator regarding human experience primarily as a subject for analysis.

Further developments compound the mystery of the extra stateroom. On the eve of the ship's scheduled departure, the narrator learns that Mrs. Wyatt will not board the ship until the hour of sailing, thus postponing his introduction to the artist's bride. Unexplained "circumstances" then delay the departure nearly a week, and when Wyatt finally comes aboard with a heavily-veiled woman, he fails to introduce her to the narrator. A greater source of bafflement, though, is the oblong box placed in Wyatt's stateroom rather than the ship's hold. Disregarding the coffin-like dimensions of the box—which, as we discover later, actually contains the corpse of Mrs. Wyatt—the narrator concocts a theory rife with grotesque irony:

> The box in question was, as I say, oblong. It was about six feet in length by two and a half in breadth;—I observed it attentively, and like to be precise. Now this shape was *peculiar;* and no sooner had I seen it, than I took credit to myself for the accuracy of my guessing. I had reached the conclusion, it will be remembered, that the extra baggage of my friend, the artist, would prove to be pictures, or at least a picture; for I knew he had been for several weeks in conference with Nicolino:—and now here was a box which, from its shape, *could* possibly contain nothing in the world but a copy of Leonardo's "Last Supper"; and a copy of this very "Last Supper," done by Rubini the younger, at Florence, I had known, for some time, to be in the possession of Nicolino. This point, therefore, I considered as sufficiently settled. I chuckled excessively when I thought of my acumen. (V, 277-278)

With all his "precision," the narrator manages to overlook the most obvious interpretation of the oblong box; the smug reference to his "acumen" in effect announces the satirical point of the tale.

Like the narrator of "The Man of the Crowd," the aspiring detective in "The Oblong Box" is both intrigued and deceived by minute details. He suspects, for example, that the "peculiarly disgusting odor" emanating from the box derives from the paint used to letter an address on its side; he attributes Wyatt's melancholy appearance to an unhappy marriage. The disparity between the narrator's assumptions and the actual situation reveals itself best, however, in his effort to elicit the secret of the box from the mournful artist:

> I determined to commence a series of covert insinuations, or innuendoes, about the oblong box—just to let him perceive, gradually, that I was *not* altogether the butt, or victim, of his little bit of pleasant mystification. My first observation was by way of opening a masked battery. I said something about the "peculiar shape of *that* box"; and, as I spoke the words, I smiled knowingly, winked, and touched him gently with my fore-finger in the ribs. (V, 281)

What the narrator believes to be cleverness is of course monumental indelicacy; the encounter throws Wyatt into a swoon and the narrator into further confusion.

Other misapprehensions beset the stupefied sleuth. Twice observing the supposed Mrs. Wyatt stealing into the extra stateroom, he concludes that Wyatt and his wife are on the verge of a divorce. Not until the end of the tale does he learn that the woman was Mrs. Wyatt's former maid masquerading as the wife of the artist to conceal from superstitious passengers the fact that the ship was transporting a corpse. More perverse than the divorce theory is his comment upon hearing Wyatt pry open his oblong box: "Mr. Wyatt, no doubt, according to custom, was merely giving the rein to one of his hobbies —indulging in one of his fits of artistic enthusiasm. He had opened his oblong box, in order to feast his eyes on the pictorial treasure within" (V, 283). The reference to the "pictorial treasure" could scarcely be more ironic, for textual evidence indicates that Mrs. Wyatt has been dead at least ten days.

Though not a major work in the Poe canon, "The Oblong Box" delivers, through the narrator's grotesque misinterpretations, a clever satiric version of the detective hero. The headnote to "The Purloined Letter" furnishes a penetrating comment on the narrator's self-deception: "Nil sapientiae odiosius acumine nimio" (There is nothing more inimical to wisdom than too much acumen, VI, 28). His failure provides another instance of the ratiocinative process run amuck. "Truth is not always in a well," Dupin remarks in "The

Murders in the Rue Morgue" (IV, 166); neither is it found in abstract analysis divorced from that world of human realities which it proposes to explain.

III

Nearly delimiting the period of Poe's interest in ratiocination by their dates of publication, "The Man of the Crowd" and "The Oblong Box" help to clarify, by the negative example of "failed" detectives, Poe's view of the nature and scope of the ratiocinative process. Both narrators resemble the comically ineffectual Prefect of Police in the Dupin stories, being "somewhat too cunning to be profound" (IV, 192). Like him, they overlook the obvious and find a way *"de nier ce qui est, et d'expliquer ce qui n'est pas."* Yet the differences between the two tales are even more significant. Initiating the ratiocinative cycle, "The Man of the Crowd" dramatizes the effort to escape the conditions of terror and hypersensitivity through a rigidly analytical system of thought. But because the narrator has not yet been delivered from the nightside experience, because the principles of ratiocination have not yet been mastered, he falls prey to the same sensational influences which distort the perceptions of Roderick Usher, William Wilson, and the narrator of "Ligeia." However, "The Oblong Box" presents the opposite extreme—a narrator so detached from the subject of his investigation, so deluded by his own intellectual pretensions, that his ratiocination achieves no resemblance to actuality. The tale portrays the *reductio ad absurdum* of rational analysis: reason dissociated from reality.

Between these two poles of experience, C. Auguste Dupin balances imaginative involvement with analytical detachment. Like his adversary in "The Purloined Letter," Dupin is both poet and mathematician. As a mathematician he understands the "Calculus of Probabilities" which ordinarily governs natural phenomena. As a poet, though, he recognizes the surprising paradoxes of human experience which make an "ordinary" case sometimes more difficult to solve than one "excessively outré." According to Poe's epistemology, the two modes of cognition are inextricably related; "the *truly* imaginative [are] never otherwise than analytic," he writes in "The Murders in the Rue Morgue" (IV, 150). But both methods of knowing are ancillary to the kind of pure reasoning to which Dupin alludes in his remark about the letter thief: "As poet *and* mathematician, he would reason well; as mere mathematician, he could not have reasoned at all" (VI, 43). The detective's ability to combine imagination and analysis causes the narrator of "The Murders in the Rue Morgue" to recall "the old philosophy of the Bi-Part Soul" and imagine a "double Dupin—the creative and the resolvent" (IV, 152). In the same tale Poe reminds us that "intuition" has nothing to do with the analyst's solutions, which are obtained "by the very soul and essence of method" (IV, 146).[12] Dupin's method typically involves both a meticulous examination of physical evidence (involvement in the world of men) and a dispassionate consideration of the case as a whole (withdrawal to the realm of abstract thought). Out of this dialectical tension between involvement and detachment, poetry and mathematics, emerges the Truth which is the detective's goal.

Significant though Dupin's conquest of the unknown may seem in the context of Poe's artistic quest for a rational vision of experience, the fact remains that the author discarded his detective hero after "The Purloined Letter." A partial explanation comes from Poe himself, who wrote to Philip Pendleton Cooke in 1846: "These tales of ratiocination owe most of their popularity to being something in a new key. I do not mean to say that they are not ingenious—but people think them more ingenious than they are—on account of their method and *air* of method. In the 'Murders in the Rue Morgue,' for instance, where is the ingenuity of unravelling a web which you yourself (the author) have woven for the express purpose of unravelling?"[13] That Poe came to see the detective story as a rather superficial and mechanical exercise in mystification seems evident from his comment to Cooke. That realization also appears to inform "The Oblong Box," where the narrator's failure illustrates the speciousness of an intellectual system out of touch with the problems of human fallibility and mortality. Poe's fundamental vision of the human condition, the vision which even through ratiocination he could not at last escape, saw man as the predestined victim of the Conqueror Worm. In abandoning the detective story, Poe finally

---

[12] The narrator of "The Mystery of Marie Rogêt" also comments on Dupin's seemingly spontaneous awareness of first causes. "The Chevalier's analytical abilities acquired for him the credit of intuition," he says, because the "simple character" of his "inductions" was never publicly explained. But the narrator adds that "his [Dupin's] frankness would have led him to disabuse every inquirer of such prejudice" (V, 3-4).

[13] August 9, 1846, *The Letters of Edgar Allan Poe*, II, 328.

acknowledged that ratiocination answers no questions of genuine importance, clarifies nothing about the hopes and fears of humankind. For a brief period in Poe's career, ratiocination perhaps offered a distraction from the recurring nightmare of death and disintegration. But he could never fully recover, through his fictional man of reason, the reassuring eighteenth-century myth of a rationally designed universe; the inescapable terrors of the imagination made that task impossible.

Usher's Hypochondriasis: Mental Alienation and Romantic Idealism in Poe's Gothic Tales
David W. Butler

ON THREE SEPARATE OCCASIONS the narrator of "The Fall of the House of Usher" refers to Roderick as a "hypochondriac."[1] It seems odd that he should do so, since he never expresses the slightest doubt that Roderick is really sick: indeed upon greeting Usher the narrator is shocked by his boyhood friend's "terribly altered" appearance (III, 278). The apparent contradiction is explained, however, when we realize that the narrator, who lays claim to some knowledge of "the history of mental disorder" (III, 292) is using the term in its medical rather than its popular sense. Although he is at least initially unaware of the broad ramifications which the disease has acquired in Usher's world, he has correctly diagnosed Roderick's peculiar combination of physical and mental complaints as symptomatic of hypochondriasis, a melancholic disorder which has been recognized for centuries and which was widely discussed among physicians in Poe's own time. The issue is of more than passing interest, since the failure of modern critics to identify Usher's illness correctly has obscured one of the most important themes in Poe's story: for only when we discover the exact nature of Usher's disease can we fully appreciate the rich parallels which Poe's tale develops between medical theories about the progressive derangement of the mind and romantic theories about the growth of the mind's perceptive powers.[2]

---

[1] James A. Harrison, ed., *The Complete Works of Edgar Allan Poe* (New York, 1902), III, 283, 287, 292. All further quotation of Poe is from the Harrison edition.

[2] The only other discussion I have encountered which purports to explain Roderick's illness in contemporary medical terms is I. M. Walker's argument that Roderick is plainly the victim of miasmatic poisoning, of the noxious effects of the "atmosphere" which his environment exhales ("The 'Legitimate Sources' of Terror in 'The Fall of the House of Usher,'" *Modern Language Review*, LXI, Oct., 1966, 585–592). Although one of the passages which Walker himself quotes suggests similarities between the two diseases (p. 589), he never indicates that all the symptoms of miasmatic poisoning which he finds in Roderick, and several of Usher's other symptoms as well, are subsumed by the medical descriptions of hypochondriasis; nor does Walker seem aware that the literature on hypochondriasis accounts much more fully than does that to which he refers for the variety of possible causes, whether physical or mental, bodily or environmental, which

Before discussing the complex case of Roderick Usher, however, some background material is necessary: we must see how the doctors of Poe's time viewed the broad relationship between mental alienation and imaginative insight, and how Poe himself approached the problem in some of his less medically intricate Gothic tales. Interestingly, the doctors saw a connection between the imaginative power which characterizes romantics like Usher and actual madness. Benjamin Rush, a well-known American doctor who was among the signers of the Declaration of Independence, follows the lead of the famous French psychiatrist Phillippe Pinel in arguing that "poets, painters, sculptors and musicians" are far more prone to madness than chemists, naturalists, mathematicians, or natural philosophers.[3] Moreover, it was commonly thought that insanity could increase artistic ability. Rush cites the case of a young woman who acquired talent as a lyricist and singer as her disease reached its latter stages, and also claims knowledge of two cases in which an aptitude for drawing was similarly evolved from madness (pp. 153–154). The renowed phrenologist J. G. Spurzheim agrees that creative artists are more inclined to insanity than mathematicians and refers to a violinist whose compositions were bettered by insanity. The case is particularly reminiscent of Usher's "wild improvisations" upon his "speaking guitar": "Dr. Cox speaks of a professor in music, whose talents for music seemed even improved; his ideas executed on the violin were wonderfully striking, singular and original, but on other subjects he reasoned absurdly."[4]

But while they recognized a relationship between the power of the creative imagination and insanity, Poe's medical contemporaries denied that the mad artist might actually achieve authentic private visions of a transcendent order. Complete madness was thought to depend upon faith in the reality of the hallucinatory, or what Rush

---

Poe's tale seems to suggest for Usher's disease. Miasmatic poisoning may aggravate Roderick's disorder, and Walker's article is valuable for the research which it offers in support of that possibility. But to insist that miasma is necessarily the source and defining factor of Usher's illness is as arbitrary as are Walker's corollary contentions that Poe's rich term "atmosphere" must be construed only as a reference to a material vapor, and that Poe's conception of the "legitimate sources" of terror must have excluded the transcendent or supernatural.

[3] *Medical Inquiries and Observations, upon the Diseases of the Mind* (Philadelphia, 1812; rpt. New York, 1962), pp. 63–64.

[4] *Observations on Deranged Manifestations of Mind, or, Insanity* (n.p., 1817), pp. 148, 98.

calls "erroneous perception" (p. 147), and Spurzheim the *"incapacity of distinguishing the diseased functions of the mind"* (pp. 71-72). John Conolly, another famous physician, sums up this typical view of madness: "In numerous instances the hallucination of the sense arises from an imagination previously over-excited; that over-excitement is disease, but not madness; it produces an hallucination, but if the hallucination is known to be an hallucination, still there is no madness; if it is mistaken for reality, then the man is mad."[5]

The criterion for error in perception is of course the sensory experience of other individuals. As Conolly puts it, insanity is a "defect in the comparing faculty," so that one way to avoid complete madness is to compare one's own sense impressions with those of other people (pp. 300, 309, 314-315). Such a definition of insanity clearly makes no allowance for that individual insight into the supernatural toward which the romantic idealist struggled and which, like Usher, he often sought to express in artistic form. The physicians of Poe's time were in this respect closer to Locke than to Coleridge. They in no way distinguished between hallucination and the possibility that the romantic imagination could break through the bounds of ordinary perception to a higher order. The moment of romantic triumph, in which the individual imagination succeeded in idealizing the real, was in medical terms the moment at which a nervous disorder turned to complete delusion.

Like the doctors, Poe saw a connection between creativity and madness, but it is by no means clear that he shared in the alienists' refusal to credit private experiences of the transcendent or supernatural. Indeed the continuing conflict between psychological and mystical explications of Poe's Gothic tales[6] suggests that in many of these stories the natural and the supernatural, or the scientific and the romantically idealistic, are deliberately paralleled rather than cautiously distinguished. The puzzle which Poe's Gothic fiction

[5] *An Inquiry Concerning the Indications of Insanity* (London, 1830), p. 307.
[6] That this persistent conflict has emerged as a major and unresolved theme of Poe criticism becomes evident upon examining two recent books on Poe: G. R. Thompson's *Poe's Fiction: Romantic Irony in the Gothic Tales* (Madison, Wis., 1973) expands the argument that the seemingly supernatural events in the Gothic stories are merely hallucinations on the part of characters within them, usually the narrators themselves; David R. Halliburton's *Edgar Allan Poe: A Phenomenological View* (Princeton, N.J., 1973) elaborates the opposite interpretation, which insists that these startling events are to be read as actual occurrences.

seems repeatedly to pose, and which modern criticism has yet to resolve, is that described by the narrator of "Eleonora":

> I am come of a race noted for vigor of fancy and ardor of passion. Men have called me mad; but the question is not yet settled, whether madness is or is not the loftiest intelligence—whether much that is glorious— whether all that is profound—does not spring from disease of thought— from *moods* of mind exalted at the expense of the general intellect. They who dream by day are cognizant of many things which escape those who dream only by night. In their grey visions they obtain glimpses of eternity, and thrill, in awaking, to find that they have been upon the verge of the great secret.
>
> . . . .
>
> We will say, then that I am mad. I grant, at least, that there are two distinct conditions of my mental existence—the condition of a lucid reason, not to be disputed, and belonging to the memory of events forming the first epoch of my life—and a condition of shadow and doubt, appertaining to the present, and to the recollection of what constitutes the second great era of my being. Therefore, what I shall tell of the earlier period, believe; and to what I may relate of the later time, give only such credit as may seem due; or doubt it altogether; or, if doubt it ye cannot, then play unto its riddle the Oedipus. (IV, 236-237)

The first period of the narrator's life is that in which he loves Eleonora as a living woman. The second is that in which he adores "the ethereal Ermengarde," whom he implicitly envisions as a spiritualized reincarnation of his earlier love. In "Eleonora," as in "Ligeia" and "Morella," the rebirth or reincarnation of the beloved suggests that the romantic idealist may, mad though he be, finally achieve some success in his quest for a higher meaning. If the rebirth is actual and not hallucinatory, then the protagonist's imagination, what Coleridge calls the "esemplastic power,"[7] succeeds in idealizing his earthly mistress: if his beloved indeed passes through the tomb, then his sensual affection is transmuted into a bond with the super-

---

[7] *Biographia Literaria,* xiii. The connections between Poe's and Coleridge's theories about the mind's creative and idealizing powers have long been recognized. See, for example, Floyd Stovall's "Poe's Debt to Coleridge," *University of Texas Studies in English,* X (July, 1930), 70-127. In 1836, just three years before he published "Usher," Poe referred to the *Biographia Literaria* as possibly "the most deeply interesting of the prose writings of Coleridge," and indicated that those who would undertake a domestic republication of the work would be "rendering an important service to the cause of psychological science in America" (IX, 52).

natural.[8] It is in the light of the connection which tales like "Eleonora" and "Ligeia" suggest between madness and the idealizing faculty that we can most profitably examine the role which Roderick's hypochondria plays in "The Fall of the House of Usher." Like the narrators of these tales, Roderick is a madman whose imaginative powers may actually increase as his mind sickens; and as in the other fictions the idealizing capacities of those powers are seemingly confirmed by supernatural events reaching their climax at the end of the tale and involving, although in the Ushers' realm the family mansion plays a part as well, the apparent rebirth of a woman to whom the madman has been closely allied. But if "Usher" is similar to some of Poe's other Gothic tales in that it suggests links between the knowledge of the alienists and the theories of the idealists, it transcends all of them in the fullness with which those suggestions are developed: nowhere else does Poe so effectively demonstrate the close similarities between contemporary romantic and medical thought.

Since hypochondriasis was thought to involve the interaction of mind and body, it offered a superb medical analogy to the romantic's concern with the bonds between the internal, subjective realm and the external world of physical objects. The value of the illness as a parallel to the romantic belief in the intimate interrelationship of mind and matter was further enhanced by the inability of contemporary physicians to agree upon the location of the seat of the disorder in their attempts to explain its psychosomatic operations. Dr. James Johnson, writing in 1827, argues that the malady inevitably affects the digestive system, and through that influences the mind. But as he points out, localizing the disease was as much a problem in his own day as it had been for the physicians of bygone eras.[9] Dr. Ralph Fletcher, writing just a few years after about the effects of the mind upon the body, maintains that hypochondriasis may sometimes be centered in the intellect, and that the physical symptoms may be wholly the creations and not the causes of mental

[8] For the development of this reading I am indebted, with many other current critics of Poe's work, to Richard Wilbur's "The House of Poe" (*Library of Congress Anniversary Lectures 1959*, rpt. in Robert Regan, ed., *Poe: A Collection of Critical Essays*, Englewood Cliffs, N.J., 1967, pp. 98–120).

[9] *An Essay on Morbid Sensitivity of the Stomach and Bowels as the Proximate Cause, or Characteristic Condition of Indigestion, Nervous Irritability, Mental Despondency, Hypochondriasis &c. &c.* . . . (London, 1827), pp. 63–74.

distress.[10] Johnson himself says that the initial causes of the intestinal affection may be mental, or as he puts it, "of a moral rather than a physical nature, as losses in business, crosses in love, disappointed ambition, or a thousand other mental afflictions." Moreover, he goes on to say that in some cases

> the original train of corporeal disorders in the digestive organs is masked, or almost entirely disappears, under the complicated sympathetic affections of remote parts. These sympathetic affections are of a mixed character, corporeal and mental. In proportion as the *causes* were of a physical nature, so will be the predominance of the sympathies:—And, on the other hand, in proportion as they were of a moral nature, so will the sympathetic disorders be of a predominant intellectual character. In general, however, they are mixed. (pp. 65–66)

By suggesting both physical and "moral" causes for Roderick's hypochondria, Poe accurately reflects the medical controversy and the intimate relationship between mind and body which it implies. As the narrator tells us, Usher calls his malady "a constitutional and a family evil" (III, 280). The belief that the tendency to nervous disorder was hereditary was widespread among physicians in Poe's time, and educated readers would have recognized that in Usher's case this predisposition must have been particularly likely, since he is directly descended from a family noted "time out of mind" for its aberrant temperament (III, 275).[11] Shortly after offering this physiological explanation for his disease, we are told, Usher adds that much of the gloom which attends the affliction, and which is reflected in his fear of the influence of the family mansion upon him, originates from the "long-continued illness" and "approaching dissolution" of the beloved Madeline (III, 281). Again the detail is medically accurate. Rush lists a number of mental disorders which might result from the psychological cause of grief, one of which is hypochondriasis (p. 318).

The doctors' descriptions of the victims of the disease also offer close parallels to the conventional romantic qualities of Roderick's temperament. His "excessive and habitual" reserve (III, 275) is not

---

[10] *Sketches from the Case Book, to Illustrate the Influence of the Mind on the Body with the Treatment of Some of the More Important Brain & Nervous Disturbances which Arise from this Influence* (London, 1833), p. 68.

[11] According to Spurzheim the longer insanity "has existed in a family, and the greater the number of generations which have been affected, the greater is the danger" that the disease will be transmitted (p. 104).

only appropriate to the romantic, who conventionally disdains society as unsympathetic to any but material pursuits, but also to the true hypochondriac, who, as both Fletcher (pp. 58-60) and Johnson (p. 67) maintain, avoids his fellowmen for fear they will deride his debility. In addition, the malady was associated with the lack of active employment (Rush, pp. 77, 90, 92; Johnson, p. 68), with the cultivation of the mind over the body (Johnson, p. 63), and with the sensitivity of feeling and activeness of imagination which are so crucial a part of Usher's—and of the romantic's—personality. Fletcher says that hypochondriasis attacks "persons of deep and delicate feelings, whose expectations from human nature are too exalted," and introduces the subject of a case study of the disease as "a lady possessed of exquisite sensibility, a most luxuriant, vivid, and restless imagination" (pp. 69, 294). Even the "morbid acuteness of the senses" of which Usher complains, and which serves to underscore his romantic sensitivity, has its parallel in the medical descriptions of hypochondriasis. Rush quotes a letter from a hypochondriac in which the writer claims to suffer so much from acuteness of hearing that he habitually stops his ears with wax (p. 87), and Johnson states that, in the higher grades of the illness, "The nerves of sense . . . are morbidly susceptible to an astonishing degree. Thus, any sudden noise will make such an impression, as if the organ of hearing was distributed over the whole surface of the body" (pp. 66-67).[12]

It is, however, through the associations which he establishes between Usher and his "house"—his dwelling, his ancestors, and his twin Madeline—that Poe most fully exploits the romantic implications of hypochondriasis. Usher's "superstitious impressions" concerning his ancestral home and the sister he entombs within it are thoroughly in keeping with the symptoms of hypochondria. Early in the story he refers to those symptoms when he tells the narrator that he dreads the future, when he must "abandon life and reason together, in some struggle with the grim phantasm, FEAR" (III,

---

[12] Roderick's pallid countenance, which is interpreted by Walker as a sign of the effects of miasma (p. 589), can also be explained in terms of his hypochondriacal disorder. According to Rush (who believes that all mental derangement is primarily seated in circulatory disorders affecting the blood vessels of the brain), in the depressive phases of hypochondria the blood vessels are "robbed of nearly all their excitement" (p. 79). Rush also refers to a scientific experiment which associated a state of melancholic depression with an abnormally slow pulse (pp. 20-21).

280). According to Rush, the characteristic mental symptom of hypochondriasis is "distress," the cause of which is an obsessive belief on the part of the sufferer that he is somehow threatened, either with regard to his person or his outward circumstances. Rush lists several examples of such obsessions, among which are the belief that one is afflicted by some specific disease, or that one has been possessed by the soul of some fellow creature (pp. 79-83).

When Usher elaborates upon his fear it becomes apparent that, like his illness, it has much in common with the romantic and transcendental belief in the interrelationship of mind and matter. Immediately after singing his composition "The Haunted Palace" to the narrator,[13] Usher describes an opinion closely linked to his obsessive terror. As the narrator tells it:

This opinion, in its general form, was that of the sentience of all vegetable things. But, in his disordered fancy, the idea had assumed a more daring character, and trespassed, under certain conditions, upon the kingdom of inorganization. I lack words to express the full extent, or the earnest *abandon* of his persuasion. The belief, however, was connected (as I have previously hinted) with the gray stones of the home of his forefathers. The conditions of the sentience had been here, he imagined, fulfilled in the method of collocation of these stones—in the order of their arrangement, as well as in that of the many *fungi* which overspread them, and of the decayed trees which stood around—above all, in the long undisturbed endurance of this arrangement, and in its reduplication in the still waters of the tarn. Its evidence—the evidence of the sentience—was to be seen, he said, (and I here started as he spoke,) in the gradual yet certain condensation of an atmosphere of their own about the waters and the walls. The result was discoverable, he added, in that silent, yet importunate and terrible influence which for centuries had moulded the destinies of his family, and which made *him* what I now saw him—what he was. (III, 286-287)

Usher has previously spoken of the demoralizing influence which the strange "physique" of his family mansion has had upon him (III, 280-281). But in stressing the relationship between the "ar-

---

[13] The parallel between hypochondria and artistic ability which Poe develops fictionally in Usher's character is reflected in his later critical treatment of the writer Thomas Hood, whose genius Poe attributes to a "vivid Fancy impelled, or controlled,—certainly tinctured, at all points, by hypochondriasis" (XII, 217; see also 233-234). Soon after penning this statement Poe decided that he should have given Hood credit for much more of the "true Imagination" (as opposed to mere "Fancy") than he had done: significantly the poem which inspired the revised judgment was Hood's "The Haunted House" (XII, 236-237; see also XIV, 284).

rangement" of that physique and the "sentience" Roderick indicates that the physical peculiarities of his house are, like the bodily peculiarities related to his own disorder, inseparably linked to intellectual forces. Moreover, just as the decadent physique of the house mirrors Usher's deteriorating physiognomy, so Roderick's discussion of the dwelling's oppressive sentience affords parallels to the melancholic qualities of his own mind. The "reduplicating" waters of the dismal tarn offer a superb correspondence to the Ushers' debilitating self-consciousness,[14] and the "atmosphere" that Roderick sees as the "evidence" of the destructive sentience is powerfully reminiscent of the dark outpourings of his own intellect, which flow "forth upon all the objects of the moral and physical universe, in one unceasing radiation of gloom" (III, 282).[15] Indeed so strong are the ties between Roderick, his house, and his twin—with whom he also shares "sympathies" (III, 288-289) which go beyond the physical—that the three have become virtually the same organism, a single diseased consciousness and constitution;[16] as the anthropomorphic structure in "The Haunted Palace" implies, the derangement which affects the Ushers is finally indistinguishable from the strange condition which affects their home.

By dissolving the distinctions between the hypochondriacal Roderick and his environment, Poe posits a world in which the alienists' belief in the capacity of the mind to interact with the body which contains it, and the romantic idealists' faith in the capacity of the imagination to interact with the world around it, are no

[14] That the reflective tarn functions as the "mind" of the Ushers' dwelling place has been suggested by Edward Davidson (*Poe: A Critical Study*, Cambridge, Mass., 1957, p. 196), and several subsequent writers.

[15] The parallel between Roderick's gloom and the "atmosphere" was noted long ago by Darrell Abel ("A Key to the House of Usher," *University of Toronto Quarterly*, XVIII, Jan., 1949, 182).

[16] Herbert Smith, to whom I am particularly indebted for my interest in Poe and science, has shown that Poe probably found a scientific source for his portrayal of Roderick's world as virtually a single living whole in Richard Watson's *Chemical Essays* ("Usher's Madness and Poe's Organicism: A Source," *American Literature*, XXXIX, Nov., 1967, pp. 379-389). Like Usher, Watson suggests that there may finally be no clear-cut division between the realms of animal, vegetable, and mineral, that all three may be organically related. But as Smith indicates, Roderick's universe is "an example of aberrant *micro*cosmic organicism" moving steadily toward destruction. While Smith has found in Watson the probable scientific source for Poe's broad concept of organicism, then, it is my contention that we can find in the medical literature on hypochondriasis the probable scientific basis for the peculiar aberration of that concept in the Ushers' world.

longer only suggestively similar, but one. In keeping with that implied unity the progress of Roderick's disorder, while it closely follows the medically recognized patterns of hypochondriasis, is inextricably linked to the fate of his dwelling place and the twin he entombs within it. The doctors could not agree as to whether hypochondriasis was ultimately physical or mental in origin, and similarly it is impossible to say whether the Ushers' family illness originated in their bodies and in the related structure of their dwelling, or in their own minds and the related intelligence of their abode. But the alienists did concur that the hypochondriac's obsessive imagination played a powerful role in accelerating his physical deterioration, and so also one suspects that the fearful minds of generations of hypochondriac Ushers, coupled with the debilitating sentience of their house, have helped to speed the fall of the family's flesh and stone. Even the violent termination of the Usher line is appropriate to the medical descriptions of the disease which afflicts it. According to Rush, the distress of the hypochondriac leads to despair, to the wish to die, and sometimes to suicide (pp. 95–97), while Johnson states that:

It is not one of the least curious anomalies in this strange malady, that the individual who appears so solicitous about every symptom of his complaint —and consequently about life, should not very rarely be the one to commit suicide. The fact is, that hypochondriacism, in its highest degree, passes into monomania or mental delusion on a single subject—and it is *despair of relief* that drives the sufferer to fly into the arms of death to escape the miseries of existence. (p. 67)

When Madeline struggles up from the bowels of their sentient dwelling and Roderick rises to meet her dying and deadly embrace, then, the two are at once fulfilling the dark fate of the family line and experiencing the ultimate crisis of the family illness. With the death of the twins their sympathetic mansion sinks into the tarn: in keeping with its disorder the "melancholy House of Usher" (III, 273) has finally surrendered to its own worst—and most fascinating—fear.

But of course the medical pattern which brings the Ushers to physical annihilation may in romantic terms be the process which brings them into absolute unity with the realm of pure mind. With its collapse the hypochondriac House of Usher may finally have achieved romantic idealism's ultimate triumph: if the narrator of "Ligeia" may actually succeed in reshaping reality in the form of Rowena's body to accommodate the undying "idea" of Ligeia herself, the Ushers may finally succeed in idealizing their reality altogether.[17] Taken as a whole, then, "The Fall of the House of Usher" brilliantly suggests that under certain circumstances there may be an exact correlation between the progress of melancholia through isolation and intellectualism, to monomaniacal obsession with a single fear, to self-destruction as a result of that obsession, and the progress of romantic idealism through reclusion and cultivation of the mind's powers, to the imaginative struggle to idealize the real, to the absolute dissolution of the real in order to achieve complete union with ideality.

When the narrator first enters the House of Usher he passes by the family physician, on whose face he sees "a mingled expression of low cunning and perplexity" (III, 277). The puzzlement he perceives in the physician's face foreshadows his own confused reaction to the Ushers' situation, the failure of his conventional and unimaginative application of scientific and medical knowledge to account fully for what he himself experiences. Given his commitment to the doctors' equation of the normal and the true, it is not surprising that when faced with the ultimate confirmation of the validity of Usher's fear, when faced with Madeline's seemingly impossible return from the armored and suffocating room in which she has been entombed, he flees "aghast."

But as in "Ligeia" and "Eleonora," we finally have no way of knowing whether the narrator is or is not to be believed. If in the light of the extraordinary events which conclude "Usher" we reject the narrator's previous commitment to normal experience, the commitment of the physicians, it is only to find that with the idealists we have committed ourselves to the unverifiable, aberrant perceptions of the individual mind. "The Fall of the House of Usher" is finally, then, Poe's most thorough and sophisticated dramatization of the impossibility of developing unquestionably valid and complete medical, or unquestionably valid and complete mystical, explanations of some extraordinary private experiences. So striking

[17] This view is of course similar to Wilbur's argument that the House of Usher collapses because Roderick has finally succeeded in becoming "all soul" ("House of Poe," p. 110).

are the parallels which the story suggests between the medical and the romantic views of mental alienation that the doctors' refusal to grant the idealists' claims for the power of the individual imagination seems arbitrary indeed. It is difficult to agree that the doctors are right. And yet given the limitations of the narrator's perception of what Usher experiences, the limitations of our ability to trust the narrator's own experience, and the fact that the tale is in any case not scientific experiment but a form of science fiction, it is difficult to agree that the doctors are wrong. Dickinson has written that "Much madness is divinest sense / To a discerning eye." Poe's tale brilliantly indicates, in terms of both the scientific and the romantic psychology of his time, just how difficult the discernment is to come by.

Poe and the Theme of Forbidden Knowledge
Jules Zanger

A CUSTOMARY DEVICE of contemporary Poe criticism is to explicate one tale in the light of several others to which it appears to have some thematic or structural or symbolic affinities. In the search in Poe's own works for what Poe spoke of as the "undercurrent, however indefinite, of meaning,"[1] it has become apparent that the Poe canon, taken together, constitutes, if not precisely a seamless garment, at least not that patchwork quilt implied by the great number of Poe source studies and publishing market analyses. The variety of modes Poe employed—arabesques, grotesques, hoaxes, parodies—are increasingly perceived as being connected by patterns of images, ideas, and concerns.

These connections permit the grouping of various tales in a variety of combinations, in order to throw light on one or another tale in the group. So, for example, "Morella," one of the subjects of this paper, is linked by Stuart Levine in "The Death of the Beautiful Woman" group to "The Fall of the House of Usher"; Patrick Quinn relates it to "Metzengerstein" in his metempsychosis group; Daniel Hoffman categorizes it with tales as diverse as "The Black Cat" and "Loss of Breath" in his "marriage group."[2] Clearly, each grouping testifies to the perceptions and concerns of the particular critic rather than to any exclusive emphases on the part of Poe. These imposed orders, however, are no less valuable for not being exclusive: underlying each is the assumption of an organic coherence uniting much of Poe's work. The multiplicity of groupings only suggests that his coherence extends further than any single critic has assumed.

A grouping I would like to discuss in order to throw light upon "Morella" first and then reflectively, upon those other stories in the group, consists of "Morella," "Ligeia," "A Descent into the Mael-

---

[1] "Philosophy of Composition," *Complete Poems and Stories of Edgar Allan Poe*, ed. A. H. Quinn and E. H. O'Neill (New York, 1964), II, 986.

[2] See Stuart Levine, *The Short Fiction of Edgar Allan Poe* (Indianapolis, 1976), p. 62; Patrick F. Quinn, *The French Face of Edgar Allan Poe* (Carbondale, Ill., 1957), p. 198; Daniel Hoffman, *Poe, Poe, Poe, Poe, Poe, Poe, Poe* (Garden City, N.Y., 1973), p. 241.

strom," and "Manuscript Found in a Bottle." I would suggest that these stories, though in many ways unlike each other, are organically linked by the shared theme of forbidden knowledge.

The idea of a body of knowledge, the gaining of which can bring destruction is, of course, a traditional one, having its major source for Western Europe in the Genesis (J) account. For the nineteenth century, when knowledge was normally perceived as a good, this idea of destructive knowledge was to receive its definitive reembodiment in Goethe's *Faust*, which became, in Jacques Barzun's phrase, the "bible of Romanticism."[3] Faust, seeking knowledge beyond that of the schools, wishes to

> learn the fabric of the world,
> see all the seeds, watch the wheels run,
> and stop this rummaging around with words.[4]

To gain this knowledge, he turns to forbidden magic ". . . although it costs my life." Impatient with books, he leaves his cloistered study to enter the world of action, and risk damnation. Goethe has Faust say, "In the beginning was"—not the Word or the Thought or the Power, but—"The Deed," and this revision of the familiar text from John suggests the iconoclastic, energetic, worldly nature of romanticism.

However, when we regard the four tales in which Poe specifically talks about forbidden knowledge, we recognize that Poe's protagonists are, at best, very reluctant seekers after revelation. Unlike Faust, who consciously and deliberately pursues his goal, Poe's protagonists are either forced or seduced into the pursuit of the knowledge they acquire. In "Morella," for example, the narrator is led by his wife, whose "pupil" he has become, into the study of "forbidden pages." "I abandoned myself implicitly to the guidance of my wife and entered with an unflinching heart into the intricacies of her studies."

In "Ligeia" the same pattern appears as the narrator tells us, "I was sufficiently aware of her infinite supremacy to resign myself with childlike confidence to her guidance . . ." and continues to describe his delight in acquiring, under her guidance, "a wisdom too divinely

---

[3] Jacques Barzun, *Classic, Romantic, and Modern* (Garden City, N.Y., 1961), p. 8.
[4] Johann Wolfgang von Goethe, *Faust, Part I*, trans. C. F. MacIntyre (Norfolk, Conn., 1941), p. 15.

precious not to be forbidden." In both "A Descent into the Maelstrom" and "Manuscript Found in a Bottle" the same motif can be found. In the "Manuscript Found in a Bottle," the narrator records, in the moment just before being impelled into the whirlpool by which his ship has been caught, "It is evident that we are hurrying onward to some exciting knowledge—some never-to-be-imparted secret whose attainment is destruction." In "A Descent into the Maelstrom," the fisherman, equally forced by the current into the vortex of the terrifying whirlpool, discovers, "After a little while, I became possessed with the keenest curiosity. I positively felt a wish to explore its depths, even at the sacrifice I was going to make...."

In all these works the protagonist acquires his knowledge either under the guidance of another as in "Morella" and "Ligeia," or under the control of forces outside of himself as in "Manuscript Found in a Bottle" and "A Descent into the Maelstrom."

The contrast with Faust reveals Poe's protagonists to be essentially passive rather than active. It also suggests withdrawal from the world rather than engagement with it, and, at least in "Morella" and "Ligeia," the protagonist is involved with exactly those words, those books, and those studies that Faust disdains. In general, we can say that the Faustian hero moves from the world of thought to the world of experience; Poe's protagonist moves in precisely the opposite direction, withdrawing both physically and spiritually from engagement with society. In "Ligeia," for example, he moves from that "dim and decaying city by the Rhine" to the "wildest and least frequented portion" of England. In "Morella," he moves into the "rigorous seclusion of my home."

Though Goethe's *Faust* throws light on Poe's protagonists in these stories, it clearly did not so provide a model for them as it did, for example, for Melville's Ahab or Hawthorne's Ethan Brand, both clearly linked to the Faustian pattern. Poe's model comes, I would suggest, from that original confrontation with forbidden knowledge, the Book of Genesis, where Adam, in response to God's question, answers, "The woman whom thou gavest to be with me, she gave me of the tree, and I did eat...."

Seen in this light, it would appear that Poe's tales of forbidden knowledge are, in one dimension at least, veiled metaphors for the Garden myth in which the Adamic hero sins, then disavows his responsibility for his sin by laying it at the feet of Eve and of God.

Certainly the Edenic theme is strongly hinted at by Poe when he has the protagonist describe the effects of the study of the "forbidden pages": "the most beautiful became the most hideous, as Hinnon [Eden] became Gehenna."

This identification of the Adamic motif is useful in that it helps throw light on the nature of that forbidden knowledge in which Poe's characters become immersed. To begin with, it appears to identify Poe's "forbidden knowledge," which on the narrative level is vaguely characterized as German mysticism or metaphysics or "theological morality," with nothing less than original sin itself. This, in turn, suggests the traditional association of original sin with sexuality. While theologians and Biblical scholars of various sects fail to agree whether original sin was itself sexuality (or concupiscence, to use St. Augustine's term) or was merely the cause of it, they tend to agree that the two were closely linked. Both Augustine in his *On Marriage and Concupiscence* and Calvin in his *Institutes,* I, 8, appear to agree that concupiscence—"the law of sin in our sinful flesh"—is identifiable with original sin;[5] and, of course, in the popular imagination this identification is widespread. Certainly, this association of the sin symbolized by partaking of the fruit of the forbidden tree of knowledge with sexuality appears to be crystallized in the King James Version's Anglo-Saxonism for sexual intercourse: "And the man knew Eve, his wife, and she conceived...."

If we can accept the linking of "Morella" and "Ligeia" and "Manuscript Found in a Bottle" and "A Descent into the Maelstrom" through the shared theme of forbidden knowledge and further identify this theme with sexuality, it would appear that the whirlpools and abysses of "A Descent into the Maelstrom" and "Manuscript Found in a Bottle" and the ladies Morella and Ligeia present alternative narrative realizations both of one another and of the principle of forbidden female sexuality originally embodied in the Garden myth.

Such a reading should not obscure the fact that, though woman and whirlpool may be accepted as metaphoric alternatives, they are not equivalents. While Morella and Ligeia act primarily as tutors and guides to forbidden knowledge, they are also, however mini-

---

[5] See St. Augustine, "On Marriage and Concupiscence," *Select Library of Nicene and Post Nicene Fathers* (Grand Rapids, Mich., 1952–1956), V, 277; John Calvin, *Institutes of the Christian Religion,* trans. F. L. Battles (Philadelphia, 1960), p. 252.

mally, women and wives. As metaphors for original sin, and, by extension, for carnality, they remain uncomfortably close to the sexual reality they are intended to suggest and disguise. Consequently their husbands must deny, as Adam did, all sinful intention toward them. Ligeia's husband tells us only of *her* love for *him,* of her "stern passion," of her "more than womanly abandonment to love." (The last phrase suggests a certain prim embarrassment.) Morella's husband explicitly tells us that "the fires were not of Eros" which Morella kindled in his soul.

On the other hand, the whirlpool as metaphor appears to have been sufficiently distant from the sexual reality it represented, at least in those pre-Freudian times, to permit a greater degree of openness to Poe's protagonists. In "A Descent into the Maelstrom," the narrator tells us ". . . I became possessed with the keenest curiosity about the whirl itself. I positively felt a wish to explore its depths, even at the sacrifice I was going to make. . . ." In "Manuscript Found in a Bottle," the narrator's confession is still more revealing: ". . . a curiosity to penetrate the mysteries of these awful regions predominates even over my despair. . . ." In these tales Poe's protagonists can be permitted to confess desire for the forbidden, the desire narrators deny in "Morella" and "Ligeia," because the metaphor is sufficiently obscure to the reader and, perhaps, even the writer. There would appear to be in operation a kind of inverse ratio by which the more opaque the metaphor the more transparent the attitude expressed towards it.

If we could accept this formulization, it would appear, then, that the desire for the forbidden confessed by the narrators of "Manuscript Found in a Bottle" and "A Descent into the Maelstrom" is that felt also by the narrators of "Ligeia" and "Morella," even though they discount or deny it and attribute it exclusively to their wives.

Such a reading might serve to identify Morella's mysterious illness, which culminates in the birth of their daughter. It might also explain that otherwise enigmatic passage in which the narrator obliquely acknowledges his own sexual guilt: ". . . Then, when poring over forbidden pages, I felt a forbidden spirit kindling within me, would Morella place her cold hand upon my own. . . ." Finally, it would suggest that to the list of Poe's narrators whose testimony must be regarded with suspicion because they are insane or alcoholic or drugged or hysterical we must add the narrator who is unreliable as self-deceiver or even as hypocrite. That possibility in turn calls into question the perception of Poe's women in Allen Tate's "Our Cousin, Mr. Poe,"[6] in which they are described as vampires "suffocating" their victims in a sexual embrace. A hypocritical narrator would support the argument that they might rather be perceived as victims. Certainly, to review the fates of Poe's women—Morella, dead; Rowena, dead; Ligeia, briefly and equivocally struggling back from the grave; Berenice, mutilated; Eleanora, dead; the painter's wife in "The Oval Portrait," dead; Madeleine, dead—suggests that to read Poe's women as destroyers rather than the destroyed evidences a very partial sympathy. The necessity to preserve the appearance of purity in the man by attributing his desire to the woman may explain both why Poe gave Morella a Hymn to the Virgin Mary to sing in the first printing of the tale and why he cut it from subsequent versions. It tipped his hand.

By the same means of interpretation, it would appear that Morella and Ligeia can be regarded not only as personalities but also as personifications of great, impersonal natural forces by which men find themselves captured and then engulfed and destroyed. It may be noted in support of this identification that Poe's protagonist in "Ligeia" speaks of her eyes in metaphors that suggest the language in which the protagonists describe their desire to explore the depths of the whirlpool in both "A Descent into the Maelstrom" and "Manuscript Found in a Bottle": "How have I, through the whole of a midsummer night, struggled to fathom it. What was it—that something more profound than the well of Democritus—which lay far within the pupils of my beloved." To corroborate this association we need only turn to the epigraph to "A Descent into the Maelstrom" taken from Joseph Glanville which speaks of "The vastness, profundity, and unsearchableness of His works, which have a depth in them greater than the well of Democritus." What Democritus actually said was, "Of a truth we know nothing, for truth is in an abyss."[7]

In "Morella" the same parallel is suggested even more strongly: "I met the glance of her meaning eye—and then my soul sickened and became giddy with the giddiness of one who gazes downward into some dreary and unfathomable abyss." The doubleness of vision

---

[6] Allen Tate, "Our Cousin, Mr. Poe," *The Forlorn Demon* (Chicago, 1953), pp. 83-85.
[7] Levine, p. 103.

in which the woman is associated both with the well of Democritus, that classic locus of truth, and with the abyss, suggesting the Christian Hell itself, reflects that combination of horror and fascination with which Poe's protagonists regard the whirlpool.

Obviously these interpretations—the male as secret sinner and the woman as engulfing sexual force—do not contradict but complement each other. The vision of women as whirlpool is essential to the male narrator if he is to keep his own true nature a secret. Like Adam in the Garden, it permits him to say, "The woman whom thou gavest to be with me, she gave me of the tree. . . ."

What, however, beyond the general religious and social taboos to which Poe was exposed, makes sexuality so threatening and full of stress in his tales? Why does it appear to be so firmly linked to ideas of sin and death? Though Poe was raised a Christian, there is no evidence to suggest that Biblical references found in his work are employed as anything but poetic metaphors of proven power and recognizability. His stories employ religious symbolism but are hardly religious in any other regard. Certainly nineteenth-century American high culture, and especially the culture of the South, conspired to avoid public acknowledgement of sexuality or the knowledge of sexuality (it was "forbidden knowledge"). That this taboo was more ritualistic than real may account for Poe's reticence. It could hardly explain his fascinated revulsion. What precisely, then, is so forbidden about sexuality for Poe?

At this point, a conventional Freudian response might take the associational cluster here described—forbidden knowledge, Garden myth, whirlpools, woman, sexuality—and conclude that the last of these elements, sexuality, is the "real" causal ancestor of the others, which would then be considered mere metaphoric variants. To do this has the apparent advantage of explaining the complex in terms of the simple. Unfortunately, however, it also devalues the public and verifiable elements of the cluster, the images and allusions and themes and plots and characters of the tales, and focuses exclusively instead on private and conjectural aspects of Poe's sexual and psychic life. While it is possible, perhaps illuminating to make such conjectures, where no adequate and reliable body of evidence exists to support them, it might be better to regard the elements of the cluster, public and private, as existing not in a causal relationship but rather in a figure within which each of the elements illuminates and is illuminated by others. Looked at this way, the anguished sexuality suggested implicitly in these tales can itself be regarded as a metaphor, precisely as forbidden knowledge and whirlpools are metaphors. If these metaphors comprise a kind of constellation in which the elements have some loose equivalency, it may be possible to clarify the more obscure elements by examining them in the light of those less so. Specifically, we may ask what the explicit metaphors of forbidden knowledge and whirlpools suggest about the significance to Poe of the implicit sexual metaphor.

To begin, it might be useful to distinguish between the forbidden knowledge metaphor and the whirlpool metaphor. The first is primarily allusive: without explicitly stating them, it refers us to a cluster of familiar ideas and images. By reminding us of the Garden myth, it links the sexual metaphor to ideas of sin and punishment and, specifically, to ideas of pain and mortality. Further, it associates the sexual metaphor with the condition of exile—both from the Garden and from childhood—into a world of drudgery, conflict, and, finally, death. The Garden, we recall, contained not only the Tree of forbidden knowledge but also the Tree of Life; and it is explicitly to deny access to the Tree of Life that Adam and Eve are exiled into the world. To be exiled from the Garden and the Tree of Life into the world and mortality was to be thrust from the condition of timelessness into time and its attendant vicissitudes—responsibility, anxiety, old age, and death. For Poe, exiled both from his native South and from his protected, pampered childhood, those associations must have been particularly relevant and painful.

The whirlpool metaphor is not so much allusive as experiential. It refers us to a cluster of dramatized states of feeling—powerlessness, confusion, lack of control, depersonalization. In both "A Descent into the Maelstrom" and "Manuscript Found in a Bottle" the narrators present themselves as rational men. The narrator of "A Descent into the Maelstrom" is a commercial fisherman clearly not prone to "fancies," one who successfully orders his life by the chart and the watch. The narrator of "Manuscript Found in a Bottle," a dealer in antiquities, boasts of a "deficiency of imagination" and his "strong relish for physical philosophy." Into both their lives intrudes without warning a sudden and terrible storm which delivers them helpless into a powerful current which propels them into a great whirlpool, by which they are engulfed. The fishing boat in "A Descent into the Maelstrom" is reduced to flotsam along with the "fragments of vessels, large masses of building timber and trunks of trees, with many smaller articles, such as pieces of house furniture, broken boxes, barrels, and staves." The confident fisherman, instead of commanding his vessel, is carried along as uncontrollably as the broken boxes and barrels. The narrator of "Manuscript Found in a Bottle" is likewise carried helplessly into a whirlpool on a mysterious ship whose captain and crew can neither see nor hear him and who totally fail to respond to his presence.

It appears, then, that in both these tales we find linked to the sexual metaphor narratives showing self-determined, self-reliant, self-confident men suddenly captured by natural forces beyond their comprehension or control and whirled against their wills into the abyss. Interestingly, these stories are quite unlike the more common Poe tales—"Berenice" or "The Black Cat" or "William Wilson"—in which the protagonist is driven by some kink in his own brain. In "A Descent into the Maelstrom" and "Manuscript Found in a Bottle" the disaster which strikes is essentially physical: the minds of the protagonists observe and plan and protest while their bodies are hurried to destruction.

Two other elements appearing in both these tales may throw light on the sexual metaphor and its meaning for Poe. One is the reiterated image of discarded mechanical devices designed to impose order on the world. In "Manuscript Found in a Bottle" the floor of the captain's cabin is strewn with "mouldering instruments of science and obsolete long-forgotten charts." In "A Descent into the Maelstrom" the fisherman's watch which normally permits him to circumvent the whirlpool mysteriously runs down on the day of the disaster, and he throws it overboard. Both these images suggest the inadequacy and breakdown of reason and order in the face of a physical universe which moves according to its own inner forces.

The other element appearing in both tales is the association of the current and whirlpool with aging. The crew and captain in "Manuscript Found in a Bottle" give "evidence of great age and infirmity." "The ship and all in it are imbued with the spirit of Eld." In "A Descent into the Maelstrom" the fisherman, who has gone only half way into the whirlpool before rescuing himself through the application of his reason, emerges from his interrupted descent transformed by his experience: "You suppose me a very old man—but I am not. It took less than a single day to change these hairs from a jetty black to white, to weaken my limbs, and to unstring my nerves."

It appears then that the sexual metaphor, itself represented by the whirlpool-woman-forbidden-knowledge cluster, is associated in Poe's mind with the entire carnal condition of man—with birth in pain, with labor, with aging, with loss of control, with debilitation, with bodily dissolution, with death. This is the condition which horrifies Poe and to which he opposes the condition of pure spirit: "If I could dwell / Where Israfel / hath dwelt . . ."—a condition which would be immortal, unchanging, autonomous, except that the spirit is trapped in its envelope of flesh which commits it to time.

Such a reading helps explain Poe's fascination with childhood ("She was a child and I was a child") and his dismay at the physical changes maturity brings. In "Morella" Poe's protagonist regards the growth of his daughter with horror:

. . . ere long, the heaven of this pure affection became darkened, and gloom, and horror, and grief, swept over it in clouds. I said the child grew strangely in stature and intelligence. Strange indeed was her rapid increase in bodily size—but terrible, oh! terrible were the tumultuous thoughts which crowded upon me while watching the development of her mental being. Could it be otherwise . . . when the wisdom or the passions of maturity I found hourly gleaming from its full and speculative eye.

That mature sexuality should be associated with pain and death, rather than with pleasure and life by Poe was by no means an idiosyncratic and personal response. Ben Barker-Benfield, in "The Spermatic Economy: a Nineteenth Century View of Sexuality," reviews a number of the most prominent and influential writers on male and female sexuality in the United States from about 1800 on. These writers, mostly clergymen and physicians, tended to agree that ". . . woman's latent boundlessness posed a threat to male energies and through them, to civilization. A woman was a sperm absorber, a drag on the energy, spirits, and resolution of her partner. . . . Desirous woman represented man's loss of control over himself."[8] Poe's perceptions, then, of sexuality need not have their roots in the im-

---

[8] *Feminist Studies*, I (Summer, 1972), 55.

potence attributed to him by Krutch and Bonaparte[9] but may rather be seen to express some of the best informed, most influential opinions of his period. The combination of fascination and horror felt by Poe's protagonists in the presence of women, whirlpools, and forbidden knowledge may be seen as, in great part, the heightened and intensified expression of nineteenth-century American opinion. Poe's narrators, then, who are self-deceived and hypocritical about their powerful male sexual motives, behave more consistently with the popular intellectual and emotional climates of Poe's time than either the biographical critics or the exotic settings of the tales would suggest. A particularly congruent passage in Simone de Beauvoir's *The Second Sex* suggests that these perceptions were limited neither to Poe nor to nineteenth-century America: ". . . man is in revolt against his carnal state; he sees himself as a fallen god: his curse is to be fallen from a bright and ordered heaven into the chaotic shadows of his mother's womb . . . . This quivering jelly which is elaborated in the womb (the womb, secret and sealed like the tomb) evokes too clearly the soft viscosity of carrion for him not to turn shuddering away."[10]

However unintentionally, de Beauvoir's images immediately suggest the metaphoric universe created by Poe's erotic imagination. He deviates from de Beauvoir's formulation only to the degree that his revulsion is modified by the attraction felt for forbidden knowledge, for beautiful women, and for imaginative voyaging.

From this interpretation it follows that, whatever else may be going on in these stories, they dramatize a conflict in Poe between his impulses toward transcendence and his impulses toward an immanence that, time-bound and committed to death though it may be, is embodied for him in forms he finds himself constrained to pursue. It may also follow that this conflict in Poe, rather than setting him off from his fellow men, binds them to him more closely than has been supposed.

[9] See J. W. Krutch, *Edgar Allan Poe: A Study in Genius* (New York, 1926), p. 62; Marie Bonaparte, *Life and Works of Edgar Allan Poe: A Psycho-Analytic Interpretation*, trans. John Roudker (London, 1949), p. 79.
[10] New York, 1961, p. 135.

"The *language* of the cipher": Interpretation in "The Gold-Bug"

Michael Williams

IN the doubled text of "The Gold-Bug" a bewildered narrator recounts, first, a series of events the full significance of which escapes him, and then, in recursion, the events as explained to him by the ingenious central figure, Legrand, on whose intelligence the disclosure of meaning depends. The protagonist's rational powers are manifested most obviously in his role as cryptographer—he decodes a cipher which points to the ultimate discovery of treasure long since concealed by Captain Kidd. Legrand's arrogance about his skills, along with Poe's own assumption of the persona of master-cryptographer in the columns of *Graham's Magazine* and *Alexander's Weekly Messenger*, has fueled literalistic complaints about flaws in the tale's cryptographic methodology.[1] The conception of literature underlying such evaluations is made explicit by J. Woodrow Hassell, Jr., who assumes that

> while a narrative based upon the solution of a cipher need not be completely realistic in every particular, it must at the very least be credible as a record of fact. The author of such a tale must be most careful to fulfill the demands of verisimilitude.[2]

Hassell's criteria for detecting "violations of realism" derive from a philosophy of language in which writing is regarded as a "transcription of the real" and the relationship between signifier and signified is believed to be secure.[3] But "The Gold-Bug," like many

---

[1] Cortell Holsapple, "Poe and Conradus," *American Literature*, 4 (1932), 62–65; Alfred Allan Kern, "News for Bibliophiles," *Nation*, 97 (22 Oct. 1913), 381–82; W. K. Wimsatt, Jr., "What Poe Knew about Cryptography," *PMLA*, 58 (1943), 778–79. See "A Few Words on Secret Writing," in *The Complete Works of Edgar Allan Poe*, ed. James A. Harrison (1902; rpt. New York: AMS Press, 1965), XIV, 114–49.

[2] "The Problem of Realism in 'The Gold Bug,'" *American Literature*, 25 (1953), 171.

[3] Rosalind Coward and John Ellis, *Language and Materialism: Developments in Semiology and the Theory of the Subject* (London: Routledge, 1977), p. 47.

other tales by Poe, subjects this very security to critical scrutiny and explores the uncertainties of referential language. In a commentary that recognizes this aspect of Poe's work, Alan C. Golding shows that *Eureka* exposes fundamental misunderstandings that can arise from a strictly referential view of language which fails to acknowledge that "words are approximations on which we cannot afford to place ultimate dependence"; at best, words "stand only as functional approximations of meaning." Consequently, Golding argues, one strategy in *Eureka* moves "toward a denotatively precise language of expository discourse which seeks accurate statements about the apprehensible universe" while confronting language's limited ability to make such statements.[4]

Although a version of this strategy can be seen in the progressive demystification of event and cipher in "The Gold-Bug," in fact the tale opens a considerably deeper perspective on the semantics of referential language than Golding's formulation suggests. At its center, as in *Eureka*, lies Poe's recognition of the instability of the arbitrary relationship between word and referent and, as a consequence, the contingency of meaning upon conventions of use and context. In a commentary that stresses how "the text requires and defines the kind of reading which can decipher its workmanship," Jean Ricardou provides a useful starting point for an examination of this tale's exploration of referential language: "It is by their way of reading [that is, of interpreting signs, linguistic and otherwise] that the nature of each of the three characters is determined. Only Legrand is capable of decoding. Jupiter and the narrator, for their part, are on bad terms with language."[5] As the following will demonstrate, Jupiter and the narrator are entrapped in opposed but equally inadequate language strategies; in contrast, Legrand is an exemplary interpreter by whose practice the reader can gauge the shortcomings of his companions. He is aware that the relationship between word and referent is ultimately arbitrary, and alert to the consequent semantic implications of changing contexts. Legrand's

---

[4] "Reductive and Expansive Language: Semantic Strategies in *Eureka*," *Poe Studies*, 11 (1978), 1-2. See also John Carlos Rowe, "Writing and Truth in Poe's *The Narrative of Arthur Gordon Pym*," *Glyph: Johns Hopkins Textual Studies*, 2 (1977), 102-21.

[5] "Gold in the Bug," trans. Frank Towne, *Poe Studies*, 9 (1976), 36. Another valuable analysis of the tale is Barton Levi St. Armand's more traditional study, "Poe's Sober Mystification: The Uses of Alchemy in 'The Gold-Bug,' " *Poe Studies*, 4 (1971), 1-7.

interpretive strategy depends on a sensitivity to the possibilities of intention which allows him to restore words to those contexts in which they convey significant meaning, contexts in which an essential consistency can be perceived.[6] Because his approach to context remains flexible, he eventually reconstitutes the "links of a great chain" leading to the treasure[7]—the tale's dramatic validation of his stance toward referential language.

I

Throughout the tale, the contingent nature of the sign is repeatedly implied. The narrative's shifting terminology for its central image, the gold-bug, emphatically illustrates the arbitrariness of the relationship between word and referent. Legrand introduces the insect by its genus, "*scarabaeus*," but he and the other characters soon fall back on the even more inclusive term "bug" (p. 808). The physical absence of the bug and the lack of a specific classification make general description necessary, but words prove inadequate to capture the attributes of this nameless insect: of the quality of the color, the mysteriously "brilliant metallic lustre," the narrator "cannot judge till to-morrow," when he will be able to see it (p. 809). Meanwhile, a sketch must suffice to give him some idea of its shape. When the narrator eventually sees the bug for himself, he refers to it indiscriminately as "*scarabaeus*," "bug," "beetle," and "insect" (pp. 815-16). The synonyms circumscribe a still-unnamed center; the connection of names to that referent is obviously arbitrary and unstable. In most cases, the narrator's terms merely point to the bug as a physical object rather than describe or classify it in a stable context.

The drawing of the shape of the bug bears a "remarkable similarity of outline" to the representation of the death's-head on the back of the parchment (p. 829). Although this similarity of form creates the possibility of confusion, the drawings have distinctive meanings, discernible, however, only by "reading" them in their intended frames of reference. The drawings are thus analogous to homo-

---

[6] On the relationship between consistency and truth, see *Eureka*, in *Complete Works*, XVI, 196.

[7] Thomas Ollive Mabbott, ed., *Collected Works of Edgar Allan Poe* (Cambridge, Mass.: Harvard Univ. Press, 1978), III, 831. Further references will be to this edition, cited in the text by page number.

phones, which also must be taken in context to be understood. A parallel instance of homophonic confusion occurs, in fact, at a crucial point in the narrative. Jupiter, out of sight in the tulip tree, signals a discovery after following Legrand's instructions to crawl out along the seventh branch:

"—o-o-o-o-oh! Lor-gol-a-marcy! What *is* dis here pon de tree?"
"Well!" cried Legrand, highly delighted, "what it is?"
"Why taint noffin but a skull—somebody bin lef him head up de tree, and de crows done gobble ebery bit ob de meat off." (pp. 820–21)

Jupiter's comments (punning on absent-mindedness) establish one meaning of the word "left." When Legrand tells Jupiter to "find the left eye of the skull," Jupiter is unable to shift his usage of "left" to the new context, replying "Hum! hoo! dat's good! why dar aint no eye lef' at all." Struggling to impose his own context on Jupiter so that the servant can drop the bug through the appropriate eye-socket of the skull, Legrand relates the abstraction to a practical function, that of chopping wood:

"To be sure! you are left-handed; and your left eye is on the same side as your left hand. Now, I suppose, you can find the left eye of the skull, or the place where the left eye has been. Have you found it?" (p. 821)

The process of instruction is beset with ambiguities of reference:

"Is de lef eye of de skull pon de same side as de lef hand of de skull, too?—cause de skull aint got not a bit ob a hand at all—nebber mind! I got de lef eye now. . . ."

But, we learn later, he has not. What he believes to be his left eye is actually his right:

"Oh, my golly, Massa Will! ain't dis here my lef eye for sartain?" roared the terrified Jupiter, placing his hand upon his *right* organ of vision. . . ." (p. 824)

Comically displaying the absence of necessary relationship between word and referent, the tale again stresses that meaning is created by conventions of use and context, which alone stabilize the interpretation of signs.

The text similarly dramatizes the obstacles to communication which arise when words are considered to be naively referential, as if word and thing were indissolubly linked. Such extreme referentiality characterizes Jupiter's use of an elemental vocabulary; he fixes on a single referent in the speech of others, recognizing familiar sounds rather than understanding meaning in context. For example, when he hears Legrand refer to the gold-bug's "*antennae*," he interrupts: "Dey ain't *no* tin in him, Massa Will, I keep a tellin on you . . . de bug is a goole bug, solid, ebery bit of him" (pp. 808–09). Jupiter believes that the middle syllable has only one referent—the metal, tin.[8] Similarly, when the narrator asks "what cause have you?" for thinking Legrand has been bitten by the bug, Jupiter replies, "Claws enuff, massa, and mouff too" (p. 812). His lexical economy admits only one name for each object in his world: when he is asked, "Did you bring any message from Mr. Legrand?" he replies, "No, massa, I bring dis here pissel" (p. 813). Legrand has given him a name for what he carries and, because his language use precludes synonyms, he does not recognize "message" as an alternate signifier.

Such a linguistic practice also inhibits abstraction, as illustrated by Jupiter's struggles with the concepts of left and right. Discovering a scythe and three spades in the bottom of the boat bound from Charleston to Sullivan's Island, the narrator asks, "What is the meaning of all this, Jup?"; "Him syfe, massa, and spade," Jupiter replies (p. 814). He can go no further than the meaning contained in naming. Thus, when the narrator ponderously asks, "to what fortunate circumstance am I to attribute the honor of a visit from you today?" Jupiter, bewildered, replies, "What de matter, massa?" (p. 813); the formulaic words, without reference to any object that Jupiter can identify, do, in one sense, lack "matter" for him.

By contrast, the narrator illustrates the dangers of language dependent upon a single, inflexible framework for controlling the relationship of word and referent. Because the narrator's language strategies are linked to a fairly broadly defined perspective and cognitive style, it is necessary to consider his character in some detail. In a tale that demonstrates the value of heightened intellectual powers, the narrator's laziness of mind is marked. His conversation with Legrand, in which he learns of the discovery of the "totally new" *scarabaeus*, is characteristic. In response to Legrand's regret that he could not show him the bug that evening, the narrator thinks

---

[8] Mabbott points out that the Southern pronunciation of "antennae" would have been "Ann-tinny" (p. 845, n. 9).

only of the chill from which he suffers and wishes "the whole tribe of *scarabaei* at the devil" (p. 808). The same intellectual torpor underlies his approach to language (typical of what Poe calls in *Eureka* "the common understanding of words"), and gives rise to contextual confusion:

[Legrand:] 'Stay here tonight, and I will send Jup down for it at sunrise. It is the loveliest thing in creation!'
[Narrator:] 'What?—sunrise?'
[Legrand:] 'Nonsense! no!—the bug.' (p. 808)

Significantly, the narrator misidentifies the referent of "it," the understanding of which demands, of course, that distant syntactic elements be held in mind in order to be linked correctly.[9] We discover as the tale progresses that the narrator's lapse is emblematic: he is irremediably obtuse to the possibilities of fixing words in displaced or alternate contexts.

Unlike Legrand, the narrator's thoughtless acceptance of the conventions of his class limits both his own use of language and his understanding of others. He recognizes only one context in which to place words, the societal, and when words and behavior violate the expectations it establishes, he is simply bewildered. The first sentence neatly establishes his manner with words:

Many years ago, *I contracted an intimacy* with a Mr. William Legrand. He was *of an ancient Huguenot family*, and had once been wealthy; but a series of misfortunes had *reduced him to want*. To *avoid the mortification consequent upon his disasters*, he left New Orleans, the *city of his forefathers*, and *took up his residence* at Sullivan's Island, near Charleston, South Carolina. (p. 806; emphasis mine)

The narrator's discourse is little more than a series of clichés and formulaic expressions that keep harsh realities at a comfortable distance. The "residence" so formally taken up is, we soon learn, a hut, and the effete nature of merely social "mortification" is exposed later in the tale by a confrontation with the results of literal mortification—the skull and the skeletons. Even his admiration of Legrand is tempered with the condescension of a socially secure urbanite for a displaced peer, as seen in his measured evaluation that "there was

---

[9] See Emile Benveniste, *Problems in General Linguistics*, trans. Mary Elizabeth Meek (Coral Gables: Univ. of Miami Press, 1971), p. 219.

much in the recluse to excite interest and esteem" (p. 807). This condescension is made explicit in his immediate reaction to Legrand's note demanding his company: "What 'business of the highest importance' could *he* possibly have to transact?" (p. 814).

The world of socially defined value sharply delimits the narrator's reactions to the unpredictable. The first part of the narrative shows his inability to comprehend events that violate his expectations as other than symptomatic of the "otherness" of insanity—a convenient catch-all for the mysterious or the ostensibly irrational. He interprets Legrand's "moods of alternate enthusiasm and melancholy" accordingly, speculating that his relatives have contrived Jupiter's guardianship of a man "somewhat unsettled in intellect" (p. 807). The narrator can only describe Legrand's enthusiasms as "fits." Unlike Jupiter, he clearly has a vocabulary to generate alternate names for the behavior, and by the very question, "how else shall I term them?" he, or rather the text, lays open the possibility of other interpretations (p. 808). He actually reacts, however, by withdrawing into the security of "prudent" silence; subsequently, he withdraws physically, having "deemed it proper to take leave" for his own world of Charleston. His incomprehensions, at the outset innocent enough, foreshadow his later settled conviction of Legrand's lunacy.

The narrator's growing persuasion of his friend's "aberration of mind" (p. 817) springs from the assumption that a man who has fallen from wealth and social prominence to unrelieved poverty and obscurity is likely to go mad: "I dreaded lest the continued pressure of misfortune had, at length, fairly unsettled the reason of my friend" (p. 814). His criterion for "madness" is whether behavior is readily comprehensible in the context of social convention. If it is not, then such behavior can be appropriated to that context only by being named as "mad"; once so labeled, it cannot threaten or force the readjustment of the narrator's point of view. The arbitrary nature of this defensive strategy is implied by the narrator's reaction to the proposed nocturnal expedition—"The man is surely mad!"—a conventional expression of astonishment which can be translated as "I do not understand you" (p. 816). For the narrator, then, words have become mere signals of social approval or disapproval. Such a use of language allows him to reserve for himself the stance of sane judgment and reaffirms the adequacy of his settled perspective in the face of experience which it cannot accommodate. Such an approach is, of course, as limited in the face of complexity as Jupiter's obsessively referential use of language, for it imposes rather than discovers meaning, the possibilities of which are severely constrained by premature closure.[10] Legrand offers an eclectic and flexible alternative.

II

Legrand's task is doubly difficult; he has not only to cope with the unreliability of language but also to discover meaning in a text which human ingenuity has deliberately rendered obscure. That meaning, which in this instance can be validated by empirical investigation, lies beneath a series of obfuscating layers: on the underside of the sketch of the bug is a text concealed by its invisibility; once the text is made visible, its words are concealed by its being in code; once the code has been broken and the words made manifest, their meaning is obscured by their use of pirate conventions and by their distance from their referents. Under such conditions, the interpreter (like the cosmologer in *Eureka*) must proceed largely on faith in the existence of some final order to which the apparently arbitrary can be reconciled.

Legrand's belief in that process of discovery by which nature appears to conform to man's need for order is clear. Having found "an unknown bivalve, forming a new genus" (p. 808), Legrand displays his awareness of how conventional taxonomy establishes likenesses, makes connections, and thus finds meaning in the natural world. Having "hunted down and secured . . . a *scarabaeus* which he believed to be totally new," he recognizes that taxonomy must also be flexible. He can make the accommodations that new circumstances require, an ability that is tested to the full by the cipher. In confronting the concealed text, he follows a process of reification, recognizing displacements and concealments in order to reach through them to original meaning. Just as he is able to reify the form of the boat at the seashore, he is able to reconstitute the text and its purposes in

[10] The narrator is in this way similar to the Prefect in "The Purloined Letter"; see Sergio L. P. Bellei, " 'The Purloined Letter': A Theory of Perception," *Poe Studies*, 9 (1976), 40–42.

order to discover its meaning. The true form of each is hidden: one has suffered disintegration by the forces of nature so that "the resemblance to boat timbers could scarcely be traced" (p. 830), while the other has been disguised by the agency of man. Legrand is successful in each instance.

That his successful strategy for reading a disguised text derives from a particular way of looking at the world is implied by a crucial juxtaposition in Legrand's account of his capture of the gold-bug and his coincident discovery of the parchment with the concealed text:

Upon my taking hold of it, it gave me a sharp bite, which caused me to let it drop. Jupiter, with his accustomed caution, before seizing the insect, which had flown towards him, looked about him for a *leaf*, or something *of that nature*, by which to take hold of it. It was at this moment that his eyes, and mine also, fell upon the scrap of *parchment*, which I then supposed to be paper. (p. 830; emphasis mine)

"Leaf" is here a middle term with a double reference, both to leaves of the natural world and to leaves of paper or parchment. This possibility is kept in view as Legrand details his pursuit of the *"rationale"* of the cipher and refers to "the natural alphabet" and "the natural division intended by the cryptographist" (pp. 837, 840).

Legrand believes in an order that lies beneath the surface of apparent coincidence; he describes the struggle of the mind to discover a "connexion—a sequence of cause and effect" (p. 829) which establishes the one significant context among the many possibilities. When this attempt meets resistance, his mind lapses into a "species of temporary paralysis." Yet even then, faced with the sudden mysterious appearance of the image of the skull, "there seemed to glimmer, faintly, within the most remote and secret chambers of [Legrand's] intellect, a glow-worm-like conception of that truth which last night's adventure brought to so magnificent a demonstration." His methodical examination of the circumstances in which he found the document leads him to establish a connection between "two links of a great chain," for the boat and the parchment are conjoined by the death's-head, "the well-known emblem of the pirate" (p. 831). He reasserts his belief in the existence of such a chain when he claims, "My steps were sure, and could afford but a single result." His steps are governed by thoughtful common sense, intuition, and an insistence that the meaning of words and signs is contingent on a multiplicity of possible contexts.

The sequence in which the elements of the message emerge from the parchment reflects a hierarchy of increasing complexity and privacy of language requiring radical shifts of perspective on the part of the interpreter. When the narrator perceives the shape on the paper as that of "a skull, or a death's-head" (p. 809), he proves himself blind to the possibility of other meanings: " 'it is a very *excellent* skull, according to the vulgar notions about such specimens of physiology. . . .' The whole *did* bear a very close resemblance to the ordinary cuts of a death's-head" (p. 810). Beyond the social labels "vulgar" and "ordinary," the narrator contemplates no other frame of reference in which to interpret the sketch. Legrand, however, immediately tests for other possibilities: "There was a boat lying on a sea-coast, and not far from the boat was a parchment—*not a paper*—with a skull depicted on it. You will, of course, ask 'where is the connection?' I reply that the skull, or death's-head, is the well-known emblem of the pirate" (p. 831). The next element to emerge, "diagonally opposite" the skull, appears to be the figure of a goat; a "closer scrutiny," however, suggests to Legrand "that it was intended for a kid" (pp. 832–33). To the narrator, goats and kids are "pretty much the same thing," and in labored humor he asserts that "pirates, you know, have nothing to do with goats; they appertain to the farming interest" (p. 833). Legrand, however, recognizes that a sign's significance changes according to the context in which it is read, and his sensitivity to the intentions of the design enables him to place the "kid" in the appropriate one. Thus he perceives, first, that the figure is a hieroglyph and, second, that it is a "punning . . . signature" of the pirate, Captain Kidd.[11] The death's-head and the kid on opposite corners of the sheet are no longer for Legrand

---

[11] John T. Irwin, "The Symbol of the Hieroglyphics in the American Renaissance," *American Quarterly*, 26 (1974), 103–26. In his discussion of Champollion's deciphering of the hieroglyphics of the Rosetta Stone, Irwin notes that the symbols could operate on one of three levels of increasing complexity—1. figurative: in which the hieroglyph stood for the thing it represented; 2. symbolic: in which it represented simple ideas associated with the objects represented; 3. phonetic: in which the hieroglyph represented sounds (pp. 106–07). The narrator of "The Gold-Bug" can make only the most elementary associations and does not recognize that the hieroglyph is phonetic. In his recent book, *American Hieroglyphics: The Symbol of the Egyptian Hieroglyphics in the American Renaissance* (New Haven: Yale Univ. Press, 1980), Irwin notes Poe's emphasis of the distinction between ideogram and phonetic hieroglyph in this tale.

merely figures; their positioning follows the conventions of letter-writing: they are "stamp" and "signature," suggesting that additional texts might emerge from the space between them. After a narrative delay, detailing Legrand's procedural difficulties, the last and most obscure elements emerge on the parchment: "figures arranged in lines" (p. 834). The narrator is lost, "as much in the dark as ever," and immediately admits his own inability to solve "this enigma." While he sees merely numbers, Legrand recognizes that they "form a cipher—that is to say, they convey a meaning" (p. 835).

Even after Legrand successfully decodes the numbers so that English words are distinguishable, the narrator cannot imagine how to "extort a meaning from all this jargon about 'devil's seats,' 'death's-heads,' and 'bishop's hotels.'" He remains "in the dark" (p. 840), for the language that emerges from the cryptograph is in another kind of code in which the meanings of some words are established by convention and those of others by reference to a particular landscape. To interpret the first group, Legrand must place them in the context of the specialized jargon of sailors, reading, for example, "good glass" as "nothing but a telescope" (p. 841). The second group of meanings is more difficult to discover for, while the features of the landscape might remain stable, the words naming them drift away from their referents, as the search for the "bishop's hostel" illustrates. The phrase modulates: "hostel," a recognizable archaism, changes to "hotel" (the narrator has already made this shift but not, like Legrand, consciously, with an awareness of the implications); Legrand changes "Bishop's" to "Bessop's," making it conform with the locality to which he hopes the message refers. The phrase when finally linked to the landscape becomes "*Bessop's Castle*," which only remotely resembles the original "bishop's hostel," and which, moreover, refers not to a castle at all but to "an irregular assemblage of cliffs and rocks—one of the latter being quite remarkable for its height as well as for its insulated and artificial appearance" (pp. 840-41).

Legrand's final superimposition of the decoded text upon the landscape presupposes, in his terms, a "definite point of view, *admitting no variation*," by which meaning can be discovered (p. 841). The conditions of the realm of the referent, at this last stage, impose "but one interpretation" upon the text (p. 842). Separate, landscape and text would remain indeterminate— the first, a wilderness "excessively wild and desolate" (p. 817), the second, obscure—and this apparent indeterminacy opens them to misreading. Without the limits provided by the landscape, the deciphered text remains a series of floating signifiers which, like the single word "blood" that Arthur G. Pym reads in the hold of the *Grampus*, can be variously and subjectively interpreted. Furthermore, without the significance conveyed to it by the text, the landscape is merely "infinitely . . . dreary" and sternly solemn (p. 817). But as text and topography are superimposed, it becomes clear, despite the fact that "no trace of a human footstep was to be seen," that the landscape is not simply unencoded wilderness; it, as well as the text, has been previously structured by Kidd so that the conformity between them will yield the meaning that is, finally, the discovery of the treasure. Landscape and text give meaning, each to the other. Legrand is able to discover the determinate relation of the two by virtue of his sensitivity both to the multiple conventions that govern the formation of the text and to the relationship between the conventions and the referential world. To a great extent, this sensitivity results from his ability to intuit Kidd's intentions. When he claims that "it may well be doubted whether human ingenuity can construct an enigma of the kind which human ingenuity may not, by proper application, resolve" (p. 835), the phrasing emphasizes the identity of the activities of construction and resolution.[12] This identification enables Legrand, once he has consciously resisted the inherent instability of language by clarifying the various contingencies affecting text and referent, to establish an ultimate determining context within which the words may be read.

III

Legrand's final explanations direct attention once more to the three interdependent factors in his method of interpretation—the identification of context, of authorial intention, and of appropriate reference—no one of which is adequate independently. The narrator, after Legrand has clarified the system of pirate signs for him, suggests that Kidd used the skull as a marker on the tree because of his desire for "poetical consistency" (p. 843). Legrand accepts this

---

[12] "The Gold-Bug" here echoes Poe's July, 1841, article in *Graham's Magazine*; see *Complete Works*, XIV, 116.

interpretation as possible but incomplete. Displacing a symbolic reading with one that takes into account the conditions of the surrounding landscape, he feels that "common-sense had quite as much to do with the matter," for "to be visible from the Devil's seat, it was necessary that the object, if small, should be *white*; and there is nothing like your human skull for retaining and even increasing its whiteness under exposure to all vicissitudes of weather." Legrand's resolutely prosaic demystification of the symbolic possibilities of the skull evidently derives from his suspicion that in attributing poetical significance to objects the interpreter runs the risk of merely creating his own subjective constructs. The risks inherent in symbolic reading are exemplified in the narrator's misinterpretation of one particular system of signs—Legrand's "grandiloquence . . . conduct in swinging the beetle . . . [and insistence] on letting fall the bug, instead of a bullet, from the skull" (pp. 843-44). As has been indicated, the narrator's unquestioning acceptance of social codes leads him to categorize this behavior as symptomatic of insanity. Such an interpretive procedure, which relies only on the internal consistency of a codification arbitrarily applied, ignores the vital consideration of intention. Here, the intention is to deceive. As Ricardou has noted (p. 39), Legrand has been fulfilling a double office, that of encoder of his own text as well as decoder of Kidd's. Having recognized the nature of the narrator's reading of events—that he, Legrand, is insane—he creates a set of signs that reinforce that interpretation, thus dramatizing its arbitrary nature and, implicitly, the arbitrary nature of all interpretations which cannot be grounded in clear evidence of intentions and frames of reference.

Legrand's confession of his authorial role encourages speculation, in turn, about the interpretation of Poe's text. The gold-bug, its most obtrusive sign and thus that element most subject to symbolic readings, serves as a test case. Throughout the tale, the narrator invests the bug with poetical significance; it, to paraphrase Ricardou, consumes his interest just as it consumed the corner of the parchment. Yet Legrand insists that it bears only a tenuous relation to the meaning of the cipher and his own actions, and that he has kept it in view only as part of his "sober mystification" (p. 844). It is not merely the narrator, however, who has been distracted by a sign that proves to be empty. Poe swings the gold-bug before the eyes of the reader right from the point of entry into the story—the title—and symbolic interpretation of the bug places the reader in the narrator's dilemma: is Poe, like Legrand, offering us a "sober mystification" which provides only a deceptive opportunity for such a reading? If we attempt to establish the validity of a symbolic reading, we are faced with that problem of intention illustrated by the narrator's interpretation of Kidd's motives for using the skull. As Legrand has shown, symbolic readings depend on subjective constructs of authorial intentions, and the reader, like the narrator, has no way to test them.

Such considerations suggest a way to account for those violations of verisimilitude that have disturbed readers such as Hassell, who points out that Legrand's explanations, while pretending to comprehensiveness, actually contain notable inconsistencies and elementary mistakes in, for example, his specification of the ink used for the cipher, his listing of letter frequencies in cryptography, and his calculations determining the location of the treasure.[13] Given Poe's generally meticulous approach to detail, it is surely inadequate to write such errors off as mere carelessness. Poe is most careful to provide that information by which the reader can judge him careless—as, for example, in the case of the muddled triangulation. These "violations" subvert every attempt to authorize Poe's fiction solely by reference to conditions outside itself. As Ricardou has shown, the text establishes a logic of its own, one aspect of which is the subversion of the priority of an *"extra-textual subject"* (p. 33). Just as it is Poe, not "Fortune," who has set up the "series of accidents and coincidences . . . so *very* extraordinary" by which Legrand becomes aware of the existence of the death's-head (p. 833), so it is Poe who wills the solutions posited by Legrand, despite any lapses in verisimilitude. Even if the reader shares Legrand's faith in an ultimate order to which the text may be reduced, in "The Gold-Bug" he is faced, as Poe's disruptive "errors" remind us, with a text lacking an external "landscape" against which to measure it: the implied realm of the referent is whatever Poe wills it to be, and our access to his intentions, as noted above, is limited to the models we can construct but cannot test.

"The Gold-Bug," then, addresses the problem of its own interpretation under those conditions of semantic indeterminacy which are

[13] Hassell, passim.

shared by every text. Though it subverts the illusion that representation is the "transcription of the real," it also offers us as consolation a limiting paradigm of the reading process. A text can be recovered by clarifying definition, establishing a determining context, and recognizing authorial intention. Some texts resist such recuperation more than others—an utterly fictional text can be as empty of reference to the empirical world as the sign of the gold-bug itself—but if we approach any text without an active awareness of the requirements of the interpretive act, we are, like the narrator of "The Gold-Bug," constantly "in the dark," moving from one bewilderment to the next.

The Psychology of "The Murders in the Rue Morgue"

J. A. Leo Lemay

IN the conclusion of "The Murders in the Rue Morgue," Edgar Allan Poe wrote three metaphors which challenge the reader. They do not make literal sense. Dupin is explaining (for the final time) the reason why the Prefect of Police failed to solve the mystery. Dupin says, "in truth, our friend the Prefect is somewhat too cunning to be profound." He illustrates the generalization with three paradoxical comparisons: "In his wisdom is no *stamen*. It is all head and no body, like the pictures of the Goddess Laverna,—or, at best, all head and shoulders, like a codfish."[1] I believe that if we fully understand the ways that these three metaphors—and the final quotation—complement the story, then we will understand the psychology of "The Murders in the Rue Morgue."

All three tropes point to a head-body dichotomy and all concern sex. The first, "In his wisdom is no *stamen*," is an obvious paradox. What does *stamen* have to do with wisdom? The *stamen*, of course, is a flower's pollen-producing organ—comparable to the male genitalia. (Since the *stamen* indicates one essential theme of the story, Poe may also have been punning on the uncommon meaning of *stamen* as "the fundamental or essential element of a thing."[2]) Literally, Dupin seems to be saying that the Prefect failed to solve the mystery because he failed to take sex into account—or because he failed to integrate the entire person, head and body, intellect and sex. The second trope, "It is all head and no body like the pictures of the Goddess Laverna," directly names the head-body dichotomy. In iden-

---

[1] *The Collected Works of Edgar Allan Poe*, ed. Thomas Ollive Mabbott, 3 vols. to date (Cambridge: Harvard Univ. Press, 1969—), 2: 568. Hereafter references to "The Murders in the Rue Morgue" will simply cite the page in Mabbott's edition. Other references to Mabbott's edition will use the formula M, 1: 360 (i.e., Mabbott, vol. 1, p. 360). References to *The Complete Works of Edgar Allan Poe*, ed. James A. Harrison, 17 vols. (New York: T. Y. Crowell, 1902), will use the formula H, 8: 170 (i.e., Harrison, vol. 8, p. 170).

[2] *OED*, s. v. "stamen," 2c. See Poe's usage at H, 11: 146: "an absolute deficiency in basis, in *stamen*, in matter, or pungency."

tifying the head with Laverna, Dupin reverses the normal, expected associations; for the head—the citadel of reason—is usually associated with intelligence and wisdom, as in the first trope. Laverna, however, is the classical goddess of the underworld, night, and thieves. She suggests crime and evil, not wisdom and good. This trope echoes at least two details in the story. The head-body dichotomy recalls the corpse of Madame L'Espanaye "with her throat so entirely cut that, upon an attempt to raise her, the head fell off" (p. 538). And the Goddess Laverna reminds us of an attribute of Dupin and the narrator, for the goddess of the night is evidently the "sable divinity" whom Dupin is "enamored of" (p. 532). The third trope is "or, at best, all head and shoulders, like a codfish." Does a fish have shoulders? Even by itself, the metaphor seems strained, since a fish appears to be an absurd choice. This comparison again reverses the normally positive associations of wisdom and instead identifies it with a fishhead, a monstrosity of mouth and jaws. The comparison again emphasizes the head-body dichotomy, thus reaffirming that "The Murders in the Rue Morgue" concerns this dualism. Further, the codfish reference, which calls attention to itself, probably does so for the sexual suggestion. Marlowe, Shakespeare, and other Renaissance writers frequently pun about cods and codfish, and Mark Twain's splendidly scurrilous poem "The Mammoth Cod" attests that the pun remained popular until well after Poe's time.[3] So when Poe drags in a reference to a codfish, I suspect that, as in the first trope, he alludes to sex, as well as to the head-body dichotomy.

The story's final sentence is at least as puzzling as these three comparisons. Poe ends with Dupin claiming that the Prefect has "attained his reputation for ingenuity" by a "master stroke of cant": "I mean the way he has '*de nier ce qui est, et d'expliquer ce qui n'est pas*'" (p. 568). The quotation, which Poe identifies as from Rousseau's *La Nouvelle Héloise,* may be translated "of denying that which is, and of explaining that which is not." But on a literal level, the quotation does not make good sense, for the Prefect neither explains nor denies what is or is not. . . . In its original context, Rousseau's

---

[3] For example, *Faustus,* II, ii, 161–62; *Love's Labor Lost,* III, i, 181; *Much Ado About Nothing,* III, iii, 133–35; and *Measure for Measure,* III, ii, 115–17. Mark Twain, *The Mammoth Cod,* intro. by G. Legman (Milwaukee: Maledicta, 1976).

statement concerns Plato's explanation of ghostly apparitions. The only direct mention of ghosts occurs when Dupin explains how he solved the mystery of the murderer's leaving the locked-room. "It is not too much to say that neither of us believe in praeternatural events. Madame and Mademoiselle L'Espanaye were not destroyed by spirits" (p. 551). The narrator of course agrees (and so, too, does the reader). Are we now supposed to think that the Prefect spent his time looking for ghosts?

Actually, throughout the story, Poe repeatedly suggests that it concerns psychology and sex, and particularly an opposition between the mind and the body.

In the tripartite introduction,[4] where Poe sets forth the story's themes and presents an analogue for its structure, the narrator begins by defining the nature of analysis. In doing so, he uses diction more appropriate to psychology and ethics than to science: "As the strong man exults in his physical ability, delighting in such exercises as call his muscles into action, so glories the analyst in that moral activity which *disentangles*" (p. 528). Notice the nature of the activity Poe's analyst "glories" in—the *moral* activity. Webster defined *moral* as "regarding vice or virtue, upright, good." But its usual meaning in Poe is the common one in eighteenth and nineteenth-century "moral philosophy," i.e., "the knowledge or study of the principles of human nature or conduct; ethics."[5] Two points concerning the meaning of moral should be stressed: it refers exclusively to humans, and it concerns motivations rather than the results of action. Poe's analysis, therefore, specifically refers to the motivations and psychology of humans. The following sentences confirm this interpretation. The narrator comments that the analyst "derives pleasure from even the most trivial occupations bringing his talent into play" (p. 528). The examples of the "most trivial occupations" are "enigmas . . .

---

[4] If we consider the main plot to be the murder mystery, then the story has a tripartite introduction: the observations on analysis (pp. 527–31), the introduction of the narrator and Dupin (pp. 531–33), and the anecdote of Dupin's "reading" the narrator's thoughts (pp. 533–37). Or one could argue that the introduction consists only of the observations on analysis.

[5] Noah Webster, *A Compendious Dictionary of the English Language* (New Haven: Hudson & Goodwin, 1806), p. 195. OED, s.v. *philosophy*, no. 4. Cf. Robert D. Jacobs, *Poe: Journalist and Critic* (Baton Rouge: Louisiana State Univ. Press, 1969), p. 132, n. 28, who suggests that Poe uses the word *moral* as "roughly equivalent to 'mental.'"

conundrums . . . hieroglyphics." Poe thus directly tells the reader that although puzzles, mysteries, riddles, and detective stories (such as, on the plot level, "The Murders in the Rue Morgue") may be amusing for the analyst or creator, they are trivial in comparison with the "glorious" fascination of psychological investigation.[6] When, in the main story, Dupin begins the investigation by saying that "An inquiry will afford us amusement," Poe is again saying that the solution of the mystery is a trivial matter. Poe even calls our attention to Dupin's diction by having the narrator remark "[I thought this an odd term, so applied, but said nothing]" (p. 546). Dupin's later references to the mystery as a "riddle" (pp. 548, 560) also trivialize the undertaking, especially when Poe uses a polyptoton which calls attention to the diction: "The riddle, so far, was now unriddled" (p. 553). According to the narrator's statement on his introductory remarks, "The narrative which follows" should be read as "a commentary upon the propositions just advanced" (p. 531).

In addition to such necessary literal matters as bringing on stage the narrator and Dupin, describing their first meeting and subsequent relationship, and telling of their characters, Part Two of the introduction (pp. 531–33) begins the particular psychological explorations that are the major undercurrent. The narrator hints that "mere self" is the theme: "I was deeply interested in the little family history which he detailed to me with all that candor which a Frenchman indulges whenever mere self is his theme." The next paragraph's paradoxical conclusion repeats this theme and hints at the ultimate unity of the characters: "We existed within ourselves alone" (p. 532). The narrator describes the "peculiar analytic ability" of Dupin. "He boasted to me, with a low chuckling laugh, that most men, in respect to himself, wore windows in their bosoms, and was wont to follow up such assertions by direct and very startling proofs of his intimate knowledge of my own" (p. 533). Poe here introduces the house-as-body metaphor ("windows in their bosoms")[7] and intimates that

---

[6] The original first paragraph of the story (as written in the fair copy of the manuscript and as printed in the 1841 and the 1843 texts), made the psychological theme more obvious. Perhaps Poe found it too obvious, for he deleted the opening in his 1845 revision. For some implications of the deleted paragraph, see Donald Barlow Stauffer, "Poe as Phrenologist: The Example of Monsieur Dupin," in *Papers on Poe: Essays in Honor of John Ward Ostrom*, ed. Richard P. Veler (Springfield, Ohio: Chantry Music Press, Inc., at Wittenburg University, 1972), pp. 113–25.

[7] Poe's poem "The Haunted Palace" is perhaps his most obvious use of the house-as-body

Dupin is a doppelgänger for the narrator. Dupin, of course, is the analyst; and the narrator, who tells the tale, is the creator. As Poe wrote in the introduction's Part One, the analyst is simply the reverse of the creator. Besides making Dupin (who, after all, tells much of the story and is thus the creator as well as the analyst) a doppelgänger for the narrator, Poe also makes Dupin a schizoid. His doubleness is directly stated after the narrator describes Dupin's voice and manner while analyzing. "Observing him in these moods, I often dwelt meditatively upon the old philosophy of the Bi-Part Soul, and amused myself with the fancy of a double Dupin—the creative and the resolvent" (p. 533). Poe thus implies that the persons in the story (or, at least, that the narrator and Dupin) are symbolically (and psychologically) aspects of a single person.[8] And in saying that the narrator and Dupin create the story, Poe puns, for he means to imply that these two characters are also the murderers, the "creators" of the mystery. Our general idea of what is meant by the "old philosophy of the Bi-Part Soul" tends to confirm the identification of the "creators" or narrators with the murderer, for the "Bi-Part Soul" usually is thought of as a division existing within the soul itself, good and evil. (That Poe probably had in mind the Epicurean, especially Lucretian, philosophy is significant for the cosmological undercurrent of the story, with which I am not here concerned.)

Part Two of the introduction also presents three motifs that will recur in the story—the two voices, the similar details in the living arrangements,[9] and the suggested homosexual relationships.

The narrator says that during analysis, Dupin's "voice, usually a rich tenor, rose into a treble which would have sounded petulantly

---

allegory. Richard Wilbur has commented on this motif in "The House of Poe," *Anniversary Lectures 1959* (Washington: Reference Department of the Library of Congress, 1959), pp. 21–38; reprinted in *The Recognition of Edgar Allen Poe*, ed. Eric Carlson (Ann Arbor: Univ. of Michigan Press, 1966), pp. 255–77.

[8] Wilbur has pointed out that the characters in a typical Poe story are "allegorical figures representing the warring principles of the poet's divided nature." "The House of Poe," in Carlson, pp. 274–75. And in Wilbur's "The Poe Mystery Case," he specifically claims that the "other 'persons' of the tale are to be taken allegorically as elements of one person, whereof Dupin is the presiding faculty." Richard Wilbur, "The Poe Mystery Case," *New York Review of Books*, 13 (July 13, 1967), 16, 25–28; reprinted in Wilbur's *Responses: Prose Pieces: 1953–1976* (New York: Harcourt, Brace, Jovanovich, 1976), pp. 127–37, at p. 136. See also Stauffer, p. 122.

[9] Richard Wilbur, "The Poe Mystery Case," first pointed out the repetitions of the voices and the similarity of the living arrangements and concluded that the repeated motifs indicated that the couples were doubles. *Responses*, pp. 135–37.

but for the deliberateness and entire distinctness of the enunciation" (p. 533). Dupin's two voices anticipate the two voices (which we later learn are the sailor and the orangutan) "heard in contention" (p. 549) in the locked room while the murders are taking place. Poe strategically emphasizes this repeated motif by describing the analysis-voice again (p. 548) just before Dupin examines the conflicting testimony concerning the voices. Dupin argues "what was *peculiar*" about "the whole testimony respecting" the voices was that while one was undoubtedly a Frenchman's "gruff voice," the other was an unidentifiable "shrill voice." Significantly, although Dupin already knows that an orangutan committed the murders and already believes that the Frenchman's voice was that of a sailor from "*a Maltese vessel*" (p. 560), he speaks of these two voices as belonging to a single person: "the voices of this third party were those heard in contention" (p. 549). Poe thus suggests that the warring voices are the outward manifestation of the conflict between good and evil that existed within the murderer. Further, as I will show, Poe suggests that the dualism itself revealed by the "voices of this third party"—and not just the "evil" half of the "third party"—is responsible for the murders. The analogue, however, between Dupin's two voices and the voices of the sailor and the orangutan implies that the sailor and the orangutan are a double for Dupin. That also means, of course, that they are doubles for one another; and since Dupin is a double for the narrator, all four characters are symbolic doubles.

Second, as Richard Wilbur has pointed out, several details of the living arrangements of Dupin and the narrator are repeated for Madame and Mademoiselle L'Espanaye. Just as Dupin and the narrator live together in "perfect" seclusion (p. 532), so too do the L'Espanayes live "an exceedingly retired life" (p. 539). The narrator and Dupin admit "no visitors" (p. 532); and the L'Espanayes' neighbors testify that "No one was spoken of as frequenting the house" (p. 539). (In passing, I might note that the arrangements of the ape and the sailor also repeat this detail, for the sailor keeps the ape "carefully secluded," p. 564.) Both Dupin and the narrator and the L'Espanayes live in large houses otherwise empty (pp. 532, 539). The L'Espanayes occupy only two rooms in the house, and evidently Dupin and the narrator do also; and both couples' rooms are on the fourth and top story (pp. 537, 539). In view of the house-as-body allegory, the symbolic significance of occupying only the top floor is that both couples live only in the mind—therefore, both deny the body. (Significantly, this motif is not necessarily true of the sailor and the ape, although in making its escape from the sailor, the orangutan does flee "down the stairs," p. 565.) And just as Dupin and the narrator are "enamored of the Night" (p. 532), so the women have not yet gone to bed at three in the morning (p. 537). This group of similarities between the living arrangements of at least the two sets of characters suggests that they are doubles. In view of our earlier identification of Dupin and the narrator with the sailor and the orangutan, we may now conclude that on at least one thematic level, all three sets of characters are symbolic doubles. The murderer and those murdered, the solver of the mystery and the teller of the tale are, symbolically, one person. One result of this too-neat duplication is an aesthetic pleasure in the extraordinary unity of the tale's formal motifs and plot. But thematic reasons, as I shall show, also exist for the characters' final unity.

Third, Poe suggests that homosexual relationships exist between Dupin and the narrator, and between Madame and Mademoiselle L'Espanaye. The narrator frankly tells of his attraction to Dupin: "I felt my soul enkindled within me by the wild fervor, and the vivid freshness of his imagination" (p. 532). The narrator says that "the society of such a man" was "to me a treasure beyond price." They decide to "live together during my stay in the city." The narrator assumes the traditional male economic role in a marriage: "I was permitted to be at the expense of renting and furnishing" the home (p. 532). And what is the narrator doing in Paris? Since he refers to Dupin as "The Frenchman" and explains in English the meaning of some French phrases, and since he is there only for a visit ("the spring and part of the summer of 18—," p. 531), the reader supposes he's an American or an Englishman.[10] Given the nineteenth-century American image of Paris, a common assumption would be that the narrator is there for a sexual fling. "Seeking in Paris the objects I then sought, I felt that the society of such a man would be to me a treasure beyond price." He adopts a supposedly traditional feminine

---

[10] Burton R. Pollin concludes that the narrator is "clearly . . . English or American." "Poe's 'Murders in the Rue Morgue': The Ingenious Web Unravelled," *Studies in the American Renaissance,* 1977, ed. Joel Myerson (Boston: Twayne, 1978), p. 238.

role in submitting himself to Dupin: "into this *bizarrerie,* as into all his others, I quietly fell; giving myself up to his wild whims with a perfect *abandon.*" Here, the connotations of the diction ("bizarrerie," "wild whims," and "perfect abandon") suggest that the narrator submits to—and relishes—the strange sexual practices of Dupin. Further, the general description of the house, of the men's habits, and of their relationships (e.g., their "absolute seclusion"), all suggest a passionate love affair. When they do venture out (and it is only at night), they sally "forth into the streets, arm in arm" (p. 533). After this series of suggestions, Poe puns on Dupin's "intimate knowledge" of the narrator's bosom (p. 533). Typical of Poe's frequent thematic and symbolic irony,[11] he concludes Part Two: "Let it not be supposed, from what I have just said, that I am detailing any mystery, or penning any romance" (p. 533). (Oh no, not Poe.) But the real "mystery" is not the detective story (although it is on the plot level— and the main story is later repeatedly referred to as a "mystery," pp. 538, 547 (2), 548, 559), the real mystery for Dupin and especially for the reader ("him who contemplates it with a kindred art")[12] concerns the "moral activity which disentangles"—i.e., the psychological solution of the tale. And just as Poe puns about the two mysteries (the literal and thematic levels), so too he puns about the two romances (the story as romance and the homosexual romance).

Why did Poe introduce the homosexual suggestions? Partially because, I suspect, it amused him to slyly tweak his Victorian readers. But he also had good reasons. Homosexuality has psychological and symbolic meanings in Poe's fictive world that complement the story's major themes. Like the psychological reading of the story that I will advance, it suggests perverse psychology. (Indeed, on one level, homosexuality is the subject of Poe's "Imp of the Perverse.") For the union of the opposites, of male and female, suggests a complete whole, as in the archetypal symbolism of a hermaphrodite. Poe repeated the theory of love Aristophanes advanced in the *Symposium*

---

[11] I coin the term thematic/symbolic irony (on the analogy with dramatic irony) to describe the common literary presentation of an ostensibly foolish or wrong statement— that actually, on a thematic and/or symbolic level, points to a truth.

[12] (H, 11: 108). Poe repeatedly condemned the obvious presentation of a theme (or allegory/undercurrent, to use his own terms) and also repeatedly expressed the highest opinion of the ideal reader's responsibility. He even claimed that the ideal reader must possess all the literary ability of the author: "In fact, to appreciate thoroughly the work of what we call genius, is to possess all the genius by which the work was produced" (H, 16: 66–67).

which held that the original humans, before Zeus split them, were both male and female, so that when humans as we know them joined together in sex, they were attempting to recapture their original unity (H, 14: 44).[13] Perhaps Poe's most obvious allegory of the final unity of male and female is the masculine "Monos" and the feminine "Una" (who were formerly earthly lovers) in "The Colloquy of Monos and Una." But Poe repeatedly posits that the actual reality allows mankind only inadequate and fleeting glimpses of "the supernal Oneness." The existing state of things necessarily reveals "the Infernal Twoness" (M, 2:342). For Poe, homosexuality symbolizes mankind's imperfect and necessarily faulty attempt to achieve wholeness. It is the way things are. On the other hand, a satisfactory heterosexual relationship would symbolize completion and unity, yin and yang. The implied final unity of the three couples—Dupin and the narrator, Madame and Mademoiselle L'Espanaye, and the sailor and the orangutan—suggests the proper ingredients of what, in Poe's vision, constitutes an achieved unified life.

The homosexual motif is repeated in the story proper. The laundress testifies that the L'Espanayes "are very affectionate towards each other" (p. 539). The tobaconnist indirectly says that Madame L'Espanaye was mannish, for he has been "selling small quantities of tobacco and snuff to Madame L'Espanaye for nearly four years" (p. 539). The truthfulness of the mother-daughter relationship is impugned by a clever sexual pun: "It was not known whether there were any *living connexions* of Madame L. and her daughter" (p. 539; my emphasis). Although they live in a large house and although another room on the fourth floor "was crowded with old Beds" (p. 542), yet the two women sleep in the same room and in the same bed (p. 539). Of course, like Dupin and the narrator, they live "an exceedingly retired life" together (p. 539). Poe even puns on their lack of male sexual relationships when he writes, "No one was spoken of as frequenting the house" (p. 539); for the phrase "to frequent a house" is often used for a house of prostitution. The rumor that "Madame L'Espanaye told fortunes" suggests that the neighbors found something not only unusual but also sexual about Madame

---

[13] Poe ignores Aristophanes' additional theories which hold that homosexuals also were originally double, and that their joining together also recaptures original unity. Plato, *Lysis, Symposium, Gorgias*, tr. W. R. M. Lamb (Cambridge: Harvard Univ. Press, 1967), pp. 135–47.

L'Espanaye; for a fortune teller, like a masseuse, is often a cover for a prostitute; and perhaps Poe meant the name itself, L'Espanaye, to suggest the word *lesbian*.[14] At any rate, taken together, these details suggest a homosexual relationship.

The main plot of the story opens with the newspaper accounts of the "Extraordinary Murders." They describe at length a key symbolic action—the breaking-in of the door, which occurs "after some delay, occasioned by a fruitless attempt to procure admission in the usual manner" (p. 537). If the action itself were not a possible symbol of rape (especially when accompanied by "a succession of terrific shrieks" and in the context of the house-as-body metaphor), the word *procure*[15] alone might alert the reader to a sexual interpretation. The second description of the breaking-in (contained in the gendarme's deposition) further emphasizes the action as a symbolic rape: "Forced it open, at length, with a bayonet—not with a crowbar. Had but little difficulty in getting it open, on account of its being a double or folding gate, and bolted neither at bottom nor top" (pp. 539–40). Just as the second description of the breaking-in more obviously suggests penetration of the vagina, so too, in the second description, the screams are contrasted with the panting moans of sexual intercourse: "The shrieks were continued until the gate was forced—and then suddenly ceased. They seemed to be screams of some person (or persons) in great agony—were loud and drawn out, not short and quick" (p. 540). If the reader—even unwittingly—suspects or feels that the forcible entry represents a symbolic rape, then Poe has accomplished several things.

First, the reader suspects—or at least feels—that something is going on in the story beside the obvious plot. Since sex in Victorian America was a taboo subject, the reader is slightly excited—and simultaneously fearful—at the prospect of a sexual undercurrent. The reader's response (the key element in Poe's esthetics) is similar to the narrator's when Dupin breaks into his thoughts with a comment proving that Dupin had read his mind. "I was even more startled than I would have been willing to express" (p. 534). Like the narrator, the normal reader (as the history of the interpretation of "The Murders in the

---

[14] The L'Espanaye/lesbian suggestion was made to me by Professor J. Gerald Kennedy at the conclusion of an oral version of this paper.

[15] *OED*, s.v. "procure," 5b.

Rue Morgue" proves) is fearful that his private thoughts may be exposed. Second, the reader begins to think (or at least to feel) in the right way—in terms of connotations, suggestions, and symbols. And third, the story's major subjects and themes are forced upon the reader. The house *is* a metaphor for the human body. The reader may have missed that implication in the introduction ("windows in their bosoms"), but he cannot avoid the emotional excitement generated by the symbolic rape. And if the doorway is the vulva, then the fourth and top floor—the area the women exclusively inhabit— is the mind. Poe believed that the reader should arrive at art's thematic truths by appreciating and analyzing his own emotional reactions. The emotions, Poe believed, pointed to the fundamental truth. Poe quoted Pascal approvingly: "*que tout notre raisonnement se réduit à céder au sentiment*" (M, 2:611). Poe's basic esthetic principle, unity of effect (his theoretical statements and practical demonstrations repeatedly reveal his overwhelming concern with the psychological response of the reader)[16] rests upon his fundamental ontological belief that emotions guided the reason—and even that emotions were truer than reason. Poe has Dupin hint at this ontology: "But it is by these deviations from the plane of the ordinary, that reason feels its way, if at all, in its search for the true" (p. 548).[17]

Like the homosexual suggestions, the symbolic rape focuses the reader's attention upon sex. The rape should make the ideal reader wonder, what is Poe saying about sex? Poe gives two direct clues that the story should be read as an exploration in sexual psychology. The second day's newspaper account (which is the primary text which Dupin will subject to a critical analysis and which is given a title— "The Tragedy in the Rue Morgue"—that obviously makes it a

[16] James Southall Wilson emphasized that Poe's "totality of effect" meant the "desired psychological effect" upon the reader. He aptly commented: "Singleness of idea, simplicity of design, and, in the story, directness and unity of plot, are means of attaining totality of effect, but they are not the end itself. It is the mind of the reader upon which he is working, not the texture and fabric of the thought expression." "Poe's Philosophy of Composition," *North American Review*, 223 (1926), 675-84, at 679 and 677. Walter Blair, "Poe's Conception of Incident and Tone in the Tale," *Modern Philology*, 41 (May, 1944), 228-40; Richard H. Fogle, "Organic Form in American Criticism, 1840-1870," in *The Development of American Literary Criticism*, ed. Floyd Stovall (Chapel Hill: Univ. of North Carolina Press, 1955), pp. 97-98; and George E. Kelly, "Poe's Theory of Unity," *Philological Quarterly*, 37 (1958), 34-44—all also emphasize Poe's concern with the reader's psychology.

[17] An indication of the importance of this hint may be found in *Eureka*, where Poe repeated the sentence and credited it to "The Murders in the Rue Morgue," H, 16:228. Poe also quotes Helvetius approvingly on the superiority of passion to reason, H, 10:131-2.

microcosm of the entire story)[18] begins: "Many individuals have been examined in relation to this most extraordinary and frightful affair." Poe then has the narrator break into the newspaper report: "[The word *affaire* has not yet, in France, that levity of import which it conveys with us]" (p. 538). Obviously the interjected comment screams out the sexual denotation of *affair*.[19] The aside also stresses arbitrary cultural influences upon sexual attitudes, particularly the relatively liberal French customs in contrast to American ones. Later in the story, Dupin says, "By undue profundity we perplex and infeeble thought; and it is possible to make *even Venus herself* vanish from the firmament by a scrutiny too sustained, too concentrated, or too direct" (pp. 545-46; my emphasis).

Throughout the story, Dupin repeatedly says that the Parisian police overlook the obvious, and Poe repeatedly hints that the story concerns psychology and sex. So we return to our original question: what is the story saying about psychology and sex? How do the final tropes and the concluding quotation complement these themes? Actually, every reader believes, as he first reads the story, that he knows the nature of the murderer, and that he knows why the murderer killed the L'Espanayes. During Dupin's analysis, the thoughts of the reader are precisely guided and verbalized by the narrator, who functions as the reader/audience within the story. The role of the narrator as Dupin's naive companion and confidante is a brilliant technical achievement, for Poe puts the reader into the story in the narrator's place, and the reader discovers that the narrator verbalizes his own thoughts and reactions. The primary effect of Poe's tales of ratiocination is, of course, a delight in analysis—or, at least, a seeming delight in a seeming analysis. But as Poe wrote in defending Longfellow from a foolish criticism, no development is possible without subsidiary ideas and effects. He praised Longfellow for having "one *leading* idea which forms the basis of his poem; but to the aid and development of this one there are innumerable others, of which the rare excellence is, that all are in keeping, that none could be well

[18] The heart of the story is Dupin's analysis (pp. 547-62) of the evidence, beginning with his interpretation of the significance of some details in the newspaper reports. Dupin's analysis is, on one "undercurrent," a paradigm of how to read a story—but this is another major theme of "The Murders in the Rue Morgue" and cannot be discussed here.

[19] Poe repeated the word in the conclusion of the newspaper report ("affairs of this nature," 544) and again in the fair copy and the 1841 and 1843 texts (p. 563).

omitted, that each tends to the one general effect" (H, 11:83). While Dupin questions the narrator and analyzes the newspaper report, we follow his supposedly superior mental exertions with admiration—but we identify with the narrator, the ostensible dummy. Poe believed that "During the hour of perusal the soul of the reader is at the writer's control" (H, 11:108). And Poe harrows the reader's soul—even in the tales of ratiocination. The tone of "The Murders in the Rue Morgue" is primarily one of thoughtful analysis—but at the very time that Poe appeals to the reader's mind with analysis, he appeals to his emotions with frightening glimpses of the "Heart Laid Bare" (H, 16:128). It is the narrator who takes us through these emotions.

Repeatedly pressed by Dupin, the narrator is forced to confront the details of the murders and called upon for an explanation. In reply to Dupin's leads and questions, he finally blurts out, "A madman . . . has done this deed—some raving maniac, escaped from a neighboring *Maison de Santé*" (p. 558). At that moment, he voices every reader's confusion, despair, and conclusion. As Daniel Hoffman says after quoting this passage, "My very thoughts."[20] The narrator does not use our modern terminology and say that the murderer must have been a psychotic sex maniac—but that is clearly what he (and every one reading the story for the first time) must think. Poe deliberately creates this impression. The physician, Paul Dumas, suggests that the murderer of the young woman knelt on her: "A large bruise was discovered upon the pit of the stomach, produced, apparently, by the pressure of a knee." He testifies that the murderer of the older woman must have been a "very powerful man," wielding a "large, heavy and obtuse weapon" (pp. 543-44). Dupin repeatedly suggests that the crime must have been committed by a sex maniac. He asks the narrator if he "had observed anything '*peculiar*' at the scene of the atrocity." The narrator finds "something in his manner of emphasizing the word *peculiar,* which caused me to shudder." When we read the narrator's reaction, we too shudder at the peculiarity of the crime. And Dupin stresses the crime's outré character: "The police are confounded by the seeming absence of motive—not for the murder itself—but for the atrocity of the murder" (p. 547). This emphasis

---

[20] Daniel Hoffman, *Poe Poe Poe Poe Poe Poe Poe* (New York: Doubleday & Co., 1972), p. 112.

plunges us into a reasonless universe where madness and crime rage amidst chaos. Dupin alone seems able to order the universe through his superior analysis—but he is grotesquely naive. Dupin is himself the astronomer unable to see Venus because his scrutiny is too abstract.

Dupin subjects a statement in the newspaper account to analysis. "The drawers of the bureau, it is said, had been rifled, although many articles of apparel still remained within them" (p. 556). The narrator and the reader must therefore suppose that some "articles of apparel" had been taken. Evidently the police found it surprising that not all the "articles of apparel" had been taken. Dupin denies the implied conclusion. "The conclusion here is absurd"—but is it? In ostensibly proving his point, Dupin relentlessly dwells on the "articles of apparel." "How are we to know that the articles found in the drawers were not all these drawers had originally contained?" By the repetition of the word *drawers,* Poe forces the reader to feel that what the police and Dupin are really talking about are panties or drawers, not a variety of "articles of apparel." Dupin continues his supposed refutation by characterizing the condition of the "apparel" stolen. "Madame L'Espanaye and her daughter lived an exceedingly retired life—saw no company—seldom went out—had little use for numerous changes of habiliment. Those found were of at least good quality as any likely to be possessed by these ladies. If a thief had taken any, why did he not take the best—why did he not take all?". . . The reader knows. Dupin has told him that the only "articles of apparel" that remained in the drawers were those in good condition. The reader knows the murderer was not interested in such panties. That crazy wanted the worn ones. Dupin is blind to the facts of life—but, then, he inhabits only the fourth floor of his "Time-eaten and grotesque mansion" (p. 532). Dupin believes that breaking-and-entering, theft, gruesome mutilations and murders might well be committed for a few pieces of new linen worth a few francs—but not for psychotic sexual drives. Dupin is an incredible egghead, an intellectual, blind to the facts of life. His refutation concludes with the following triumphant statement of foolish logic: "In a word, why did he abandon four thousand francs in gold to encumber himself with a bundle of linen?" (p. 556). When he reads this statement, every reader is driven to conclude that he knows why. The murderer is a psychotic sex maniac.

Poe forces the reader to feel—and the careful reader to acknowledge—the reality and power of libidinous drives. Although the reader is rushed through Dupin's analysis by the rapid-fire verbal constructions ("saw no company—seldom went out"), he nevertheless impatiently assigns more force to the sexual psychosis than to the desire for money. The real point of Dupin's analysis is to make the reader *feel* the greater validity of the libidinous drives as a motive. For the reader can only know this truth by empathy—i.e., by putting himself in the place of the murderer. Throughout Dupin's analysis of the police deduction, Poe carefully shifts the implied question from whether or not the thief took anything at all from the room to why the murderer would abandon the money and steal worn panties. The reader's answer—that the murderer is a psychotic sex maniac—is at the same time a revelation that we all are potential psychotic sex maniacs, for the basic facts (that the "articles of apparel" were panties, and that the thief preferred to steal worn panties) have been supplied by the reader. To be sure, Poe intended we should make these associations and deductions, but they are certainly not stated by Dupin. Indeed, if we analyze his thinking in this passage, we must judge him a complete naif. Poe thus succeeds in making the reader imaginatively guilty of the murders in the Rue Morgue. Further, the reader, through his combination of head and body, has entirely superior analytical powers to Dupin.[21]

For the following three paragraphs, Dupin continuously fastens our attention upon "the butchery itself": "Here is a woman strangled to death by manual strength, and thrust up a chimney, head downward. . . . In the manner of thrusting the corpse up the chimney, you will admit that there was something *excessively outré*—something altogether irreconcilable with our common notions of human action, even when we suppose the actors the most depraved of men" (p. 557). During the time that Dupin stresses the supposed abnor-

---

[21] Poe here exemplifies the criticism that he made of Macaulay's reputation. He claimed that the public was fooled into thinking Macaulay was a "profound thinker" because the public admired "logic for logic's sake," because the public confounded "the vehicle with the conveyed," and because the public could be "so dazzled by the luminousness with which an idea is set forth as to mistake it for the luminousness of the idea itself" (H, 10:156). Compare Poe's observation on Dupin's logic in a letter to Philip P. Cooke: "These tales of ratiocination owe most of their popularity to being something in a new key. I do not mean to say that they are not ingenious—but people think them more ingenious than they are—on account of their method and *air* of method." *The Letters of Edgar Allan Poe,* ed. John Ward Ostrom (Cambridge: Harvard Univ. Press, 1948), 2:265.

mality of the crime, Poe deliberately makes the reader's flesh crawl. One high point in the reader's reaction occurs when Dupin finally finishes stressing the "*grotesquerie* in horror absolutely alien from humanity" which characterizes the murders and asks "What impression have I made upon your fancy?" (p. 558). In the manuscript, and in both the 1841 and 1843 printed versions, the narrator tells us "I shuddered as Dupin asked me the question." But Poe had used "shudder" for the narrator's reaction before (p. 547) and he wanted to intensify the effect, so in 1845 he revised the sentence to heighten the emotion and to force the reader to experience it: "I felt a creeping of the flesh as Dupin asked me the question" (p. 558). At the very time that Poe is making the reader experience the uncanny effect, he also makes the reader acknowledge—through Dupin's denial—that such crimes are *not* "irreconcilable with our common notions of human action." Similar crimes of mutilation and murder appear in every large-city newspaper nearly weekly. They are a fact of life— and of human nature. Dupin denies this gruesome reality. We want to agree, but we know better—and so we say that the murderer must have been a "raving maniac" (p. 558). Literally, the narrator is wrong, but as Dupin concedes, "In some respects . . . your idea is not irrelevant" (p. 558).

Poe's thematic irony expresses a symbolic truth. A psychotic sex maniac did murder the L'Espanayes. It is a great detective story— but the solution does not lie with the proof that an orangutan murdered the women. That solution, in terms of the story's own fictive world, is merely a "trivial" example of analysis. The "glorious" detective-work that Poe demands of the ideal reader is to solve the murders in terms of "that moral activity which *disentangles*" (p. 528). Poe challenges the reader to explain the murders as necessary outcomes of his characters' psychology. Dupin and the narrator, the sailor and the orangutan, and the L'Espanayes, are all the murderers—and the murdered. Indeed, every reader is made imaginatively to feel (and the ideal reader will ultimately perceive) that he is the murderer and the murdered.

The facts seem straightforward. A woman and her daughter live "an exceedingly retired life" (p. 539). From a small income provided by "some property" (p. 541), the mother "made frequent deposits in small sums" in the same bank for eight years. For that entire time, she never withdrew any money until three days before her death "when she took out in person the sum of 4000 francs" (p. 541). Obviously Madame and Mademoiselle L'Espanaye planned a major change. Evidently they were about to give over their "exceedingly retired life." The normal reasons for great seclusion are extraordinary sensitivity and/or fear. The newspaper reports prove that Madame L'Espanaye possessed both these qualities. The tobacconist testified that the L'Espanayes' house "was formerly occupied by a jeweller, who under-let the upper rooms to various persons." But Madame L'Espanaye "became dissatisfied with the abuse of the premises by her tenant, and moved into them herself, refusing to let any portion." The tobacconist's common-sensical judgment is "The old lady was childish." Clearly Madame L'Espanaye was extraordinarily sensitive to "the abuse of the premises" (p. 539). The "abuse" was presumably the normal wear and tear caused by daily occupancy. The tobacconist judges her neurotic. Symbolically, in terms of the house-as-body allegory, Madame L'Espanaye objects to any use of the body. The underlying cause of her neurosis is also suggested by what we are told concerning the way she lives. The locked doors and windows, the seclusion, and the safe under the bed—all directly show her fear and all symbolically point to sexual suppression.

It may seem contradictory that Poe suggests both that the two women are extraordinarily fearful of sex and that they are homosexuals. But one nineteenth-century theory supposed that lesbianism often accompanied—indeed, was caused by—fear of heterosexuality.[22] Besides, Poe had other good reasons for including these seemingly conflicting implications. Like the homosexual suggestions, the fearfulness of the L'Espanayes calls the reader's attention to sexuality and (like the possible allusions to prostitution) emphasizes the L'Espanayes' lack of heterosexual activity. It also recalls the symbolic and psychological suggestions raised earlier by the implied relationship between the narrator and Dupin. But primarily, it suggests the nature of the transformation which the L'Espanayes are about to undergo. Madame L'Espanaye has withdrawn four thousand francs from the bank. The two women are doing something with the safe open

[22] G. J. Barker-Benfield, *The Horrors of the Half-Known Life: Male Attitudes Toward Women and Sexuality in Nineteenth-Century America* (New York: Harper and Row, 1976), p. 39.

(counting the money?) as they conclude their last-minute preparations for the coming change. Based upon what we have learned about them, we may predict the nature of that change. They are going to change from seclusion to an active participation in society; from fearfulness of heterosexual contacts to flirtation; and from an asexual or homosexual relationship to heterosexual relations. Yet, as all the evidence suggests, they greatly fear activity and heterosexuality.

Before drawing together the major strains of the story in a psychological solution to the murderer's identity, I should comment on the orangutan and the sailor. Both the sailor and the orangutan suggest unrestrained sexuality and animality. The idea of a sailor in port (like the old popular attitude toward a visit to Paris) has always been synonymous with gluttonous, abandoned sexuality. And the orangutan (commonly called the "wild man of the woods") is a version of the traditional "wild man," whose attribute is the club and who symbolizes lust and aggression.[23] The sailor and the orangutan are doubles. When the sailor enters Dupin's room, "He had with him a huge oaken cudgel" (p. 562). Although the orangutan has no club, the physician Paul Dumas testified that the mutilations of Madame L'Espanaye could have been caused by "A heavy club of wood" (p. 544). It may be symbolically significant that the gendarme (the representative of society's force and power) breaks in the door of the L'Espanayes' house "with a crowbar" (p. 537) or, as we later learn, "with a bayonet—not with a crowbar" (p. 539). For the club and other weapons recur in the story, forming a minor motif, always threatening violence. Even Dupin and the narrator prepare for violence, pistols ready (pp. 548, 562, 563). They will meet violence with violence. After Dupin shows his pistol, the sailor "started to his feet and grasped his cudgel" (p. 563). As Poe wrote in "The Philosophy of Composition," a change in mood on the part of the student was "intended to induce a similar one on the part of the reader" (H, 14: 206). The pistols and the sailor's cudgel make the reader anticipate violence. The reader experiences an emotional heightening—an eagerness for violence—even if he does not acknowledge the possibility of violence lurking within himself.

[23] James Hall mentions that the wild man's attribute is the club and identifies the ape with the wild man. *Dictionary of Subjects and Symbols in Art*, rev. ed. (New York: Harper and Row, 1979), pp. 22 and 341. See also Richard Bernheimer, *Wild Men in the Middle Ages* (Cambridge: Harvard Univ. Press, 1952).

The gendarme's breaking into the house with his bayonet is really the third symbolic rape, for the first and the second, as Marie Bonaparte has shown, are the orangutan's entry into the room and its subsequent murders.[24] The gendarme is thus identified with the orangutan (for both are symbols of lust and aggression), only the gendarme uses his bayonet/billy-stick/pistol to defend society, whereas the ape/sailor uses his razor/club against it. The symbolic reading of the story need not (contrary to Bonaparte) represent Poe's recapitulation of his infantile memories of his mother's love-making.[25] Instead, the symbolic reading reveals Poe's artful dramatization of characteristic and cultural ills within a context that presents Poe's remedy.

The sailor testified the events of that fearful night began when he returned "from some sailors' frolic on the night, or rather the morning of the murder" and "found the beast occupying his own bedroom, into which it had broken from a closet adjoining, where it had been, as was thought, securely confined" (pp. 564-65). This passage, suggesting confinement and repression, symbolically portrays the outbreaking of repressed libidinal urges. It is of course a psychological truth that repressed drives will seek some outlet, perhaps with greater rigor because long repressed.[26] The orangutan, in imitation of its master, is shaving. Although this act had humorous and burlesque overtones (Mabbott notes that the story about a barber's pet monkey who shaves the customers is an old favorite of comics), it also admirably reinforces the story's main themes. The usual ending of the stories and broadside ballads about a monkey who shaves himself is that he cuts his own throat.[27] Symbolically, shaving is an act

[24] Marie Bonaparte, *The Life and Works of Edgar Allan Poe: A PsychoAnalytic Interpretation*, tr. John Rodker (New York: Humanities Press, 1971), pp. 454 and 447, respectively.

[25] Bonaparte, pp. 445-56.

[26] William Bradford offers this psychological explanation as one cause of the Plymouth colony's 1642 crime wave. *Of Plymouth Plantation*, ed. Samuel Eliot Morison (New York: Knopf, 1952), pp. 316-17.

[27] For numerous references to such broadside ballads, see G. Malcolm Laws, *American Balladry from British Broadsides* (Philadelphia: American Folksong Society, 1957), p. 279, no. Q14. Henry M. Belden first called attention to the ballad "The Monkey Turn'd Barber" as Poe's possible source in "The Vulgar Ballad," *Sewanee Review*, 19 (1911), 222-24. And Charles Clay Doyle, "The Imitating Monkey: A Folktale Motif in Poe," *North Carolina Folklore Journal*, 23 (1975), 89-91, pointed out that this folktale appears in various languages from the sixteenth century to the present and is common in the South.

of castration.[28] In an ape's shaving himself, the symbolic castration becomes a literal decapitation. The orangutan's shaving in the denouement of the story recalls the gruesome description of Madame L'Espanaye "with her throat so entirely cut that, upon an attempt to raise her, the head fell off" (p. 538). And since, as I will show, Madame L'Espanaye psychologically and symbolically decapitated herself, the orangutan's shaving is thus a splendid analogue for the murders.

Poe even suggests that the Judeo-Christian ascetic tradition is responsible for the sexual illness of his characters and Western society. The sailor "had been accustomed, however, to quiet the creature, even in its fiercest moods, by the use of a whip" (p. 565). The image of whipping, used in connection with suppressing sexual symbols, calls up the masochistic repression of sexual desire by medieval ascetics. In his "Marginalia," Poe linked an absurd "*self*-infliction of punishment" with "the Dervishes, the Simeons, the monastic hair-cloths and shoe-peas, the present Puritanism and cant about the 'mortification' of the flesh" (H, 16:93). Poe's diction supports this interpretation, because *creature* ("to quiet the creature") in most Christian contexts means unregenerate man, that is, man viewed merely as a beast.[29] Poe's image of the sailor quieting the "creature" with a whip summons up the traditional Western—and specifically Christian—attitudes toward sex. Within the fictive world of "The Murders in the Rue Morgue," these ascetic attitudes are blamed for dividing man into body and soul and blamed for producing such symbolic grotesques as the ape and the sailor, who represent headless bodies, sheer sexuality and animality.

The other two sets of doubles, who live only in the fourth story, are also symbolic grotesques—bodiless heads. Dupin and the narrator, like the L'Espanayes, live in the fourth and top story of their house.

---

[28] "To represent castration symbolically, the dream-work makes use of baldness, hair-cutting, falling out of teeth and decapitation." Sigmund Freud, *The Interpretation of Dreams*, v. 5 of *The Standard Edition of the Complete Psychological Works* (London: Hogarth Press, 1953), p. 357.

[29] Surprisingly, this common Christian meaning of *creature* is not defined in the *OED*, even though the examples (s.v. *creature*) under definition no. 2 for 1667 from Milton and under no. 3 for 1837 from Newman both illustrate it. The meaning descends from the Augustinian tradition wherein unregenerate man is viewed merely as a beast. The key Biblical text is 2 Corinthians v. 15: "Therefore if any man *be* in Christ, *he* is a new creature: old things are passed away; behold, all things are new" (King James version).

In Poe's common house-as-body metaphor, they inhabit the mind only. Furthermore, in his analysis, Dupin completely denies the validity—and even ignores the existence of—sexual drives. Their denial of the body is their illness—and, in the case of the L'Espanayes, the cause of their death. The severed head of Madame L'Espanaye symbolizes both couples' psychological state. Poe presents us with a key to the psychological reading of the story in the three concluding metaphors—but they only serve as an epilogue for the ideal reader, who has felt the truth of the symbols as they appear throughout the story and who applies analysis to the truth of the emotions. During his analysis, Dupin says "It is not too much to say that neither of us believe in praeternatural events. Madame and Mademoiselle L'Espanaye were not destroyed by spirits" (p. 551). Poe uses thematic irony as a clue to the truth. On the psychological level, they were indeed killed by spirits. Their mutilation and death enact the most grotesque possibility of their subconscious fears. Their nightmares come true. Madame and Mademoiselle L'Espanaye are killed by a psychotic sex maniac—but it lives within them, in their fears and in their dreams.

That is the significance of the story's final sentence. In Rousseau's *La Nouvelle Héloise,* Julia or the new Eloisa discusses the possibility of the soul's being separated from the body. As she lies on her death bed, the Enlightenment rationalist Julia ridicules the simplicity of those persons who have, in similar situations, promised to return to their friends to tell them about the other world. Julia claims that such promises are as absurd as the stories of ghosts and apparitions who are said to commit a thousand disorders and to torment credulous good women. In a note, Rousseau makes fun of Plato's psychological explanation of such fantasies, and ends by saying that such explanations are common to philosophers of all ages, who commonly deny what is, and explain what is not.[30] So "The Murders in the Rue Morgue" ends with Dupin saying he admires the Prefect G. for his "one master stroke of cant, by which he has attained his reputation for ingenuity. I mean the way he has '*de nier ce qui est, et d'expliquer ce qui n'est pas*' " (p. 568).

In the conclusion, Dupin (who has previously in the story been an

---

[30] Jean-Jacques Rousseau, *La Nouvelle Héloise,* ed. Daniel Mornet, 4 v. (Paris: Hackette, 1925), 4:314-5.

egghead—a version of the Prefect G.) speaks for Poe, using thematic irony. Dupin and Poe are affirming the existence of spirits—in the subconscious.[31] By their mental illness, by their deliberate suppression of sexuality, by their denial of the body, the L'Espanayes have created the monster who kills them. The psychological level of the story suggests that a man's penis is the bludgeoning instrument of death. Not, to be sure, a real penis—but such a one as might exist in the imagination of a severely repressed female neurotic: "Any large, heavy, and obtuse weapon would have produced such results, if wielded by the hands of a very powerful man. No woman could have inflicted the blows with any weapon" (p. 544). When the narrator (and the reader) concludes that some psychotic sex maniac has committed the crime, he is right. The "raving maniac" (p. 558) exists in the L'Espanayes' minds. Their continual suppression of the body and sex, their heightened fears as they make their last preparations before breaking away from their old patterns of suppression, result in creating at this three A.M. climactic moment the monster who kills them. Psychologically, the L'Espanayes cut off their own heads. Poe portrays a violent and horrible murder, but it is not rare in Poe's or our own society. The literal murders symbolize common psychological murders. Perhaps, as Poe suggests, the traditions of Western and specifically Christian society are partly to blame. But Poe also suggests that archetypal symbols of separation and schizophrenia are found in classical times as well as modern, in France as well as America. They are an aspect of being human—and are characteristic of humanity.

The newspaper report stresses that Madame L'Espanaye's head was "fearfully mutilated . . . so much so as scarcely to retain any semblance of humanity" (p. 538), which might well make us wonder about Poe's definition of humanity. Dupin twice, in speaking of the

---

[31] Since Dupin earlier ignores the obvious sexual interpretation (see notes 15 and 19), he is thus an inconsistent character—or, rather, one whose basic principles for analysis are inconsistent. Of course he appears to be consistent. And even the most obvious allegories in Poe's tales, when closely examined, yield contradictory undercurrents. My reading of the psychological undercurrent in the tale strengthens the suggestion that Poe was influenced by "A Chapter on Goblins," *Blackwood's,* 14 (1823), 639–46, where the writer argued for "the reality of apparitions"—on the basis that not to believe in apparitions is to give up romance. Poe goes that author one better—and proves that apparitions exist in every dreaming or subconscious mind. Benjamin Franklin Fisher IV, "Poe, Blackwood's, and 'The Murders in the Rue Morgue,'" *American Notes and Queries,* 12 (1974), 109–10.

peculiarity of the murders, claims that the crime contradicted "our common notions of human action" (p. 557), that it was "a *grotesquerie* in horror absolutely alien from humanity" (p. 558). But, as we have seen, the reader naturally assumes that the murderer was a psychotic sex criminal—a species perhaps unique to humanity and certainly one characteristic of humanity, as newspaper reports show. Further, every reader believes that a madman has committed the murder: not only because he knows that mankind is capable of such actions but because he finds himself excited by—and identifying with—the murderer. Poe proves that every reader will find that his own subconscious lusts and aggressions make the crime explainable. It is thematically ironic that the murderer is ostensibly non-human. We are, on the literal level of the story, relieved that mutilation and murder are perpetrated by something sub-human; that the *ingress* and *egress,* the shrill and gruff voices, may be so logically explained; but, actually, the symbolic and psychological truths of the story prove that we live in a non-rational, chaotic world, where man is the most inhuman of all animals. When Dupin reveals the ostensible truth to the narrator that the murderer was an orangutan, Poes drags in a reference to the "imitative propensities of these mammalia" (p. 559). Poe also stresses that the orangutan, after escaping from the closet, was imitating the sailor: "Razor in hand, and fully lathered, it was sitting before a looking-glass, attempting the operation of shaving, in which it had no doubt previously watched its master through the key-hole of the closet" (p. 565). Those very details which Dupin singled out as proving the mutilations to be "altogether irreconcilable with our common notions of human action" (p. 557) are the ones caused by the *humanness* of the orangutan's response when he sees the face of the sailor in the window. "The fury of the beast, who no doubt bore still in mind the dreaded whip, was instantly converted into fear. Conscious of having deserved punishment, it seemed desirous of concealing its bloody deeds, and skipped about the chamber in an agony of nervous agitation" (p. 567). Fear, shame, and consciousness are the human characteristics that cause the orangutan to thrust the corpse of Mademoiselle L'Espanaye up the chimney and to hurl the old lady out the window. "In the manner of thrusting the corpse up the chimney, you will admit that there was something *excessively outré*—something altogether irreconcilable with our common notions of human action, even when we suppose the actors the most depraved of men" (p. 557). Dupin is wrong again. The thrusting of the corpse up the chimney is perfectly accounted for—in human terms. Only the strength necessary to do it is super- (or sub-) human. What is *peculiar* is that an orangutan would do it; but then, give the orangutan human characteristics, and his shame and fear perfectly explain the action.

The story proves that spirits exist—in man's subconscious—and the story attacks the Enlightenment enthroning of reason. It was poetic justice that caused Poe to set the story in Paris, for the guillotining of French intellectuals proved that the Enlightenment ideas inadequately defined man. Like Dupin, Rousseau is an emotional and psychological naif. Poe's story of decapitation, proving the fallacy of the Enlightenment ideal of man, recalls the French Revolution which, for the Romantics in general, was historical testimony to the psychological and ontological truth of "The Murders in the Rue Morgue."[32] Not that Poe believed man to be merely or even primarily body and emotions. He testifies elsewhere that he thought reason was man's distinguishing characteristic (H, 16:6–7). All three qualities should be integrated. A headless body is as grotesque—bears as little resemblance to true humanity—as a bodiless head. That is the ultimate significance of the characters all being doubles for one another. Dupin and the narrator represent the analyzing and creative intelligence—aspects of reason; the L'Espanayes represent the suppression of the emotions—another aspect of the head's supremacy; and the orangutan and the sailor represent animality and sexuality—the body alone. As the reader perceives the true nature of the murderous assailant (the breaking out of repressed libidinal drives), he also perceives the need for the integration of the entire self. Dupin frees Le Bon when he reveals that the murderer was an orangutan. Poe implies that we will free the good in man when we correctly identify the murderer as the repressed libido, for then we acknowledge it necessary to unify the opposing forces that exist in man.

[32] Brigid Brophy, "Detective Fiction: A Modern Myth of Violence," *Hudson Review*, 18 (1965), 11–30, and Albert D. Hutter, "Dreams, Transformations, and Literature: The Implications of Detective Fiction," *Victorian Studies*, 19 (1975), 181–209, have previously linked the French Revolution and the rise of the detective story, but they both believe that the genre embodies Enlightenment principles.

Poe's Re-Vision: The Recovery of the Second Story

Cynthia S. Jordan

I

WHILE the longstanding debates over Hawthorne's treatment of women characters have been reinvigorated and refined by feminist critics in the last fifteen years or so, feminist criticism has as yet had little to say about Poe's women-centered fictions.[1] This lack of attention might have surprised—or more probably, annoyed—the egotistical Poe, since he himself suggested the terms by which his treatment of women characters might be compared with Hawthorne's. In an 1842 review of *Twice-Told Tales*, Poe praised "The Minister's Black Veil" as "a masterly composition" whose underlying meaning would probably be lost on most readers, for the "*moral* put into the mouth of the dying minister will be supposed to convey the *true* import of the narrative; and that a crime of dark dye, (having reference to the 'young lady') has been committed, is a point which only minds congenial with that of the author will perceive."[2]

Poe's use of the term "crime" was perceptive in this instance and virtually prophetic of the direction Hawthorne's tales would take in the next few years. Nina Baym has observed, for example, that in "most of the stories written before . . . 1842, the destruction or damaging of the woman seems to result accidentally as a by-

---

[1] Nina Baym has made the strongest and most persuasive case for regarding Hawthorne's treatment of women characters as feminist, in a series of articles, two of which will be cited below, and a full-length critical biography, *The Shape of Hawthorne's Career* (Ithaca: Cornell Univ. Press, 1976). For opposing views, see Wendy Martin, "Seduced and Abandoned in the New World," in *Woman in Sexist Society*, ed. Vivian Gornick and Barbara K. Moran (New York: Basic Books, 1971), pp. 329–46; and Judith Fryer, *The Faces of Eve: Women in the Nineteenth-Century American Novel* (New York: Oxford Univ. Press, 1976).

[2] *Graham's Magazine*, May 1842; rpt. in *Hawthorne: The Critical Heritage*, ed. J. Donald Crowley (London: Routledge & Kegan Paul, 1970), p. 92.

American Literature, Volume 59, Number 1, March 1987. Copyright © 1987 by The Duke University Press. CCC 0002-9831/87/$1.50.

product." The question of the male character's having a "covert intention" to cause such harm, however, "cannot be entirely absent," especially since in the years which followed, Hawthorne's stories "escalate" the male character's ambiguous intentions to "an attitude more clearly hostile."[3] In stories such as "The Birthmark" (1843), "Rappaccini's Daughter" (1844), "Drowne's Wooden Image" (1844), "The Artist of the Beautiful" (1844), and "Ethan Brand" (1849), "crimes" against women are indeed laid bare.

A chronology of Poe's women-centered tales written during these same years suggests a reason for his apparently inside knowledge of Hawthorne's "true import" in 1842. Having already published "Berenice" (1835), "Morella" (1835), "Ligeia" (1838) and "The Fall of the House of Usher" (1839), Poe had clearly established his own "congenial" interest in the fictional possibilities to be found in covert crimes against ladies. With the publication of "The Murders in the Rue Morgue" in 1841, he had begun to highlight such crimes and would continue to do so in the two subsequent detective stories in the Dupin series, "The Mystery of Marie Rogêt" (1842) and "The Purloined Letter" (1845). Thus the evolution of Hawthorne's women-centered tales followed the same pattern as Poe's: both authors gradually changed their fictional focus from covert to overt victimizations of women.

A brief look at individual works reveals more similarity between the authors, because the recurring crime in all of the above-mentioned tales is that one or more women have been criminally silenced; the speech that would allow them self-expression has been denied or usurped by male agents. Poe was especially prolific in creating images of violently silenced women, their vocal apparatus the apparent target of their attackers, who, in the earlier stories, are the storytellers themselves. One remembers the forcible removal of Berenice's teeth by her professed "lover"; the premature shroud that "lay heavily about the mouth" of Ligeia[4]—and of Madeline Usher, no doubt; and later, the throat-cutting and

---

[3] "Thwarted Nature: Nathaniel Hawthorne as Feminist," in *American Novelists Revisited: Essays in Feminist Criticism*, ed. Fritz Fleischmann (Boston: G. K. Hall, 1982), pp. 64–65.

[4] "Ligeia," in *Collected Works of Edgar Allan Poe*, ed. Thomas Ollive Mabbott (Cambridge: Harvard Univ. Press, 1978), II, 330. Subsequent references to this edition will appear parenthetically in the text.

strangulations in "The Murders in the Rue Morgue" and "The Mystery of Marie Rogêt." The psychological violence in such tales is no less pre-emptive. Morella's narrator-husband comes to a point where he can "no longer bear . . . the low tone of her musical language," and after she dies she is denied a place in his own speech: "Morella's name died with her at her death. Of the mother I had never spoken to the daughter . . ." (II, 231, 235). Even in "The Purloined Letter," the least violent of Poe's tales about women, the Queen who sees her "letter" stolen before her very eyes cannot speak to save herself for fear of jeopardizing her position with the King, who fails to understand the crime taking place.

In Hawthorne's tales about victimized women, silencing is most often effected by the artifices of male characters who are ostensibly obsessed with "perfecting" women according to their own ideas of what women should be. Georgiana in "The Birthmark" and Beatrice Rappaccini are imprisoned, both literally and figuratively in male fantasies, their self-expression limited and finally extinguished altogether. In "Drowne's Wooden Image," in which the process appears to be reversed and the image of a woman comes to life, the woman is still not allowed to speak for herself. This man-made creature is led silently away by another male character, which surely accounts for the broad gold chain around her neck: she is marked from first to last as a slave to male image-making. Hawthorne continued to explore the idea of the male artist's thinly veiled misogyny in "The Artist of the Beautiful." There, Owen Warland originally fantasizes Annie Hovenden as a fitting "interpreter" of his works to those of lesser sensibilities, but he eventually forecloses his own fantasy and any pronouncement she might have made by convincing himself that Annie "could never say the fitting word . . . which should be the perfect recompense of an artist."[5] Finally, in "Ethan Brand," the recurring crime against women is labeled as such—"the only crime for which Heaven could afford no mercy," and the prototypical victim of the Unpardonable Sin is Esther, the girl whom, "with such cold and

[5] In *Mosses from an Old Manse*, Volume X of *The Centenary Edition of the Works of Nathaniel Hawthorne*, ed. William Charvat et al. (Columbus: Ohio State Univ. Press, 1974), pp. 468, 472.

remorseless purpose, Ethan Brand had made the subject of psychological experiment, and wasted, absorbed, and perhaps annihilated her soul, in the process."[6]

It is crimes of silencing such as these which have understandably fueled the feminist critical debate over Hawthorne's responsibilities as an artist. Judith Fetterley has argued of "The Birthmark" in particular that Hawthorne "is unwilling to do more with the sickness [of the male victimizer] than call it sick," and of such stories in general that they expose "the imaginative limits of our literature." This type of "storytelling and art," she claims, "can do no more than lament the inevitable"—the criminal nature of our culture's sexism—and the "lament is self-indulgent; it offers the luxury of feeling bad without the responsibility of change."[7] Baym has taken a more approving view of Hawthorne, basing her argument on the gradual evolution of his art which culminates, she maintains, in "the triumph of *The Scarlet Letter*." Like Fetterley, she acknowledges "the responsibility of change": while condemning his male characters' crimes against women, he must nevertheless "represent them, and thus the question of his own motivation as an artist enters his discourse. He must hold himself responsible along with other men for injuries done to women; he inflicts imaginary injuries on imaginary women through the stories he creates, in which women are injured. To some degree, he has a higher degree of responsibility than other men, because he has an awareness that others lack. . . ." Baym argues, however, that Hawthorne's art accedes to that responsibility. His progression from the delineation of ambiguous or covert criminality to blatantly condemnatory portrayals of the injuries done to women by "warped" male mentality brings him at last to that groundbreaking moment in "The Custom House" when "the Hawthorne narrator accepts the woman's story as his subject and, putting her scarlet letter on his own breast, loses his identity in hers."[8] In *The*

---

[6] In *The Snow-Image and Uncollected Tales*, Volume XI of *The Centenary Edition of the Works of Nathaniel Hawthorne*, ed. William Charvat et al. (Columbus: Ohio State Univ. Press, 1974), pp. 88, 94.

[7] *The Resisting Reader: A Feminist Approach to American Fiction* (Bloomington: Indiana Univ. Press, 1978), pp. xiv–xv.

[8] "Thwarted Nature," pp. 63, 62, 61, 73.

Scarlet Letter "the woman's story" is finally told, and in crossing gender boundaries Hawthorne thus goes beyond "the imaginative limits" of male-authored fictions.

What I propose to do in this essay is to bring Poe into the critical arena on Hawthorne's coat-tails, as it were. Given the similar progression of his fictional focus from covert to overt crimes against women, and given his similar understanding of what in fact constitutes such "crimes," Poe's women-centered tales raise the same issues as Hawthorne's: "the imaginative limits" of male-authored fictions and "the responsibility of change." What makes Poe an equally apt candidate for a feminist inquiry is that, like Hawthorne, he incorporates those issues into his own discourse, and his fictional response to both problems is also to cross gender boundaries in order to tell "the woman's story."

Poe's villainous narrators in tales like "Berenice," "Morella," and "Ligeia" do indeed tell one-sided stories, and the warped nature of their sexual crimes has been well documented.[9] Poe's search for a solution to such crimes is my main subject here, and "The Fall of the House of Usher" marks the beginning of that search. Starting with Roderick Usher, Poe began his experiments with the androgynous male character whose developing empathy with a woman enables him to reject one-sided male-authored fictions and finally to engender a new fictional form—a second story that provides a text for female experience. In the Dupin tales that follow, in which the task of solving crimes against women calls for a detective with an awareness that other men lack, the androgynous Dupin becomes virtually a feminist critic. In Dupin, Poe created a new caretaker of social and political order, and Dupin fulfills these responsibilities by going beyond the imaginative limits of the male storytellers around him and recovering the second story—"the woman's story"—which has previously gone untold. Whether that act of recovery establishes Poe as a writer of feminist sensibility is an issue I will take up in my conclusion.

---

[9] Michael Davitt Bell has shown the narrators of "Berenice," "Morella," and "Ligeia" to be "lover-murderers," repulsed by sexuality, in *The Development of American Romance: The Sacrifice of Relation* (Chicago: Univ. of Chicago Press, 1980), pp. 101, 112–17. See also Terence J. Matheson, "The Multiple Murder in 'Ligeia': A New Look at Poe's Narrator," *Canadian Review of American Studies*, 13 (1982), 279–89.

II

The crime against the Lady Madeline Usher is that she is prematurely entombed, and while Roderick has traditionally been considered solely responsible, he is but a character in the story himself, and his actions are at least in part the product of his narrator's construction. That is, while critics have credited him with a variety of personal motives for trying to kill his "tenderly beloved sister" (II, 404), including self-defense, euthanasia, and a vampiristic "creative impulse,"[10] the fact remains that he could not have incarcerated Madeline without the narrator's help, as Roderick himself comes to realize: "*We have put her living in the tomb!*" (II, 416). Thus it is the male narrator's actions in this story, his influence over Roderick and his misogynist strategies of textual control, that first warrant a reader's attention—and suspicion.

A boyhood friend of Roderick, the narrator arrives on the scene at the outset to bolster his friend's waning manhood, and from hints variously placed in his narration, it soon becomes clear that he views Roderick's acute nervous condition as arising from his sister's presence, perhaps from her overcloseness or her unmanly influence. The longstanding critical consensus regarding the narrator is that he is a well-intentioned man of reason, valiantly, albeit naively, trying to make sense of a world skewed by irrational forces.[11] His animosity towards Madeline, however, which is foreshadowed in his first description of the mansion upon his arrival, seems if anything unreasonable, irrational. The "vacant and eye-like windows" (II, 398), the "fine tangled web-work" of fungi "hanging . . . from the eaves" (II, 400), and the crack which runs from roof to foundation prefigure Roderick's "luminous" eyes, his "hair of a more than web-like softness and tenuity" (II,

---

[10] J. O. Bailey, "What Happens in 'The Fall of the House of Usher'?" *American Literature*, 35 (1964), 445–66; Maurice Beebe, "The Universe of Roderick Usher," in *Poe: A Collection of Critical Essays*, ed. Robert Regan (Englewood Cliffs, N. J.: Prentice-Hall, 1967), pp. 129–30; and Daniel Hoffman, *Poe Poe Poe Poe Poe Poe Poe* (New York: Doubleday, 1972), pp. 310–11.

[11] See, for example, Charles Feidelson, Jr., *Symbolism and American Literature* (Chicago: Univ. of Chicago Press, 1953), p. 35; Joel Porte, *The Romance in America: Studies in Cooper, Poe, Hawthorne, Melville, and James* (Middletown, Conn.: Wesleyan Univ. Press, 1969), p. 62; and Stefano Tani, *The Doomed Detective: The Contribution of the Detective Novel to Postmodern American and Italian Fiction* (Carbondale: Southern Illinois Univ. Press, 1984), p. 12.

401–02), and his oddly split personality, all of which seem ominous enough to the narrator. But he experiences "a shudder even more thrilling than before" when he looks at the reflection of the House in the tarn, the "remodelled and inverted images" (II, 398) which represent Madeline, Roderick's physical and psychological counterpart. In particular, the "silent tarn" (II, 400) foreshadows Madeline's ill-fated exclusion from the narrator's story, for she will be buried at a "great depth" (II, 410) in the House, in a chamber that lies beneath the surface of the tarn and of the narrative.

The narrator's first encounter with Madeline confirms the conflict between the male storyteller and the lady of the House, for he frames the encounter as one between mutually exclusive presences. "I regarded her with an utter astonishment not unmingled with dread. . . . A sensation of stupor oppressed me," he tells us, and the effect of his presence on her is equally oppressive: "on the closing in of the evening of my arrival at the house, she succumbed . . . to the prostrating power of the destroyer." What is of interest here is the periphrastic description of her lapse into a cataleptic–speechless–stupor and the narrator's passive construction in the phrasing that follows: "the lady, at least while living, would be seen by me no more." Without implicating himself as an agent in her immediate demise, the narrator uses language covertly to relegate Madeline to a passive position in relation to himself, and in the next sentence he tries to exclude her from the text altogether: "For several days ensuing, her name was unmentioned by either Usher or myself" (II, 404). Although he ostensibly remarks on this to demonstrate his concern and sensitivity for his friend's grief over his sister's deteriorating condition, the effect is to show the narrator making sure that Madeline has no place in their masculine language or in this male-authored fiction.

Similarly, on the verge of her return from the tomb, the narrator will try not to hear what he dismisses as her "indefinite sounds" (II, 411) as she breaks through steel and a copper-lined vault, sounds which emanate from the tomb "beneath . . . [his] own sleeping apartment" (II, 410) on a night when he tries unsuccessfully to sleep. The suggestion here of a guilty conscience, or more specifically, of a consciousness plagued by its repressed underpinnings, is heightened by the fact that the narrator is awakened to such ominous sounds by the nightmare vision of "an incubus," which he wants to believe is "of utterly causeless alarm" (II, 411). His word is ill-chosen, however, or at least revealing of the psychological processes he has previously tried to conceal, for "incubus" is the archaic name for a male spirit that visited women in their sleep and aroused female sexuality. If his word choice is a conscious misnomer, that is, if he has substituted "incubus" for "succubus," the female counterpart supposed to visit sleeping men, then the choice is but another narrative strategy intended to exclude any female agency from his text. If, as seems more likely, we are to take "incubus" as an authentic report of a mind that is losing conscious control (for on this night of nights the return of the repressed is imminent), then Poe would seem to be suggesting that the narrator's homoerotic attraction to Roderick has caused him to see himself in some way feminized. If this is the case, then the nightmare status of this identification with female sexuality is no less proof of the narrator's misogyny—of his fear and hatred of the female sexuality incarnate in Madeline Usher.

It is Roderick who finally admits to hearing Madeline, and it is Roderick's growing consciousness of the crime perpetrated against his sister that finally allows her back into the text. Before he can make such an admission, however, he has first to undergo a mighty transformation for a fictional character and free himself of his narrator's control. Essentially, the conflict between the male storyteller and the female character is internalized in the androgynous Roderick, whose dual gender is depicted in behavior that is "alternately vivacious and sullen" and in a voice that varies "rapidly from a tremulous indecision" to a "species of energetic concision" also described as a "guttural utterance" (II, 402). That he is Madeline's twin more obviously implies a merging of gender identities in this story, and there are other suggestions of his partly feminine nature. Given the year of publication for "The Fall of the House of Usher," for example, when the "feminization of American culture" was well under way, the fact that Roderick is an artist is itself enough to insure his effeminate status.[12] In addition, his

[12] I have borrowed the phrase from Ann Douglas' *The Feminization of American Culture* (New York: Knopf, 1977), in which she discusses the feminized status of nineteenth-century American artists at length.

composition of a musical ballad is reminiscent of Morella and Ligeia, who had been characterized by their musical language (II, 227, 311), which their male narrators had also found unsettling. Poe's physical description of Roderick is in fact, as D. H. Lawrence recognized, very similar to that of the beautiful Ligeia.[13] He has the same large, pale brow; eyes "large, liquid, and luminous beyond comparison"; lips of "a surpassingly beautiful curve"; and "a nose of delicate Hebrew model" (II, 401). Thus it is not surprising that the narrator speaks distastefully of his friend's "peculiar physical conformation and temperament" (II, 402) or that he will try to cure him of the effeminacy he denigrates as a "mental disorder" (II, 410).

We may speculate that it was the masculine side of Roderick's character, or rather, his desire for an exclusively masculine identity, that originally motivated him to summon the narrator to him, "with a view of attempting . . . some alleviation of his malady" (II, 398). Once the narrator is in authorial possession of the House, however, and Madeline's effeminizing influence has been dispatched, Roderick begins to have second thoughts about what he will finally come to see as the crime of masculine exclusivity, and his change of mind is imaged in his search for a narrative form that will allow him to express what the narrator has so artfully excluded.

Roderick's first attempt to communicate his inner turmoil after Madeline has been confined to her sick chamber, for example, is through a "perversion and amplification" of a waltz by Von Weber. That Roderick gives an unusual interpretation of this musical score suggests his desire to deviate from male-authored compositions. But the single-minded narrator characteristically refuses to confer such meaning on his friend's deviation from a masculine script and thus labels it merely a "perversion" (II, 405). The next of Roderick's creations we see, a small painting of an interior vault that suggests both Madeline's femaleness and her fate, is illuminated, the misogynous narrator would have us believe, with "inappropriate splendor," and again he resists assigning meaning to his friend's subversive attempt to communicate otherness, claiming that Roderick's subject may be "shadowed forth, [only]

---

[13] *Studies in Classic American Literature* (Garden City, N. Y.: Doubleday, 1923); rpt. in *The Shock of Recognition*, ed. Edmund Wilson (New York: Random House, 1955), p. 979.

feebly, in words" (II, 405-06). Roderick's third formal experiment, the musical ballad of "The Haunted Palace," has its own verbal component, which implies Roderick's growing abilities as a storyteller in his own right. But here, perhaps sensing a rival narrative voice for the first time, our narrator escalates his textual control. Acknowledging that there is an "under or mystic current of . . . meaning," he nevertheless exerts editorial authority over Roderick's text in phrasing that hints at partial censorship: "The verses . . . ran very nearly, if not accurately, thus:" (II, 406).

"The Haunted Palace," like "The Fall of the House of Usher," tells the story of a mind ("Thought's dominion") assailed and enervated by nameless "evil things," and as in the prose narrative, where Madeline's enshrouded body is graced by "the mockery of a faint blush upon the bosom and the face" (II, 410), "the glory / That blushed and bloomed / Is but a dim-remembered story / Of the old time entombed" (II, 406-07). The narrator of "The Fall of the House of Usher" has used his narrative strategies to suppress the "story" of Madeline's victimization, and Roderick's ballad, while it is an improvement over the nonverbal suggestiveness of his music and his painting, is no more explicit about the crime perpetrated against his sister: it tells its tale in symbolism, metonymy, allegory—all misnomers sanctioned historically by a male-dominant literary tradition. It is Roderick's task finally to retrieve that "dim-remembered story" from the obfuscating language of male-authored fictions, and to do so he must become fully conscious of his own complicity in the crime of excluding-by-misnaming. It was Roderick after all who had first invited the narrator's misogynistic intrusion into the House of Usher by labelling his "sympathies" with his lady sister a "malady" (II, 410).

Roderick's reviving sympathies with and for his sister precipitate her return from the tomb to the text, and in the climactic closing scenes of this tale, where Roderick at last acknowledges and renounces his crime, the narrator struggles to maintain his textual control. As Madeline makes headway up from the lower regions of the House, the narrator, finally showing his true colors, tries desperately to shut out her noisy return with the language of another male-authored fiction, "the only book immediately at hand." Trying to hold Roderick's divided attention with "a gentle violence" (II, 413), he reads him the story of Ethelred, a manly hero and "conqueror," who is challenged by a dragon with "a shriek so horrid and harsh, and withal so piercing, that Ethelred had fain to close his ears with his hands against the dreadful noise of it" (II, 414). But Roderick here becomes virtually "a resisting reader." He rejects both the model of manliness the narrator has tried to impose upon him and the misnaming of the sound he hears, and he replaces the narrator's death-dealing text with a new, second story in a dramatic act of "re-vision"[14]:

Not hear it?—yes, I hear it, and *have* heard it. Long—long—long—many minutes, many hours, many days, have I heard it—yet I dared not—oh, pity me, miserable wretch that I am! I dared not—I *dared* not speak! *We have put her living in the tomb*! . . . And now—tonight—Ethelred—ha! ha! the breaking of the hermit's door, and the death-cry of the dragon, and the clangor of the shield!—say, rather, the rending of her coffin, and the grating of the iron hinges of her prison, and her struggles within the coppered archway of the vault! . . . MADMAN! I TELL YOU THAT SHE NOW STANDS WITHOUT THE DOOR! (II, 416)

By momentarily freeing himself of the narrator's control and authoring a second story that explicitly reveals the crime perpetrated against femaleness, Roderick has succeeded in bringing Madeline to the threshold of the narrator's tale. And indeed, the unmasked "MADMAN" in Poe's story is here forced to acknowledge in unambiguous words the irrefutable truth of Roderick's narrative: "without those doors there *did* stand the lofty and enshrouded figure of the lady Madeline of Usher. There was blood upon her white robes, and the evidence of some bitter struggle upon every portion of her emaciated frame" (II, 416; Poe's emphasis). The narrator is still not willing to admit his role in her long "struggle" for acknowledgment, however, any more than he is willing to wait around for her to speak her own mind. Claiming that Madeline and Roderick reunite only to die in each other's arms, this eminently unreliable narrator flees the chamber, the House, and his own misogynistic narrative endeavor.[15] "The Fall of the

---

[14] Adrienne Rich, "When We Dead Awaken: Writing as Re-Vision," in *On Lies, Secrets, and Silence: Selected Prose 1966–1978* (New York: Norton, 1979), p. 35. I will give Rich's full definition of "re-vision" later in the text.

[15] G. R. Thompson has also argued the unreliability of the narrator, but for different reasons. He claims that the narrator gradually comes to accept Roderick's mad interpreta-

House of Usher" ends with the narrator's fragmented sentences, the last fragments of his control. But control, nevertheless, for his final act of "sentencing" is to dispatch Madeline and her too-familiar twin into the "silent tarn," out of mind and out of language one last time: "the deep and dark tarn at my feet closed sullenly and silently over the fragments of the '*House of Usher*' " (II, 417).

In this tale, Roderick's growing abilities as a storyteller are parallelled by his growing terror at the implications of what he must finally do: act as a free agent and virtually rupture the narrative proper with a second story that lays bare the crime of male-authored fictions. The rupture is momentary, lasting just long enough to allow the woman character to get a foot in the door, but it is a significant moment in the evolution of Poe's artistry. Roderick Usher was a new character in Poe's repertoire, an androgynous spokesperson capable of giving voice to female experience and critiquing male-authored fictions which mute that experience, and despite what his madman-narrator must have hoped, his unusual talents were not so easily laid to rest. They would surface again two years later in the service of C. Auguste Dupin, Poe's great detective. The new genre that serves as a vehicle for this androgynous mastermind may be said to be Poe's own "second story," for it too is a new narrative form that critiques male-authored interpretive paradigms which fail to do justice to women. In the three detective stories published between 1841 and 1845, Poe moved from the timeless, dreamlike worlds of remote gothic mansions, turrets, and dungeons to the social realm of neighborhoods, shops, newspapers, and political intrigue, where the investigation of seemingly isolated crimes against women uncovers a network of covert gender-related "crimes" that pervades the entire social order. And Dupin, like Roderick Usher before him, is the detective-critic who brings such "crimes" to light.[16]

---

tions and that the scene of Madeline's return is thus a dual hallucination. See *Poe's Fiction: Romantic Irony in the Gothic Tales* (Madison: Univ. of Wisconsin Press, 1973), pp. 68–104, and "Poe and the Paradox of Terror: Structures of Heightened Consciousness in 'The Fall of the House of Usher,' " in *Ruined Eden of the Present: Hawthorne, Melville, and Poe*, ed. G. R. Thompson and Virgil L. Lokke (West Lafayette, Ind.: Purdue Univ. Press, 1981), pp. 313–40.

[16] Tani, p. 4, likens Dupin to Roderick Usher on the grounds that each is a poet-figure suffering from a "diseased" imagination. For other readings of Dupin as a poet-figure, see

The epigraph to the first tale, "The Murders in the Rue Morgue," introduces the idea of crossing gender boundaries to recover the now "dim-remembered story" of female experience: "What song the Syrens sang, or what name Achilles assumed when he hid himself among women, although puzzling questions, are not beyond *all* conjecture" (II, 527). Like Roderick, Dupin exhibits a "Bi-Part Soul," which leads his narrator to imagine "a double Dupin," and he speaks in dual modes, his normal speaking voice "a rich tenor" which rises "into a treble" when he delivers his analysis of a crime, i.e., when he recounts the experience of a female victim (II, 533). That he represents a second draft of Roderick's character, however, is evident in his greater ability to speak, literally, for the silenced woman, to imagine her story in her own words. In "The Mystery of Marie Rogêt," for example, Dupin goes so far as to recreate the thought-pattern of the murdered Marie in the first-person: "We may imagine her thinking thus—'I am to meet a certain person . . .' " (III, 756).

The most significant difference between Dupin's ability to recover the story untold by male-authored fictions and Roderick's, however, is that the detective's skill is presented as the desired model. Unlike Roderick's closed-minded narrator, for example, Dupin's narrator greatly admires his friend's mental powers (as do the police), and Dupin in fact tries to teach his lesser-skilled narrator how to read in a new way. In this, the evolution of his character may be traced back to Ligeia, whose deeper knowledge of texts had threatened her narrator-husband by revealing his lesser abilities. In "Ligeia," the narrator had described his attempt to attain to Ligeia's knowledge as being like "our endeavors to recall to memory something long forgotten": "we often find ourselves *upon the very verge* of remembrance, without being able, in the end, to remember" (II, 313–14). In "The Murders in the Rue Morgue," Dupin tells his narrator his own partial interpretation of a newspaper text reporting the grisly murders of two women and asks for the man's conclusion: "At these words a vague and half-formed conception of the meaning of Dupin flitted over my mind. I seemed to be upon the verge of comprehension, without power to

---

Leslie A. Fiedler, *Love and Death in the American Novel*, 2nd ed. (New York: Stein and Day, 1966), p. 497; and Hoffman, pp. 114–22.

comprehend—as men, at times, find themselves upon the brink of remembrance, without being able, in the end, to remember" (II, 555). One critic has claimed that readers rightly identify with this "ostensible dummy," rather than with the detective, whom he sees as "grotesquely naive" in this story. He argues in particular that the story is a lesson in the dangers inherent in sexual repression: while the overly intellectual Dupin fails to see the obvious sexual nature of the crime and thus tries to rationalize the evidence in a way that the narrator finds incomprehensible, the narrator, who represents "every reader," more naturally sees evidence of rape. "Every reader," this critic explains, knows that "he" is potentially "capable of such actions" and all-too-humanly "finds himself excited by—and identifying with—" the putative rapist-murderer.[17] The similar phrasings above, however, suggest that Poe conceived of Dupin as being like Ligeia, or at least as thinking like her, and it seems unrealistic to fault a character who apparently thinks like a woman for failing to identify with or be excited by the idea of a rapist. Indeed, this seems to be the point of the similar phrasings, that men and women think and see things differently; specifically, that Dupin, like Ligeia, has mental abilities of which most "men" are unconscious, their conceptions merely "half-formed." He is thus able to read beyond the surface narrative of male-authored texts, to perceive the gap between text and reality, as we are shown in "The Mystery of Marie Rogêt," where he criticizes virtually point by point a newspaper journalist's attempted reconstruction of the crime. "The sentence in question has but one meaning, as it stands," Dupin instructs his narrator, "but it is material that we go behind the mere words, for an idea which these words have . . . failed to convey" (III, 739).

What I have called the gap between text and reality is, of course, a gender gap. In the Dupin tales, male-authored texts exclude femaleness because their authors are incapable of imagining women's experience; which is to say, they fail to recognize the various ways in which women are victimized. Such failures of imagination, recognition, and empathy are thus "crimes" in their own right, for

---

[17] J. A. Leo Lemay, "The Psychology of 'The Murders in the Rue Morgue,'" *American Literature*, 54 (1982), 177, 178, 187.

although these male authors are less obviously misogynistic than Poe's earlier narrators, the texts they create continue to leave the woman's story untold, the overt crime unsolved. In "The Murders in the Rue Morgue," for example, Dupin is able to track down the murderer of the old woman and her daughter because he can recognize what has gone unnamed by the newspaper account of the crime: the strange "voice" of the attacker, which none of the "witnesses" could identify, is that of an orangutan. Once this fact is established, the detective is then able to recover the entire scenario—the second story, which reveals at last what the women actually suffered. Not surprisingly, that story presents a grim parody of what in Poe's tales constitutes normative masculine behavior. The trained animal had been acting out a masculine script, first flourishing a razor around the face of one of his victims, "in imitation of the motions of a barber"; then silencing both women when they put up a struggle; and finally trying to conceal all evidence of the crime (II, 566–67).

The issue of masculine norms, or rather, masculine conceptions of normative behavior, is continued in "The Mystery of Marie Rogêt." In this tale Dupin criticizes several conflicting newspaper articles on the grounds that they are indeed male-authored "fictions": "[I]t is the object of our newspapers rather to create a sensation—to make a point—than to further the cause of truth" (III, 738). Specifically, the "truth" of a woman's experience gets lost sight of because the language of each text is informed by a rigidly masculine perspective. In discussing attempts to identify Marie's body, for instance, one journalist had argued that the fact that garter clasps had been set back to accommodate smaller legs, as Marie was said to have done, was not admissible evidence that the corpse was the petite Marie, because after buying them, "most women find it proper to take a pair of garters home and fit them to the size of the limbs" (III, 745). "Here it is difficult to suppose the reasoner in earnest," Dupin comments, revealing the flaw in the male author's generalization: the "elastic nature of the clasp-garter is self-demonstration of the *unusualness* of the abbreviation" which Marie undertook (III, 746). That men cannot imagine what the life of a woman is like and that they thus define all experience in masculine terms is more explicitly demonstrated in Dupin's criticism of another newspaper's argument. "It is impossible," this text urges, "that a person so well known to thousands as this young woman was, should have passed three blocks without some one having seen her." But, Dupin explains, this

> is the idea of a man long resident in Paris—a public man—and one whose walks to and fro in the city, have been mostly limited to the vicinity of the public offices. He is aware that *he* seldom passes so far as a dozen blocks from his own *bureau*, without being recognized and accosted. And, knowing the extent of his personal acquaintance with others, and of others with him, he compares his notoriety with that of the perfumery-girl, finds no great difference between them, and reaches at once the conclusion that she, in her walks, would be equally liable to recognition with himself in his. This could only be the case were her walks of the same unvarying, methodical character, and within the same *species* of limited region as are his own. (III, 749)

In the third and final tale in which Dupin appears, the "limited region" whose boundaries are set by masculine minds is shown to be the province of the Parisian police. Their failure to recover "the purloined letter" results, as Dupin explains, from the narrow "limits of the Prefect's examination—in other words, had the principle of [the letter's] concealment been comprehended within the principles of the Prefect . . . its discovery would have been a matter altogether beyond question" (III, 986). In this tale the plot-lines we have seen previously are reduced to their essence and the issue of gender conflict is in fact given a political dimension, for the crime is the theft of a text that rightfully belongs to the Queen; the thief is the Minister D____, "who dares all things, those unbecoming as well as those becoming a man" (III, 976); and "the power thus attained," as even the Prefect of police recognizes, "has . . . been wielded, for political purposes, to a very dangerous extent" (III, 977). Once again Dupin, acting according to his "political prepossessions" as "partisan of the lady" (III, 993), is able to recover the lost text (and replace it with a clever substitute) because he alone can decode the artifice by which the woman has been disempowered: the male criminal had merely disguised her "letter" to look as if it was his own. And once again this second story acts as a gloss upon the first. The Minister's conscious concealment of the Queen's letter is but the external manifestation of the police's interpretive paradigm, by which they unconsciously define all human action only according to "their *own*"—masculine—"ideas" of it. In Dupin's words, "They have no variation of principle in their investigations." Their unchanging principle is "based upon . . . one set of notions regarding human ingenuity" (III, 985), and one set of notions, as the "double Dupin" demonstrates, is not enough to accommodate both halves of humanity.

This tale has a new ending, suggesting perhaps that Poe felt he had taken his critique of male-authored fictions to its logical conclusion: the victimized woman lives to benefit from Dupin's recovery of the second story, and the male criminal faces imminent retribution. As Dupin reveals at the end, for "eighteen months the Minister has had her in his power. She has now him in hers; since, being unaware that the letter is not in his possession, he will proceed with his exactions as if it was. Thus will he inevitably commit himself, at once, to his political destruction" (III, 993). Dupin's criticism of the police's interpretive paradigm, however, is obviously not new; it merely rounds out the metaphorical arguments begun in "The Fall of the House of Usher." The police's "one set of notions," like the earlier depictions of "half-formed conception" and male-authored texts which failed to convey "but one meaning," represents a blind spot in masculine interpretations of reality that keeps men from seeing how women are victimized. What the men in these tales cannot see, they cannot include in their own "story" of events, but the crime metaphor that provides the basis for Poe's detective tales insists on the criminal nature of such oversights. The death-dealing misogyny of Roderick Usher's narrator differs from the half-formed conceptions of Dupin's newspaper writers and police only in degree, not in effect. The second story, or perhaps finally, the second half of the human story, must be recovered by a mind capable of "looking back, of seeing with fresh eyes, of entering an old text from a new critical direction,"[18] and Poe's solution to the problem of such much-needed "re-vision" is the androgynous mind that had first so terrified Roderick Usher and had finally so distinguished C. Auguste Dupin.

[18] Rich, p. 35.

III

I have twice referred to Adrienne Rich's definition of "re-vision" to help explain Roderick's and Dupin's recovery of the second story, so it seems only proper to repeat it here as she originally articulated it: "Re-vision—the act of looking back, of seeing with fresh eyes, of entering an old text from a new critical direction—is for women more than a chapter in cultural history: it is an act of survival. Until we can understand the assumptions in which we are drenched we cannot know ourselves. . . . We need to know the writing of the past, and know it differently than we have ever known it; not to pass on a tradition but to break its hold over us." Read in sequence, "The Fall of the House of Usher" and the three Dupin tales suggest that Poe was considering what Fetterley has called "the responsibility of change" and experimenting with the idea of the androgynous mind which would be capable of imaginative re-vision. The androgynous Dupin accomplishes what Roderick Usher so tentatively began, a fully-specified critique of "the imaginative limits" of one-sided male-authored fictions. The end-product of such a critique is the recovery of "the woman's story," which, in the last tale in the sequence, breaks the hold of male domination and finally insures the woman's survival by restoring her honor and her socio-political power.

There is no question that Poe's depictions of acts of physical violence committed against women are particularly gruesome, and some feminist readers might feel that having to encounter such grisly surface details is too big a price to pay to get to the final acts of recovery and restoration Poe seems to have had in mind. A greater stumbling block to any acceptance of Poe as an author capable of feminist sensibility must surely be his now infamous statement that "the death . . . of a beautiful woman is, unquestionably, the most poetical topic in the world." Certainly at first glance it would seem to contradict any argument that his tales show an evolving feminist ethos, a growing awareness and renunciation of death-dealing male-authored fictions, and indeed, it appeared a year after "The Purloined Letter," in "The Philosophy of Composition," published in 1846.

When feminist critics cite the statement, however, they tend to leave off the second half of the sentence: "—and equally is it beyond doubt that the lips best suited for such topic are those of a bereaved lover."[19] While I do not intend to justify the images of death which Poe habitually chose as a vehicle for his vision, I do believe that the halves of this statement constitute a conceptual whole which is not inconsistent with his use of the androgyny metaphor, and to argue this final point, I will extrapolate from Baym's reading of Hawthorne one last time: "The domain of his work is the male psyche, and throughout his writings 'woman' stands for a set of qualities which the male denies within himself and rejects in others. . . . The ability to accept woman—either as the 'other' or as part of the self—becomes in his writing a test of man's wholeness."[20]

The domain of Poe's work is also the male psyche, and the loss of "woman" throughout his writings represents a halving of "man's" soul, his human potential, and—for the male artist—his imagination. Telling the story of that loss seems to have been for Poe a compelling need, for he told it obsessively again and again and clearly derived a kind of perverse pleasure from doing so. Nevertheless, that such works are cautionary tales is confirmed by the heroic stature of his androgynous heroes. Roderick Usher does come to accept woman both as the "other" and as part of the self, but it is Dupin who stands finally as Poe's greatest achievement. "The double Dupin" represents his creator's fullest expression of the need for wholeness and the need to tell not only the story of loss, but the second story as well: the story of recovery and restoration, "the woman's story." I have to conclude that Poe's ability to tell both stories, or both halves of the human story, is—like Hawthorne's—the sign of what we would today call feminist re-vision.

---

[19] See, for example, Sandra M. Gilbert and Susan Gubar, *The Madwoman in the Attic: The Woman Writer and the Nineteenth-Century Literary Imagination* (New Haven: Yale Univ. Press, 1979), p. 25. Also, *The Complete Poems and Stories of Edgar Allan Poe, with Selections from his Critical Writings*, ed. A. H. Quinn (New York: Knopf, 1951), II, 982.

[20] "Hawthorne's Women: The Tyranny of Social Myths," *Centennial Review*, 15 (1971), 250–51.

Index

This index is centered on Edgar Allan Poe. The titles of his writings appear as main entries, and unqualified entries such as "music" or "narrators" refer directly to the content of those writings.

Alexander's Weekly Messenger, 44–45
Allen, Hervey, 26, 39
Alterton, Margaret, 56, 67–68, 76
"Annabel Lee," 99
anti-rationalism, 172, 183–84, 246. *See also* romanticism
Arnold, Matthew, 131
"Assignation, The," 72, 75
Auden, W. H., 123, 132

"Bargain Lost, The," 143n
Barrett, Elizabeth, 56, 126
Baym, Nina, 247, 250
beauty, concept of, 63–64, 67, 77, 100–101
"Bells, The," 99–100
"Berenice," 72, 156, 202, 205, 248, 251
Bergson, Henri, 133–34, 137–39
"Black Cat, The," 14, 73, 197, 205
Blackwood's Magazine, 145, 153, 158, 167–68, 244
Bonaparte, Marie, 207n, 241
"Bridal Ballad," 94, 96
Briggs, Charles F., 112–14, 118n
Broadway Journal, 109n, 110–11, 114n
Bryant, William Cullen, 1, 4, 36n, 60, 130
Bulwer-Lytton, Edward, 32
burlesque, 142–44, 149, 153. *See also* comedy; hoaxing; humor
"Business Man, The," 174
Butler, Samuel, 125
Byron, George Gordon, Lord, 31n

Campbell, Killis, 26, 40n
Canby, Henry Seidel, 26, 143n
Carlyle, Thomas, 29, 108–9
Child, Lydia Maria, 31n
childhood, fascination with, 206

Chivers, Thomas Holley, 36n, 76, 110, 111n
"City in the Sea, The," 69–70, 75
Clark, Lewis Gaylord, 102–21
Clark, Willis Gaylord, 103
Coleridge, Samuel Taylor, 58, 62, 74, 122, 123, 127, 131, 188
"Colloquy of Monos and Una, The," 13, 35–36, 152–55, 231
Columbia Spy, The, 28
Combe, George, 2–8, 11n, 18–21
comedy, 125, 133–42. *See also* burlesque; hoaxing; humor
"Conqueror Worm, The," 71, 75
"Conversation of Eiros and Charmion, The," 154
Cooper, James Fenimore, 74
Craig, Hardin, 56, 76–77
critic of fiction, Poe as, 72–74, 123–24
critic of poetry, Poe as, 6–7, 57–69, 124–25, 128–30. *See also* "Philosophy of Composition, The"
cryptography, 40–54, 208–22
current taste, alertness to, 144

Davidson, Edward H., 142n, 143, 144, 149, 150n, 172, 174, 177n, 193
death as motif, 125, 152, 207, 264–65
"Decided Loss, A," 143n
Defoe, Daniel, 124
"Descent into the Maelström, A," 158–60, 164n, 169, 171, 172, 197, 199–205
detective stories. *See* ratiocination, tales of
Dickens, Charles, 127, 140
didacticism in poetry, 59–63, 125–26, 129
"Diddling Considered as One of the Exact Sciences," 11, 16
"Domain of Arnheim, The," 36, 152n

Drake, Joseph Rodman, 6–7, 77
"Dream-Land," 97–98, 144
"Dream Within a Dream, A," 100
"Duc de L'Omelette, Le," 143n
Dupin, C. Auguste, 15–16, 172, 175–77, 181–84, 229–30, 251, 258, 265. *See also* "Murders in the Rue Morgue, The"; "Mystery of Marie Rogêt, The"; "Purloined Letter, The"
Duyckinck, Evert A., 7, 24, 107n
Duyckinck, George, 24

"Eldorado," 96
"Eleanora," 72, 188–89, 195, 202
Eliot, T. S., 123, 130, 140
Eureka, 29, 35, 209, 210n, 213, 233n

"Facts in the Case of M. Valdemar The," 155
"Fall of the House of Usher, The," 16–20, 73, 75, 152, 168, 185–97, 202, 252–58
Faust, Goethe's, 198–99
feminism, 31–33
Fetterley, Judith, 250, 264
"Few Words on Secret Writing, A," 42–45
Fielding, Henry, 125
"Fifty Suggestions," 36n, 38n
"For Annie," 99
"Four Beasts in One," 26n, 134–40
Fuller, Margaret, 33

Gall, Franz Joseph, 2, 4, 5n, 11n, 12, 13
Garden, myth of the, 199–201, 203–4
Godey, Louis, 120
Godey's Lady's Book, 112, 114n, 115n, 120
Godwin, William, 144
"Gold-Bug, The," 52–53, 73, 208–22
gothicism, 142–49, 176, 185–96
Graham, George R., 118, 121
Graham's Magazine, 42–43, 46, 50, 51, 53, 107, 109, 118, 208, 219n
Griswold, Rufus Wilmot, 102, 105n, 108n, 110n, 114n, 118–20, 144, 148, 149

Halleck, Fitz-Greene, 6–7, 77
"Hans Pfaall—A Tale," 38n, 103–4, 137n, 157

"Haunted Palace, The," 19, 70, 74, 120, 256
Hawthorne, Nathaniel, 72–73, 113, 170, 199, 248–51, 265
Hazlitt, William, 124n, 128
head-body dichotomy, 223–46
hoaxing, 142–43, 149. *See also* burlesque; comedy; humor
Hoffman, Charles Fenno, 8
Hoffman, Dan, 172, 197, 235n, 252n
Hoffman, E. T. A., 119
homosexuality, 230–32, 239–40
Hood, Thomas, 74, 192
"Hop-Frog," 134–40, 143, 147
Horne, Richard H., 36n, 58, 61, 74
"How to Write a Blackwood Article," 144, 147, 149
humor, 133–41, 174n, 176. *See also* burlesque; comedy; hoaxing

"Imp of the Perverse, The," 14–15, 230
Ingraham, Joseph Holt, 31n
Ingram, John H., 78, 91
irony. *See* burlesque; comedy; hoaxing; humor
Irving, Washington, 25n, 147

Jackson, Andrew, 26n
James, Henry, 150, 164n
Jones, Howard Mumford, 26, 143n, 148n
"Journal of Julius Rodman, The," 25n, 105, 174n

Keats, John, 124
Kemble, Frances, 32
Kennedy, John Pendleton, 27, 31n, 104n, 133
"King Pest," 134n, 137n
Kirkland, Caroline M., 25n
Knickerbocker Magazine, 102–20
Krutch, Joseph Wood, 38n, 40, 53n, 173, 207

language, theory of, 209–22
Lawrence, D. H., 151, 157
Lazarus figure, 156–58, 160–63, 165, 168–69
"Lenore," 75, 100

lesbianism, 238–40. *See also* sexuality
Levin, Harry, 122, 152, 156, 166n, 172
"Ligeia," 20–23, 64, 72, 75, 152, 158, 160–63, 164n, 168, 169, 176, 188, 195, 197–205, 248, 251, 259
"Lionizing," 36n, 134n
"Literary Life of Thingum Bob, Esq., The," 10, 109n
literary theorist, 57–69, 72–74, 122–32
"Literati of New York City, The," 7, 9, 33, 104n, 111n, 112, 114, 119–20
Longfellow, Henry Wadsworth, 111–13, 118n, 119–20, 125, 129, 234
"Loss of Breath," 144, 149, 197
Lowell, James Russell, 35–37, 109

Mabbott, Thomas O., 14, 49, 103, 106, 142n, 143, 148n, 212n
Macaulay, Thomas Babington, 237
Macnish, Robert, 4n, 11n, 17n, 19
"Maelzel's Chess-Player," 78–91, 173
"Man of the Crowd, The," 169, 174–79, 180
"Man That Was Used Up, The," 32, 134–40
"Marginalia," 29, 30, 36, 37n, 126, 150–53, 155–56, 158, 161, 242
"Masque of the Red Death, The," 73, 75, 144n, 147
"Mellonta Tauta," 29–30, 31n, 35, 36n, 37n, 38n
Melville, Herman, 170, 178, 199
mental illness, 232–44. *See also* psychology
"Mesmeric Revelation," 155–57
meter, theory of, 68–69
"Metzengerstein," 142–49, 197
Miles, Mrs. L., 4–7, 11n, 19n
Milton, John, 66, 67, 127
"Minor Contemporaries," 65–66
Moore, Thomas, 58, 66, 74
"Morella," 72, 75, 136n, 145n, 188, 197–205, 248, 249, 251
"MS. Found in a Bottle," 164n, 169, 198–205
"Murders in the Rue Morgue, The," 15, 73, 175, 182–84, 223–46, 248–49, 259–61

music, 66, 125n, 127n
"Mystery of Marie Rogêt, The," 172, 179, 183n, 248–49, 259, 260–62

Narrative of Arthur Gordon Pym, The, 104–5, 137n, 150, 152, 156, 163–71, 219
narrative technique, 150–71
narrators, 176–79, 180–82, 214–15, 251–58
New Critics, 122–23
Norman Leslie, 121
North American Review, 105, 106n, 118, 120

"Oblong Box, The," 179–83
"Oval Portrait, The," 148n, 202

Paulding, J. K., 33, 35n
Penn Magazine, 105
"Philosophy of Composition, The," 56, 64, 66, 67, 92–94, 97, 101, 131, 197, 240, 264
phrenology, 1–23, 62n, 226n
"Pit and the Pendulum, The," 119, 145
Poe, Henry, 83
"Poetic Principle, The," 56, 57, 59, 63, 67, 125
political attitudes. *See* socio-political ideas
Pope, Alexander, 125
Poulet, Georges, 151
"Power of Words, The," 152–54
Prentice, George Dennison, 109–110, 118n
psychology, 185–96, 223–46
"Purloined Letter, The," 172, 182–83, 215n, 248–49, 262–63

Quinn, Arthur Hobson, 105n, 119n, 133n, 137, 143n
Quinn, Patrick F., 172, 174, 197

racial stereotypes, 33–35, 166
Ransom, John Crowe, 129
ratiocination, tales of, 79, 172–84, 234. *See also* Dupin, C. Auguste
"Rationale of Verse, The," 56, 68–69. *See also* critic of poetry, Poe as

"Raven, The," 59, 66–67, 71, 75–76, 96–97, 100, 109, 110–11, 157
refrains in poetry, 92–101
reviewer, Poe as, 5, 25, 31n, 35n, 42, 107–17, 120–21, 124, 127–28, 247
romanticism, 130, 177n
Rousseau, Jean-Jacques, 243
Rush, Benjamin, 186, 190–91

Sand, George, 31n
sexuality, 200–202, 206–7, 223–46, 254–55, 264–65
Shelley, Percy Bysshe, 59, 62, 124
short story, theory of, 72–74
Simms, William Gilmore, 118
slavery, 33–35, 166
"Sleeper, The," 66, 71, 75
Smollett, Tobias, 125
socio-political ideas, 24–39, 137
"Some Words with a Mummy," 12, 28, 36n, 38n
"Song (I saw thee on thy bridal day)," 94
"Sonnet to Science," 35
Southern Literary Messenger, 5, 78, 103, 144n, 145
"Spectacles, The," 134–40
"Spirits of the Dead, The," 74
Spurzheim, Johann Kaspar, 2, 4, 12, 15, 21, 186–87
Stovall, Floyd, 55, 76–77, 122n, 188
style of Poe's critical prose, 76
"System of Doctor Tarr and Professor Fether, The," 10, 134–40

"Tale of Jerusalem, A," 143n, 149
"Tale of the Ragged Mountains, A," 155, 172

"Tales of the Folio Club," 133, 142n
Tamerlane and Other Poems, 83, 94
Tate, Allen, 123n, 138, 140–41, 156, 202
"Tell-Tale Heart, The," 72, 176–77
Tennyson, Alfred Lord, 57, 58, 62, 68
terror, tales of. See *Blackwood's Magazine*; "How to Write a Blackwood Article"
Thomas, F. W., 27, 33, 35, 49
Thompson, G. R., 177n, 187n, 257n
" 'Thou Art the Man,' " 172
"To Helen," 74
"To One in Paradise," 74, 75, 94, 95

"Ulalume," 59, 66, 70–71, 74, 97–100, 110–11
Usher, Roderick, 17–19, 152, 185–96. See also "Fall of the House of Usher, The"
utilitarianism, 29–30, 35. See also socio-political ideas

"Von Kempelen and His Discovery," 25n

Ward, Thomas ("Flaccus"), 107–8
Whitman, Sarah Helen, 120
Whittier, John Greenleaf, 35
"Why the Little Frenchman Wears His Hand in a Sling," 174n
Wilbur, Richard, 152, 162n, 189n, 195n, 227n, 228
"William Wilson," 74, 174, 205
Willis, N. P., 7, 74, 118, 127
Wilson, James Southall, 26, 233n
Winters, Yvor, 93n, 100-101
woman-centered stories, 247–65
Woodberry, George Edward, 55, 57, 78, 79n, 84n, 120

Notes on Contributors

David W. Butler. University of Kentucky, 1972–1978.

Anthony Caputi (1924–). University of Buffalo, 1953–1967; Cornell University, 1967–. *John Marston, Satirist* (1961); *Buffo: The Genius of Vulgar Comedy* (1978); *Pirandello and the Crisis of Modern Consciousness* (1988). Edited *Modern Drama: Authoritative Texts ... Backgrounds, and Criticism* (1966).

Paul John Eakin (1938–). Indiana University, 1966–. *The New England Girl: Cultural Ideals in Hawthorne, Stowe, Howells, and James* (1976); *Fictions in Autobiography: Studies in the Art of Self Invention* (1985). Edited *On Autobiography* (1989); *American Autobiography: Retrospect and Prospect* (1991).

Benjamin F. Fisher (1940–). University of Pennsylvania, 1967–1973; Hahnemann Medical College, 1973–1979; University of Mississippi, 1979–. *The Very Spirit of Cordiality: The Literary Uses of Alcohol and Alcoholism in the Tales of Edgar Allan Poe* (1978); *Frederick Irving Anderson (1877–1947): A Bibliography* (1987); *The Gothic's Gothic: Study Aids to the Tradition of the Tale of Terror* (1988); *William Dunlap, American Gothic Dramatist* (1988). Edited *Poe at Work: Seven Textual Studies* (1978); *Poe and Our Times: Influences and Affinities* (1986); *Poe and His Times: The Artist and His Milieu* (1990).

William F. Friedman (1891–1969). Cryptologist, Army Signal Corps, 1921–1930; Chief of Signal Intelligence Service, U.S. Army, 1930–1946. *Elements of Cryptoanalysis* (1926); *Report on the History of the Use of Codes and Code Language ...* (1938); (with Elizabeth S. Friedman) *The Shakespearean Ciphers Examined* (1957).

Edward Hungerford (1900–1988). Beloit College, 1922–1923; Northwestern University, 1928–1970. *Shores of Darkness* (1941). Edited *Poets in Progress: Critical Prefaces to Ten Contemporary Americans* (1962).

Cynthia S. Jordan (1949–). Indiana University, 1982–; College of the Holy Cross, 1991–1992. *Second Stories: The Politics of Language, Form, and Gender in Early American Fictions* (1989).

J. Gerald Kennedy (1947–). Louisiana State University, Baton Rouge, 1973. *The Astonished Traveler: William Darby, Frontier Geographer and Man of Letters* (1981); *Walker Percy* (1981); *Death and the Life of Writing* (1987). Edited *American Letters and the Historical Consciousness: Essays in Honor of Lewis P. Simpson* (1987).

J. A. Leo Lemay (1935–). University of California, Los Angeles, 1964–1977; H. F. duPont Winterthur Professor of English, University of Delaware, 1977. *Ebenezer Kinnersley, Franklin's Friend* (1964); *A Bibliographical Guide to the Study of Southern Literature* (1969); *A Calendar of American Poetry in the Colonial Newspapers and Magazines and in the Major English Magazines through 1765* (1970); *Men of Letters in Colonial Maryland* (1972); *"New England's Annoyances": America's First Folk Song* (1985); *The Canon of Benjamin Franklin, 1722–1776: New Attributions and Reconsiderations* (1986); *The American Dream of Captain John Smith* (1991). Edited *The Oldest Revolutionary: Essays on Benjamin Franklin* (1976); *Essays in Virginia Literature Honoring Richard Beale Davis*

Contributors

(1977); *The Autobiography of Benjamin Franklin: A Genetic Text* (1981); *Deism, Masonry, and the Enlightenment: Essays Honoring Alfred Owen Aldridge* (1987); *Robert Bolling Woos Anne Miller: Love and Courtship in Colonial Virginia, 1760* (1990); *The American Dream of Captain John Smith* (1991).

Ernest Marchand (1898–1985). Oregon State College, 1926–1928; Stanford University, 1935–1946; San Diego State College, 1946–1968. *Frank Norris* (1942). Edited C. B. Brown, *Ormond* (1937).

Emerson R. Marks (1918–). Newark College, Rutgers University, 1945–1956; Southern Illinois University, 1956–1957; Wayne State University, 1957–1969; University of Massachusetts in Boston, 1969–. *Relativist and Absolutist: The Early Neoclassical Debate in England* (1955); *The Poetics of Reason: English Neoclassical Criticism* (1968); *Coleridge on the Language of Verse* (1981). Translated and edited *Literary Criticism of Sainte-Beuve* (1971).

Stephen L. Mooney (1913–1971). University of Alabama, 1946–1960; University of Tennessee, 1960–1964; University of Southern Alabama, 1964–1965; University of Tennessee at Martin, 1965–1971.

Sidney P. Moss (1917–). Murray State University, 1954–1964; Southern Illinois University, Carbondale, 1965–1987. *Poe's Literary Battles: The Critic in the Context of His Literary Milieu* (1963); *Poe's Major Crisis: His Libel Suit and New York's Literary World* (1970); *Charles Dickens' Quarrel with America* (1984).

Michael Williams (1949–). Washington State University, 1985–1989; University of Wisconsin, Stevens Point, 1989–. *A World of Words: Language and Displacement in the Fiction of Edgar Allan Poe* (1988).

W. K. Wimsatt, Jr. (1907–1975). Portsmouth Priory School, 1930–1935; Yale University, 1939–1975; Frederick Clifford Ford Professor, 1965; Sterling Professor of English, 1974. *The Prose Style of Samuel Johnson* (1941); *Philosophic Words: A Study of Style and Meaning in the "Rambler" and "Dictionary" of Samuel Johnson* (1948); *The Verbal Icon: Studies in the Meaning of Poetry* (1954); (with Cleanth Brooks) *Literary Criticism: A Short History* (1957); *The Portraits of Alexander Pope* (1965); *Hateful Contraries: Studies in Literature and Criticism* (1965); *Versification: Major Language Types* (1972); *Day of the Leopards: Essays in Defence of Poems* (1976). Edited *English Stage Comedy* (1955); (with F. A. Pottle) *Boswell for the Defence, 1769–74* (1959); *Samuel Johnson on Shakespeare* (1960); *Explication as Criticism* (1963); *The Idea of Comedy: Essays in Prose and Verse* (1969); *Literary Criticism: Idea and Act* (1974); (with Frank Brady) *Selected Poetry and Prose: Samuel Johnson* (1977).

Yvor Winters (1900–1968). Stanford University, 1928–1966; Albert Guerard Professor of Literature, 1961. *Primitivism and Decadence: A Study of American Experimental Poetry* (1937); *The Anatomy of Nonsense* (1943); *Edwin Arlington Robinson* (1946; rev. ed. 1971); *In Defense of Reason* (1947); *The Function of Criticism: Problems and Exercises* (1957); *On Modern Poets* (1957, 1959); *Forms of Discovery: Critical and Historical Essays on the Forms of the Short Poem in English* (1967). Edited *Twelve Poets of the Pacific* (1932); *Quest for Reality: An Anthology of Short Poems in English* (1969).

Jules Zanger (1927–). Ohio State University, 1954–1957; Illinois Institute of Technology, 1957–1960; Southern Illinois University, Edwardsville, 1960–. Edited *The Beauchamp Tragedy* (1963).

Library of Congress Cataloging-in-Publication Data
On Poe / edited by Louis J. Budd and Edwin H. Cady.
(The Best from *American Literature*)
Includes index.
ISBN 0-8223-1311-1 (acid-free paper)
1. Poe, Edgar Allan, 1809-1849—Criticism and interpretation.
I. Budd, Louis J.   II. Cady, Edwin Harrison.   III. Series.
PS2638.O5   1993
818'.309—dc20   92-28839   CIP